THE EXECUTION OF
BRIDGET NOBLE

ii

THE EXECUTION OF BRIDGET NOBLE

The Missing Woman of the Beara Peninsula Troubles

Sean Boyne

Published, Dublin, Ireland 2021

ISBN: 9798717322782

Cover photo: The arch under the road at Collorus, in the County Kerry part of the Beara Peninsula, where some local people believe that Bridget Noble was executed.

Readers who find errors in this book, or who wish to clarify matters or who have additional information are invited to make contact, in confidence, through nobleresearch27-ctb at yahoo dot com

Table of Contents

Introduction   1

Chapter 1: The Abduction   7

Chapter 2: Éamon de Valera and the Two Missing Women   17

Chapter 3: Bridget Noble – Early Years   26

Chapter 4: Alexander Noble's Beara Romance with Bridget 37

Chapter 5: Bridget Noble Goes to Court   48

Chapter 6: The Shooting of William Lehane   57

Chapter 7: Punishment Attack   67

Chapter 8: Bridget Noble's Complaint to the Police   79

Chapter 9: 'Save me, Jack, save me!'   91

Chapter 10: A Curious Anomaly   107

Chapter 11: 'Fortified with the Rites of the Church'   117

Chapter 12: Noble to de Valera: 'It Is Not Clean Work...'   125

Chapter 13: Relatives of Disappeared Seek Help from IRA
Liaison Officers   140

Chapter 14: Alexander Noble Returns to County Cork   151

Chapter 15: Death Sentence In Breach of IRA Rules   162

Chapter 16: Witnesses In Other Hair-Shearing Attacks Not
Targeted as Informers   181

Chapter 17: Fate of Mary Lindsay and Kate Carroll   190

Chapter 18: Release of Prisoners   197

Chapter 19: Rejecting the Treaty   209

Chapter 20: Firefight at Castletownbere   219

Chapter 21: Free State Forces Occupy Beara Peninsula   228

Chapter 22: The Capture of Patsy Dan Crowley   234

Chapter 23: Bridget Noble Excluded from Accounts of
Conflict in Beara   253

Chapter 24: The Disappeared: The Youngest Victim   264

Chapter 25: Exile from Ireland   274

Chapter 26: Alexander Noble's Troubled Life   288

Epilogue   297

Acknowledgements   303

Appendix   305

Picture Section   307

Bibliography   320

Notes and References   326

Index   355

'And some there be who have no memorial, who are perished, as though they had never been.'
Ecclesiasticus, 44:9.

List of Abbreviations

Batt.	Battalion
BMH	Bureau of Military History
CDBI	Congested Districts Board for Ireland
CnB	Cumann na mBan
C.I.	County Inspector (RIC)
CO	Colonial Office
Cork WR	Cork West Riding
Comdt.	Commandant
D.I.	District Inspector (RIC)
GAA	Gaelic Athletic Association
GHQ	General Headquarters
HO	Home Office
IE/MA	Ireland, Military Archives
IRA	Irish Republican Army
LE	Liaison and Evacuation [Papers]
MSP	Military Service Pension
MSPC	Military Service Pension Collection
NLI	National Library of Ireland
O/C	Officer Commanding
PIRA	Provisional IRA
RIC	Royal Irish Constabulary
RUC	Royal Ulster Constabulary
TNA	The National Archives (United Kingdom)
TD	Teachta Dála [Member of Dáil Éireann]
UCDA	University College Dublin Archives
WO	War Office
WS	Witness Statement
YMCA	Young Men's Christian Association

Introduction

It was early 2013, and I was trawling through files of letters, almost yellow with age, in the Irish Military Archives in Dublin when I came across references to a disturbing incident during the War of Independence I had never heard about before. In early 1921 a woman called Bridget Noble was abducted while walking alone along a lonely road near her home in West Cork and never seen again by her loved ones. The kidnapping occurred during a time of particular turbulence in West Cork. Very little about Mrs Noble entered into the public domain over the years – some important information has emerged in more recent times. I was most intrigued when I came across correspondence to do with her disappearance while carrying out research in the archives centre at Cathal Brugha Barracks. The Military Archives were then located in an old redbrick building dating from the British Army era, before the new state-of-the-art archives centre was formally opened in 2016. It appeared that Mrs Noble had fallen foul of local elements of the insurgent Irish Republican Army (IRA) and that she had been taken away and killed, and her body disposed of in a secret location. I wondered what could this ordinary, middle-aged woman from Ardgroom in the Beara peninsula have done to merit such draconian punishment? And why had there been so little publicity about the case?

Despite the lack of public attention to the fate of Mrs Noble over the years, I came to realise that this Beara woman had her own special place in the history of the Troubles of the 1920s. She is one of only two women known for certain to have been disappeared by the IRA during the War of Independence. The other woman was Mrs Mary Lindsay, whose abduction received considerable publicity at the time, and also in more recent decades. (As will be explained, one cannot rule out the possibility that one or two other women were disappeared in County Cork during the same period, whose names have never come to light.) In the more recent Troubles in Northern Ireland, there was just one woman who was disappeared by the Provisional IRA (PIRA) –

widowed mother of ten, Jean McConville, whose murder became a *cause célèbre*.

I found the correspondence concerning Mrs Noble, quite by chance, in what are known as the Liaison and Evacuation Papers when I was carrying out archival research for my biography of Major General Emmet Dalton, published in 2014.[1] (I mention the Noble case briefly in the book.) It emerged that Bridget, a Catholic, had married a man from outside her ethnic and religious community. Her husband, Alexander Noble, was a cooper by trade and a Scotsman of Presbyterian background. He had left the couple's Ardgroom home to seek work in England some time before Bridget was kidnapped, and in late 1921 was making strenuous efforts to find out what happened his wife. The file of letters I saw in the archives did not reveal how his quest ended. My curiosity was aroused, and thus began my fascination with the story of Bridget Noble.

During the revolutionary period there was a taboo about killing women, but there were two well-known cases where females had been shot by the IRA after being accused of being informers. The afore-mentioned Mrs Lindsay, an elderly Protestant widow, had been abducted and shot in County Cork, and in County Monaghan a woman called Kate Carroll had been taken from her home at night and shot, and her body left by the side of the road. Both were put to death in 1921, and various details had come into the public domain. But why was there so little known about the 'Third Woman' who was taken away and killed by the IRA? Why had there been so little publicity about the sad case of Bridget Noble?

I wondered what kind of person she was, what kind of life did she lead, who were her parents and siblings, how did she come to marry a Scotsman, and how could it all end in such tragedy? It appeared that some local people knew about the Noble saga but over the decades it was not something that was normally discussed in a public forum. I wondered if there was a code of silence, a kind of *Omerta*, an agreement not to talk publicly about this episode, that had prevailed among those members of the IRA who knew the details of her disappearance.

Despite the lack of publicity surrounding Mrs Noble's fate, her disappearance was known about, and was a matter of historical record. I had not uncovered something that had been totally secret. I would eventually discover that there were brief mentions of Bridget Noble in at least two books, one published in 1992 and the other in 2012. Later, in 2016, Mrs Noble would figure in an academic study of 78 'suspected civilian spies' killed by the IRA in Cork city and county in 1920-21.[2] She would subsequently feature in other studies published in 2020 dealing with the Disappeared, the dead of the Irish revolutionary period, and the punishment of women during that era.

In the meantime, before coming across these references, I tried the internet. I put Bridget's name and other relevant details into the search engine Google and I found only one result, but a most remarkable one. Bridget was commemorated on the website of the musician and composer Skully. His family roots are in the Beara peninsula and he had learned of Bridget's sad fate from his grandmother, Mrs Elizabeth O'Sullivan, who had been horrified at what was done to her, and was appalled at the actions of those who had abducted and killed her. It was a very dark story that made a deep impression on Skully.

The musician had never forgotten the story of Bridget Noble and he had located the remote area where Bridget lived at Reenavaude and put photos onto his website. He had written a piece of music in Bridget's memory, called *Mrs Noble* – it's a track on his album *Scent of a Moment*. The music is electronic, and the track conveys a sombre air of menace, in tune with the terrible fate of the woman from Reenavaude. In a blog, he wrote that Bridget had been harassed and humiliated, firstly by having her hair forcibly cut off, which was a warning for what was to come – eventually she would be kidnapped and murdered. He comments: 'Biddy Noble has no grave, there is nowhere to leave flowers, nowhere to remember her.' People who posted comments on his website were moved by his memorial to the missing woman. One person wrote: 'Your tribute of song is a most beautiful monument. Her spirit shall be honoured with remembrance for all time yet to come. I thank you, for sharing the emotion of your heart...' Another person wrote: 'You have paid her a fine tribute. Though we may never know her final resting place, her memory and the injustice done unto her was just waiting for someone like you to unearth it and give her a proper eulogy.'

I was now even more intrigued by the story of Bridget Noble. Then, on a field trip to the idyllic Beara Peninsula in 2015 with the Military History Society of Ireland to visit historical sites, I happened to meet a local man familiar with the Ardgroom area. I asked him if he had ever heard of Bridget Noble. He looked at me with astonishment. How had I heard of Mrs Noble? I explained how I had found letters in the Military Archives about her disappearance. He was clearly intrigued by what I had found and was eager to know more. As I made further inquiries, I gained the impression that among people on the Beara peninsula who knew of Mrs Noble, there was a lingering sense of horror at what had been done to her, but that it was also a sensitive subject. An elderly man, whose forebears lived near Mrs Noble, seemed troubled as he recalled accounts that had come down in his own family about her fate. 'Jaysus, it was bad. They were terrible times.'

As I delved into the archives, details emerged of allegations made against Mrs Noble, although one has to bear in mind that we do not have her side of the story. She had come under suspicion by the IRA after being seen in contact with the crown forces – she had made visits to the local Royal Irish Constabulary (RIC) station and was apparently friendly with a local RIC sergeant. Was she passing on information about the IRA to the police? What would she have known that might have been of interest to the RIC? Some believe there was an innocent explanation for her visits to the police, and this is one of the topics I explore. Anecdotal evidence indicates she was a rather naïve, unsophisticated person, who may not have fully realised the potential dangers of having contacts with the RIC, and that she could be suspected of being an informer. It is also possible that the RIC took advantage of her naivety to get information. The local IRA alleged that she gave the names of two men (both prominent IRA members) as having been involved in the fatal shooting of a local farmer in an agrarian dispute. Nobody was ever arrested for the killing, and as will be outlined, there is a remarkable anomaly in the local IRA commandant's account of the alleged consequences of Mrs Noble's 'informing'. Relevant information was omitted from his report to GHQ, to her detriment.

After coming home from hospital, Bridget Noble was subjected to a punishment attack by a number of IRA men in which her hair was forcibly shorn. The indications are that the major reason for her subsequent abduction and execution was that she complained about the attack to the RIC, naming alleged perpetrators. Subsequently, a man who was a member of a prominent republican family received a six months sentence; another man would later be interned after her death. Anecdotal evidence suggests that Mrs Noble was a person of considerable courage and independence of mind, and clearly she was prepared to stand up for herself and defend her dignity as a woman. Unfortunately, her defiance of the local IRA would have very dark consequences. After being kidnapped she was held prisoner for a period of time before a death sentence was carried out, and the body secretly disposed of.

A statement issued by the British administration in Dublin Castle would later claim that Mrs Noble was subjected to this outrage because she was a 'loyalist'. The British would also accept liability for paying compensation to her husband, Alexander, arising from her death. (There was a considerable number of other cases in which the British agreed to provide compensation in cases of loss, injury or death arising

4

out of the Troubles in Ireland.) Nevertheless, despite being given the label of 'loyalist' or 'British supporter', one wonders, in light of anecdotal information, if this unsophisticated woman really held strong political views of any type.

It also emerges that the republicans who decided that she should die were in breach of the IRA's own rules for dealing with women accused of being informers – an IRA order laid down various punishments for women convicted of spying, but not the death penalty. The order also laid down various procedures for dealing with such cases, and the indications are that the local IRA battalion had not followed these procedures either.

As I researched and wrote the story of Bridget Noble, the narrative gradually expanded to include events that occurred in the Beara region during the 1916 Rising, the War of Independence and the Truce period, and also during the Civil War and its aftermath. Also examined is the ultimate fate of the local battalion of the IRA, often known as the Beara Battalion. The battalion was composed mainly of young men, some only teenagers, and without seeking to make excuses for some very dark deeds, one has to bear in mind that anything that happened, occurred in a very different era, during a period of great pressure and turmoil.

One local person who was very disturbed by Mrs Noble's fate and who greatly assisted my research, commented on the young Beara Volunteers at that time. He said they were 'fighting for a noble cause', adding: 'I suppose we shouldn't judge them too harshly from the comforts of the 21st Century…' It emerged that one of the staff officers of the Beara Battalion, at the time of Mrs Noble's abduction, had a particular educational distinction – he had been taught by Pádraic Pearse at the latter's renowned college, St Enda's [Scoil Éanna]. It appears he was Pearse's pupil in 1915, the year prior to the Easter Rising that would result in Pearse's execution.

To give additional context to the story of Mrs Noble, I include details of the other two women executed by the IRA in 1921, Mrs Lindsay and Kate Carroll. I examine how women were punished by both sides during the revolutionary period, and I reflect on the woman who was disappeared by the PIRA in the more recent Troubles, Jean McConville. (The most recent female victim of republican violence is, of course, the journalist Lyra McKee, who was shot dead in Derry by a gunman from a dissident republican group when he opened fire on police in April 2019.) I also consider the issue of the Disappeared of the 1920s, the scores of people who were taken away by the IRA, killed and their remains secretly disposed of, in unknown locations. Probably the youngest was a 15-year-old Protestant boy, William Edward Parsons, who was abducted in Cork city.

As regards the two women who were abducted and killed in 1921, one is struck by how little Bridget Noble and Mary Lindsay had in common during the years they lived in County Cork. Mrs Noble was a Catholic and native Irish speaker who lived in a small, thatched cottage and was a person of humble background. Mrs Lindsay, a Protestant, resided in a big house with servants and was a lady of high social status. In death, they did have something in common – they came to occupy their own sad niche in the turbulent history of Ireland's War of Independence by joining the ranks of the Disappeared.

Researching the story of Mrs Noble has been very a very challenging experience, at times frustrating, but also fascinating. At first, it seemed only very basic information was available. But as one delved more deeply into archives, gradually more information came to light, and more pieces in the jigsaw puzzle could be put into place. I was intrigued, for instance, to discover that in the 1920s Alexander Noble paid an emotional tribute to his missing wife in notices published in a Scots newspaper. I discovered more about Alexander himself, and his remarkable seafaring family in Scotland. I made visits to the Beara peninsula and with the aid of local sources I found various places associated with Mrs Noble, such as the ruins of her former home and the ruined farmhouse in a remote valley of haunting natural beauty where she was held prisoner. As local people shared their knowledge and provided guidance, a far fuller picture of the Noble saga emerged. In so far as one can piece together the facts so long after these tragic events, this is the story of Bridget Noble.

Chapter 1: The Abduction

It was on Friday, 4 March 1921 that Bridget Noble set out on a fateful journey from her cottage on the tiny family farm at Reenavaude near Ardgroom on the Beara Peninsula. It must have been a tense time for the middle-aged woman and her elderly father John Neill, with whom she had resided all her life. Mrs Noble had been the target of a punishment attack at her home by members of the IRA some days previously. Her hair had been forcibly shorn off – a severe public humiliation. The first part of Mrs Noble's journey took her along a narrow, winding road to the village of Ardgroom, about two miles from her home.

According to an internal IRA report on the Noble case, it was on 4 March also that IRA members carried out another raid on the humble dwelling. It was claimed that they found a letter from the RIC Head Constable inviting Mrs Noble to see him at the police station in Castletownbere. This was the main town and sea port on the Beara peninsula. If the report is true, it is unclear when exactly, on 4 March, this raid would have taken place – maybe it was after she left the house. In that case, the IRA must have been able to move extremely quickly to mobilise a party to abduct her before she reached Castletownbere. Whatever the sequence of events may have been, and regardless of whether or not the IRA statement is accurate, this would be Bridget Noble's last day of freedom. John Neill would never see his daughter again.

It appears that the IRA men, with their extensive local knowledge, planned the abduction well. They were probably keeping Bridget under surveillance as she walked along the main street of Ardgroom. She went into the local shop/post office run by Mrs Brigid McCarthy where she often bought groceries and other items. (In that era the post office was located in a house on the western side of the main thoroughfare in the village. It would have been on the right-hand side of the street, coming from Reenavaude direction.) According to the accounts book which has survived, Mrs Noble often purchased items on account, with the bill being settled later – a common practice in that era. It was recorded, for instance, that on 8 January 1921 she bought a quarter pound of tea, a pound of sugar, two candles and a pot of jam, as well as a packet of notepaper and a stamp. She paid five shillings, but still owed 14 shillings and 7 pence from previous transactions. Mrs Noble would also get the occasional small loan – it is recorded that on 20 February 1921 she was loaned the sum of ten shillings.

Then, on 2 March, there is an unusual item in the account – she buys a woollen shawl. A shawl can be used to cover the head, and one wonders if she bought the shawl to cover her embarrassment, in the wake of the forcible shearing of her hair by members of the IRA a few days earlier, after she was seen making visits to the local RIC station. On this visit to the shop, she also bought a tin of syrup (she seemed to have a sweet tooth) and a pillow case. The money she now owed amounted to four pounds and seven pence. This must have been a matter of concern to her because when she called to the post office a couple of days later, on 4 March, she had gathered together the sum of 13 shillings and ten pence, which she paid over. She now owed a balance of three pounds, six shillings and ninepence. She would never get to clear that debt. The transactions under her name in the accounts book, written in Mrs McCarthy's precise, elegant handwriting, come to an abrupt end at that point. Mrs McCarthy, aged 36 years at the time, would never see Bridget Noble again.

Anecdotal evidence indicates that around this period, as part of the investigation into Mrs Noble, members of the IRA broke into the letter box at the post office to check on any letters she might have posted. After her visit to the post office, it appears the next item on Bridget's agenda was to travel to Castletownbere, about nine miles away. An internal IRA report claimed, as indicated above, that she had been summoned to see the RIC Head Constable there. If this is correct, one could speculate that this visit was in connection with the police investigation into the forcible shearing of her hair by members of the IRA. As will be explained in more detail later, it appears that she had complained to the police, naming the men whom she accused of attacking her; one was arrested on 4 March and this may have been the catalyst for the IRA decision to abduct her on that day.

The Recording

An account of what happened next was given many years later by a woman from the Beara peninsula, Eva O'Sullivan, who said that she based her account on information provided by a man who was in the IRA at the time. (If there was a pact between local IRA men to observe strict secrecy about the fate of Mrs Noble, the information given by

Eva's informant would have been a rare example of the rule of silence being broken.) Eva came from Bridget Noble's own district of Reenavaude, and although she was only aged about 12 years when Bridget was abducted, she may have been acquainted with the woman whose disappearance would have a major, disquieting impact on this small, close-knit community.

Eva was the great-grandaunt of Skully, the composer who would go on to write a piece of music to commemorate Mrs Noble. Most of those called Sullivan or O'Sullivan in County Cork were Catholic – Eva O'Sullivan was unusual in that she came from a Church of Ireland family. Her parents were Dan O'Sullivan and his wife Fanny Jones – the family farm was in West Reenavaude. According to the 1911 Census, there was just one other Church of Ireland family in the quaintly-named townland of Ardgroom Inward – they were also called Sullivan, and had a farm at Carrigaphrechane. (During the 19th century a church building catered for the small Church of Ireland congregation in the district, consisting largely of families that had converted from Catholicism. As the number of worshippers dwindled in the early 20th Century, the building located in the Reenavaude area near Ardgroom was disposed of and later dismantled, the materials being used in the locality for other purposes.) Despite her tender years at the time, records show that in 1921 Eva was a member of the 85-member Ardgroom Company of Cumann na mBan (CnB), the IRA's female auxiliary organisation. Eva's older sister Nell was also a member. (Eva was marked down as having been 'neutral' during the Civil War.[3])

A recording was made, possibly in the 1950s or 1960s, of Eva discussing the Noble abduction with two male friends. (The recording was made by Skully's grandmother, Mrs Elizabeth O'Sullivan. She had a keen interest in local history and was unusual in that era in that she had a reel-to-reel tape recorder, and liked to tape the reminiscences of relatives and friends.[4]) Eva referred to Mrs Noble's hair being 'bobbed' and suggests that Mrs Noble knew that a more dire punishment would follow. 'After the hair being bobbed, she knew what was coming.'

Eva provides some intriguing detail about the IRA operation to seize Mrs Noble, as related by her IRA informant. According to Eva, the local IRA men knew that Bridget often took a lift from Ardgroom to Castletownbere with the driver of a horse-drawn bread delivery car, Dan Holland. He worked for Warner's, a grocery and bakery concern in Castletownbere – the firm's main base was in Bantry. On this day, the IRA men warned the driver not to give her a lift. When Bridget asked for a lift, he told her to walk on, that he would catch up with her on the road. 'Be walking away, and I will pick you up.' The unsuspecting Mrs Noble set off walking towards Eyeries, en route to

Castletownbere. One could speculate that as she moved along the road she wore her shawl or a hat or scarf to cover her head, to hide her humiliation – the fact that her hair had been forcibly shorn off.

Assuming that Eva's informant is correct in his account of the events that day, it must have been a difficult moment for Dan Holland, who lived with his wife and family in West End, Castletownbere. Aged in his mid-forties, he was a popular figure in the region, and made deliveries not only to the shops but to the homes of local people, and was probably on friendly terms with Mrs Noble. Dan probably felt he had no alternative but to obey the order from the IRA men – it appears he stayed in Ardgroom as instructed. As Mrs Noble walked away from Ardgroom she would have quickly left houses behind and entered a lonely, sparsely populated area, with rugged mountains to her left and in the distance to her right, across open moorland, a line of low, green hills beyond which lay the sea. It was a good place for an abduction. Perhaps Mrs Noble began to feel uneasy when there was no sign of the bread car. Eventually, it was not the bread car driver but members of the IRA who caught up with her. In Eva O'Sullivan's words: 'She was just going down the hill towards Eyeries when they came along and captured her.'

Presumably, the IRA could have commandeered a motor car to carry out the kidnapping. However, a more humble means of transport may have been used – a donkey and cart. As will be explained in more detail below, at a later stage in her captivity Mrs Noble was heard calling out in great distress for someone to save her as she was being taken in a donkey and cart along a boreen towards the sea, from where, apparently, she would be taken by boat further along the coast, to the place of execution.

Because of local road conditions, a donkey and cart would have been a more effective means of transport than a motor car. Even the local ambulance, drawn by a sturdy horse hired at five shillings a day, sometimes failed to reach patients in remote areas to bring them to hospital in Castletownbere. Other means of transport had to be used to get sick people to the infirmary. A donkey could negotiate the narrow, unpaved boreens along which Mrs Noble would be transported, boreens that would have been inaccessible to a motor vehicle. The donkey and cart was a traditional part of rural life in the Ireland of the past. It was a mode of transport that can summon up charming images from the whimsical world of the John Ford film, *The Quiet Man* – but in this area, back in March 1921, it would be used for a more ominous purpose.

Having grabbed Mrs Noble as she walked along the Ardgroom-Eyeries road, her captors could now take her along quiet country roads towards a place of detention. They could choose a route that would enable them to avoid the security risk of returning through Ardgroom village. The fewer people who knew about the kidnapping and the identity of those involved, the better from a security point of view. One could speculate that scouts were deployed in various directions to warn the captors of any movements by the crown forces. Eva O'Sullivan, quoting her IRA informant, states that Mrs Noble was taken to a shed in Ballycrovane where she was 'gagged and tied up'. (Ballycrovane townland lies roughly to the southwest of the townland of Ardgroom Inward, where Bridget Noble resided, and has a coastline facing onto Coulagh Bay – Ballycrovane pier is also located here.)

Eva did not know how many days and nights Mrs Noble was kept in the shed. According to Eva, a contingent of crown forces landed at the nearby pier and moved by the shed, unaware that a prisoner was being held there. 'They passed as close as I am to ye now, to that shed where she was tied up…' This may have occurred, although clearly Eva was mistaken about the date – she said it happened when crown forces were bringing petrol ashore to burn the home of IRA leader Liam O'Dwyer – the house was not burned until much later, in the latter part of May.

Guarding the 'Lady Prisoner'

Members of Cumann na mBan (CnB) were called in to assist IRA men in guarding Mrs Noble, later described by one former CnB activist as a 'lady prisoner'. There was liaison between John Sheehan, Captain of the IRA's Ardgroom Company, and officers of the Ardgroom branch of CnB. A number of men were assigned to guard the prisoner in the places where she was held captive, and also to escort her when she was being moved. Some of the young men involved in these duties would later move to America, as did many men who had been active in the IRA on the Beara peninsula. A notable aspect of those assigned to keep watch over the prisoner was their youthfulness. Some were teenagers, or in their early twenties, when deployed to guard Mrs Noble. Some of the female 'minders' from CnB were also very young.

Cumann na mBan was well-organised on the Beara peninsula. Dublin-born Leslie Price was the CnB Director of Organisation, and had played a role in setting up branches in Castletownbere, Eyeries, Ardgroom and Adrigole. The RIC noted Ms Price's presence in Castletownbere in the summer of 1918 and it was reported that she was giving tuition in 'ambulance work' to members of the local branch of Cumann na mBan in a local hall. (District Inspector Thomas J. Oates, based in Castletownbere reported to his RIC superiors in Bandon that one of Ms Price's CnB associates in Castletownbere was

Kathleen Downing, who was an assistant in the town's post office. This would prove to be a matter of concern to the post office authorities in Dublin. Ms Downing's brother Daniel Downing, the local postmaster, informed his superiors that his sister denied being a member of Cumann na mBan 'but that she is acquainted with some lady who was in the town recently in connection, it is understood, with that association.'5)

Another key figure in the work of organising CnB on the peninsula was Bella O'Connell, from Eyeries, a sister of Christopher O'Connell, a prominent figure in the Beara IRA – Ms O'Connell became the head of CnB in Beara, holding the position of District Council Secretary.6 Sighle Humphreys, a notable republican who was a member of the CnB Executive, visited Beara in 1921. It was said that she found the area 'very thoroughly organised by Miss Bella O'Connell', and was 'astounded as to the strength and efficiency of the branches…'7

One of the CnB members deployed to attend Mrs Noble in captivity was a young woman called Hannah O'Neill (1901 – 1990), from Eyeries village. (Details of her involvement only emerged into the public domain in October 2017, when her Military Service Pension file was among the latest tranche of pension records to be released online.) Ms O'Neill was not a member of Ardgroom Cumann na mBan – she was the Captain of the neighbouring Eyeries branch of CnB which covered four IRA Company areas – Inches, Urhan, Eyeries and Ballycrovane. She was aged about 20 years at the time. Her superior in CnB was Bella O'Connell. Ms O'Neill would go on to marry John Hanley, from East End, Eyeries, in 1926. He had previously emigrated to Toledo, Ohio, was conscripted into the US forces, and fought in France during the Great War. In the late 1930s under her married name Hannah Hanley, she applied for a Military Service Pension (MSP) and outlined a range of activities during the revolutionary period. Her service began in Easter Week 1916, when, under Volunteer Captain Sean Driscoll [O'Driscoll] she 'picked up information in connection with activities of military and police'.

At a later stage, in 1921, her activities included carrying out a 'special duty', attending to a 'lady prisoner'.8 'I travelled under darkness of night to attend to a lady spy prisoner in our area whose arrest caused considerable excitement by the British military.' It is unclear how the military would have known at this early stage that Mrs Noble had been abducted. As part of her pension application, Mrs Hanley told an interviewer from the Department of Defence that she was 'called on by the Commandant to attend to her'. This would suggest a 'hands on' approach by the Commandant of the local battalion of the IRA to the guarding of the prisoner. The battalion, often known as the Beara

Battalion, was part of the Cork No. 3 Brigade of the IRA, covering West Cork. Prominent local republican, Liam O'Dwyer, would emerge as one of the best-known of the men who, at various times, acted as Commandant.

Asked how long she attended the prisoner, Mrs Hanley replied: 'Two nights in the area. She was moved on then and I got other girls to attend to her.' However, in a revised statement about her activities in the revolutionary era, Mrs Hanley stated that she attended the prisoner 'occasionally' during her period of captivity, 'up to the time of Mrs Noble's execution'. It is unclear from this statement if she was actually present with Mrs Noble when she was killed, or if she was simply attending the prisoner up to a period shortly before she was put to death. (The former Ms O'Neill gets a particular mention in Liam O'Dwyer's memoir, when he paid tribute to the role of members of Cumann na mBan during the War of Independence, stating: 'In Eyeries, Bella O'Connell, Hannah O'Neill and others saved IRA men on many occasions.'[9])

At some stage, possibly after two nights in Ballycrovane, Mrs Noble was taken on a further journey by her captors. It may have been at this stage that she was brought along a rough track leading into a hidden valley close to the sea in the area of Kilcatherine. At the end of the boreen an extraordinary vista opens up – a natural amphitheatre formed by green hills in a place of magical beauty known locally as Feith Bhui. A secluded farmhouse was the only structure in the valley, and it is known that this is where Mrs Noble was held prisoner for a period. The location was identified in later life by an elderly woman who had been a member of Cumann na mBan and who attended Mrs Noble at the farmhouse. Today, the house is in ruins, but on the floor of the valley there are still green fields, bounded by low, stone walls. On one of the hills overlooking the ruins, there is the spectral outline of an ancient monument, a standing stone.

The house is said to have been owned at the time by a woman called Kate Sullivan. She came from the Cohu branch of the Sullivan clan, and was known as Kate Cohu. The house may have been unoccupied when it was taken over as a prison for Mrs Noble. According to a local source, it was 'boarded up' at the time. On a day in March 2017 I stood on high ground by the sea and was shown the valley below, with the ruined house at one end. It was an isolated area of great tranquillity and might have been the location for a film. But one was also conscious of something sinister - the fact that this was the place where a very frightened woman was held prisoner back in the troubled times of 1921.

In this remote hide-out, CnB members assisted IRA Volunteers in guarding Mrs Noble, the female custodians staying with the prisoner overnight. One of the CnB 'minders' was a 17-year-old girl from Kilcatherine Point. She would have been able to take a short cut to the improvised prison from her home – there was a path that led across a hill into the valley where Kate Cohu's house was located. In old age, in 1995, she recalled memories of her long life. She told how she had been a member of Cumann na mBan – you were 'expected' to join the organisation, she said. She also told what she knew of the action taken against Bridget Noble, and details have emerged of the account that she gave.[10] She was a naïve teenager and seemingly unaware that the IRA planned to kill the female prisoner. She referred to Mrs Noble as Biddy, and also with much sympathy as 'the poor soul'. She said that members of CnB took it in turns to 'mind' the prisoner at night at Kate Cohu's house in the valley. It seems that Biddy was in fear of her life and was afraid of being poisoned. When they made tea for her, they would have to taste it themselves before Biddy would drink it. The teenager seemed to like Biddy, and was sorry for her. She heard that Biddy had come under suspicion because she had been seen talking to the crown forces, and then somebody saw her going into a shop and she had silver – a couple of shillings. There was a suspicion that Biddy had got the money in return for giving information. The girl had her doubts about Biddy's guilt, and thought maybe Biddy had given no information at all. (The internal IRA report on the execution of Mrs Noble outlines various allegations against her but does not contain any suggestion that she was suspected of receiving payment for giving information to the crown forces.)

The teenaged 'minder' was related to William Lehane, the farmer who had been shot and fatally injured at nearby Cleandra the previous year following an agrarian dispute. Even though the girl was a member of CnB, she felt angry towards the IRA which she blamed for the killing. She heard that an IRA man, Patsy Dan Crowley, was involved in the shooting. 'They said it was Patsy Dan Crowley and them that shot him.' (So, according to the rumour, was Patsy Dan just one of the masked men who went to Lehane's house on the night of the attack, or was it suggested that he was the actual shooter? A knowledgeable local source believes that another member of the IRA may have shot Lehane.) The former CnB 'minder' said she was told by a prominent IRA member, Liam O'Dwyer, that Lehane would not have been shot had he himself been around – he was in jail at the time of the shooting. (Even in old age, the former CnB member seemed unaware that one of the IRA allegations against Mrs Noble was that she had given information to the RIC about the Lehane shooting.)

14

And then, one evening, the IRA took Biddy away. The girl was horrified later to hear a rumour that the IRA men had put Biddy into a bag or a sack and thrown her live into the sea off Ardgroom to drown, and that local people heard her screaming. It was 'bad work' to drown Biddy, she said.

Some local men who happened to be in the IRA came to the girl's house one day in a horse and cart to inquire about buying a boat. (From the names mentioned, at least one seems to have been a well-known member of Ardgroom Company.) The girl confronted them over what had been done to Mrs Noble – she suggested that if they went fishing in the boat in Ardgroom Harbour the first item they might dredge up would be Biddy. The men were stunned by her comment. They said nothing but looked at each other and glared at her, and gathered around her. But despite their threatening attitude she did not care. She was glad that she had shocked them. They left and did not take the boat. She described the IRA at that time as 'outlaws', i.e. they were a law unto themselves. They would go into a shop and demand clothing and other items, she said. On one occasion a local farmer found that one of his bullocks was missing – it emerged that the animal had been taken away and slaughtered to feed IRA men staying in a house in the locality. Her father was furious that she had challenged the IRA men who called about the boat, and warned her to keep her mouth shut. The fate of Bridget Noble would remain a sensitive topic in the Ardgroom area.

Eva O'Sullivan recalled in the taped conversation that Mrs Noble's husband was not around at the time she was abducted – she was living with her father. 'She married this cooper, Noble. I don't know if he was an Englishman or not. We never knew Noble. I do not know if he died or not, or if he ran away from her or what, but she was there with her father, on her own.' As previously mentioned, Alexander Noble was a cooper by trade and was in England when his wife Bridget was disappeared in March 1921. He would explain later that there was no work available in the Ardgroom area where the couple resided. Bridget may have decided to remain in the area to look after her aged father John Neill and the small family farm rather than accompany her husband when he went to England to look for work, eventually taking up employment in the major English fishing port of Grimsby, situated by the North Sea in Lincolnshire.

At some stage Alexander learned of Bridget's disappearance. It is unclear if he returned home on a visit to find her missing or if he learned through some other means. He discovered that the last time John Neill had seen his daughter was when she set off from the cottage in Reenavaude to go to Castletownbere on 4 March. Clearly anxious over Bridget's fate, and hoping she might still be alive, Alexander embarked on a drive to find out what had happened to her. As will be shown, in his quest for answers, Alexander would engage in correspondence with a legendary Irish leader, Éamon de Valera.

Chapter 2: Éamon de Valera and the Two Missing Women

Alexander Noble must have been in a quandary as he tried to find out what happened Bridget. If a man's wife has been taken away by members of a secret, underground organisation, who does he contact for information about her fate? Despite his years of residing in Reenavaude, he was still an outsider, and he may have lacked the contacts on the Beara peninsula, and the local knowledge, that might have elicited some answers. Then there was a development that must have opened up a glimmer of light at the end of a very dark tunnel. The newspapers reported that a Truce had been arranged in what would become known as the War of Independence. The Truce, between the British and the IRA, came into operation on 11 July 1921. It was also reported that, in the wake of the Truce, Éamon de Valera, President of the Irish parliament, Dáil Éireann, which the British had tried to suppress, had gone to London for talks with British Prime Minister, David Lloyd George. De Valera's delegation included Arthur Griffith, Austin Stack, Robert Barton, Count Plunkett and Erskine Childers.

These initial talks on a settlement between the Irish and the British were the prelude to negotiations on an Anglo-Irish Treaty that would start later that year. De Valera had achieved considerable fame as one of the leaders of the Easter Rising in Dublin in 1916. The tall former mathematics teacher with the austere, priestly air popularly known as 'Dev' had narrowly avoided the firing squad after the Rising. Soon after arriving in London, it was widely reported in the British newspapers, in editions published on 15 July, that de Valera made a statement to the press the previous day, 'at the Grosvenor Hotel'. This would have been a vital piece of information for Alexander. He now had an address in England where de Valera could be contacted. It seems he decided to take a chance, and to avail of the opportunity that had opened up. He wrote a letter to de Valera, apparently addressed to him care of the

Grosvenor Hotel, and it actually reached the Irish leader at this opulent establishment located at Victoria railway station. De Valera was not actually booked in at the hotel – he was staying with friends at West Halkin Street.[1] But he was using the Grosvenor as a base, and members of his delegation were staying there. In his letter, Alexander explained how Bridget had been taken away, and appealed to de Valera for help in finding out what had happened to her.

De Valera had great matters of state to deal with – another letter he received at the Grosvenor Hotel and that survives was a handwritten note from Prime Minister Lloyd George, dated 14 July, inviting Dev to a meeting.[2] Nevertheless, despite the pressures he was under, de Valera found time to write back to Alexander on Monday, 18 July, even though he had an important engagement that day – a meeting with Lloyd George, who was also conferring with Sir James Craig, the Premier of Northern Ireland. Two female secretaries formed part of de Valera's entourage, and this doubtless helped the Irish leader to deal with correspondence. (One of the secretaries was Lily O'Brennan, sister-in-law of the executed 1916 Rising leader, Éamonn Ceannt. The other was Kathleen O'Connell, a native of Caherdaniel, County Kerry. Noted for her reliability and discretion, Ms O'Connell would be Dev's devoted private secretary for 37 years, until her death in 1956.) De Valera, in his reply to Alexander, said he had passed his letter to the proper authorities in Ireland for 'enquiry and investigation'.[3] However, Alexander would experience considerable difficulty in clarifying Bridget's fate.

Mrs Noble was not the only missing woman to be brought to de Valera's attention at this period. He had also been asked for help in getting information about the fate of another woman who had been kidnapped by the IRA in County Cork during the War of Independence. Relatives of elderly Protestant widow Mrs Maria Georgina Lindsay (generally known as Mary Lindsay) were extremely anxious to know what happened to her. Armed men had abducted Mrs Lindsay, a staunch Loyalist aged about 60 years, and her middle-aged servant, James Clarke, from her fine country residence, Leemount House, Coachford. This was in the area covered by the Cork No. 1 Brigade of the IRA. (Mrs Lindsay was a member of the Church of Ireland, while James Clarke was a Presbyterian.)

De Valera had set up an office at the Mansion House, Dublin in late June 1921. It was a period when senior British official Alfred Cope, based in Dublin Castle, was seeking to develop a rapport with de Valera as part of a peace process, while ensuring that Dev was not arrested by over-enthusiastic members of the crown forces. During July, having emerged from the shadows, de Valera had received letters from Mrs Lindsay's sister, Mrs Ethel Benson, seeking news of her sister. She originally wrote to de Valera on 6 July and received a reply, dated 11 July. It was similar to the letter he would send days later to Alexander Noble. De Valera wrote that her letter had been referred to his Army Headquarters for 'immediate attention'. Time passed and when she heard nothing more, the very determined Mrs Benson wrote further reminders to de Valera on July 21 and 26. She stated later that in her correspondence with de Valera she also sought news of James Clarke, adding that they had communicated with his aged mother in County Down 'who was dependent on him'. (Clarke came from Ballydown, Banbridge, and his mother, Mrs Sarah Clarke, was said to be aged 85 years, and an invalid.) Mrs Benson was said to have declared to friends that she got 'neither sympathy nor support' from de Valera.[4]

Unlike the kidnapping of Bridget Noble which had gone unreported in the newspapers, the abduction of Mrs Lindsay and her butler/chauffeur Mr Clarke in February 1921 had received considerable publicity in Ireland, England and further afield, and powerful figures in England began taking an interest in the case. Then, in April, the IRA in County Monaghan shot Kate Carroll for alleged informing and left her body by the side of the road. The abduction of Mrs Lindsay and the shooting of Kate Carroll caused embarrassment for the Irish republican leadership in Dublin. They had not been told in advance about the action to be taken against the women, and they had not been informed about the fate of Mrs Lindsay. The abduction and the killing had given their British opponents a propaganda advantage.

In May 1921, Erskine Childers, the English-born former Royal Navy officer who had thrown in his lot with the Irish republican cause and was now Director of Publicity with Dáil Éireann, had sent a memo to Michael Collins, IRA Director of Intelligence, about the case of the two women. Childers, author of the renowned spy thriller, *Riddle of the Sands*, had landed rifles for the Volunteers at Howth, County Dublin in 1914 and had Anglo-Irish family connections. In his memo, he seemed concerned about the kidnapping and killing of females. With his background as an officer and a gentleman, the targeting of women may have conflicted with his sense of chivalry. He was particularly concerned that 'enemy propaganda' was making 'mendacious but damaging use' of the 'spy question'. In his note to the charismatic Collins, known as 'The Big Fellow', he seemed anxious for guidance as to how to deal with the adverse publicity that had resulted. 'Shall we say (a) the execution of women spies is forbidden, and that Kitty Carroll was not killed by the IRA? Or (b) Kitty Carroll was killed in contravention of orders by the IRA, and that (c) Mrs Lindsay is now in prison for giving information to the enemy?'[5]

It would later emerge that Mrs Lindsay had been shot several weeks before, the previous March, but that Sean O'Hegarty, the secretive commandant of Cork No. 1 Brigade, had not informed GHQ about her death, even though it appears that he was fully aware of her fate. On 15 March a communication was sent to Michael Collins by the wily Cork No. 1 Brigade Adjutant, Florence O'Donoghue (who was also the Brigade Intelligence Officer), indicating that James Clarke had been dealt with 'in the usual way' [i.e. shot and secretly buried] but that Mrs Lindsay was too old for deportation and was dying, and the local Battalion Commandant proposed to hold her 'until she died'.

Historian Dr Andy Bielenberg has pointed out that O'Donoghue's account 'is completely at variance with the subsequent report on her death by the O/C of the Cork No 1 Brigade, Sean O'Hegarty'. Bielenberg went on: 'This [report by O'Hegarty] alleged that they were both shot together, Clarke and Lindsay, and they were buried in the same grave. This is an altogether more likely scenario since it is corroborated by testimony of Frank Busteed, the 6th Battalion [Cork No 1 Brigade] Flying Column leader, who supervised the executions. So in other words, she was already dead when this letter was written on 15 March...' He said the Cork No. 1 Brigade 'were trying to make it look' like they were conforming to an IRA directive that women spies were 'not to be shot' but were to be 'deported'.[6]

The claim that Mrs Lindsay was dying in captivity seems to have been a remarkable piece of disinformation conveyed to Collins by O'Donoghue – a case of deceiving not the enemy, but his own leadership. Ironically, O'Donoghue would later play an important role in setting up the Bureau of Military History, which collected personal accounts of the Rising and the War of Independence. (There was also an unconfirmed report, or theory, that the IRA may have tried to poison Mrs Lindsay as a prisoner. It appears that in the 1970s Moss Twomey, who was IRA Chief of Staff from 1926 to 1936, tried to enlist the assistance of the Provisional IRA to prevent the publication of Sean O'Callaghan's book *Execution*, because he feared it would disclose that in 1921 the IRA poisoned Mrs Lindsay, as they did not want to shoot a woman.[7])

It is noteworthy that the case of Bridget Noble, who had also been secretly killed in March, remained 'below the radar', and does not figure at all in the deliberations at GHQ level about the fate of women who had been abducted or shot by the IRA. Members of the IRA's Beara Battalion had clearly managed to maintain strict secrecy around the fate of Mrs Noble. Alexander's letter to de Valera may have been the first that Dev heard about her abduction. Michael Collins, in his role overseeing counter-intelligence, was ruthless in his drive to eliminate spies and informers. But there are indications that he would have spared Mrs Lindsay had the Cork No. 1 Brigade referred the case to him. He is reported to have said: 'They should have referred it to me for decision. But they did not do so… That's why I said I was sorry about it, as I don't think I'd have shot her on account of her age.'[8] Perhaps Collins would have taken action to spare Mrs Noble as well, had her case been referred to him.

Lloyd George Makes Inquiries

Meanwhile, the disappearance of Mrs Lindsay continued to be a matter of concern to the British. During their July talks in London, Prime Minister Lloyd George is reported to have personally asked de Valera for information about the missing woman.[9] It appears that prompt action would then be taken by de Valera to clarify the situation regarding Mrs Lindsay, while it would take longer to establish what had happened to Mrs Noble. Unfortunately, there were no powerful statesmen inquiring about the woman from Reenavaude. On his return to Dublin, de Valera asked Cathal Brugha, the feisty Dáil Minister for Defence, to make inquiries regarding Mrs Lindsay. Cathal Brugha was a hard-line republican who had taken part in the Easter Rising and would later be killed fighting on the anti-Treaty side in the early days of the Civil War. He would go on to clarify matters regarding the fate of Mrs Lindsay.

De Valera had also been asked by the British about the fate of the elderly Earl of Bandon, one of a number of Justices of the Peace who had been abducted by the IRA in West Cork, with the threat that they would be shot if the British executed any IRA captive. De Valera sent Leslie Price, the Cumann na mBan organiser, to West Cork to inquire about the earl, and after apparently conferring with prominent IRA officer Tom Barry (whom she would later marry) she reported back that the prisoner was alive and in good health.[10] There is an indication that men from IRA GHQ were sent to another part of County Cork to inquire into the Lindsay case.[11] They were said to include Sean O'Connell, a tall, very discreet Clareman who was very close to Michael Collins, and was a member of Collins's special unit, The Squad. O'Connell, who always shunned publicity and kept an extremely low profile, was in command of the troops in Collins's convoy when they were ambushed at Bealnablath during the Civil War, and a distraught O'Connell recited an Act of Contrition into Collins's ear as he lay dying after being shot.

Cathal Brugha ascertained that Mrs Lindsay had been put to death by the IRA along with her servant James Clarke. This was communicated to Mrs Benson who immediately informed the newspapers. She paid particular tribute to Clarke. She said that Mr Clarke gave a promise to her late brother-in-law John Lindsay that he would always take care of Mrs Lindsay in her old age. 'So to his promise he was "faithful unto death".'[12] The revelation about the fate of Mrs Lindsay and her driver would spark outrage in Britain. It emerged that Mrs Lindsay had learned of plans by the local IRA to ambush a contingent of Auxiliaries, paramilitary police, in January 1921 at Dripsey, County Cork. In order to save the lives of members of the crown forces, Mrs Lindsay, acting in accordance with her own lights, tipped off the authorities. She also tried to do the decent thing by saving the lives of the IRA men due to take part in the ambush. She talked to the local Catholic priest, Father Shinnick, and through him word was passed to IRA leaders that their ambush plans were known to the authorities. (In his book on the fate of Mrs Lindsay, author Sean O'Callaghan, who was in the IRA before joining the Irish Defence Forces, then becoming a journalist, portrays the elderly Protestant woman in a highly unfavourable light as an anti-Catholic 'bigot'. However, her attempt to save the lives of IRA men might suggest that her alleged prejudices were not of the extreme variety as portrayed in the book.[13])

In what would turn out to be a major error of judgement, the IRA did not accept the word of a priest who was seen as anti-IRA and decided to go ahead with the ambush. According to a book written by journalist Tim Sheehan,[14] Jackie O'Leary, commander of the 6th Battalion of the Cork No.1 Brigade wanted to heed the warning, but his second-in-command, Frank Busteed, 'led the opposition' to O'Leary's cautious approach, and the latter finally relented. Busteed's impetuosity and gung-ho attitude overcame wiser counsels – with disastrous results.

Busteed, who, as mentioned, was also O/C of the battalion Active Service Unit, or 'flying column', may have hoped to emulate the action of Tom Barry who, with his column, had wiped out an Auxiliary patrol at Kilmichael the previous November. Referring to the two lorry-loads of Auxiliaries who were being targeted at Dripsey, Busteed told Ernie O'Malley, the republican who, in the 1940s and 1950s, interviewed many former colleagues from the revolutionary period: 'If Mrs Lindsay had not told the British, it would have been complete annihilation for them.'[15]

In a newspaper article, Tim Sheehan described Busteed as 'exceptionally trigger-happy' and quoted the 6th Battalion Staff Driver Maurice Hinchion as saying he could never understand how O'Leary put up with the 'arrogance and bullying of Frank Busteed'.[16] Another author, Sean O'Callaghan, in his book *Execution*, says that the decision on whether or not to abandon the ambush was one for Frank Busteed – and he decided that the ambush party would remain in position.[17]

The IRA men would have had plenty of time to disperse, but despite the priest's warning, the Volunteers were still in place when Manchester Regiment troops took them by surprise, mounting a major operation to surround the ambush party. One Volunteer was fatally injured, while others were captured. Members of the IRA ambush group would later go on trial in a military court in Cork. The IRA abducted Mrs Lindsay and her servant, Mr Clarke and held her hostage to ensure that the men would not be executed. The IRA sent a letter signed by Mrs Lindsay to the British military commander in Cork, General Strickland, warning that her life would be in danger if the men were put to death. Five men were duly sentenced to death, a decision that was particularly harsh, as the crown forces had not suffered any casualties, thanks to the intervention of Mrs Lindsay.

According to author Sean O'Callaghan, Frank Busteed had the idea of burning local 'big houses' to prevent the executions. O'Callaghan wrote: 'In the Coachford-Dripsey area, which his Flying Column covered, there were twenty or more big houses: Shandy Hall, Innisfail House, Riversdale House, Rock Lodge, Classis, Leemount, all owned by rich Protestants. He had enough men to burn every bloody one of them on that same night. That would give Strickland and some of his high military officers something to think about. The Protestants would raise such an outcry that the executions would not be carried out, particularly if they knew the houses that remained standing would be next on the list.' According to O'Callaghan, Busteed believed 'that there was only one way to get the British out of Ireland, burn them out', and had proposed his views at Brigade meetings.[18]

Draconian Punishment

Meanwhile the British pressed ahead with arrangements to inflict a draconian punishment, and the five IRA men were shot by firing squad. (In addition, John Allen, from County Tipperary, whose offence was the possession of a revolver and ammunition, and a military manual, *Night Fighting*, was also executed on the same day.) Punishments imposed by British courts martial during the revolutionary period were sometimes comparatively mild. As will be shown, some young Volunteers from Beara who appeared before a military court were sentenced to just one month in prison for IRA membership. Nevertheless, it is noteworthy that no mercy was shown to the five men captured at Dripsey, or to John Allen. The historian, Dr Andy Bielenberg, has told of finding an entry in Strickland's diary indicating that it was only after the IRA men had been shot that he received Mrs Lindsay's letter warning of the consequences for herself were the executions to go ahead.[19] After the five were put to death, the IRA shot Mrs Lindsay and Mr Clarke as a reprisal, and buried their bodies in a secret grave. The IRA also burned Mrs Lindsay's residence, Leemount House. (Busteed seems to have abandoned the idea of burning other big houses in the locality owned by 'rich Protestants'.)

It was apparently through Mrs Lindsay's contact with Father Shinnick that the IRA learned that it was she who informed the British about the ambush. Ironically, by trying to save the lives of IRA men, Mrs Lindsay was putting her own life on the line. In press reports in Britain and further afield, Mrs Lindsay was compared to the heroic English nurse Edith Cavell, executed by the Germans during the First World War for helping Allied soldiers escape from occupied Belgium. It has been suggested that while the local IRA leadership had responsibility for the debacle by unwisely ignoring Father Shinnick's warning, Mrs Lindsay was made a 'scapegoat' for the disaster.[20]

By comparison with the politically-charged and highly publicised case of Mrs Lindsay, the issue of Bridget Noble's disappearance may have seemed a far less urgent problem for the Irish leaders to deal with. There is no indication that any emissaries from IRA GHQ were sent to the Beara peninsula to inquire into Mrs Noble's fate. As already indicated, Bridget's husband Alexander would have a longer quest to get some answers about his wife's disappearance. Mrs Lindsay's two sisters, Ethel Benson and Lady Annie Catherine Forde, were sophisticated and well-connected and ensured that her plight was brought into the public domain. They were daughters of a man who had been a prominent solicitor and landowner, Richard Rawson, of Baltinglass, County Wicklow. (It was reported in August 1881 that Richard Rawson, 'a highly respected gentleman', was boycotted by members of the Land League, the organisation that campaigned against the landlord system, 'for having entertained the sheriff'.[21])

Mrs Benson, whose late husband Arthur Benson was an eminent ophthalmologist, lived at 40 Morehampton Road in the affluent Donnybrook district of Dublin. She wrote letters to the newspapers, ensuring that the kidnapping and fate of Mrs Lindsay was publicised. Bridget Noble's aged father in a remote part of the Beara peninsula would have lacked the skills to publicise his daughter's disappearance. Also, living in an isolated area, he would probably have been more subject to intimidation than Mrs Benson, who resided in an upper middle-class suburb in the capital, where crown forces still maintained considerable control. Bridget's husband Alexander probably also lacked the lobbying/publicity skills and the contacts that might have elicited speedier answers about his wife's fate. He would eventually learn the truth.

Chapter 3: Bridget Noble – Early Years

Bridget Noble was unfortunate to have been the youngest child in the family. Her older siblings either died or emigrated, leaving her to look after elderly parents and the tiny family farm. One could speculate that she would have liked to move to America like her older sisters. But circumstances dictated that she would stay in Beara where, in her mid-forties, she would meet a terrible fate. She was born Bridget Neill on 30 January 1876 – she was baptised on the following 3 February in the Catholic church (known then as a 'chapel') at Eyeries, a village on the Beara peninsula. In that era, Catholic baptismal registers were written in Latin, and Bridget appears in the records as 'Brigida Neill'.[1] The sponsors were James McCarthy and Ellen Lyne. Bridget, also known as Biddy or Bridgie, was the daughter of John Neill (also known as Jack O'Neill) and his wife Mary Sullivan Neill – Mary's address at the time of her marriage was Sleave, the name by which Ardgroom village was then known, but she came from Collorus, a place of great scenic beauty beside the sea, in the area of Lauragh, in the County Kerry part of Beara. The couple had married at Eyeries church in February 1864. Bridget grew up on her parents' small farm at Reenavaude, near Ardgroom, on the northern side of the Beara peninsula, close to the Kerry border. The farm was situated on high ground overlooking the sea and with a view across to the mountains on the far side of Ardgroom Harbour.

Bridget's grandfather, Daniel O'Neill, came from Bere Island and around the beginning of the Great Famine married Mary Rahilly and thus 'married into' her farm at Reenavaude North.[2] In the Irish language phrase used locally, he came *cliamhain isteach*. It was a small farm, as the original holding had been divided in three, Mary getting one portion and a sister and brother getting the other portions.[3] The sub-division of farms was a feature of life on the Beara peninsula at the time, as tenant farmers tried desperately to provide a living for family members by providing small parcels of land. However, the system meant that a farm that might have supported one family as well as generating money to pay the rent, was now divided into smaller holdings that were often uneconomic. Daniel and Mary went on to have four children, one of whom, John, also known as Jack, settled down on the farm – he and his wife Mary would have six children, one of whom was Bridget. The sub-division of the original holding would account for the very small size of the farm where Bridget was raised.

As indicated above, Bridget's mother Mary had the maiden name of Sullivan – her father was John Sullivan. The Beara peninsula was historically the territory of the Sullivan clan, and Sullivan is a dominant family name in the region. A local genealogist has recorded that in Eyeries parish [which included the Ardgroom district] there were 23 branches of the Sullivan clan.[4] Bridget's mother, who came from the adjoining Tuosist parish, belonged to the Suonish branch. With so many people called Sullivan or O'Sullivan living in Beara, the use of family branch names was a useful way for local people to distinguish informally one person from another with a similar name. 'Suonish' is derived from the Gaelic word 'suaimhneas', meaning 'tranquillity', 'quietness' or 'rest'. It was a suitable word to describe the tranquillity of the magnificent Collorus seascapes on a mild summer's day, but an ironic appellation in light of the tragedy that would later engulf Bridget. (In tithe records for 1824, a Collorus farmer, Darby Sullivan, was given the additional appellation 'Sounish', obviously another way of spelling 'Suonish'.[5])

Sullivans and Beara History

The Sullivans and Beara have a remarkable history. On the last day of 1602 the leader of the Sullivan clan on the peninsula, Donal O'Sullivan Beare, set off with about 1,000 followers on an epic 14-day march to seek refuge with an ally in County Leitrim. One of the last of the Gaelic chieftains, he had refused obeisance to the English crown, and had lost his Dunboy Castle stronghold. Most of his followers died on the march from hardship or attacks by enemies, and the event entered into Irish history. In the years following the Famine of the mid-19th century, there was much emigration from the region and Beara natives were to be found in many far-flung corners of the globe. Migrants sent back money to their families at home, and this often proved a vital lifeline. Bridget Noble had two aunts, sisters of her father, who also emigrated to distant places. Mary went to Michigan, USA, while Catherine went to Queensland, Australia.[6] A third aunt, Nora, stayed in Beara and married John Crowley of Dreenacappra, Ardgroom – Nora and John acted as sponsors when Bridget's eldest sister Mary was baptised in February 1865. Nora and John would have ten children, and a number of them would also emigrate to America, settling in Michigan (at Vulcan, Dickinson County), or Butte, Montana.[7]

There was a tradition of copper mining in Allihies, at the western end of the peninsula, and the result was that men from Beara went to work in mining in America, especially Butte, in the Rocky Mountains, where many Beara migrants settled. (In 1918, the afore-mentioned Liam O'Dwyer had two uncles and three aunts residing in Butte.[8]) The Anglo-Irish Puxley family ran the mines at Allihies, and Daphne du Maurier's 1943 novel *Hungry Hill* was based loosely on the colourful saga of the Puxley clan. In 1754, during a feud, John Puxley, a local revenue officer and magistrate, was shot dead by Murty Óg O'Sullivan, who had a distinguished career as a 'Wild Geese' military officer in continental armies. Murty, a smuggler and a charismatic figure who was popularly recognised as clan chieftain O'Sullivan Beare, was killed by soldiers who raided his Eyeries home, and his head was displayed on a spike in Cork. (A very fine biography of Murty Óg by Beara man Gerard J. Lyne was published in 2017 – sadly, the author has since passed away.[9]) In the 19th century, the Puxley family built a mansion close by the ruins of Dunboy Castle, and as will be explained, it would later be burned by the IRA in 1921, during the War of Independence.

The Beara peninsula, where Bridget's family roots ran deep, juts out into the Atlantic in the southwest corner of Ireland. The rugged Slieve Miskish and Caha Mountains run down the central spine of the peninsula, which is bounded to the north by Kenmare Bay, sometimes called the Kenmare River, and to the south, by the broad sweep of Bantry Bay. The Caha Mountains are dominated by the massive, brooding presence of Hungry Hill which, of course, also supplied the title for Daphne du Maurier's novel, as mentioned. The Beara region is still an unspoilt, idyllic haven of magical scenery and magnificent landscapes. Over the generations, visitors have been inspired by the mountains, the secluded bays, the deserted beaches and the tranquil lakes of Beara, as well as its rich history, its Gaelic heritage, the many archaeological remains and the hospitality of the people. Reenavaude, close to the sea, was a place of great natural beauty, but it would have been difficult for Bridget's family to make a decent living from the small holding.

Life was peaceful on the Beara peninsula when Bridget came into the world. Samuel Waters was District Inspector (D.I.) of the RIC and he wrote of his happy memories of the period he was based in the main town on the peninsula, Castletownbere, from 1874 to 1877. 'The district was absolutely peaceful. I could inspect all my stations in two days… To me, it was a paradise of sport. I had free shooting over twenty miles of bog and mountain. There were lakes and small rivers alive with trout. Grouse, woodcock, partridge, and snipe were plentiful... One lake at Glenbeg so teemed with moderate sized fish that it was only a question of how many I wished to bring home. Fifteen dozen was an average take...'

D.I. Waters was referring to a remarkable fjiord-like lake with deep waters set among mountains, close to Ardgroom. The writer Rudyard Kipling would also fish in the lake at Glenbeg. Having landed from the Royal Navy ship, HMS *Pelorus* at Castletownbere in September 1898, Kipling journeyed with some friends on a jaunting car to Glenbeg for the fishing. He wrote later: 'It was a land of blue and grey mountains, of raw green fields, stone-fenced, ribbed with black lines of peat, and studded with clumps of gorse and heather and the porter-coloured pools of bog water.'[10] And then they encountered the lake: 'At last we came on an inky-black tarn, shut in by mountains, locked and lonely and lashed into angry waves by a downward-smiting blast.' Kipling and his friends did not achieve the level of success in their fishing that day as enjoyed by D.I. Waters, but the renowned writer would retain fond memories of his outing to Glenbeg.

Despite the idyllic experience of D.I. Waters, there were storm clouds gathering even as he was posted by the RIC to another part of Ireland. Eventually conflict and strife would disrupt the tranquillity of life on the Beara peninsula. In 1877, the year that Waters departed from Beara, a man called William Dwyer became Principal of Eyeries school, a few miles from Castletownbere. On the Beara peninsula, he was the organiser of the rebel Fenian movement and of the Land League, which opposed landlordism and fought for the rights of tenant farmers. (Around this period it was reported that a major landowner in the region, the Earl of Bantry, owned 69,500 acres, a statistic that helps to explain the local agitation against the landlord system.[11]) William Dwyer would provide much inspiration for his nephew, Liam O'Dwyer, a future leader of the IRA in the Beara region and who, as we shall see, would figure in the Bridget Noble saga. (Liam O'Dwyer records in his memoir that land activist Fanny Parnell, sister of Land League leader Charles Stewart Parnell, once spent a week in his father's house at Cailroe, near Ardgroom.[12])

As for Glenbeg, the secluded valley that was so beloved of D.I. Waters and that had bewitched Rudyard Kipling, it would also have a bearing on the story of Mrs Noble. A young man from Glenbeg, who had been a toddler about two years old when Kipling came calling, would emerge as one of the IRA members who investigated Mrs Noble's visit to the RIC station, when she complained to the police about the shearing of her hair. It would even be claimed locally that he was her executioner although this allegation cannot be confirmed.

Alexander Noble and his Seafaring Forebears

There is a mystery surrounding one aspect of the story of Alexander Noble, the man who would marry Bridget Neill. What brought him to the Beara peninsula, a remote area on the edge of Europe, to pursue his trade as a cooper? He could hardly have chosen a more distant location from his native Fraserburgh, while staying within the bounds of what were then known as the British Isles. It is recorded that the Congested Districts Board for Ireland (CDBI) sent a 'foreman cooper' to Castletownbere and neighbouring districts in 1907 to instruct curers 'in the cleaning and curing of herrings'.[13] Could Alexander Noble have come to Beara under a similar scheme? The CDBI, which had the role of alleviating poverty and promoting industry, had connections with Alexander's home area of Fraserburgh. In the 1890s the board had arranged to have two fishing boats built in Fraserburgh and fitted out by local fishermen, and it was reported that three Fraserburgh fishermen accompanied the boats to Ireland.[14]

There was also a practice whereby some English and Scottish commercial concerns involved in the fish curing business would bring Scots coopers to Ireland to assist with local operations.[15] It was further reported that in 1896, on the section of coast from Ardgroom to Dursey Head, there were more than 60 fish curing stations, owned by more than a dozen firms.[16] In the 1920s at least one fish curer based in Fraserburgh, John Dunbar, also operated in Ireland.[17] While it cannot be confirmed that Alexander Noble was linked to any of the above enterprises, it is very possible that he found employment as a cooper with a fish curing firm operating in Beara.

A couple of older people from Beara, probably reflecting what they heard from their own forebears who would have been contemporaries of Alexander, believe that he had been a member of the British forces. This prompted the question – could he have been connected in some way with the navy? Britain's Royal Navy had long maintained a presence in Berehaven, the magnificent anchorage between Bere Island and the Beara peninsula at the mouth of Bantry Bay, with Castletownbere as a major port. Some of the bigger naval ships at that period carried various artisans including coopers. One of the cooper's roles was to look after the casks containing the rum that was issued to the crew – a most important task. In the naval service, there were two ranks connected to the trade – 'cooper', and a lower rank, 'cooper's crew'. One theory is that Noble was a cooper on a naval ship, and that having arrived in Berehaven, he decided to settle down there, but this cannot be confirmed – no record has come to light to show he ever served in the navy or in any other branch of the crown forces. A man from an old Beara family assured me that regardless of the factors that drew Alexander Noble to the peninsula, it was virtually certain that Alexander would have arrived by ship, rather than by road, given the challenges posed by overland travel at the time.

Alexander Noble may not have been in the navy but he certainly had some remarkable personal connections in the shipping world – there was a strong seafaring tradition in his family going back generations, to the 18th century. Some of the Nobles were very intrepid mariners. Alexander's father, grandfather and great-grandfather were all shipmasters, going to sea in command of sailing ships. Alexander was born in Scotland on 8 August 1873, the eldest of seven children of sea captain Alexander Sim Noble and his wife Helen. The place of birth has been variously given in records as Fraserburgh, or Findochty, Banffshire, or Rathven, Banff. Helen also came from a seafaring family – her father John Noble was a fisherman, as was her mother's father, James Thain.

Alexander's siblings were John, Charles, Helen, Isabella, Jessie and William. The family lived in the bustling fishing port of Fraserburgh, Aberdeenshire, on the northeast coast of Scotland. Many locals made their living in occupations linked to the sea. The father, Alexander Sim, himself the son and grandson of Fraserburgh sea captains, had been baptised in the local Church of Scotland [Presbyterian] parish in June 1847.[18] Alexander Sim probably learned seamanship through going to sea as a boy with his own father (Alexander 'Sandie' Noble 1805-1862), and he made steady progress in his sailing career. He obtained his merchant navy mate's certificate in December 1876 and, after an examination at Aberdeen port, his master's certificate in April 1881.[19]

He had honed his seafaring skills while still only in his early twenties by skippering, or helping to skipper, a schooner of the type known as a billy-boy, registered in the Aberdeenshire port of Peterhead, taking cargoes to and from the Continent. (The small schooner was called the *Jessie*, a name by which his mother was often known – she was the former Janet Carle; one of Alexander Sim's daughters would also be called Jessie.) In September 1870, while bound from Hamburg to Middlesbrough with a cargo described as 'manure salt', the vessel was caught up in a storm and lost her mainsail. Alexander Sim and his two crewmen were rescued by the crew of the fishing smack *Pathfinder* after being found in a disoriented state below deck, and the *Jessie* had to be towed into Yarmouth.[20] Following an adjudication hearing in Yarmouth, certain payments had to be made to the salvors, and the matter was reported in a local newspaper.

This must have been a harrowing, and indeed embarrassing experience for Alexander Sim. Seafaring under sail was a tough, hazardous and demanding way of life. A severe storm could blow you off course or lead to shipwreck; navigating in bad visibility due to mist or fog posed its own dangers; another hazard was becoming becalmed due to lack of wind. (Alexander Sim was a traditionalist who never embraced steam power, the propulsion method for ships that was becoming increasingly dominant in the shipping world.)

Seafaring had also brought about a great family tragedy. Alexander Sim's older brother Peter, born in 1828, decided to follow in the family seafaring tradition and as a young man was progressing well in his nautical career. In 1851 Peter had secured his seamaster's certificate from the Board of Trade. In 1853, like some other British sea captains at this period, he became a Freemason – he was master of the vessel *Eliza* at the time. In July 1856, at Fareham, Hampshire, he married 25-year-old Rosina Frances Fynmore, daughter of a swashbuckling Royal Marines officer, Lieutenant-Colonel Thomas Fynmore (1797-1866).

The officer had seen much action in many far-flung corners of the globe. As a boy in the Marines he had taken part in the capture of a French privateer schooner in 1811; in 1827 he was at the naval Battle of Navarino which resulted in the defeat of the Otttoman navy, and among other exploits, in 1837 he landed in Albania at the head of a force to fight pirates.[21] As for Peter Noble, in 1858 he was master of the ship *Albatros* and, accompanied by wife Rosina, he set sail from Liverpool bound for Singapore on 18 February that year. The ship never reached its destination and was reported to have been destroyed by a hurricane off the coast of Central Sulawesi, in what is now Indonesia.[22] There were no survivors. As will be shown, decades later, the sea would inflict another great tragedy on the Noble family.

In addition to the 1870 rescue mentioned above, Alexander Sim Noble would have some other scarey experiences at sea. It was reported in November 1879, for instance, that his schooner *Milky Way* was 'run down' by the steamer *Spray* off the Danish coast, and five crew had to be rescued.[23] Alexander Sim was subsequently master of the 127-ton brigantine *Isabel*. In September 1888 the two-masted sailing ship was being towed out of its home harbour of Aberdeen by a steam-tug when a 300-ton schooner-rigged steamer, *St Clair*, crashed into it while entering the port, carrying away the main rigging and causing much other damage.[24] The following February there was a newspaper report of how a vessel called the *Isabel* from Aberdeen, probably Alexander Sim's ship, almost foundered after losing her sails in a gale. The *Isabel* was being driven towards rocks when a tug managed to get a line on board and she was towed into Tyne harbour.[25]

Instead of going to sea in sailing ships, two of Alexander Sim's sons took up a rather safer and perhaps more mundane occupation – Alexander junior and his youngest brother William became coopers, making wooden barrels for use in the fish curing industry. It was a very good, lucrative trade requiring considerable skill, and a lengthy apprenticeship was necessary. Coopers were considered among the elite of tradesmen. The herring industry in Fraserburgh was flourishing and fish were cured and packed in air-tight barrels for export. It is not known where Alexander learned his trade as an apprentice but records show that his brother William had an apprenticeship with the long-established Fraserburgh fish curing concern, J. Cardno & Sons – he finished serving his time in April 1913.[26]

Tuberculosis Takes Its Toll

It was a period when a common cause of death in Great Britain and Ireland was Tuberculosis (TB), and the disease would take a terrible toll on young adult members of the Noble family – Alexander junior's siblings John, Charles and Isabella would all succumb to what was known as 'consumption' while still in their late teens or early twenties. They were all single and died within a few years of each other. The first to go was John – he had joined the Royal Navy in 1891 at age 16 years, having previously worked as a clerk. In time-honoured sailor tradition, he soon acquired tattoos. His navy file records that marks on his body consist of: 'Tattooed letter "J" on left hand. Bracelets tattooed on both wrists.' He was said to be 5 foot 8¼ inches tall, with light brown hair, blue eyes and fresh complexion.[27] He steadily worked his way up through the ranks, becoming an Ordinary Seaman and then Able Seaman, his character being consistently described in naval records as 'VG' [Very Good]. His first ship was the *Clyde*, and he would go on to serve on other vessels, including the *Caledonia, Pembroke, Dolphin, Victory I* and *Gibraltar*.

After five years in the navy, Able Seaman Noble was invalided out on 13 March 1896 and died the following year, on 25 August 1897, at 27 High Street, Fraserburgh. He was aged 22 years. The death registration record indicated that he had been ill from TB for a year. John's brother Charles was among those with him when he died.[28] Charles himself would die from the contagious disease just a couple of years later, on 13 December 1899, at the same location, 27 High Street. He was aged 20 years, and worked as a fish merchant's clerk. It was his brother Alexander who reported the death to the registration authorities.[29]

At the time of the 1901 census Alexander was still living at the family home at Fraserburgh. Then it seems he decided to spread his wings and move on to the big city of Aberdeen, about 40 miles away, where he lived in rented accommodation at 35 Walker Street in the Torry district. Meanwhile, the family moved from their previous address in Fraserburgh, taking up residence at 65 Charlotte Street. The period of the early 1900s would prove an eventful and challenging time for Alexander Noble. Alexander's father, Alexander Sim, was far away from home at this time, his career as a mariner having taken him to the southern hemisphere. He was chief mate on a sailing ship, the *Acacia*, a 200-ton barque registered in Hobart, Tasmania.

In 1903 Alexander [junior] made a return visit to Fraserburgh where yet another family tragedy was unfolding. His younger sister, Isabella, a dressmaker, was dying of Tuberculosis. Records show that Alexander was present when she passed away at age 19 years at 11.15 pm on Tuesday, 27 January, at 65 Charlotte Street.[30] Isabella had been ill for 15 months, and the cause of death was recorded as Phthisis Pulmonalis, also known as 'consumption' or TB. It was Alexander who reported her passing to the death registration authorities. The loss of his three siblings in such a short space of time must have weighed heavily on Alexander, and perhaps deepened the bond with his surviving brother William. Unfortunately, as will be shown, another of Alexander's sisters would later also succumb to TB. The disease had also attacked a previous generation of Nobles – when Alexander's shipmaster grandfather, Alexander 'Sandie' Noble passed away in 1862, the cause of death was given as 'Phthisis Pulmonalis'. The death registration record noted that he was the son of shipmaster William Noble, now deceased.[31]

Paternity Suit

Later in 1903, Alexander faced another difficult situation, this time in his own personal life. It appears that he had a relationship with an older, single woman, Mary Ann, who worked as a domestic servant on a big farm at New Byth, Turriff, about 15 miles southwest of Fraserburgh. Court records show that on 11 September, at Peterhead Sheriff Court, Mary Ann brought a paternity suit against him.[32] (Mary Ann already had a young son from another relationship.) The court ordered Alexander Noble, 65 Charlotte Street, Fraserburgh, to make certain payments to Mary Ann as he was 'the father of an illegitimate male child' of which she was delivered at New Byth, in January 1903. He was instructed to pay £2 for 'inlying charges' and £6 for the first year, thereafter £5 per annum for six years 'as aliment for said child'. It was also decreed that Noble pay the sum of £3.16s.9p to Mary Ann's solicitor. Little is known about the relationship between Alexander and Mary Ann, and it is unclear to what extent Alexander kept in touch with the boy whose birth gave rise to the paternity suit.

Shipwreck Tragedy

In the summer of 1904 Alexander's father was about to set off from Tasmania on a lengthy sea passage aboard the three-masted sailing ship on which he served. Alexander Sim Noble, aged 57 years, proposed that this would be his final working voyage before retiring home to Fraserburgh. He planned to be back with his family by Christmas. On 20 June the 118-foot *Acacia* left Port Esperance, Tasmania with a cargo of timber bound for Port Adelaide, South Australia, more than 900 nautical miles away. The ship was under the command of Captain A.V. Saunier; second-in-command was Chief Mate Alexander Sim, and there were seven crew. The vessel never reached its destination. Alexander Sim's family learned later that year that the ship was missing. The fact that a well-known Fraserburgh mariner was 'lost at sea' was reported by the local press in October, the *Fraserburgh Herald* stating that Captain Noble is survived by widow and family 'for whom the utmost public sympathy is expressed'.

Then, in early 1905, fishermen came across wreckage from the *Acacia* south of the Mainwaring Inlet, on the remote west coast of Tasmania. A naval ship, HMS Cadmus went to the scene and on 17 March 1905 searchers found the wreckage spread along three miles of beach. Naval personnel recovered the remains of five skeletons, one of which was judged, by the height and remnants of clothing, to be that of the mate, Alexander Sim Noble, who was six feet tall. One theory was that the vessel foundered after being driven onto offshore rocks by heavy gales and that the men drowned, their bodies then being washed ashore. Another theory was that the men survived the wreck but died of starvation. An inquest in Hobart found that there was no evidence to show how the men came by their death. At least remains were recovered – there was no such conclusion when Peter Noble and his young wife were lost at sea decades previously.

The funeral of the *Acacia* victims took place in Hobart on 20 March. The remains of the five men were placed in one coffin draped with the Union Jack, and there was a service at St Andrew's Presbyterian Church, attended by local dignitaries. The hearse was drawn by four black horses, escorted by naval personnel, and the procession to Queenborough Cemetery was led by the band of HMS Euryalus, while local people respectfully lined the route, the men with heads uncovered. Back in Aberdeenshire, the local press provided sympathetic coverage of the tragedy, the *Fraserburgh Herald* stating that Captain Noble came from 'an old and well-known seafaring family' in Fraserburgh, and noting that his wife and family resided at 65 Charlotte Street. The report went on: 'The pathetic part of the story is that

Captain Noble, before leaving Port Esperance, wrote home to his wife [Helen] saying that the voyage on which he was entering was to be his last as immediately on its completion he was to finally retire from the sea, and settle down in Fraserburgh.'

Having lost his father to the sea, and three siblings to Tuberculosis, and having been the target of a paternity suit, Alexander Noble may have hoped that his move to the Beara peninsula would usher in a period of tranquillity in his life, but once again tragedy would eventually intrude.

Chapter 4: Alexander Noble's Beara Romance with Bridget

Shortly before he moved to Ireland, Alexander Noble was living in Montrose, a coastal town in Scotland to the south of Aberdeen, where there was a major fish curing industry. Then he came to West Cork, where he pursued his trade as a cooper, once again working in the fish curing industry. One wonders if family tragedy was one of the factors that led him to make a fresh start in a very different location. On the Beara peninsula many local men fished for mackerel and there was also a practice of curing mackerel for export. It was a period when the fish curing industry on the Beara peninsula was flourishing, and there was a high demand for barrels for the export market – thousands were required every year.[1]

The most prominent merchant in Castletownbere, Denis F. McCarthy, known as 'D.F.', was a major exporter of cured mackerel. (The spelling of the family name was later changed to 'MacCarthy' in order to differentiate Denis and his family from others of similar name. Denis's son Aidan MacCarthy became a medical doctor in the RAF and as a prisoner of war in Japan famously survived the atomic bombing of Nagasaki.) Steamships and schooners visited Castletownbere to load barrels of cured mackerel for transport to destinations in England and as far away as the USA and Norway. Anecdotal evidence suggests Alexander lived on Bere Island for a period. Then it appears he worked as a cooper at Pallas Pier in Ardgroom Harbour, a place of enchanting scenery with panoramic views of the sea and the mountains. He may have been the only Presbyterian in Ardgroom Inland – as mentioned, there were just a couple of Church of Ireland families in the townland at the time of the 1911 census, and there are no Presbyterians recorded in either the 1901 or 1911 census.

With the arrival of Alexander in the Beara peninsula, it seems that love entered Bridget Neill's life. She may have encountered the

Scotsman as she walked by Pallas Pier on her way to and from Ardgroom village. A romance developed and the pair decided to marry. Perhaps Bridget fell under the spell of this young man who was very different from the other young men in her district, mainly farmers' sons, and almost all Catholic. He may have seemed rather exotic, in light of the fact that he was from Scotland and was from a different religious background. On 12 February 1907, Alexander, aged 33 years, married Bridget, aged 31 years, in the Catholic church at Eyeries. The small church, with its narrow nave and two small transepts and its air of tranquillity, is dedicated to St. Kentigern, and lies on the narrow, winding main street of the quiet village, nowadays noted for its neat, terraced houses, each painted a different colour.

The witnesses were Johanna Sullivan and William Noble, Alexander's younger brother. William, aged 17 years, was still an apprentice cooper. The celebrant was the Rev. Michael Costello C.C. The marriage certificate describes Alexander as a bachelor, a cooper by profession, with his residence at the time of marriage as Montrose, and the profession of his father as 'ship master'. (The fact that he gave Montrose as his place of residence might suggest that he did not have a permanent address at this stage in Beara.) Bridget is stated to be a 'spinster' and a 'farmer's daughter'.[2] Although commonly known as 'Bridget Neill', her surname is rendered as 'O'Neill' on the marriage register. As for the witness, Johanna Sullivan, the name was quite common, but one could speculate that it was a 19-year-old woman who lived near Bridget in Reenavaude. A few years later she would marry a farmer in an adjoining district, but tragically died in 1926 at age 38 years from broncho-pneumonia and heart failure.

Alexander and Bridget took up residence with her parents, John and Mary, in their small thatched cottage at Reenavaude North, within easy walking distance of Pallas Pier. The cottage lay only about a half mile from the pier. The 1911 Census shows that all four were in residence at that time in the three-roomed house. Alexander's new surroundings would have been very different from the urban environment that he had previously known in Scotland. The ruins of the old cottage are still there, located off the road, in a field. The stone walls are obscured by trees and, for a visitor without local knowledge, difficult to find. As previously indicated, the ruined dwelling is in an area of great natural beauty, with haunting views of the sea and the mountains, the tranquillity of the landscape in stark contrast to the tragedy associated with the cottage. Census data indicates the house was a very modest dwelling, with two windows to the front, and one outhouse. Alexander came from a Protestant family, his father having been baptised in the Church of Scotland, as previously indicated, but in the Census returns for 1911 Alexander is surprisingly recorded as being a Catholic. If the entry is correct, it would suggest he converted on getting married to Bridget, although no record has come to light to show that he was received into the Catholic church. (Alexander's parents were married in Fraserburgh on 31 October 1872 under the auspices of the Congregational Church, an off-shoot from the Church of Scotland, with the Rev. John Wemyss, a notable preacher and temperance crusader, overseeing the nuptials.[3])

Bridget had wed later in life than some other women on the Beara peninsula who married very young and had large families. The Catholic church approved of big families and in the Beara region, as in Ireland generally in the late 19th and early 20th centuries, some of the families were very big by modern standards, or indeed by any standard. Towards the top of the child-bearing league in the Beara region were Tim Harrington and his wife of Finaha, Castletownbere, who had 24 children[4]; Tade Hanley and his wife Kate of Scrahan, Urhan, had 21 children[5]; Dan and Mary McAuliffe of Clash, Derrycreeveen on Bere Island had 17 offspring, as did Jeremiah O'Sullivan and his wife Mary Harrington of Gortnabulliga, Eyeries. Sadly, Julia O'Sullivan, wife of Pats O'Sullivan of Gortahig, Allihies, died while giving birth to her 20th child.[6] In the midst of all this fecundity, it would appear that Bridget herself remained childless – there is no record of her having any children.

As mentioned, Bridget was the youngest in her own family. The 1911 census indicates that she had five siblings with only two still alive. The latter had emigrated to America, leaving Bridget as the family member who drew the 'short straw', so to speak – it would fall to her to provide care and support for elderly parents. Had she decided to join her two sisters in America, no doubt they would have given money towards the fare and helped her make a new start in the USA. But family circumstances ensured that Bridget would remain in Beara, where she would fall foul of the IRA and become one of the Disappeared. In the 1901 Census she is recorded as the only child of the family living with the parents. Research by a genealogist, and information from birth registry records, indicates that Bridget's siblings were Mary, born February 1865; Patrick, born January 1867, who died young; Dora, born September 1869 and Martha [Mattie], born April 1872, who both went to New York, and Laurence, born 30 December 1874, who died as a baby.[7]

Bridget's Sisters in America

Little is known about Bridget's eldest sister Mary, who had passed on by the time of the 1911 Census. Bridget's remaining two sisters, Dora and Martha, took the emigrant ship to America. They both settled on the east coast of the US, got married, and realised the American dream, raising families in pleasant New England neighbourhoods and leading lives of modest prosperity. Dora was aged 20 years when she embarked on her great adventure to find a better life in America – she boarded the liner *Teutonic* at Queenstown [Cobh], on 7 August 1890 arriving in New York six days later.[8] Ship records show that a young man called James Scully (the name was rendered as 'Skully' in the passenger list) was on the same voyage to New York. They had consecutively numbered tickets – Dora's was numbered 2892 while his was 2893, suggesting they were bought around the same time. This may have been the James Scully that Dora would marry in September 1891, the year after they both arrived in America – it appears that her new husband was from the Caharagh, Drimoleague area of West Cork. They were wed in the picturesque coastal town of Scituate in Plymouth County, Massachusetts, where many Irish immigrants settled. For a time after arrival, Dora had lived in the Brooklyn borough of New York City, working as a milliner. After their marriage, Dora and James lived on Rockingham Street in Portsmouth, New Hampshire.

After 25 years of marriage, there was a significant development – Dora divorced her husband in September 1916, citing his 'extreme cruelty' but in a remarkable turn of events they were reconciled and married again in 1919. They would then stay together until parted by death. He worked at various jobs – including coachman, sexton of a church, and hospital attendant. They had four sons, John, James, Paul Vincent and Edward (also known as Everett), and a daughter Mary. Census records indicate that four other children were born but did not survive or died young. John and Mary may have been named after Dora's parents back in Reenavaude.

Dora seems to have had Irish nationalist sympathies. In June 1919 her name was included in a long list of local citizens who had donated money to the Irish Victory Fund, organised by the Friends of Irish Freedom in support of the campaign for Irish independence from Britain.[9] It was also reported that she became a member of the Ladies auxiliary section of the Ancient Order of Hibernians (AOH).[10] Another group she joined was a patriotic American association, the Companions of the Forest of America, which, among other aims, was said to promote devotion to the home, respect for other people's religious beliefs, loyalty to the American flag and obedience to God's commandments.

Martha, usually known as Mattie, took the emigrant ship a couple of years after Dora. This would have been a very notable event in the Neill family life. Bridget, now aged 16 years, would no longer have any siblings in Ireland and she may have felt an additional burden of responsibility towards the parents. It was not unusual in that era for migrants going to America never to return to the home country. The term 'American wake' was often used for the last family gathering, perhaps involving an all-night party, before a son or daughter made their last emotional farewells to parents, siblings, friends and neighbours before heading to Queenstown/Cobh to board the ship to the New World. The word 'wake' arose from the fact that people regarded going to America as like going to the grave, so unlikely was it that the departing migrant would ever return. There is no indication that Bridget ever saw either of her sisters again.

Records indicate that Mattie sailed on the *Brittanic* from Queenstown, arriving in New York in May 1892. It appears that she came through Ellis Island, the now-legendary immigration inspection station that had been opened the previous January and that was to become the gateway to the United States for millions of immigrants.[11] 'Mattie O'Neill' was recorded in the ship's manifest as being a Servant by occupation, and it was stated that she carried one piece of baggage. It was also recorded that she proposed to have a 'Protracted Sojourn' in America, i.e. she planned to stay there. Dora probably helped her settle in America. In February 1895, at age 22 years, Mattie married 29-year-old John Monahan, the son of immigrants who left Ireland at the time of the Great Famine. Mattie's address was given as Scituate, the same town where Dora was married. Mattie's new husband was also recorded as being a native of Scituate, his occupation described as 'laborer'. (In recent times Scituate has been described as 'the most Irish town in America'. Data from the 2010 US Census indicates that the town has a higher concentration of people who trace their heritage to Ireland more than any other place in the United States.[12]) When Mattie married John Monahan, the Rev. Ignatius P. Egan presided over the ceremony at St Anthony's Church, Cohasset, Massachusetts. The couple took up residence at 131 Myrtle Street in Rockland, Plymouth, Mass., and ran a grocery store for many years. They had three sons, Harry, Arthur and Bernard.

After the departure of her sisters to America, Bridget Neill, the stay-at-home daughter, must have found life on the farm at Reenavaude particularly challenging. She had no brothers to help with the farm, and as her father grew older, she may have had to take greater responsibility for the heavier manual work traditionally carried out by male members of farming families. One wonders if she regretted missing out on the adventure of going to America, and joining her sisters there. After Alexander moved in, he assisted with the farm work, although he came from an essentially urban background, with little experience of agriculture. It would have been difficult to make a living from John Neill's extremely small farm. The fact that Bridget had found herself a husband with a good, lucrative trade must have greatly eased the parents' economic burden and transformed the family finances. Alexander's earnings from his work as a cooper would have been an extremely valuable addition to the household income. Bridget's life must also have been transformed. From being the daughter of an impecunious farmer, she was now the wife of a tradesman who, it can be assumed, was making good money in a highly-skilled and respected occupation.

John Neill's Farm

Valuation records indicate that in the 19th century John Neill's land stretched to just over four acres, divided in two parts. (Using the land measurements of the period, the main part consisted of 2 acres, 3 roods and 25 perches, while the other part was 1 acre, 1 rood.) In the parlance of the time, it was probably 'the grass of two or three cows'. Eventually, John would acquire a little extra land and by the time of Bridget's death, the farm would consist of just over five acres – still a very small holding.[13] Like many of his neighbours, John was a tenant of the Earl of Bantry estate, later known as the Leigh-White estate. Eventually, under British land reform legislation (seen as one of the achievments of Irish constitutional nationalism), the tenants would purchase the land and become the proprietors of their own farms. The division of the farm into two sections was not unusual in that area at that period, and the Neill family would also have had the use of commonage.

It was said that local youngsters were amused at Alexander's Scots accent as he drove the cows along the road, calling out to them by their names. One cow was called 'Star' or 'Starry' and Alexander would call out, 'Hi, go, Starry!' It seems the locals, many still Irish-speaking, did not bother putting names on their own cows. A local man heard from his own family that the children would imitate Alexander's call to the cows. Some of the land around the house was quite good, facilitating the growing of vegetables, including potatoes. Records in the local shop suggest that Bridget preferred the Champion variety – there is at least one note showing that she bought seed potatoes of that type.

Remarkably, as previously indicated, the accounts book in the local shop/post office has survived and gives an insight into the everyday life of Bridget and family members through the purchases that were made. For quite some time the account was in the name of Bridget's father John Neill, but it was often his wife Mary or Bridget herself (referred to as 'Bridgie' in the accounts book) who made purchases 'on account', later settling the bill when money became available, or when it was convenient to do so. Ultimately, after Bridget's mother passed on and her father became advanced in years, the account was in the name of 'Mrs B. Noble, Reenavaude'. Among the items bought on a regular basis were loaves of bread, tea, sugar, bacon, eggs, and occasionally fish. In regard to the latter item, Catholics were obliged by church rules to abstain from meat on Fridays, and fish became a regular substitute for meat on that day.

As regards meat, apart from bacon, the accounts show that the occasional 'pig's head' or 'pig's cheek' was purchased. Porridge would have been an important breakfast staple, and oatmeal is another regular item cropping up in the accounts book. Bridget seemed to like sweet things, and jars of jam and marmalade formed part of the family shopping list. In so far as her budget allowed, Bridget liked the occasional treat. On 22 April 1909, for instance, it is recorded that Bridgie paid over six shillings, and purchased a quarter of tea, a loaf of bread, and '8 crown cakes' – the latter must have been a particular luxury, and were probably baked by Warner's in Castletownbere. On this occasion it is also recorded that she bought 'an ounce of tobacco'. This would indicate that her father and/or her husband smoked a pipe, as many men did in the Ireland of that era.

Bridget and her mother probably had dressmaking skills, and in an era when money for new clothes was in short supply, mending clothes already in the wardrobe would have been important. On one occasion, '2 ½ yards of calico, and 2 ½ yards of lace' were bought. Trouser buttons and spools of thread were also among items purchased. One entry in the accounts book refers to '34 inches of coat lining'. Attention was obviously paid to one's appearance, and on one occasion '2 cakes of blacking' are purchased – this is the term used at the time for black shoe polish. Items for the house were also bought – cups, saucers and a saucepan. Miscellaneous items purchased on a one-off basis included a pinafore, a 'box of hairpins', 'lining for a quilt' and a bath towel. Simple home-cure remedies popular at the period appear in the accounts book – Castor Oil (used for a variety of health conditions and as a laxative) and Epsom Salts which, among various uses, was seen as a cure for constipation. Occasionally a newspaper was bought, referred to simply as 'a paper' in the accounts, possibly the *Cork Examiner* or the *Southern Star*. Another occasional purchase was notepaper and a stamp – possibly a sign that Bridget kept in touch with her sisters in America, and/or that Alexander was writing to his own relatives back in Fraserburgh.

Adapting to life in the simple cottage in Reenavaude may have posed its own challenges for Alexander. In the urban environments he had known in Scotland, he probably enjoyed amenities that were unavailable in his new abode. He would have been familiar with the convenience of gaslight back in Fraserburgh, where there was a town gas supply, while some public buildings were linked up to electricity. In the cottage at Reenavaude, lighting was by candle and oil lamp, and candles and oil figure regularly among purchases recorded in the accounts book of the local shop/post office. Alexander would also have lived in urban locations in Scotland where there was a piped water supply, whereas in Reenavaude water would have been carried by bucket from a well.

With little real crime in the area, it seems that RIC constables busied themselves with enforcing minor laws such as ensuring that people had licences for their dogs. Records indicate that in the years after she married, it was often Bridget who paid the annual 2/6 licence fee for the family dog. Court records show that John Neill of Ardgroom Inward was fined one shilling at Castletownbere Petty Sessions on 26 July 1901 for having a dog not 'licenced according to law'. It may be the case that this was Bridget's father and that the incident encouraged her to ensure the licence fee was paid. The last recorded occasion when Bridget took out a licence was in March 1919, when the fee was paid in respect of a 'red and white cur' [mixed breed or mongrel]. At this stage the couple had a second dog and that year Alexander also paid for a licence for a Collie.[14] A time of turmoil and conflict was fast approaching when the enforcement of dog licencing laws would become the least of the worries of RIC members as they came under attack from militant republicans.

'Simple and Naïve'

Anecdotal evidence suggests that Bridget was a simple, naïve and unsophisticated person. This is the description of her given to Skully through his own Beara connections. Another man on the Beara peninsula, whose family knew Bridget, gives a similar account, even using the unflattering term 'simpleton'. Yet another Beara native whose grandmother knew Bridget well, summarised what he himself heard about her personality — he was told of her quality of 'innocence' or naiveté. Despite the occasional 'paper' being bought, one wonders if Bridget read newspapers on a regular basis, or was fully aware of the quickly developing politics of the time. Nevertheless, she had enough understanding of the legal system of the period to avail of its support if she felt her rights had been threatened or infringed. Perhaps a little like her sister Dora who had divorced her husband when she objected to the way she was being treated, Bridget seems also to have been a person inclined to stand up for herself, and possessed of a feisty independence of mind. This latter trait was illustrated by the fact that she had married a man from outside her closely-knit ethnic and religious community. Perhaps by doing so, she became something of an 'outsider' in the minds of some, even though Alexander may have converted on getting married.

An academic study of mixed marriages in the early years of 20th century Ireland has referred to the 'general public disapproval of couples who married across the religious divide'. The study also found that mixed marriages were quite rare in Ireland – at the time of the 1911 Census less than one per cent of married couples comprised a Catholic married to a spouse from another religious denomination.[15] In Castletownbere parish, which adjoined Bridget's Eyeries parish, the local parish priest, Canon Thomas Carmody, recorded in 1890 that no mixed marriages had taken place in the parish in the previous ten years.[16] This absence of mixed marriages among his flock must have been a source of considerable consolation for the Canon.

The Catholic church disapproved of mixed marriages, and insisted that the children of any such marriages be raised as Catholics. One solution was for the Protestant partner to convert to Catholicism before being married. In August 1907, just a few months after Bridget and Alexander were wed, the Vatican issued its *Ne Temere* decree. Contrary to widespread belief, it did not refer to the religious upbringing of children in a mixed marriage – it laid down various rules that had to be followed so that such a marriage would be valid in the eyes of the church. For instance, it had to be witnessed by the Catholic partner's parish priest or his nominee. The stipulation that children of mixed marriages be raised as Catholics had been in force long before *Ne Temere*. The latter decree was a reminder that the church would only accept mixed marriages under certain stringent conditions.

Gaelic Culture

Many aspects of the old Gaelic culture survived on the Beara peninsula and in the earlier part of the 20th century there were still local people, especially among the elderly, who were native speakers of Irish, although the English language was making major inroads. The 1901 Census returns indicate that there were still some elderly people in the Ardgroom area who spoke only Irish. Anecdotal evidence indicates that Irish was still spoken in Reenavaude when Alexander came to live there after his marriage to Bridget. Sadly, it is said that some Beara people felt at this period that speaking Irish was a sign of backwardness. The Irish language activist and writer Peadar Ó hAnnracháin who spent time in Beara in 1906 as a Timire [organiser] for Conradh na Gaeilge [Gaelic League], described, in a memoir, visiting the remote Claonach area in Allihies parish and finding that everyone had very good Irish but were ashamed to speak it. '*Tá Gaeludhig bhlasta ag gach aoinne acu ach bíonn náire orthu í a labhairt, na créatúirí!*'[17] In his memoir he remarks that many people in Beara depended on the Royal Navy presence to make a living, and seems to imply that this was an important factor in the spread of the English language.

Bridget's parents were born before the Great Famine of the late 1840s, and grew up at a time when Irish was the main language of the people of Beara. (The parents seem to have been uncertain about their exact age. In the 1901 census they are said to be aged 70 years, while in the 1911 census that are stated to be aged 73 years.) According to the 1911 census returns, the parents could speak Irish and English, as could Bridget herself. In a 1925 government report, Ardgroom was included in areas regarded as 'Irish-speaking or partly Irish-speaking'.[18] A factor that may have played a role in the survival of Irish in Ardgroom was its comparative remoteness – the nearest railway station was at Kenmare, about 20 miles away. The town of Bantry, at the head of Bantry Bay, lay about 30 miles from Castletownbere. There was a road transport service between the latter towns but many locals used the ferry operated by a steamship company.

A prominent native Irish speaker from the Ardgroom area was James Bartley Shea (1870-1959). Although born a Catholic, he broke a taboo and became a Church of Ireland clergyman and for a period was an itinerant preacher, often preaching in Irish. He attended Trinity College Dublin, wrote articles in Irish and contributed translations to the Gaelic version of the church hymnal. A native of Cummeendeach in Ardgroom Inward, he retained a sentimental attachment to the Ardgroom area, and in a poem *My Brown-Haired Girl in Beare* recalled the local sea caves, the sounds of the ocean, the dancing and the young woman who won his heart.[19] According to local anecdotal evidence, Douglas Hyde [Dubhghlas de hÍde], a founding member of Conradh na Gaeilge and future President of Ireland, also visited Ardgroom to explore the richness of the Irish language as spoken locally.

In Ardgroom village, native Irish speaker Sean Crowley [Seán Ó Crualaoich], known as Jack or Jackessy, was a notable authority on Irish language and folklore. His daughter, Mrs Brigid McCarthy ran the shop/post office on the main street and was probably one of the last people to talk to Mrs Noble before she was abducted. It is very likely that Mrs Noble herself knew Jackessy – he was still in residence at the shop/post office on the day of her last visit on 4 March 1921. Seven months later, he passed away at age 95 years on 23 September. The above-mentioned Peadar Ó hAnnracháin was an internee at the

46

detention camp on Bere Island when word filtered through in October that Seán Ó Crualaoich had died. Ó hAnnracháin had enormous respect for him, and during his time as a Conradh na Gaeilge organiser had visited his house, had drunk whiskey with him and taken copious notes as Seán shared his knowledge of Gaelic culture. Ó hAnnracháin made a sorrowful note in his prison diary, written in Irish, reflecting on the passing of the Gaelic sage. He remarked that Seán had more than 100 songs, and many stories, and while he was blind [*dall*], his mind was 'not blind'.[20] (By coincidence, the house that accommodated the shop and post office was later sold to Ted O'Sullivan, who became a Fianna Fáil TD having been a notable IRA commander in West Cork.[21] He was also known as Ted 'Ríoch' O'Sullivan.)

Jackessy was originally from Carrigaphrechane in the townland of Ardgroom Inward, and opened the first post office in Ardgroom. He and his wife Margaret O'Shea had seven children. Jackessy himself was famous locally for having survived a sea tragedy. He was on a boat taking sheep across Kenmare Bay to Sneem, County Kerry when the vessel overturned. Three people drowned, but Jackessy managed to survive, also saving his sister Mary.[22]

Surprisingly, Bridget's Scots husband Alexander was listed in the 1911 census returns as having both Irish and English. If the entry is correct, one presumes that he picked up some Irish after coming to live at Reenavaude and through his work as a cooper at Pallas Pier. It is also possible that he had a few words of Scots Gaelic – many Gaelic-speaking migrant workers from the Hebrides travelled to his home town of Fraserburgh to work in the fish curing industry in which he himself made a living. There is also the possibility that Constable Thomas Keane from Eyeries RIC station who acted as enumerator may have made errors while assisting the family in completing the Census form. In the 1901 census, both Bridget's parents are stated to be unable to read, and her father signed the census form with a mark rather than a signature. Remarkably, in the 1911 Census, the father is listed as having reading and writing skills and there is a signature on the form, purporting to be that of John Neill. (Constable Keane, a Catholic from County Kerry, would later receive an award from the RIC for his role in defending the police barracks at Farran, County Cork, when it was attacked by a large party of men on 20 June 1920.[23]) As regards Bridget's literacy skills, she was certainly able to read and write, as is clear from the Census returns for both 1901 and 1911. As will be shown, a letter that she would write in early 1921 would have a crucial significance. Her letter to the police would name the IRA men whom she accused of attacking her and shearing her hair. By writing that letter, she may well have signed her death warrant.

Chapter 5: Bridget Noble Goes to Court

In late 1914, just after the start of the Great War, Bridget Noble was experiencing difficulties in her own locality of Reenavaude. She considered that she was being bullied by a neighbour, a young married woman Mrs Katherine Sullivan, and felt so strongly about the issue that, either on her own initiative or at the urging of someone close to her, she brought the matter to court. Anecdotal evidence suggests that Bridget's family, the Neills, were feisty people inclined to stand up for themselves. The trip to court was an early example of Bridget insisting forcefully on her rights, as she would have seen it.

It may not have been the first time she called on the courts for assistance. Records show that on 12 October 1894, Bridget Neill, of Ardgroom Inward, complained at Castletownbere Petty Sessions Court that James Shea did 'maliciously assault and beat' her in Ardgroom village on 16 September.[1] Shea was convicted and bound to the peace. It cannot be confirmed with absolute certainty that the complainant was the Bridget Neill who would later marry Alexander Noble, but the tendency to stand up for herself would fit the profile of Bridget Noble – she would have been aged 18 years at the time of this court hearing.

It is unclear why the friction with Mrs Sullivan developed or why Bridget might have been the target of hostility in her own neighbourhood. It was a portent of more serious trouble to come, although the trouble with the neighbour seems to have been personal, rather than anything to do with politics or religion. Bridget availed of the services of a notable Skibbereen-based solicitor, Jasper Travers Wolfe who practised in the court in Castletownbere and who had a reputation for fighting vigorously for his clients and achieving success. Some years previously Wolfe had pulled off a notable legal victory in Castletownbere Petty Sessions when, against the odds, he secured the acquittal of a 16-year-old youth, Michael Murphy, despite clear evidence that the defendant had thrown a stone that injured a bailiff during an eviction at Gowlane, Eyeries.[2]

The catalyst for Bridget Noble's court action was a confrontation between herself and Katherine Sullivan on Thursday, 3 December 1914. Bridget decided to take the case to court by means of a summons issued to her neighbour, who lived close by in Reenavaude. (Mrs Sullivan would later move with her family to a rather fine house beside the sea, further along the road to Ardgroom. According to a relative, she had spent some time in Butte, Montana before returning to Ireland, and had relatives in the RIC. He told me: 'Nobody now knows the reason for the friction that arose with Mrs Noble.') The case was heard at Castletownbere Petty Sessions in January 1915, and was reported in the *Cork Examiner*.[3] Presiding on the bench was the resident magistrate, B.R. Purdon R.M. Two local medical doctors, Dr Hayes and Dr Lyne, who served as Justices of the Peace, were also on the bench. Through Bridget's solicitor Jasper Travers Wolfe, an application was made to have Mrs Sullivan bound to the peace. Mrs Sullivan, in turn, took a cross-case against Bridget.

Mrs Noble told the court that Mrs Sullivan set a dog at her and came out on the road and jostled and struck her against the face. According to Bridget, the woman used 'vile language' against her, and had 'made a habit' of abusing her every Sunday. [These difficulties may have arisen when Bridget was passing by the house on her way to or from Mass in Ardgroom.] Bridget told the court: 'I am afraid of this woman.' Cross-examined by Mr G.J. Hegarty for the defendant, he put it to Bridget that the dog was a 'young one'. Bridget denied taking up a stone to Mrs Sullivan. Mrs Sullivan, examined by her own solicitor, said she was waiting with her daughter for a merchant to come, and Mrs Noble came by, called her a 'bad name' and said, 'Here I am now, come on.' Mrs Noble stooped to pick up a stone, and Mrs Sullivan pushed her. Mrs Sullivan said she did not 'knock or stagger' Mrs Noble. Mr Hegarty contended that the case against his client was not proved. The bench decided to bind Mrs Sullivan to the peace, herself in £3 and two sureties of £1 10s each. During the same court session, the resident magistrate, Mr Purdon, said they had heard with much regret of the retirement and departure of Head Constable Dobbyn, remarking that during his 22 years in Berehaven, 'he had always acted to the entire satisfaction of the magistrates, the police and the people…' It may be case that Mrs Noble's venture into the courts brought her into contact with the RIC – her later connections with the police would have serious repercussions for her.

Funeral Customs

When Bridget's mother Mary Neill passed on, it appears the death was not registered with the authorities – this was not unknown in that era. (When even somebody as notable as the National Army Commander-in-Chief Michael Collins was killed in an ambush in West Cork in 1922, it appears that nobody thought of formally registering his death with the proper authorities.) While no record of Mary Neill's passing has emerged in death registration archives, one could speculate that she died in 1915. On 25 August that year, it is recorded in the accounts book of the local shop/post office in Ardgroom that 'Bridgie' [Bridget Noble] bought '3 dozen pipes'. This is an indication that a wake was being held at Bridget's home. It was the custom at the time to provide clay pipes, tobacco and snuff for mourners who called to maintain a vigil in the house where the corpse was laid out.

Another funeral custom that survived in Bridget's district of Ardgroom was the ancient practice of 'keening', whereby women loudly lamented a dead person, the word 'keening' being derived from the Gaelic word for lament, 'caoine' or 'caoineadh'. In December 1921 Mrs Elizabeth O'Sullivan, a teacher in Ardgroom National School who had been ill for some months, died at the age of 47 years. A newspaper reported: 'When the funeral neared Ardgroom village it was met by a number of local women who stopped the hearse and started an old Irish caoine which was most mournful to listen to.'[4] There was no keening for Bridget, no lamentation, no 'songs for the dead' as, of course, she was not accorded a funeral when she was done to death secretly earlier that year.

First World War

The outbreak of the First World War in 1914 would have an impact on many families in Ireland. Bridget Noble's own brother-in-law William Noble, who had been a witness at her wedding, was one of the vast numbers of British soldiers to experience the horrors of the trenches in France. As will be outlined, Bridget's niece in America showed much pioneering spirit by joining the US Navy as soon as it began accepting females into the service, as America entered the war. It has been estimated that more than 200,000 men from Ireland served in British and allied forces during the Great War with estimates of the dead ranging from between 30,000 and 35,000, to up to 50,000. John Redmond, the leader of the Irish Parliamentary Party, which attracted the votes of most Irish nationalists, and which had made considerable progress towards its objective of Home Rule through its activities at Westminster, had urged Irish nationalists to join the British Army.

Redmond had re-united the party in 1900 after a split over the involvement of previous party leader Charles Stewart Parnell in a sensational divorce case. Another potential leader of the party at the time was a native Irish speaker from Beara, Timothy C. Harrington (1851 – 1910), who took a major role in the Land League campaign, was close to Parnell, became an MP and a barrister, and who campaigned to clear the names of the men hanged for the infamous Maamtrasna murders in 1882. When the Home Rule Bill was passed by the House of Commons in May 1914 there were massive celebrations in Bridget Noble's home area of Ardgroom. It was reported that on the evening of 26 May, hundreds of people gathered and took part in a procession through the village. They addressed by members of the United Irish League, and there were cheers for Redmond and Home Rule. Patriotic songs were sung, there were displays of Irish dancing, and the festivities, amid blazing tar barrels, went on into the early hours.[5]

In urging his followers to aid the British war effort, Redmond, was hoping to build bridges with Ulster Protestant Unionists who were demanding exclusion from Home Rule and who had formed a militia to enforce their demands. The Home Rule measure had been placed on the statute book but largely due to Unionist opposition, implementation had been postponed while the Great War lasted. Redmond probably did not anticipate that the war would drag on so long and that so many would die. His hopes of a peaceful progress towards Home Rule (which some believe would have been a stepping stone to full independence) would be dashed by various developments, especially the Easter Rising of 1916, which was followed by the War of Independence and the Civil War.

The First World War brought an unprecedented economic boom to Castletownbere and the Beara peninsula. Squadrons of Royal Navy ships began using Berehaven on a scale never seen before. The visiting naval ships with their huge crews needed vast amounts of food supplies. Local merchants made fortunes and farmers had an outlet for their produce. Alexander Noble, working as a cooper in the cured fish industry, must also have seen the benefits. After America entered the war in 1917, the economic boom became even greater, with major US warships appearing in Bantry Bay. Berehaven also became a vital base for the submarines of both Britain and the US. Among the US vessels to visit Berehaven were the battleships USS *Utah* and the USS *Oklahoma*, later to be sunk during the Japanese attack on Pearl Harbour in 1941. (The sinking of another US naval ship in 1942, the *Juneau*, led tragically to the deaths of five Sullivan brothers from Iowa who had enlisted in the navy and who were of Beara descent – their Sullivan forebears left Adrigole around the time of the Famine to seek a new life in America.) Some Royal Navy personnel who died during the Great War were buried at St Finian's Cemetery, Castletownbere. Alexander Noble may have known one of them, a Scotsman from Alexander's home town. Engineman Peter Rourk, from High Street, Fraserburgh died of disease in October 1918 aboard a Royal Navy vessel, HM Drifter *Girl May*.[6]

The naval connection with Berehaven went back a long way. The British had become seriously alarmed in 1796 after Theobald Wolfe Tone, leader of the revolutionary organisation, the United Irishmen, arrived in Bantry Bay with a French naval fleet. Bad weather prevented Napoleon's invasion force from landing, and the ships withdrew, much to Tone's frustration. A local landowner, Richard White, who lived in an impressive mansion, Bantry House, at the head of Bantry Bay, organised a loyalist force to resist any French landing, and for his efforts was ultimately made the 1st Earl of Bantry. As will be shown, a dispute over a farm in the Beara peninsula that had been rented from one of the earl's landowning descendants would figure in the story of Bridget Noble.

As the Royal Navy was a familiar presence in Bantry Bay, it was not unusual for men from West Cork to join up, as previously indicated. During the Great War itself, men from Beara served in the navy, while others were in the British Army. Private James McCarthy from Eyeries was killed in 1917 while serving with the Irish Guards in Flanders. At least two men from Castletownbere were also killed in the war – Sapper James Doyle (Royal Engineers) and Private Denis O'Neill (Connaught Rangers). One of the West Cork men from a previous generation to join the Royal Navy was William Deasy, from the Bandon area. He was demobilised from the navy in 1902, and then served with the Royal Navy Reserve.[7] His son Liam Deasy would become an important IRA leader in West Cork during the War of Independence and Civil War.

Bridget Noble's Niece Joins the US Navy

In America, there was a remarkable development when Bridget Noble's niece, Mary Agnes Scully, became one of the first contingent of women to join the US Navy. Mary, born in November 1895, was the daughter of Bridget's sister Dora. As mentioned, the Scullys lived in Portsmouth, New Hampshire – it was the location of an important naval shipyard. America entered the war on 6 April 1917, and on 21 April, Mary Scully, a 21-year-old stenographer, enlisted in the US Naval Reserve Force. The previous month, the US Navy authorities had authorised the recruitment of females for the first time. It could be said that Mary, like perhaps her aunt Bridget and other women in her extended family, was displaying a sense of adventure and independence of mind. Designated as Yeomen (F), and sometimes referred to as Yeomanettes, female naval personnel like Mary generally served in shore installations to free up male colleagues for duty at sea. In June 1917 Mary further consolidated her links with the naval forces when she married another Yeoman in the navy, William Calvin Rutland, from Birmingham, Alabama. The Rev. John P. Moran performed the wedding ceremony in Portsmouth and the couple took up residence in the city. Mary served in the navy for three years, before being demobilised. She would later become a saleslady in a millinery shop.

William Noble in the Trenches

Having already lost three siblings due to Tuberculosis, Alexander Noble must have been particularly concerned when his only remaining brother William went off to fight on the Western Front. William had joined the 5th Battalion of the Gordon Highlanders as a Private at age 21 years on 27 February 1911. This was a part-time Territorial unit which recruited in Fraserburgh and other areas but with the start of the war it would be mobilised for full-time service. William's name was included in a list of battalion personnel who had 'volunteered for foreign service' and which was published in a local newspaper in October 1914.[8]

After his unit was sent to France, William saw considerable action when he was deployed at Festubert, in the Artois region. He was wounded in the knee by shrapnel in early June 1915 when his unit's trenches came under heavy German artillery fire. He was fortunate – a number of his comrades were killed in the bombardment. On 7 June Sergeant Macgregor wrote a letter about the action experienced by the 5th Gordons in the trenches, and it was published in the *Fraserburgh Herald*.[9] The sergeant listed the names of six men of B Company who were killed and 13 wounded – 'Private W. Noble' was among the latter. The sergeant referred to the Fraserburgh soldiers as the 'Broch boys' – Broch was a popular name for Fraserburgh, derived from the Gaelic for 'shore'. Macgregor wrote that he regretted to say 'we have lost a good few of our company'. He went on: 'We were in the trenches for four days, and during all that time we were under a severe fire from the enemy, whose trenches were in some places only 70 yards from ours. It so happened that the portions of our line occupied by A and B Companies came in for the worst of it, time and again our trenches were blown in and the men buried, but time and again our men built them up again under a galling fire.' He added: 'Nothing would have pleased our men better than to have got the command to fix bayonets and charge, for then they would have got a chance of getting their own back.' (A total of 411 men from Fraserburgh lost their lives in the Great War – they are commemorated by a War Memorial in the town.)

Probably because of his injuries, William Noble (Service Number 1278) was discharged from the army in February 1916.[10] There is an indication that he had been promoted to Corporal at this stage.[11] No doubt to the great relief of Alexander over in Ardgroom, William returned to Fraserburgh, took up residence again with his mother at the family home, 35 College Bounds, and resumed his work as a cooper. William was extremely lucky to survive the carnage in France. But if he saw himself as a local hero, he was soon brought rudely down to earth. Shortly after his return from the war, a policeman stopped him on 30 April while cycling on a public road after sunset without a light. He was duly brought before Peterhead Court on 5 May 1916 where he pleaded guilty to 'not displaying the regulation lights' on his bicycle. Sheriff Young fined him the sum of ten shillings.[12]

Beara and the Easter Rising

At first, Bridget Noble's district of Ardgroom and the Beara region generally seemed unaffected by the 1916 Rising, the most significant rebellion against British rule since the 1798 rebellion. The Volunteer movement had split, with the majority, known as the National Volunteers, following John Redmond and his policy of supporting the British war effort against Germany, and taking the constitutional route towards Home Rule. The smaller Irish Volunteer movement took a more militant, separatist line, and a Company of the Irish Volunteers had been formed in Eyeries, on the northern side of the Beara peninsula, a few miles from Ardgroom, in 1915. The moving force behind this development was Sean O'Driscoll, from Eyeries. Christy O'Connell was another founder member. O'Connell's life-long friend, Liam O'Dwyer, born in 1896, alao joined Eyeries Company and would go on to play an important role in organising the Irish Volunteers on the Beara peninsula. Local companies were set up and they would form part of the IRA battalion on the peninsula, the Beara Battalion, also sometimes known as the 'Castletownbere Battalion', or the 'Berehaven Battalion'.

Liam O'Dwyer came from a strongly nationalist family at Cailroe, Ardgroom. He had several brothers who were active in the Volunteers. Robert, John, Tim, Pat, Richard and Michael were all listed as members of Ballycrovane Company. (Robert would die in a drowning tragedy in November 1918 along with four other men when their fishing boat foundered on a reef in Coulagh Bay.) As indicated above, Liam O'Dwyer was greatly inspired by his uncle, William Dwyer, a local

Fenian leader. O'Dwyer described his uncle as 'professor of Irish and professor of French' who 'during his short life wrote thirty-two books in English and French'.[13] None of the books survived – according to O'Dwyer, they were taken by crown forces in a raid on his uncle's home and never seen again.

Liam O'Dwyer was deeply religious, and his Catholicism was intertwined with his republican faith. From his own memoir, he clearly resented how the English tried to force on the Irish their 'king religion' – O'Dwyer's dismissive term for the Anglican Church founded by King Henry VIII.[14] He wrote of how, during the Penal Law period, Catholic priests hid in caves, emerging on Sunday to celebrate Mass on the Mass rocks for their people. O'Dwyer also wrote of Protestant attempts to proselytise among starving Catholics by means of soup kitchens during the Great Famine. He resented the tithe system that operated into the 19th century, whereby Catholics had to contribute towards the upkeep of what was then the established church, the Church of Ireland.

However, he did admire one Church of Ireland clergyman, the Irish-speaking and uilleann pipe-playing Rev. James Goodman who ministered in the Ardgroom area in the 1860s, who collected traditional Irish music and who was 'loved and respected by the people'.[15] (Canon Goodman may well have been a familiar figure to Bridget Noble's parents. He lived in a fine house – now in ruins - overlooking Ardgroom Harbour, not far from the cottage where Jack and Mary Neill resided in Reenavaude.)

In his statement to the Bureau of Military History (BMH) O'Dwyer told how Eyeries Company mobilised after Mass at Eyeries on Easter Sunday, 1916, numbering about 100 men and officers.[16] The company marched towards Lauragh in the County Kerry part of Beara while four men on bicycles, including O'Dwyer, proceeded to Kenmare where they learned that 'things had gone wrong'. (He was referring to the failure of a mission to land arms provided by Germany for the Rising. In addition, an instruction had gone out from the Irish Volunteers commander, Eoin MacNeill, countermanding the order for manoeuvres that weekend – he had been kept in the dark about the Rising, and tried to stop it going ahead. The rebellion had been masterminded by activists from the Irish Republican Brotherhood, who had infiltrated the senior ranks of the Irish Volunteers.) When O'Dwyer and his colleagues cycled back to Lauragh they found the Company sheltering from heavy rain in Lauragh church. The officers instructed all the men to return home. One of the men, Joe Foley of Ardacluggan, Eyeries, was arrested by the RIC and would later be interned for a period at Frongoch camp in Wales.

Jack O'Sullivan and Captain Robert Monteith

It would later emerge that one of Bridget Noble's neighbours in Reenavaude had carved out his own niche in the history of the Rising. Jack O'Sullivan, from West Reenavaude, was an employee of the Great Southern Railway in County Kerry when he, along with his wife Nellie and his sister Elizabeth, provided shelter to Captain Robert Monteith who had landed from a German submarine at Banna Strand on 21 April 1916 as part of an unsuccessful operation to deliver German arms for the Rising.[17] Jack was an older brother of Eva O'Sullivan who, as indicated previously, would go on to record an account of the abduction of Bridget Noble, based on information from a man who had been in the IRA. (Jack and Eva's collateral descendant is, of course, the musician and composer Skully who would play an important role in perpetuating the memory of Mrs Noble.) Monteith met O'Sullivan at the AOH [Ancient Order of Hibernians] hall in Tralee, of which he was caretaker, and O'Sullivan ensured that the weary traveller was well looked after. Monteith recalled how he stayed the night in O'Sullivan's flat, and was provided with a much-needed hot bath, followed by a good night's sleep. 'O'Sullivan worked on the railway, and was on night duty, but his wife and her sister-in-law, Miss Elizabeth O'Sullivan took good care of me.' Jack O'Sullivan warned him next morning that two trains loaded with troops had arrived in Tralee.[18]

While Captain Monteith would evade capture with the crucial assistance of Jack O'Sullivan and others, his comrade Roger Casement, who had landed from the same German U-boat, was less fortunate. The former British diplomat who had exposed the cruel treatment of native workers in the Congo and Brazil, was taken prisoner and would later be executed for treason following a trial in London at the Old Bailey. In later years, as will be shown, Liam O'Dwyer would have some difficult encounters with Monteith in America.

Chapter 6: The Shooting of William Lehane

One night in 1920 the spectre of violence intruded into Bridget Noble's own secluded area of the Beara peninsula, and it would form part of her story. It was the year after the start of what became known as the Anglo-Irish War or the War of Independence, and the conflict had spread to Beara. Late on the night of Friday, 7 May, a man was shot and died of his injuries. Although all the indications are that the shooting was the work of IRA men, it is unclear if the incident can be seen as an 'official' IRA operation, or as an 'unofficial' vigilante attack carried out by republicans. The shooting occurred after three masked men called to the home of a farmer, William Lehane (also known as William Lyons). A widower aged about 47 years, he lived at Cleandra, further west along the coast from Reenavaude. One of the men was armed with a shotgun.

After Mr Lehane opened the door, the gunman fired at very close range, inflicting serious injuries on the farmer. His daughter Mary Ellen later described how he called out: 'Oh God, I am killed.' The farmer was then shot a second time. A Castletownbere general practitioner, Dr Patrick Valentine Murphy, was called. Dr Murphy, who had been practising in the area since he qualified in 1917, had the difficult task of extracting grains of shot from the traumatized victim's legs. (While Dr Murphy was greatly helpful to the IRA during the War of Independence by treating IRA men who were wounded or ill, the Lehane shooting may have been one of the incidents that would lead him to abhor certain actions of local republicans, as will be explained.)

Lehane was in considerable agony and Dr Murphy conveyed him in his motor car to Castletownbere Hospital. There, in consultation with Dr Hayes and Dr Lyne, it was decided that amputation would be necessary to save his life, and his relatives were informed. Accompanied by a nephew, Lehane was transferred by car to the Mercy Hospital in Cork where it was proposed to carry out the amputation. He died on 10 May before the operation could be carried out. It was believed he was shot over a land dispute. Mr Lehane's daughter Mary Ellen told the inquest that her father took over a farm from the Congested Districts Board for Ireland (CDBI) five years previously.[1] A man named Timothy O'Shea [also known as Timothy Shea] had been evicted from it. Since her father took over the farm a potato crop had been destroyed, and he had received compensation. She did not think the gunman fired to kill her father, but rather to frighten him. She said that Mr O'Shea was not one of the men at the door that night. Representing the authorities at the inquest was District Inspector Thomas J. Oates of the RIC. The inquest jury found that Lehane died from gunshot wounds 'inflicted by a person or persons unknown'.

It was in 1914 that Timothy Shea was evicted from his farm by the CDBI over rent arrears. (The CDBI had embarked on the purchase of the lands held by the Leigh-White estate. This was done under land reform legislation, which facilitated tenant farmers in purchasing the land that they rented, so that they became 'peasant proprietors'. However, in the case of the Leigh-White estate, there were delays in finalising the project, and the CDBI acted, in effect, as interim landlord. Bridget Noble's father John Neill was also a tenant of the Leigh-White estate and his farm would also be taken over by the CDBI.) William Lehane made the fateful decision to take the 'evicted farm'. According to one version of events, Lehane received a visit from his brother-in-law, Pats O'Driscoll, who advised him not to take the Shea farm, saying it was not right, and perhaps 'dangerous' to do so, but Lehane did not heed the advice. (O'Driscoll's wife Julia was a sister of Lehane's.) It appears that Lehane had spent time in America, and there was a belief locally that, as a result, he may not have fully appreciated the possible consequences of taking over a farm from which a neighbour had been evicted.

Timothy Shea found it very difficult to accept being ejected from the farm, and continued to resist his exclusion from the land. Lehane's taking of the land caused resentment that would later explode into violence. Meanwhile, in December 1915, at the High Court in Dublin, an injunction was granted restraining Shea and his wife Mary from entering the lands, pulling down fences, cutting the meadows and driving cattle.[2] The injunction was granted by Mr Justice Barton in the Chancery Division to the CDBI; Edward E. Leigh White of Bantry [the original landlord] and Timothy Lehane of Kilcatherine, County Cork [son of William Lehane] who, it was stated, was now in occupation of the land, under a grazing letting.

Trouble would continue. In June 1917, most of a crop of potatoes on the land was found destroyed. This led to a claim for compensation by William and Timothy Lehane at Skibbereen Quarter Sessions in October 1917.[3] Represented by Mr J.M. Burke BL, instructed by Castletownbere solicitor Mr G.L. Hegarty, the Lehanes claimed £150 compensation. The court heard that a crop of one and a half acres of growing potatoes 'was wantonly and maliciously destroyed, and cut down with a scythe or other sharp instrument'. Burke told the court that the case 'reeked of malice'. He said that the applicant had two farms, 'one of which was an evicted one, Timothy Shea having been evicted from it in 1914'. After eviction, Shea 'continued to use the grazing' with the result that the CDBI 'had to get an injunction against him in the Superior Courts'.

Sergeant Thomas Nugent from Eyeries RIC station inspected the damage. He said that he saw the potato garden on 28 June and 'barely five per cent of the potatoes were uninjured – the rest were destroyed'. The judge gave a decree of £35, to be levied on the electoral division of Kilcatherine. Now, in 1920, William Lehane would pay a heavy price for taking the farm – it would cost him his life. Even though Lehane had broken a taboo, the shooting was a punishment that shocked members of the local community. It was said that at Sunday Mass the killing was forcefully condemned from the altar by the priest, who prophesied that the violence would come back on those responsible. As indicated above, there was a belief locally that it was the IRA that shot William Lehane, and it would be alleged by the IRA Battalion Commandant, Liam O'Dwyer that 'information reached us from the RIC' that Bridget Noble gave information to the police about the killing.

Many years later, O'Dwyer referred to the Lehane shooting in a letter to an official in the Department of Defence in Dublin, in connection with a local man's application under military pensions legislation – the man himself was not involved in the attack on the farmer. O'Dwyer stated that Lehane was 'shot for "land-grabbing" by members of this company' – a reference to Ardgroom Company. O'Dwyer stated that he himself 'was in prison at the time' and claimed that 'the actual shooting was an accident during a visit to threaten him'.[4] (The fact that Lehane had been shot twice would raise questions as to whether the shooting was 'accidental'.) Some weeks after the shooting of Lehane, in July, father-of-seven John Dwyer, who worked as a herd for a landlord, was found shot dead in the Drombane area of County Tipperary. He had apparently been targeted as a result of an agrarian dispute. Commenting on incidents of agrarian violence during the revolutionary period, the historian Charles Townshend remarked: 'The rebels of 1920 were the heirs not only to the exalted legacies of the United Irishmen and the Fenians, but also to a deeper and darker tradition of agrarian secret society terrorism.'[5]

RIC Patrol in Eyeries Comes Under Attack

Thomas J. Oates, RIC District Inspector at Castletownbere, was shocked to learn how some of his men had been ambushed. The D.I., who would figure in the story of Bridget Noble, had been informed of an attack on a police patrol near Eyeries, and he was appalled. Gunmen opened fire on a sergeant and three constables, wounding three of them. The police returned fire. It was April 1919 and the incident was an early example of violence in Beara following the outbreak of the War of Independence. Inspector Oates, who occupied an upstairs office in the solidly-built, detached police building in the West End of Castletownbere, wrote a report on the incident for his superiors. He said that he was satisfied that the policemen would have been shot dead 'only that their assailants were saving their own skins by keeping behind land cover at fairly long range'. He asked that the military be sent to Eyeries to back up the police, and this was done.[6]

The attackers, armed with shotguns, were men from Inches Company of the Volunteers, under Peter Neill,[7] who would later become Commandant of the Beara Battalion and would be succeeded in that post by Liam O'Dwyer. According to a statement in his Military Service Pension file, O'Dwyer also took part in the attack.[8] One of the policemen injured was Constable John F. Cummings. The following year he would resign from the force – perhaps one of the many who left the RIC as a result of increasing pressure from the IRA.

What are generally seen as the first shots of the War of Independence had been fired some months before, on 21 January, when members of the Irish Volunteers shot dead two RIC men at Soloheadbeg, County Tipperary during an operation to seize gelignite being escorted by the two policemen. Like most members of the RIC, the two victims were Catholics – one was a widower and father of seven. The attackers included two men aged in their twenties, Dan Breen and Sean Treacy. The killings had not been authorised by Volunteer GHQ, and Breen told later of being castigated by Volunteer Chief of Staff Richard Mulcahy, who said that the GHQ could not stand over what had been done at Soloheadbeg. In a statement to the Bureau of Military History, Breen said: 'Treacy had stated to me that the only way to start a war was to kill someone, and we wanted to start a war, so we intended to kill some of the police whom we looked upon as the foremost and most important branch of the enemy forces which were holding the country in subjection.'[9]

There was an indirect Beara connection to Soloheadbeg. Dan Breen and Sean Treacy were greatly impressed when a Volunteer called Michael O'Callaghan shot dead two RIC men who tried to arrest him after a shooting incident in Tipperary in 1916. O'Callaghan fired on Sergeant Thomas Rourke first and then shot Constable John Hurley in the head as he tried to run away. Hurley, a 23-year-old Catholic from Fuhir, Castletownbere, was given a big funeral in his native town. The victims were the only members of the crown forces to die in County Tipperary during the period of the Easter Rising. Breen told how Treacy considered that O'Callaghan saved 'the honour of Tipperary' in 1916.[10] At Soloheadbeg, Breen and Treacy had now followed the example of the man they admired. The attacks on the RIC spread to other parts of the country, including Beara, and hundreds of policemen would die before a Truce was called. In the meantime, in 1920, as a result of the IRA campaign and because men were resigning from the RIC, the British reinforced the embattled police force with a new element, temporary constables who were mainly former British soldiers known as Black and Tans; a paramilitary police unit, the Auxiliary Division of the RIC (ADRIC) then arrived. It was composed mainly of ex-army officers, known as Auxiliaries. Some of the new police would become notorious, developing a reputation for ruthlessness, brutality and ill-discipline.

RIC Career of District Inspector Oates

Thomas J. Oates was an experienced officer who had previously served in various parts of Ireland. Before the period of conflict, service in the RIC had been considered a good career by young Irish Catholic men. Few of the country lads who joined the force would have considered they were representing an alien power. District Inspector (D.I.) Oates was himself a Catholic, born in County Roscommon at Northyard, Strokestown in early 1871 or 1872 – the records differ.[11] He had made steady progress through the ranks since joining the force as a constable at the age of about 20 years. The RIC authorities kept a note of men who showed promise and who could merit promotion and in 1911, while serving as an acting sergeant, Oates was recorded as being 'good and smart'.[12] (In December that year he was given a Favourable Record, First Class, for 'Good Police Duty' and a gratuity of £5.)

In May 1918, Oates was transferred from the tranquil surroundings of Ballymoney, County Antrim to a rather more challenging posting on the Beara peninsula. From his base at Castletownbere RIC barracks, Oates also had responsibility for outlying police stations in Eyeries, Allihies and Adrigole. He would get to know Bridget Noble and would give evidence at a court hearing arising out of her disappearance.

During his time in Castletownbere, he would also face difficulties in his personal life as well as major challenges in his professional life. Just a couple of months before Oates assumed his duties in Castletownbere, Volunteers had carried out a raid on Eyeries barracks getting away with four carbines. This must have been a severe blow to police morale in the local constabulary district. An RIC inquiry led to the dismissal of two constables. It fell to Oates to prosecute two leading Volunteers, Sean O'Driscoll and Charlie Hurley, for unlawful assembly on the day of the raid – they each got two months imprisonment at the local court in Castletownbere. (Hurley would receive a further jail sentence in December 1918, imposed by a military court in Cork, after the discovery of documents indicating plans to attack crown forces' installations and other public buildings in Castletownbere.) On 30 September 1918, amid increasing tension, the British established a Special Military Area covering much of West Cork, and in Beara, a military presence was established in Eyeries, as mentioned.

As tension escalated in Beara, personal animosity developed between RIC personnel at Eyeries and local Volunteers. In October 1918 Patrick Malvey was arrested in his native Ardgroom village by the RIC, along with Mortimer McCarthy of Ballycrovane – they would later get 28 days imprisonment with hard labour, for refusing to answer questions 'reasonably addressed to them by the police'. Patrick's brother James Malvey would later figure in the story of Bridget Noble, as will be shown. Later in 1918, D.I. Oates had to deal with a tragedy in the RIC contingent at Eyeries. One dark night Constable John Moriarty was shot dead by a police colleague after being mistaken for a gunman. Moriarty had jokingly called out 'hands up' to a group of fellow policemen coming along the road from Castletownbere.

In 1918, just after being assigned to Castletownbere, Oates suffered the embarrassment of being sued for £500 in a Dublin court for 'breach of promise'.[13] The case was brought by Catherine Moloney, who worked as a typist in Dublin. Described as the daughter of a 'respectable farmer' from County Clare, it was stated that she had met Thomas Oates about seven years previously in Kilkee when he was a Head Constable. She claimed they became engaged but that after he was promoted to District Inspector he became cool towards her and broke off the relationship. Oates pleaded that if there had been any promise to marry, it had been rescinded by mutual consent. After the opening remarks by counsel for the plaintiff, there was a consultation between the lawyers for each side and Mr Justice Kenny was told that the case had been settled. In this pre-conflict era, many young Irish women would have regarded RIC men as good 'husband material', before the policemen became the targets of boycotting and violence.

Attack on Allihies RIC Station

In February 1920, there was a significant escalation in the conflict in the Beara region. An attack was carried out on Allihies RIC station, and two constables were wounded, one of whom died – he was Michael Neenan, a Catholic from County Clare. Neenan was not the first policeman to die in County Cork during the Troubles but he was the first to die in a barracks attack in the county. The sergeant in charge was a tough-minded Catholic from County Leitrim, Thomas Nugent. (He will figure further in the narrative in connection with Bridget Noble.) Sergeant Nugent refused to surrender even though the barracks was badly damaged by an explosion, and he fired off two rockets to summon assistance.

After the attack, the RIC evacuated the station which was then destroyed by the IRA. Sean O'Sullivan, who took part in the attack, wrote an account afterwards summarising the RIC casualties – he included a particular detail that illustrates the psychological torment that can impact on individuals in incidents of this type: 'One RIC man was killed and another wounded and one man went insane.'[14] Following the raid, a number of men from the Eyeries area were arrested on suspicion of involvement in the attack, including Sean O'Driscoll and his brother Jeremiah. On 3 March, Sergeant Nugent and the other policemen who defended Allihies police station were awarded the Constabulary Medal for Bravery. Constable Neenan was the first RIC man ever to be awarded the medal posthumously.[15]

In the Ardgroom area, local Volunteers pressed on with attempts to procure arms. It was reported that during February 1920 two sportsmen who had been shooting in the Ardgroom district were held up while travelling in their motor car near the village, and two shotguns seized. Police subsequently searched houses in the village and district, but there is no indication that the guns were found.[16] Shotguns would become a useful element in the armoury of the Beara Battalion, and as mentioned, a shotgun was used to inflict fatal injuries on William Lehane, a killing that would figure in the story of Bridget Noble.

Meanwhile, Liam O'Dwyer was being targeted by the crown forces. He was arrested by police and military at Bantry on Friday, 21 January 1920, after arriving from Cork. A dispatch to do with the Volunteers was found hidden in his hat. At Bantry Petty Sessions he was jailed for a month for 'unlawful association'. He was taken by military lorry to Cork where he was imprisoned at Cork Male Gaol. According to the prison records, he was 5 foot 7½ inches tall, with red hair, blue eyes and a fresh complexion.[17] In his statement to the BMH, he records that he 'took part in a three day hunger strike for political treatment, which was granted.'[18] Some time after his release, he was arrested again and would go on to serve a further period of incarceration, part of this period of detention being served in a London prison, Wormwood Scrubs, where, as will be outlined in more detail, he took part in a more extended hunger strike.

Alexander Noble's Visit to Scotland

As previously indicated, Alexander Noble seems to have remained close to his younger brother William. Records show that in late 1919 Alexander visited his native Fraserburgh to act as witness when William was married. William had acted as a witness when Alexander married Bridget, and now Alexander was providing a similar service to his brother. William, now aged 30 years, wed Williamina Hutchinson Noble, a 23-year-old shop assistant, from Cross Street, Fraserburgh. The ceremony was conducted on 3 December by Rev John Robson of St Andrew's Church, part of the Presbyterian 'United Free Church of Scotland'. The other witness was Jessie Noble, sister of William and Alexander, who was seriously ill.[19] Jessie's illness may have been another reason for Alexander to pay a return visit to Fraserburgh. Just 12 days after William's marriage, the family would suffer yet another tragedy – the death of Jessie from Tuberculosis. She passed away on 15 December at 35 College Bounds. William, who was at her bedside as she died, reported the death to the registration authorities. The record shows that she was aged 32 years, worked as a shop assistant, and was single.[20]

Attacks on Coastguard Stations

The local IRA on the Beara peninsula had been building up its capabilities, organising its members and gradually acquiring arms by various means. One of the significant operations mounted by the IRA in the Beara region at this period was an attack on Eyeries Coastguard station at Ballycrovane, on Sunday, 25 July 1920. One of the aims was to seize arms held at the station. Men from a number of different companies of the IRA came together for this operation. Taking a prominent role were Liam O'Dwyer and his friend Christy O'Connell, two of the leading IRA officers in the region. According to one account, among the members of the Ardgroom Company who took part were John Sheehan, Captain of the company and Patsy Dan Crowley, who was armed with a shotgun, as well as Michael D.J. O'Sullivan, 2nd Lieutenant, and John Sheehan, Barrakilla.[21] O'Dwyer later told the BMH how he shot dead two coastguard officers in a firefight.[22] He said it was a matter of 'kill or be killed'. Chief Officer Philip W. Snewin (aged 51 years) and Petty Officer Charles Brown (aged 44 years) were the men who died. Snewin was a widower who was buried at Scarborough, Yorkshire. He had been a Chief Petty Officer in the Royal Navy before transferring to the Coastguard in 1919. He and his late wife Charlotte had four children, aged 15 to 25 years. Brown, who was shot in the presence of his hysterical wife Caroline, was buried at Middlesborough, Yorkshire. The Browns had two children – Charles, aged about 14 years and Charlotte Elsie, aged about 12 years.

The raiders got away with a very useful haul of war materiel. According to Liam O'Dwyer in his MSP file, there were 14 rifles, up to ten revolvers and 12,000 rounds of ammunition. In addition to Liam O'Dwyer, Patsy Dan Crowley would also figure in the story of Bridget Noble, as would John Sheehan, Captain of Ardgroom Company. After the raid, the RIC and military scoured the countryside, seeking the perpetrators. According to a report that emerged in 2004, two brothers, Pat and John O'Neill, from Eyeries, were the only ones arrested and in a highly unusual development, after a period of imprisonment, it was also reported that they were deported to Canada.[23] During the raid at Ballycrovane, a simultaneous attack was carried out on Castletownbere coastguard station but with less success. One Volunteer, James Mullins, was injured and taken prisoner – he would later get a 12-year sentence. Jackie McCarthy was another of the Volunteers wounded and was lucky to evade capture.

During the War of Independence the Beara Battalion was designated as the 6th Battalion of Cork No. 3 Brigade which, as indicated above, covered West Cork. This was one of the most active brigades during the period of conflict, and encompassed the formidable Brigade Column, or Flying Column, led by Tom Barry which took part in notable engagements against crown forces in the Kilmichael ambush (November 1920) and the Crossbarry ambush (March 1921). The various battalions that made up the brigade would contribute members to the flying column, some serving on a permanent basis. Rifles and ammunition were also supplied to the column by the various battalions. Barry, the son of an RIC man, had served in the British Army in the Great War. Some republicans were initially suspicious of him because of his background. Nevertheless, with his military training and combat experience, he proved a major asset to the IRA after he became head of the Flying Column. He proved adept at guerrilla tactics, had considerable leadership qualities and was decisive and also ruthless.

The raid on Ballycrovane coastguard station was just one of a number of attacks on crown forces covered by the RIC Inspector General in his monthly report for July 1920.[24] He was particularly concerned about the situation in Cork West Riding [West Cork], and the shooting dead of policemen and other members of the crown forces. On the same day as the Ballycrovane attack, the Inspector General noted that Sergeant William Mulherin, the special sergeant at Bandon, 'was foully murdered by three masked and armed men as he was entering the R.C. church'. (It would later emerge that Tom Barry acted as scout for the attack on the sergeant, as he went to attend Sunday Mass.) The report went on: 'The police were boycotted everywhere and could do little more than defend themselves and their barracks. Their lives were a misery to them and applications to resign were frequent. The men were disheartened in several ways and regarded themselves as mere pawns in a political game with no adequate support.'

It appears that an RIC man in Castletownbere had a lucky escape in December 1920. In a statement in his Military Service Pension file, Liam O'Dwyer tells how he 'prowled Castletownbere by night, in disguise', along with Captain Chris Connell, 'in an attempt to shoot a marked policeman'. O'Dwyer did not identify the policeman who was to be shot.

Chapter 7: Punishment Attack

The period of early 1921 was a difficult time for Bridget Noble. She had health problems which required hospital treatment, and she did not have the immediate support of her husband Alexander, who had moved to England. Alexander's departure must have been a particularly challenging development for Bridget, both in emotional and practical terms. She was left alone to run the small farm and take care of her elderly father. According to one account, Mrs Noble underwent an operation in hospital. The nearest hospital to Ardgroom was the one in Castletownbere, and it is likely that this is the facility she attended. Nuns, members of the Sister of Mercy congregation, whose local superior was Sister Benignus O'Dea, played an important role, along with lay staff, in running the hospital. Simple surgical operations were carried out at the facility by Dr. Michael J. Hayes, Medical Officer of the Workhouse, while more complex cases would be referred to hospitals in Cork city or Dublin.

In some cases Dr Hayes was assisted in surgical procedures by Dr. Daniel J. Lyne, who was Medical Officer of the Castletown [Castletownbere] Dispensary District. (Dr Lyne was related to one of the notable figures of 19th century Ireland, Daniel O'Connell – his mother was a grand-niece of the Liberator.[1]) In such cases Dr Lyne was entitled to a fee for his assistance – the usual amount in 1920-21 was £1.1s, and approval for the payment of the fee would be given by the Castletown Board of Guardians, which oversaw the operation of the hospital, the workhouse and other local services including midwifery, and it would be recorded in the minutes of the regular Board meetings that were held. Dr Hayes was assisted by Dr Lyne in carrying out operations on three patients on 21 December 1920, one of them being James Dwyer of Kaelroe [Cailroe], a younger brother of Liam O'Dwyer. There appears to be no record in the Board's minutes of an operation carried out on Mrs Noble – one could speculate that any such procedure was handled by Dr Hayes without the assistance of Dr Lyne, and since the question of a fee to Dr Lyne would not arise, the matter would not have been brought to the attention of the board.

(The spending of money was carefully monitored by the Board of Guardians. Board members were, for instance, displeased to receive a bill for £4 in May 1920 from Dr O'Mahony, Bantry, for 'examining two lunatics'. It was noted in the minutes that the Guardians 'pay only £1 for lunacy fees' and it was agreed to write to Dr O'Mahony on this matter.[2])

In the period 1920-21 the Board of Guardians was dominated by members of Sinn Féin, and there were very active IRA men among them – one was Mícheál Óg O'Sullivan, who had returned from a sojourn in Dublin to take up residence at the family home in Inchintaglin, Adrigole, and who became Vice Commandant of the Beara Battalion. Also a member was Michael Crowley from Castletownbere, who became Adjutant of the Battalion. Another prominent IRA member on the Board of Guardians was Mark Sullivan, from West End, Castletownbere, who was Intelligence Officer of the Battalion at the time of the Truce, and would go on to become Battalion Adjutant in place of Crowley when the IRA brigade structure in West Cork was re-organised.[3] It is ironical that when Bridget Noble received hospital treatment, it was probably in a facility overseen by a board that included members of the staff of the Beara Battalion – as mentioned above, it would later be stated in an internal IRA document that the staff of the battalion were responsible for her execution.

After gaining places on the Board of Guardians, the republicans, who ensured that their names were recorded in Irish in the minutes, quickly made their presence felt. On 15 August 1920, following a motion proposed by Michael Crowley, and seconded by Mícheál Óg O'Sullivan, it was resolved that 'anybody in our employment holding the commission of JP-ship [Justice of the Peace] under the alien government resign same within two weeks of the date hereof.'[4] This resolution seems to have been aimed at medical doctors who served in various roles under the Board. Dr Lyne, in addition to his role as a dispensary doctor, served as JP as did his late father, also a medical doctor. Dr Hayes had also served as JP as had Dr Charles Harrison, the Kilcatherine dispensary doctor. It will be recalled that Dr Lyne and Dr Hayes were on the bench along with the resident magistrate in Castletownbere Petty Sessions when Bridget Noble had Mrs Katherine Sullivan bound to the peace in 1915. Jasper Travers Wolfe, who acted for Mrs Noble on that occasion, was also adversely affected by the republican takeover of the Board of Guardians – he was replaced as solicitor to the Board. He also lost his role as solicitor to the Castletownbere Rural District Council.[5]

The Board of Guardians, in another important move, resolved on 11 October 1920 to reject the authority of the Local Government Board, which operated under British auspices, and to accept the authority of Dáil Éireann. While republicans dominated the Board of Guardians, life in the hospital and workhouse seemed to continue much as before. Despite the War of Independence, members of the crown forces received treatment at the hospital, for which payment was duly made to the Board. It was recorded in October 1920, for instance, that Britain's Admiralty paid £1.7s for the maintenance at the hospital from 5 to 14 August of Able Seaman J.W. Beard, of HMS Veteran.[6] (This was a Royal Navy destroyer, destined to be sunk with all hands by a German U-boat south of Iceland in September 1942, during the Second World War.)

After treatment in hospital Bridget Noble returned home to the cottage in Reenavaude and to her elderly father John Neill. Mrs Noble's return home may have been monitored by members of the IRA. Assuming that she had been treated in Castletownbere hospital, it is possible, but perhaps unlikely, that IRA members on the Board of Guardians were involved in compiling intelligence on her return home to Reeenavaude, where she would face a punishment attack. While Board members attended regular meetings, and while there was micro-management of financial matters, it did not necessarily follow that they would have been familiar with all the day-to-day workings of the hospital, and the movements of patients. Around the time Mrs Noble left hospital, it seems that the leadership of the Beara Battalion had marked her down for punishment after her contacts with the RIC in Castletownbere had been observed. One wonders if she was even aware at this point that she had come to the adverse attention of the IRA. As will be explained, it would also be alleged that when IRA members searched her home they found evidence that she had been in correspondence with the RIC – the discovery may have been made some time after the punishment attack.

Meanwhile, there were other events occurring in Beara to grab the attention of local republicans. Early 1921 was a turbulent period in the northern part of the peninsula. On Sunday, 30 January, a force of Auxiliary police from Glengarriff threw a cordon around Eyeries church and as the congregation left after 10 o'clock Mass, seven young men were arrested and taken to Glengarriff in lorries. (At this period, 'J' Company of the Auxiliaries was based at the Eccles Hotel, Glengarriff. According to IRA officer, Ted O'Sullivan, these Auxiliaries were 'not bad'.[7]) For Catholics, attendance at Sunday Mass was compulsory, and church services provided good opportunities for crown forces to arrest republican suspects, who were usually practising Catholics. The IRA also made use of the tactic to shoot policemen on their way to or from Mass. As mentioned, gunmen shot dead RIC

Sergeant William Mulherin as he entered the church at Bandon for Sunday Mass, causing much anger among the clergy. According to the *Cork Examiner*, among those arrested at Eyeries were Timothy Dwyer [brother of Liam O'Dwyer], whose address was given as Kaelroe [Cailroe]; Patrick Sullivan, also of Kaelroe and John Cadogan, Croumhane, Eyeries. (As will be explained, the latter would be fatally injured while serving with Free State forces during the Civil War.) The newspaper reported that there was 'considerable firing to stop some parties who got through the cordon', but there was 'no report' of anybody being injured.

Tim Dwyer may have been detained only temporarily. Subsequently, a number of young men from the Eyeries area, including some who were detained after Mass in Eyeries, would serve time in Cork Prison. Among them was 17-years-old Richard Dwyer, a brother of Tim and Liam O'Dwyer. The prisoners were convicted by a summary military court in Bantry on 1 February 1921 of an offence against martial law – 'being a member of IRA [and] refusing to take the oath of allegiance'.[8] They were sentenced to one month's imprisonment with hard labour. The others jailed on this occasion were the afore-mentioned Patrick Sullivan and John Cadogan, as well as Jeremiah Sullivan, Croumhane; Cornelius O'Neill of Eyeries, and Stephen Murphy and Daniel Sullivan, both of Urhan, Eyeries. The latter name seems to have been a reference to Dan 'Red' Sullivan as opposed to Beara Battalion Quartermaster Dan T. Sullivan, who was also from Urhan. The one-month sentences were quite light – nowadays a person convicted at the Special Criminal Court in Dublin of membership of an illegal paramilitary organisation can face a term of imprisonment of years rather than months. Nevertheless, the roundup in Eyeries must surely have increased tension in the area.

'Bobbing' Assault

According to one account, it was on Wednesday, 23 February 1921, after Mrs Noble returned home from hospital, that the blow fell.[9] Members of the IRA raided Mrs Noble's home to inflict the punishment that had been decreed by the Beara Battalion leadership. According to the internal IRA report, written some months later by Liam O'Dwyer, Commandant of the Battalion, 'when she came home from hospital she was bobbed by order of Battn [Battalion].' It is unclear from this phrase if the order was given by the Battalion Commandant on his own initiative, or if the order was given by the Commandant acting in conjunction with staff officers. Being 'bobbed' meant that Mrs Noble's hair was forcibly cut off – a most severe public humiliation. The word 'bobbed' sounds innocuous and understates the nature of the act, and seems more indicative of a pleasant trip to the hairdressers rather than a severe punishment designed to shame the victim. It would later be alleged that a wool shears, normally used for shearing sheep, was used to cut her hair. Allegations would also emerge that she was beaten around the head, kicked, and knocked unconscious, and that she was robbed of her savings.

It was claimed that up to eight Volunteers were deployed to carry out the punishment. It is unclear why so many Volunteers, probably young men, farmers' sons in their teens or twenties, would have been mobilised to punish one lone female who had just emerged from hospital and who was probably in a physically fragile state. Eight men against one woman would have been a rather unequal contest – it was not exactly Kilmichael or Crossbarry. Possibly there were fears that this independent-minded woman would resist efforts to punish her, and that she would have to be subdued. Some of the Volunteers may have had the role of providing security for those wielding the shears in the unlikely event of somebody trying to intervene. The presence of a number of men to observe or to actively participate in the degrading punishment being inflicted on the female victim may have exacerbated her sense of shame and embarrassment. If her aged father witnessed the attack it must have been a most traumatic experience for him also.

Bridget Noble's visits to the RIC station in Castletownbere and other contacts with the crown forces probably led the IRA to suspect that she was an informer. Was she passing on information about the activities of local IRA men? Or was there another explanation? According to information from a local source in Beara, whose family were neighbours of Mrs Noble, she would ask members of the crown forces, when they came into the area, if anybody had seen her husband or had news of him. This would suggest that she was worried and upset over Alexander's departure, and perhaps feared that something untoward had happened him. There is a belief locally that concern over her husband may have led her to make visits to the police station to inquire about him. Had there been a breakdown in communications between herself and Alexander as he travelled in England, looking for work? Or did she fear he was under threat in some way?

There was a rumour that amid increasing political tension Scots-born Alexander Noble was 'forced out' of Beara but this could not be confirmed. In a letter to de Valera, Alexander indicates that he had gone to England in order to support Bridget, because there was no work in Ireland. This would suggest that his work at Pallas Pier had dried up. Alexander's departure from the family home in Reenavaude may have sparked a crisis in Bridget's life. She had waited longer than other women in her neighbourhood for love and marriage to enhance her life. She did not have children, Alexander was all she had, and now he was gone from the family home. From a practical point of view, any help he might have provided in running the small family farm was also gone. It is not known if there were difficulties in the marriage that might have been a factor in Alexander's decision to move away from the house in Reenavaude. Whether or not there were marital problems, it would appear that a bond remained between Alexander and Bridget. After her disappearance, he made strenuous efforts to find out what happened to her and, as will be outlined, it is recorded that he 'wept bitterly' for Bridget. He also placed *In Memoriam* notices in his local newspaper in Fraserburgh on the anniversaries of her death 'in ever loving remembrance of my dear wife…'

It is possible that the RIC took advantage of Bridget's naivety to get information. Bridget's contacts with the police were in violation of the IRA-enforced boycott of the RIC, and as previously indicated, it may have raised suspicions that she was an informer. The above-mentioned source suggests that Bridget may not have fully understood the political situation and the dangers involved in having contact with the crown forces. She was attracting adverse attention to herself that would have terrible consequences. It might have been helpful if somebody from the IRA could have advised Mrs Noble that having these contacts with the crown forces was most unwise and could get her into serious trouble. There is no indication in the internal IRA report on the Noble case that such an approach was made. Instead, it appears a decision was made by the local leadership to take a hard-line, punitive approach, and to deploy a group of Volunteers to humiliate her and cut her hair off.

Watching Mrs Noble

According to the internal IRA report drawn up by Liam O'Dwyer, Mrs Noble was seen by men of 'C' Company, Castletownbere, 'going into the police barracks on four or five occasions and in conversation with the police sergeant in a private house in Castletownbere on two occasions'. The historian, Professor Eunan O'Halpin, considers that O'Dwyer's account 'hinted that the IRA disapproved of what they saw as her improper friendships with a number of RIC men in Castletownbere'.[10] When Bridget Noble walked down the narrow, winding main street of Castletownbere to visit the RIC barracks (now the garda station) she may have been unaware that she was under observation, that she was moving through 'the valley of the squinting windows'.

It is not known which members of 'C' Company were involved in watching Mrs Noble and compiling the intelligence on her visits to the police station. The Company had about 70 members at this period. The Company Captain in 1920-21 was a young man in his early twenties, William O'Neill, also known as Willie or Billy Neill, from Churchgate, Castletownbere. (His nickname was 'Billy the Kid', after the gunfighter of the American Old West, and he would later spend some years in America, before returning to Ireland.) His father Cornelius O'Neill (also known as Neill) has been variously described as a shopkeeper or baker. It is not known if Billy O'Neill was directly involved in the Bridget Noble case, although, as will be shown, he would later be cited as a witness when two other women from the Castletownbere area were accused, in internal IRA intelligence reports in early 1922, of being constantly 'in company' with the police over the previous two years, and of being 'hostile' to Volunteers. There is no indication that these women were subjected to a punishment attack, unlike the case of Mrs Noble.

Two of Billy O'Neill's sisters, Nora O'Neill (later to be known by her married name of Nora O'Sullivan) and Margaret [Maggie] O'Neill, were very active members of Cumann na mBan – Nora was head of the CnB branch in the town. The two young women worked at MacCarthy's stores, where a prominent Volunteer, Charlie Hurley, was also employed.[11] Billy O'Neill was Captain of the Company at the time of the attack on Castletownbere coastguard station on 25 June 1920, an operation in which he took a prominent role. (According to Billy O'Neill's statement to the Bureau of Military History, he was still O/C of the Company at the time of the Truce in July 1921. However, another record in the Military Archives indicates that John Cronin, Knockoura, Castletownbere was O/C at the Truce.[12] It is thus unclear who was O/C at the time Mrs Noble was under surveillance.)

As previously indicated, Mark Sullivan, who became a member of the Board of Guardians, was described in IRA records as Battalion Intelligence Officer at the time of the Truce, and he was a member of 'C' Company, Castletownbere. He also came from the West End area of Castletownbere, where the police station was located. Gathering intelligence on suspected spies would have been part of his role but there is no indication as to when exactly he took up intelligence duties, and it is not known if he was directly involved in the Noble case. Nora O'Neill, referred to above, also had an intelligence role with the battalion, according to Liam O'Dwyer in a letter supporting her application for a Military Service Pension. He stated: 'Under trying conditions, including that of Martial Law, she continually did the duties of Assistant Battalion Adjutant and Assistant Battalion I.O. [Intelligence Officer] for the IRA, together with her duties as Cumann na mBan Captain.'[13] However, as in the case of Mark Sullivan, there is no indication in available records that she was involved in gathering intelligence on Mrs Noble.

One could speculate that the police sergeant with whom Mrs Noble was apparently friendly was Thomas Nugent. Sergeant Nugent had been based for some years in Eyeries station, which covered Mrs Noble's home area of Ardgroom, and it is possible he was acquainted with her. He investigated the malicious damage done to the potato crop of the ill-fated farmer William Lehane at Cleandra in 1917 and he was sergeant in charge of Eyeries station in March 1918 when Volunteers raided the barracks and seized carbines. At the time of the raid he had been lured away to Castletownbere where Volunteers had assembled as a diversionary tactic. He was sergeant in charge of Allihies RIC station when it was attacked by the IRA in February 1920, resulting in the death of one of his men, Constable Neenan.

Ironically, Hannah O'Neill, the young woman who was a member of Cumann na mBan and who would later guard Mrs Noble as a prisoner, was herself involved in a relationship with an RIC man, but this would not have brought her to the adverse attention of the IRA. She was very active in CnB, and she could claim, no doubt truthfully, that associating with the policeman produced intelligence for the movement. She stated in her application for a Military Service Pension: 'There was one RIC who was previously stationed in Eyeries Station, we were doing a "line". I got information from him.' She indicated that the information was in relation to the 'change of guard', in advance of the IRA raid on Allihies RIC station. She also mentioned supplying milk to the wives of the Coast Guards but once again she stated that she used this contact to get information. 'I found out about the garrison there.'[14] Since Mrs Noble was not a member of CnB, nor an 'insider' in republican circles, the IRA would view her contacts with the crown forces in a rather more sinister light.

The Accusations

Judging by the way the IRA report on Mrs Noble is structured (see Appendix), it may be the case that the factors that led to the punishment attack were primarily her visits to the RIC station and her conversations with the police sergeant in a house in Castletownbere, while additional factors led to the decision to execute her, although this cannot be confirmed with absolute certainty. According to one report, published in a unionist newspaper in Northern Ireland, the raiders made particular reference to Mrs Noble's connection with the sergeant when they came to her home to carry out the punishment. 'They accused her of being on friendly terms with one of the RIC sergeants at Castletown, and told her to prepare for death.'[15]

As will be discussed in more detail, an important allegation against Mrs Noble is that she told the RIC that Liam Dwyer [Liam O'Dwyer] and Pat [Patsy Dan] Crowley shot the farmer William Lehane for 'land grabbing'. The two men were, of course, very active in the Beara IRA, as mentioned. The internal IRA report on her execution claims that the IRA heard from the RIC that Bridget Noble had provided the police with the names of the two men, but the report does not say exactly when the IRA received the intelligence from an RIC source. The structure of the IRA report might suggest that the allegation of informing was not being advanced as one of the reasons for the 'bobbing' attack, but was part of the case against Mrs Noble after she was abducted and put on trial for her life.

On the other hand, if the Lehane affair was one of the infractions for which she was being punished in the 'bobbing' operation, various thoughts occur. While a man could be shot for passing on information about the alleged killers of a local farmer, would the hair-shearing have been considered sufficient punishment for a woman, especially since nobody had been arrested? Had Mrs Noble not complained to the police about the 'bobbing' assailants, would the hair-shearing have been the end of the matter, so far as the IRA was concerned? These are matters about which one can only speculate. The claim that Mrs Noble gave the RIC the names of the Volunteers whom she accused of the 'bobbing' attack emerges as the most serious allegation against her.

Letters from the RIC

Among the additional allegations against Mrs Noble, it was claimed that she received letters from the RIC, and that on one occasion her home was visited by crown forces. According to the IRA report, there was a military raid on the district, and 'two officers' [presumably British Army officers] were seen going into her house. This was possibly after the punishment attack – Mrs Noble may have come under additional surveillance by the IRA in the wake of the 'bobbing' incident. The visit of the 'two officers' prompted a search of her house by order of a local IRA officer, the Officer Commanding 'H' Company, Ardgroom. (John Sheehan, as mentioned, was Captain of Ardgroom Company – he was recorded as holding this position on 11 July 1921. Another officer was Dan Harrington, Droumard, a 2nd Lieutenant.[16] Sheehan was aged about 30 years, and was a farmer's son from Canfie East, Ardgroom.[17])

According to the IRA report, those who searched Mrs Noble's home found 'part of a letter from the Head Constable, Castletown [Castletownbere]; five half-torn letters from other members of the RIC and two photos of RIC men'. The report did not give details of the contents of the letters said to have been received by Mrs Noble. The implication was that they were letters in relation to information she was supplying to the police. The question could also be asked – were they letters in reply to requests for information about the whereabouts of her husband? Or could they have been letters arising from a complaint she made to the RIC about the IRA men who had assaulted her – a complaint that will be dealt with in more detail below. Receiving letters from the RIC would not necessarily prove Mrs Noble was an informer, although it may have bolstered IRA suspicions.

It is unclear how the possession of two photos of RIC men might have been seen as incriminating, although it could be seen as evidence of social interaction with one or more members of the RIC, which would also have been anathema to the local IRA. In a reference to the three women known to have been abducted and killed by the IRA in 1921, Mrs Lindsay, Kate Carroll and Bridget Noble, Professor Eunan O'Halpin commented: 'Two of the victims had a reputation for social deviance: Kate Carroll kept an illicit still and Bridget Noble, although married, was held to be too friendly with a number of RIC men on the Beara peninsula. These killings caused acute embarrassment locally and at GHQ.'[18]

Newspaper Reports on Punishment Attack

In early March 1921, more than a week after Mrs Noble was assaulted, there were newspaper reports of an attack on a woman in the Castletownbere area and while the reports do not mention the name, the details clearly refer to Bridget Noble.[19] The 'bobbing' attack does not figure in the RIC County Inspector's report for February covering offences committed in Cork West Riding. The Inspector had many other matters to occupy his attention, including twelve murders. (Incidentally, there was also a single case of the strictly non-political offence of bigamy.)[20] Despite the omission, it seems likely that the RIC sent a report on the incident to Dublin Castle, the historic nerve centre of British administration in Ireland, and that press officers there decided to release the details to the newspapers in order to discredit the republicans responsible for the attack. The British ran quite a sophisticated press publicity operation at this period, based in Dublin Castle. One report published in England, in the *Northern Daily Mail*, stated: 'A peculiarly brutal attack on a woman is reported from the Castletownbeare district. [Ardgroom was part of the constabulary district of Castletownbere.] The victim was a woman farmer, whose house was broken into by eight masked men, one of whom carried a gun. She was robbed of £35 and then dragged into the yard where her hair was shorn with wool shears. The motive of the crime appears to be that the woman visited the police barracks recently and was suspected of imparting information. She was in delicate health at the time, having recently passed through an operation.'

The claim that Mrs Noble possessed the sum of £35, which was then robbed, is noteworthy, and at first glance may not appear to tally with the fact that she was buying items on credit in the local shop. If she did indeed have £35, it may have been money accumulated by Alexander through his work as a cooper, and it is possible that she wanted to safeguard the lump sum, while using current income to purchase groceries and other items in the shop. Her father John Neill may have had an Old Age Pension – in 1909 the British had introduced non-contributory pensions for those aged 70 years and over, who satisfied certain criteria. As the accounts book in the local shop/post office shows, Mrs Noble's parents and many of her neighbours had a tradition of buying items on account, with the debt being settled later. The internal IRA report on the fate of Mrs Noble makes no mention of any money being confiscated from her during the 'bobbing' attack. As previously mentioned, while the report makes various allegations against Mrs Noble, it does not include any suggestion that she was suspected of receiving money from the crown forces for giving information.

During research, I was told of an incident that allegedly occurred during the Troubles and that was said to have led members of the IRA to regard Mrs Noble as an informer. A local source described how a Beara man was given an account of the incident by a relative who was in the IRA at the time. According to this account, members of the IRA intercepted a mail car in the area of Adrigole, found a cheque in a letter addressed to Mrs Noble from the crown forces, and this led to her being targeted as an informer. The mails were often intercepted by the IRA during the War of Independence as part of intelligence-gathering, and the practice was particularly common in West Cork. The mail car travelling through isolated countryside between Castletownbere and Bantry was particularly vulnerable.

There was one particular interception of the mail car that could be relevant from the point of view of timing. There was a report in the *Cork Examiner* on 15 February 1921 that the motor mail car 'was held up between Castletown and Glengarriff, and subsequently between Glengarriff and Bantry, and all the mails taken'. It is unclear if this is the incident referred to in the account that came down in the oral tradition. The hold-up would have occurred some days before the reported date on which Mrs Noble was 'bobbed'. However, the claim that an incriminating letter was intercepted is very much open to question, in light of the fact that there is no mention of the cheque allegation in Liam O'Dwyer's internal IRA report to GHQ giving the reasons for Mrs Noble's execution. It is difficult to understand why O'Dwyer, in seeking to justify the execution of a female, would have omitted the story of the intercepted cheque, had the account been true. The alleged informing activities of Mrs Noble, as outlined in O'Dwyer's report, are unlikely to have attracted payment from the crown forces. If she did inform on the alleged killers of William Lehane, as claimed by O'Dwyer, it is unlikely the RIC would have paid her for information that was patently incorrect or unreliable – this will be explained later in more detail. It also seems unlikely that the police would have paid her for complaining about the alleged assailants who 'bobbed' her.

As regards the punishment attack on Mrs Noble, the Belfast unionist newspaper, the *Northern Whig*, carried the story about the assault on the unnamed woman farmer, with the headline: 'Delicate Woman Attacked: Sinn Fein "Gallantry" in Cork'.[21] Another report in a local unionist newspaper in Northern Ireland which appeared some months later, in August, actually names Bridget Noble as the victim and makes the additional allegation that she was kicked and beaten over the head and knocked unconscious by her assailants. No source is given for this information in the *Londonderry Sentinel* and the allegation that Mrs Noble was beaten and knocked unconscious does not figure in other news reports based on the Dublin Castle statement released in March – the text of the original statement has not come to light.[22] According to the *Londonderry Sentinel* report, although her attackers were masked, Mrs Noble was able to identify the leader, and 'seven of the eight assailants'. As mentioned, the newspaper also claimed that the raiders accused her of being friendly with an RIC sergeant in Castletownbere, and made a death threat against her.

From this newspaper report, it would appear that Mrs Noble was now in fear of her life and decided to dispose of her farm and flee the country. However, there were probably factors that would have disrupted any attempt at speedy flight. If it was true that her savings had been seized by the Volunteers, how would she finance a new life in another location? Then there was her elderly father who depended on her – what was to happen to him? There would have been livestock on the farm – probably two or three cows, as well as some hens and one or two dogs. Neighbours might take in the animals but the real challenge would have been ensuring the care of her father in his final years. In the meantime, Mrs Noble embarked on a course of action that was extremely courageous but highly dangerous and ill-advised – she decided to complain to the RIC and to name the men she accused of attacking her.

Chapter 8: Bridget Noble's Complaint to the Police

The humiliating punishment inflicted on Bridget Noble by the Volunteers may have pushed her over the edge, and impelled her to go to the RIC. She was a middle-aged married woman, and perhaps she considered that the punishment cast her in the role of a pariah and social outcast, perhaps even as a 'loose woman' consorting with RIC men, even though there is no indication that there was ever any impropriety. It appears that in her anguish and her anger, she could not accept what the Volunteers had done to her, she could not accept being abused and degraded. Sadly, by standing up to the men who had attacked and humiliated her and violated her femininity, she would forfeit her own life. Perhaps it was the case that Mrs Noble's personal traits combined to form a lethal cocktail that would destroy her. She obviously had courage, and a tendency to stand up for herself, but she combined these traits with naivety, and an apparent disregard for the consequences of defying the IRA.

It may have been the case that there were few people around to persuade her not to put her life on the line by going to the police. Being childless, there were no young adult sons or daughters who might have better understood the security situation and the politics of the period and who could have provided counselling. In addition, her sisters had emigrated, her Scots-born husband was in England and her father was a man of advanced years. According to a local source in the Ardgroom area, another person, a young married woman with a family, also came under suspicion by the IRA around this period. It was suspected that she had given information about IRA hide-outs and she was apparently threatened with being executed by being tied up on a beach and left to drown by the incoming tide. However, her father was a man of some standing and influence in the community, he went to the IRA and the matter was resolved, with no further action being taken against the woman. Bridget Noble was a woman of modest social background, and even though she married a man with a good trade and, as will be outlined, had a relative who was an officer in Cumann na mBan, she may have lacked influential connections in the local community that might have helped her when she was accused of informing.

As regards Bridget's complaint to the RIC, any action taken by the police against the alleged perpetrators on the basis of her accusation would point to her as the source of the information. If there was no hard proof previously of her being an 'informer', the IRA would have it now. She would be in a very vulnerable situation and the RIC would be unable to protect her. (It is noteworthy that in his monthly reports for February and March 1921, the RIC County Inspector for Cork West Riding, which included the Beara region, recorded the 'Number of Persons Protected' as 'Nil'.[1]) It would only be a matter of time before the IRA learned that Mrs Noble had provided the police with the names of the men accused of shearing her hair. It would later be alleged that Mrs Noble went to the RIC station, accompanied by a young woman called Nora Sullivan (a name very common in County Cork), and that she handed in a letter to the Head Constable naming seven men whom she accused of having 'bobbed' her.

A young single woman called Nora Sullivan lived with her family in the next farm along the road from Bridget in Reenavaude. (The 1911 Census shows her residing here with her widower father Daniel Sullivan and siblings.) Nora was in her mid-twenties and was related to Bridget – their grandmothers, Nora and Mary Rahilly, were sisters. It is possible that it was this Nora Sullivan who accompanied Bridget when she made her fateful visit to the RIC station in Castletownbere, although this cannot be confirmed with absolute certainty. Nora Sullivan's former home, with a rusty corrugated iron roof, still stands, although derelict and in an area overgrown by trees. It would have been the closest house to Bridget's cottage. Nora continued to live in the house in later years, until she died. A neighbour remembered her with great affection, describing her as very small in stature, and an extremely kind person. He recalled how people used to play cards in the house, which was always kept extremely tidy. He remembered also the many religious pictures, including portraits of the Popes, that adorned the walls. ('Nora Sullivan' from Reenavaude was listed as a member of Ardgroom Cumann na mBan – it is unclear if this is Bridget's cousin.[2]) Another neighbour recalled Nora as being 'as tough as nails'. He ruefully recalled how, as a boy, he angered her over the way he was riding his bicycle – he could still remember the tongue lashing she gave him. He considered that she would have been more than capable of accompanying Bridget to the police station to complain about the 'bobbing' attack. He said he 'could not imagine anyone else' having the courage to do so.

By an odd coincidence, another relation of Bridget's, Katie Sullivan, was an officer of the Ardgroom branch of Cumann na mBan which, of course, also covered Bridget's home area of Reeenavaude. Katie, who was aged 23 years at the time of Bridget's abduction, was also a grand-daughter of the above-mentioned Nora Rahilly, sister of Bridget's grandmother Mary Rahilly. Katie's father Paddy Sullivan was a tailor, residing on the main street of Ardgroom, and he was a son of Sean (Philib) Sullivan (also a tailor) and his wife, the former Nora Rahilly.[3] Although records in the Military Archives concerning the leadership of Ardgroom Cumann na mBan are contradictory, the indications are that Katie was Captain of Ardgroom branch, while her neighbour in Ardgroom village, Julia O'Sullivan, was the Secretary of the branch. As will be shown, Katie and Julia would later become aware that Mrs Noble was being held as a prisoner. It is unclear what role Katie would play during the Civil War – one archival record indicates she was neutral during that conflict.[4] Katie later emigrated to America.

John Dwyer Taken Prisoner

Following Mrs Noble's complaint about the punishment attack, it appears that the RIC moved quickly, and matters came to a head on Friday, 4 March 1921. John Dwyer was one of a number of men arrested in a military sweep that day and according to the internal IRA report on the execution of the Reenavaude woman, he would later be charged in connection with the 'bobbing' of Mrs Noble. Dwyer was an active local republican, brother of Liam O'Dwyer, and he himself was an officer of Ballycrovane Company. The names of the arrested men were given in a report in the *Evening Echo*, obviously based on a statement from the military. According to Liam O'Dwyer's report on Bridget Noble, John Dwyer, after being arrested on 4 March, 'was charged with having bobbed Mrs Noble and got six months imprisonment for same'.

It must have come as a shock to young men of the local IRA that a lone, middle-aged female was displaying such rebelliousness, and was challenging the authority of the organisation in such an obstinate manner. It was claimed that John Dwyer was not the only republican to be rounded up on the basis of Bridget Noble's complaint to the police. According to the IRA report, Michael Sullivan, 'whose name was given by Mrs Noble as having taken part in the bobbing was arrested in the month of May and interned'. Sullivan's internment took place, of course, after Mrs Noble was put to death. Michael Sullivan was a member of the Ardgroom Company of the IRA.[5]

According to the report in the *Evening Echo*, it was at 9 am on 4 March that the military 'took up positions around Eyeries and made a search of the village and some houses adjoining, and afterwards continued the search to the Ballycrovane district, going as far as Ardgroom'.[6] It was stated that six young men were brought back to the military camp [obviously a reference to the Furious Pier military camp located east of Castletownbere, by the coast]. The men were named as Michael Sullivan, Eyriesbeg (not to be confused with the afore-mentioned Michael Sullivan from Ardgroom, who would be interned in May); Patrick Murphy, Eyeries; James McCarthy, Boffickil; Mortimer McCarthy, Ballycrovane; John O'Dwyer [or Dwyer], Kailroe [Cailroe], and John O'Shea, Faunlaiv [Faunleave]. Michael Sullivan, Eyriesbeg, was a member of Eyeries Company of the IRA, as was James McCarthy – the latter became 2nd Lieutenant of the Company. Mortimer McCarthy, who as previously mentioned was jailed along with Patrick Malvey in 1918 for failing to answer police questions, was a member of Ballycrovane Company and became 2nd Lieutenant of that unit, while John Dywer was Captain of Ballycrovane Company. John O'Shea from Faunleave was a member of Ardgroom Company. British military records indicate that these five men would all be sentenced to six months imprisonment by a military court, and subsequently interned, although they would all be released towards the end of the year. It is unclear if the sixth man, Patrick Murphy from Eyeries, was a member of the IRA.

John Dwyer seems to have been arrested during a time of mourning for his mother Ellen Dwyer who had passed away at the family home. As will be described in greater detail, his brother Liam was lucky to escape a raid that occurred during a wake for Mrs Dwyer, although it appears that another man was arrested while also attending the wake. The *Evening Echo* report stated that 'the prisoner John Sheehan, of Ardgroom, arrested at Kailroe on Monday night, was released near his home on the arrival of the military there'. The man in question was probably the John Sheehan who was a Captain of Ardgroom Company, although this cannot be confirmed with absolute certainty. [Confusingly, there was another officer of Ardgroom Company called John Sheehan – he came from Barrakilla.] Another newspaper report indicates that 'J. Sheehan' was arrested at 2 am while attending a wake at Kaelroe [Cailroe] – almost certainly a reference to the wake for Mrs Dwyer, although Liam O'Dwyer, in his writings, does not mention anyone being arrested during the wake.[7]

The roundup that netted John Dwyer and other local men is mentioned in a statement to the Bureau of Military History by one of those detained, James McCarthy. He told how, on 4 March he met the

82

Parish Priest, Father Daly, who informed him that 'a strong force of military from Furious Pier were carrying out a roundup in the area'.[8] The military were in Ballycrovane at this period and were moving towards Eyeries, McCarthy stated. He tried to avoid the roundup but was arrested. He was taken to Furious Pier. He states that at this location, 'I was tried by an officer and sentenced to six months imprisonment.' He was removed to Bere Island [where there was a detention centre] and later to Spike Island where he was interned after completing five months of his sentence. He was released from Maryboro [now Portlaoise] Prison on 8 December 1921 following the signing of the Treaty.

Liam O'Dwyer Under Pressure From Crown Forces

It was a period when Liam O'Dwyer was under particular pressure from the crown forces. In mid-January 1921, following the Christmas break, Christy O'Connell and a number of other men from the Beara Battalion went off to serve with the Brigade Column, i.e. the Flying Column headed by Tom Barry. (A contingent would also depart in March to serve with the column.) O'Dwyer recalled in his statement to the BMH that he himself was prevented from travelling as, being a Battalion Officer, he was instructed by Brigade HQ to remain in his own area to keep the local organisation going. O'Dwyer told in his memoir how, with some reluctance, he complied with an order to transfer all the battalion's rifles to the Flying Column, although he retained two rifles that were damaged and that he spent a week repairing. He gave one of these rifles, with a plentiful supply of ammunition to Patsy Dan Crowley, who was 'on the run'.

By this time, in early 1921, he states in his memoir that the British military, 'through their experienced intelligence men', knew that the battalion's arms and best fighting men were gone from the area, and 'they scoured the country, night and day, for those of us who were left'.[9] He told how one night he and Patsy Dan Crowley slept on the floor of Dan O'Shea's house in Coomindagh [Cummeendeach]. Early in the morning they heard the dog barking - the house near Ardgroom was being surrounded by the military. O'Dwyer told how he and Crowley shot their way out, covering each other by taking turns to fire at the military while they ran to the mountain and safety.

Another close associate of O'Dwyer's was Connie Healy, a member of the IRA's Ardgroom Company, and in his memoir O'Dwyer describes how he was sleeping overnight in the Healy home when the crown forces came raiding, and he had a narrow escape out the back door.[10] Yet another of Liam O'Dwyer's comrades in arms was Jerh O'Connor, another member of Ardgroom Company. O'Dwyer told in his memoir how a local girl [Katie Reilly] warned himself and O'Connor of a military roundup and they had just enough time to squeeze themselves into a drain, where they had to remain for more than two hours with water flowing over them.[11] As will be shown, Jerh O'Connor would be among those who would figure in an internal IRA report on the case of Bridget Noble – he was stated to be one of the Volunteers who interviewed Nora Sullivan about Mrs Noble's complaint to the police about the 'bobbing' attack.

Hiding Under The Bed

Around the end of February or the beginning of March 1921 O'Dwyer's widowed mother Ellen died at age 48 years. The death certificate gives the cause of death as 'hemiplegia cardiac failure', the duration of illness as three days, and the date of death as 29 February. The latter detail is erroneous as there was no such date in 1921 as it was not a leap year. Possibly the actual date was 1 March.[12] O'Dwyer said that the house at Caolrua [Cailroe] was searched at least four nights a week by the crown forces and his mother had become 'overwhelmed with fear and sleeplessness'. He recalled in his memoir that she had only the young children of the family with her, as all the rest were 'on the run', in the Column and in jail. He was probably referring to himself, who was certainly 'on the run', his brother Tim who served with the Flying Column, and his brother Richard who had been sent to prison. Richard's scheduled release date was 28 February 1921 – it is unclear if he made it home before his mother passed away. Another brother, John, would of course spend time in prison after his arrest on 4 March. It may have been during one of the raids on the family home that John Dwyer was taken into custody. His brother Liam was fortunate to evade capture.

In her comparatively short life, Mrs O'Dwyer had given birth to 14 children, two of whom died at birth. The former Ellen Lynch had been married at age 18 years to Johnny O'Dwyer who was a widower, his previous two wives having died. Johnny himself had passed away in 1920 at age 72 years. On the night of Ellen's wake, Liam O'Dwyer told in his memoir how he was in the kitchen when the dog barked. Julia O'Sullivan, Secretary of Ardgroom Cumann na mBan, looked out and saw British soldiers in the yard. (Local anecdotal evidence suggests that the soldiers, in at least one of the raids on the house, tried to maintain the element of surprise by approaching from across the fields, rather than moving down the long, narrow lane leading to the very isolated farmhouse.) The soldiers saw O'Dwyer as he ran to the stairs. Julia O'Sullivan slammed the door and tried to keep it shut but the military burst in. O'Dwyer hid under the bed in the corpse room upstairs. His grandmother pretended to fall and threw herself along the front of the bed so he could not be seen underneath it. An officer came in, saw the grandmother [Mrs Nell Lynch] crying aloud on the floor beside her daughter's corpse, and told the soldiers to leave the room. The soldiers kept watch outside the house, so O'Dwyer dressed in his mother's clothes, and with a shawl over his head sauntered out towards the turf rick and when the coast was clear, ran until he was safe.[13]

According to an extraordinary account that would later emerge, it was claimed that the officer in charge knew that O'Dwyer was hiding under the bed, but made a last-moment decision to let him go. The officer was Irish, and was possibly moved by the sight of the grandmother wailing over her daughter's corpse. He may have had the traditional Irish respect for a wake. It was said that decades after the raid, a local man, Denis Murphy, from Ahabrock, Eyeries, would encounter the officer in America. Murphy had emigrated to the US in 1949 and was working in construction in Chicago. During a card game one night, one of his fellow players was a man from Tipperary who had been in the British forces. When the latter found that Murphy was from Beara, he inquired if he knew Willie Dwyer [Liam O'Dwyer]. The ex-officer revealed that it was he who ordered the troops out of the corpse room. He said he knew O'Dwyer was under the bed but made a snap decision to leave him alone. He asked that his regards be passed on to O'Dwyer. This account may explain how Liam O'Dwyer escaped capture, although his brother John was arrested around this period. Denis Murphy died in 2007 in Cook County, Illinois, aged 80 years.

The action of Julia O'Sullivan in slamming the door and in delaying the entry of the soldiers, bought O'Dwyer vital seconds to dash upstairs and hide under the bed. It was a crucial factor in his escape. O'Dwyer always remained grateful to O'Sullivan for her help that night and, as will be shown, many years later he would reciprocate, assisting O'Sullivan in her own hour of need. As will be explained in more detail, Julia O'Sullivan, who was a shopkeeper in Ardgroom village, would marry John Sheehan, the Captain of Ardgroom Company who, according to the internal IRA report on Mrs Noble's execution, had ordered a search of her home, which uncovered letters sent to her by members of the RIC. Julia's fellow officer in Ardgroom Cumann na mBan during the War of Independence was, of course, the afore-mentioned Katie Sullivan, a cousin of Bridget Noble.[14]

The crown forces' raid occurred during a period of considerable upheaval, and it would not be until the following September that Liam O'Dwyer would register his mother's death with the interim registrar for the locality, Dr Patrick V. Murphy, referred to above. (As will be shown, there would later be a rather tense, difficult encounter between

O'Dwyer and Dr Murphy during the Civil War.) Liam O'Dwyer makes no mention in his memoir of his brother John being arrested on 4 March although, as indicated above, he does refer to brothers 'on the run', in the Column or 'in jail'.

Sentencing of John Dwyer

British military records show that John Dwyer, described as a farmer, aged 23 years, with an address at 'Castletown Bere', received six months Imprisonment with Hard Labour (IHL) following a Summary Court hearing on 8 March 1921.[15] (Military Courts were divided into different tiers – the lower level Summary Courts were used to try smaller infractions, while upper level Military Courts tried more serious offences. The court hearing probably took place at the British military camp at Furious Pier. As noted above, this is the location where a trial took place of another Volunteer, James McCarthy, arrested on the same day as Dwyer.)

It was recorded that John Dwyer was sentenced for 'offences against martial law'.[16] The record seems to indicate that he was originally held in detention on Bere Island for some days, then taken to Cork Male Gaol and transferred from there to the military prison on Spike Island on 2 June 1921.[17] Apart from stating that he was jailed for 'offences against martial law', the available records do not give details of the nature of the offences. The only indication that he was jailed as a result of the allegation that he took part in the 'bobbing' attack on Bridget Noble comes from the internal IRA report on her execution, compiled by his brother Liam. (A British military record shows that James McCarthy was also convicted in a summary military court on 8 March of an 'offence against martial law' and given six months with hard labour. Mortimer McCarthy was likewise convicted and given a similar penalty.[18])

John Dwyer was due for release on 8 August 1921. On 3 August a British officer, an Assistant Adjutant General at British HQ in Cork, wrote a memo for a superior officer listing various prisoners who were due for release from Spike Military Prison on various specified dates, with the request: 'Please state what action you wish taken.'[19] One of the names on the list was that of John Dwyer. The letter 'I' for 'Internment' was subsequently written in red ink alongside his name. Also on the list were the names of four men arrested along with John Dwyer in the same roundup on 4 March, as mentioned, and who were also due for release on 8 August. They also were marked down for internment with the letter 'I' in red ink appended to their names – Mortimer McCarthy, James McCarthy, John Shea [or O'Shea] and Michael Sullivan. Also ordered to be interned was another Volunteer from Beara, Jim O'Donnell, whose release date was 9 August. In the document, five prisoners were marked 'R' for 'release', while a question mark was written alongside the names of two others.

The British military commander in Cork formally approved John Dwyer's internment. The relevant memo from Lt. General Strickland, commander of the 6th Division to GHQ at Parkgate, Dublin, reads: 'I have approved of the internment of the following rebel: 17 I.B. 476 John Dwyer of Eyeries.'[20] Dwyer would spend just over three months as an internee, and because of political developments would be free by the following December. John Dwyer was recorded as being Captain of Ballycrovane Company of the IRA, although incarcerated, on 11 July 1921. He also held the same position of Captain on 1 July 1922.[21]

The IRA report on the Noble case, as indicated above, stated that Michael Sullivan was interned in May following Bridget Noble's complaint to the police about the men who 'bobbed' her. In this regard, a British military record shows that Michael Sullivan, from Gurteen, Ardgroom, was interned in May 1921, the date of his arrival in the detention centre being given as 28 May.[22] The record did not provide details of the reasons why he was interned. Once again, the only indication that he was interned as a result of his alleged involvement in the 'bobbing' of Mrs Noble comes from the IRA report on her execution. One cannot assume that the guilt of Michael Sullivan and John Dwyer in the 'bobbing' attack has been established beyond a shadow of a doubt.

Michael Sullivan of the same address, Gurteen, was later recorded by Liam O'Dwyer as being 2nd Lieutenant of Ardgroom Company on 1 July 1922.[23] Military records indicate that Sullivan's brothers Eugene and Peter were also interned at Spike Island around the same period, for reasons that are not apparent. The brothers came from a family of 13 children in Gurteen, most of whom emigrated to America. Their mother, Mrs Margaret O'Sullivan, the former Peig Minihane-O'Driscoll from Kilcatherine, was a native Irish speaker and a noted source of local stories and folklore.[24] Michael Sullivan was himself an Irish language enthusiast, and is said to have taught the language to other prisoners at Spike Island.[25]

The IRA Closes In On Bridget Noble

It was on 4 March, as mentioned, that the IRA moved once again against Mrs Noble, this time with much more lethal effect. The arrest of John Dwyer may have been the catalyst for IRA action. Volunteers raided her house and according to the IRA report, as previously indicated, a letter was found addressed to her from the RIC Head Constable, asking her to meet him in Castletown [Castletownbere] that evening. 'She was arrested on her way to the police barrack,' the report said. One of the possible reasons for the IRA decision to abduct Mrs Noble was to ensure that she would not be available to give evidence against John Dwyer in any trial that might take place. After Mrs Noble was abducted, arrangements for the guarding of the prisoner had to be made by officers of the IRA, in cooperation with officers of Cumann na mBan. Information that emerged in a file in the Irish Military Archives indicates that a meeting was held at the home of Patrick Lynch, Droumbeg, Ardgroom Inward in regard to the guarding of Mrs Noble and that those present included John Sheehan, Captain of Ardgroom Company, and officers of Ardgroom Cumann na mBan, Katie Sullivan and Julia Sullivan.[26]

Nora Sullivan, who accompanied Mrs Noble to the police station, was apparently interviewed by a number of Volunteers. According to the IRA report on the Noble case, on being questioned by the Volunteers, she told of seeing Mrs Noble handing a letter to the RIC Head Constable 'containing the names of seven Volunteers and stating that these were the men who bobbed her'. There is no indication in the report as to how this young woman was encouraged, induced or pressurised to provide this crucial information. Possibly, she was seen entering the police station with Bridget, as it appears little happened in Castletownbere that was not observed by republicans. If Nora Sullivan was seen by the IRA as complicit in Bridget's complaint to the police, she was fortunate to escape punishment. The information provided by Nora may have sealed Mrs Noble's fate.

District Inspector Oates, who was acquainted with Mrs Noble through her visits to the local RIC station, was away from Castletownbere at this period, being based temporarily in Bantry. RIC records indicate that the Head Constable was Michael Goaley, aged 33 years, an Irish-speaking Catholic from Annaghdown, County Galway. Goaley had joined the RIC in 1907 and was stationed in County Mayo. During the Great War he served as a sergeant in the Royal Dublin Fusiliers in France, later becoming a 2nd Lieutenant in the Machine Gun Corps. After being demobilised he re-joined the RIC and on promotion from Sergeant to Head Constable was transferred from County Mayo to the turmoil of West Cork, being assigned to Castletownbere on 1 February 1921.[27] (It appears that during Oates's six-month absence from Castletownbere, the RIC District Inspector at the latter location for a period was Forbes Le Blount Croke.[28] A solicitor's son from Pinner, Middlesex, Croke had come to Ireland as a member of the Auxiliaries. A former army officer, he held the rank of 3rd District Inspector, the lowest D.I. rank – Oates was a 1st D.I.)[29]

The IRA report names the men who questioned Nora Sullivan about Mrs Noble's letter to the Head Constable as Pat Crowley, Jerh O'Connor, James Malvey, Con Crowley and Tim Rahilly [otherwise Reilly]. These men were members of the Ardgroom Company of the Beara Battalion – the company had about 55 members.[30] Pat Crowley, better known as Patsy Dan Crowley, would succeed John Sheehan as Captain of Ardgroom Company and hold that position on 1 July 1922.[31]

The afore-mentioned Con Crowley came from Glenbeg, the same valley that was home to Patsy Dan. Con's brothers and a sister, Nora Mary Crowley, were also active in republican activities. One brother, Daniel Crowley, while not listed as a member of Ardgroom Company, was said to have been involved in secret intelligence work known only to Battalion officers while working as a shoemaker apprentice in Ardgroom village.[32] Another brother, Jack Crowley, was a member of Ardgroom Company and in 1928 he would marry Lizzie Healy, a sister of fellow Company member Connie Healy, from Canfie, Ardgroom. Lizzie herself had been a member of the Ardgroom branch of Cumann na mBan from 1918.[33] It is noteworthy that Ardgroom republicans Connie and Lizzie Healy were connected indirectly by marriage to Bridget Noble. In April 1915, at Ardgroom church, their sister Margaret Healy, at age 23 years, married Peter Crowley, Bridget's first cousin, and a farmer who resided at Dreenacappra. One of the witnesses at the ceremony overseen by the parish priest, Father O'Callaghan, was the bride's sister Lizzie. (Peter was a son of Bridget's aunt Nora who, as mentioned, married John Crowley of Dreenacappra.)

The sentencing of John Dwyer on 8 March occurred during the period that Mrs Noble was being held prisoner, and may have boosted the resentment of IRA members towards her – she would now be seen as somebody whose complaint to the RIC had resulted in one of their number, a brother of the man who became Battalion Commandant, being sent to prison. Records also show that James Malvey, referred to above, was himself interned later in 1921, although the reasons for his incarceration are not given. A memo signed on 25 July by Lt. General Strickland, the British commander in Cork, approved the internment of a number of men, including 'Jim Malvey'.[34]

The day after Bridget Noble was taken prisoner by the IRA, the *Irish Independent* published a short, two-sentence summary of the Dublin Castle statement, referred to above, about a woman farmer who had been attacked by a group of men. As already indicated, the story was also published in newspapers in England and in Northern Ireland. The *Irish Independent* version stated: 'Dublin Castle reports a raid on the house of a woman farmer in Castletownbere district by 8 masked men who cut off her hair and carried away £35 in notes. The motive is alleged to be that she was suspected of having given information to the police.'[35]

The Editor of the *Irish Independent* at this period was Timothy R. Harrington, who probably would have had a personal interest in news items from the Beara peninsula as he was a native of the area. He had been appointed to the post by a fellow Beara man, the businessman William Martin Murphy who, as a major employer, famously clashed with trade union leader James Larkin during the Dublin Lockout of 1913. (Murphy was born at Derrymihan, near Castletownbere.) Timothy Harrington, born in 1869, was the son of Jack and Catherine Harrington of Bawrs in Eyeries parish, and the Harringtons were close neighbours of Liam O'Dwyer's family. The Harrington residence was just across the road from the entrance to the long lane leading to the O'Dwyer family home at Cailroe. Timothy Harrington and Liam O'Dwyer differed on politics, and as Editor, Harrington would take a strong pro-Treaty stance during the Civil War. (Another Beara native working as a journalist on the *Irish Independent* at this period was Michael J. Spillane, born in West End, Castletownbere, who had a major scoop in 1915 when he interviewed survivors after the sinking of the *Lusitania*.[36])

Mrs Noble's captors are unlikely to have been pleased with the *Irish Independent* report on the punishment attack. They may have seen it as additional evidence that Mrs Noble complained to the RIC about those who had 'bobbed' her. They may also have resented the negative publicity that had resulted from her complaint to the police. As will be demonstrated in more detail, the leaders of the Beara Battalion were very sensitive about the reputation of their organisastion. They demanded respect from civilians, and showed little tolerance towards anyone who made a comment, even in private, considered damaging to the 'good name' of the IRA.

Chapter 9: 'Save me, Jack, save me!'

As she was being taken away by her captors along a narrow lane towards the sea, Bridget Noble was in great distress and she cried out for someone to save her. Probably tied up, she was being taken in a donkey and cart down a remote boreen towards Cleandra harbour, in the townland of Kilcatherine. It was in an isolated area called Darrigroe. From Cleandra, it is believed that she would be taken by boat to another location further east along the coast. She had been held prisoner in the isolated house in the valley by the sea at Kilcatherine for some time and, it seems, the time of execution was drawing near. As the prisoner and her captors were passing the home of Jack O'Sullivan, she cried out, 'Save me, Jack, save me!' It was probably her last chance to summon help from a neighbour, a last desperate attempt to save her life. In the way it was described to me, it seemed that this was a despairing cry with something almost biblical about it, a cry that was *De Profundis* – 'out of the depths…'

According to an account that has survived locally, it was dark, early in the morning, when Jack and his young son Den, aged about nine years, heard the chilling sound of the woman crying out. A man, obviously one of Mrs Noble's captors, knocked on the door to say, 'Everything is all right.' A modern equivalent might be: 'Nothing to see here.' The family would learn that the woman who was calling out for help was a neighbour from down the road in Reenavaude, Mrs Noble. Her IRA captors would not have allowed anyone to intervene as they pressed ahead with their task of transporting her to a location where she would face death. There was nothing Jack could have done to save his neighbour. The horrifying events of that morning made a deep impression on Jack and the boy Den, and the memory would stay with Den all his life – he passed away in comparatively recent years, in 1999. (Jack came from the Derrihy branch of the Sullivan clan, and was known as Jack Derrihy.)

According to an informed source, when Mrs Noble's captors reached the sea shore, they took possession of a rowing boat that was stored in a shed, for a further journey along the coast. The use of a boat to transport the prisoner may have been for security reasons, to maintain an element of secrecy and to avoid the danger of encountering crown forces patrolling the roads. Travelling by boat during the hours of darkness may have been for a particular purpose – to avoid being seen from the coast. It was pointed out to me during research that many parts of the Kenmare River are visible during daylight from the high ground along this stretch of coast. Those escorting Mrs Noble by boat would doubtless have been anxious to ensure that they were not observed by anyone looking out to sea from local farms or from the roads that ran parallel to the coast.

Many local men had boat-handling skills, and engaged in seine fishing at night for mackerel – they would thus have acquired experience of navigating at night. One local person heard that Mrs Noble was tied up as she was being transported by boat. (The peninsula's maritime tradition proved useful on occasion to the IRA during the revolutionary period. The afore-mentioned Mrs Hannah Hanley told of drawing up plans to assist escapees from the Bere Island internment camp to get away by boat to safety on the mainland; she also told of organising a rowing boat and crew to undertake a 28 mile night-time journey by sea 'at risk of our lives' to take petrol from Beara to the 'headquarters' of Lady Broderick in Caherdaniel, County Kerry.[1] Lady Albinia Broderick was unusual among the ascendancy class in that she had republican sympathies. It is also reported that a man who had served with the Flying Column and was wanted by the British was assisted in eluding capture by being taken by boat on a similar voyage from Beara across Kenmare Bay to County Kerry in 1921.)

According to the internal IRA report on her fate, Bridget Noble was held prisoner for nine days, until a trial was held on 13 March. This happened to be a Sunday, and those involved in the proceedings probably attended Mass that day, possibly at Ardgroom or Eyeries or Castletownbere. In the Catholic liturgical calendar, 13 March is the feast day of Saint Ansovinus, a 9th century bishop in Camerino, in what is now central Italy. Ansovinus is the patron saint of small farmers – an ironic coincidence in light of the fact that those involved in the detention and trial of Mrs Noble were probably of small farm background themselves.

Professor Eunan O'Halpin has explained IRA procedures for dealing with alleged spies and informers. 'They were to be brought before an IRA court martial, which would determine guilt and impose penalties ranging from fines and confiscation of property to exile and death. In most cases a handful of officers would decide on someone's fate, whether or not the person was present to defend themselves or was even aware of the proceedings. If not already in custody, the guilty party would then be captured and the penalty enforced. Sometimes the brigade Officer Commanding (O/C) was consulted before an execution, but often he was not.' O'Halpin remarked that 'contemporary accounts of IRA courts martial indicate that they were generally cursory affairs…'[2]

A history of the local company of the IRA at Knockraha, County Cork, in the Cork No 1 Brigade area, where captives were often held, gives an account of how the fate of prisoners was decided. The history was written with the cooperation of Martin Corry, who was Captain of the Knockraha Company, as mentioned, and of other local men who had been active in the Volunteers. According to the history, in some instances, the decision on a prisoner's fate was made 'by the brigade or battalion personnel' and in some instances 'by the officers of the local company'.[3] The latter comment would suggest that in this area at least, some life-or-death decisions were made at quite a low level in the IRA hierarchy, by low-ranking personnel.

Details have not emerged as to how the court martial of Mrs Noble was conducted or where it was held. One could speculate that the trial took place at the remote farmhouse in the Kilcatherine area where she was detained. In a rather simplistic phrase, the IRA report drawn up by Liam O'Dwyer says that she 'admitted guilt on all the charges'. We do not, of course, have Mrs Noble's version of events. She had undergone the terrifying experience of being kidnapped and locked up as a prisoner. Even a person with a strong personality could succumb to dread and despair in such conditions. From the account of one of her minders, it appears she was in fear of her life, and would not even drink tea unless shown that it was not poisoned. She was under enormous pressure and the reliability of any confession made under such extreme duress is open to question.

Bridget Noble had been held prisoner for more than a week before her trial, and this would have given her captors ample opportunity to interrogate her. Did they ask her why she was making visits to the RIC barracks, or why she was in correspondence with the RIC? And if so, how did she answer? Could she have given a valid explanation? Liam O'Dwyer's report gives no indication. Neither is there any indication in the report that any questioning of Mrs Noble that might have taken place produced much in the way of useful information. While it is claimed that Mrs Noble 'admitted guilt on all the charges', the IRA report does not state specifically that her contacts with the police were for the purposes of informing – with the obvious exception of what may have been her final visit to the police station, when, apparently, she handed a letter to the Head Constable naming the men she accused of the 'bobbing' attack.

Death Sentence

Mrs Noble was sentenced to death. Details are unavailable as to the processes involved in reaching the decision to impose the ultimate penalty. While members of Cumann na mBan had a role in guarding Mrs Noble as a prisoner, the decision on her fate would have been a matter for male republicans, for IRA men. Condemning a person to be executed was the ultimate expression of power and authority. Perhaps those involved considered they were carrying out an act of patriotism, and were furthering the cause of the republic. There appears to have been no facility for an appeal against the verdict or prescribed punishment. Liam O'Dwyer's report notes that the 'date of execution' was two days later, 15 March 1921. The date reminds one of the soothsayer's warning in Shakespeare's *Julius Caesar*: 'Beware the Ides of March.' (On 13 March, the day that Mrs Noble received the death sentence, there was another tragic event on the Beara peninsula. A young Volunteer called Richard Newman was shot and fatally injured by crown forces near his home at Cluin, Allihies, after he tried to run away.[4]) The IRA report did not give details of how Mrs Noble was put to death or the location where she was killed.

After travelling by boat from Darrigroe, some locals believe that Mrs Noble was taken ashore further along the coast at a very isolated place, Cuas pier, and that she was kept in a shed at the pier for at least one night. This would probably have involved the attendance of at least one member of Cumann na mBan to assist the male captors in guarding the female prisoner. On 13 March 2017, which happened to be the 96th anniversary of Mrs Noble being sentenced to death, I re-visited the Beara peninsula. On that day, I travelled along the road from Darrigroe to Cuas pier. At Darrigroe, I saw the boreen along which Mrs Noble was taken on the donkey and cart down to the sea on her way to the place of execution – it had probably changed little since that harrowing event back in March 1921.

A short distance further east along the coast is the area where William Lehane lived and where he was shot. The house, now in ruins, is obscured by trees and close to the sea – a local person gave directions as to where it is located. One can look down on the site from the road. It was a fine, clear day, but I was conscious of the dark history associated with the ruined house in the woods. Arriving shortly afterwards at Cuas pier, I found a very tranquil, beautiful spot. There was nobody around, no boats at the slipway and the only sound was the sound of the sea. There was an old stone shed near the pier and I wondered if this was the place where Mrs Noble was kept prisoner.

Guarding Bridget Noble; Conflicting Reports of Execution & Disposal of Remains

A trawl though the Service (1917-1921) Medal records in the Military Archives relating to applicants from the Ardgroom-Eyeries area produced some information about the guarding of Mrs Noble while she was being held captive. (There is a summary of each application for a Medal on the Military Archives website, but one has to visit the archives centre to inspect the full file, and in some cases certain details are withheld for data protection purposes.) Details of Volunteers said to have been engaged in guarding the prisoner emerged from one particular file.[5] They included Dan Harrington, Droumard, an officer of Ardgroom Company who later resided in Somerville, Boston. Another was Tim Reilly [Rahilly] who was aged 18 years at the time, and who in the late 1960s was residing in New York City at East 209 Street, The Bronx. It will be recalled that he was one of the Volunteers said to have questioned Nora Sullivan who told of Mrs Noble's letter to the Head Constable complaining about the men who had allegedly 'bobbed' her. Also named as one of those guarding Mrs Noble was Mike Shea, from Ardgroom Inward, who also moved to America, residing in the 1960s at College Avenue, Medford, Massachusetts. Another man mentioned as guarding the female prisoner was Mike Lynch, who later resided in Chicago. Shea, Lynch and Harrington were all aged about 20 years at the time Mrs Noble was being held captive. A teenaged youth, not listed as a Volunteer, was also said to have guarded the prisoner.

It was also stated that a party [of Volunteers] were engaged in the 'conveying of the prisoner, Bridget Noble, from Coose to Poleen in 1921'. This appears to be a reference to Mrs Noble being brought from Cuas pier to Pulleen, which lay in the northern part of the townland of Ardgroom Inward, and not far from her home area of Reenavaude. Pulleen is in an isolated area of small farms and rugged countryside intersected by narrow roads and boreens, with a long coastline and spectacular views of the sea and Ardgroom Harbour. There is no indication as to whether the journey was undertaken by sea or by road.

There are conflicting accounts locally as to how Mrs Noble was put to death, where she was killed and how her remains were disposed of. Liam O'Dwyer's very brief internal IRA report on Bridget's execution does not address these issues and the anecdotal evidence varies greatly. According to one version of events, Bridget was drowned at Pulleen or nearby Pallas Pier, both places located in Bridget's own townland of Ardgroom Inward; another version has her being hanged or shot at an arch under the bridge at Collorus, in the County Kerry part of Beara, near Lauragh.

It is noteworthy that the afore-mentioned file in the Military Archives indicates that a party of Volunteers brought Bridget Noble on a journey from Cuas to Pulleen. There is no mention of a further trip to another location, which might suggest that Pulleen was the final destination for the prisoner. Execution at Pulleen might arguably fit with the timescale outlined in the internal IRA report on Mrs Noble's fate. According to the report, as previously mentioned, she was put on trial on Sunday 13 March – probably at the house in Feith Bhui, Kilcatherine where she was held prisoner. She may then have been taken away that night on the sea journey from Cleandra to Cuas pier. It was while being taken to Cleandra harbour, during the hours of darkness, that she called out for help while passing the home of Jack 'Derrihy' O'Sullivan at Darrigroe. Then the night of the 14th may have been spent by Mrs Noble as a prisoner in the shed at Cuas pier; it may have been the following day, the 15th, that she was taken to Pulleen. It was, of course, on 15 March that she was put to death, according to the internal IRA report on her fate.

As regards anecdotal evidence suggesting that Mrs Noble was executed by drowning, one method would have been for her captors to take the prisoner out in a boat and throw her overboard while tied to a heavy object. It will also be recalled that a former Cumann na mBan member who attended Mrs Noble as a prisoner told of hearing a rumour that Bridget had been put into a bag or sack and thrown into the sea to drown. (She also stated that a local man with whom she discussed the matter also believed that Mrs Noble was drowned, and quotes him as hearing her screaming.) She seemed to accept that Mrs Noble's body lay beneath the waters off Ardgroom, and recalled how she challenged a group of IRA men, saying that if they went out fishing in Ardgroom Harbour, the first thing they might dredge up would be Biddy Noble.

Other versions of the drowning story have also emerged. It is known that a man, whose father was in the IRA, told of hearing that Mrs Noble was drowned at Pulleen, by being left tied up on the shore while the tide engulfed her – this would have inflicted a most barbaric, slow death on the prisoner. Another man, whose father was close to various members of the IRA of that era, told me that he also heard that Mrs Noble was put to death in this manner, but thought it happened at Pallas Pier, a short distance to the south of a narrow promontory at Pulleen jutting out into the sea. There would have been obvious security risks about drowning a prisoner in such a public place at Pallas Pier, in Ardgroom Harbour. It has not been possible to confirm the above reports, although one cannot rule out the possibility that Mrs Noble did indeed meet her death by drowning.

Then there are the reports that Mrs Noble was shot, and that this happened in an entirely different location, in the County Kerry part of Beara. An important source in regard to this version of events is Eva O'Sullivan, who gave a taped interview based on what she learned from a man who had been in the IRA. Eva, quoting her IRA contact, says that Mrs Noble was 'taken by boat along the Kenmare River' and that 'she was taken in at Collorus', where she was killed. Collorus is much further to the east from Pulleen and, as mentioned, is located across the county boundary in County Kerry. Did IRA members put out a story that Mrs Noble was shot in County Kerry, to conceal that she had been subjected to a slow death by being drowned, and to divert attention from the area where this occurred? (In terms of archival records, the last recorded location of Bridget Noble, shortly before her death, was Pulleen.) Or is it the case that another team of Volunteers, for whatever reason, brought Mrs Noble on a further voyage, from Pulleen to Collorus, where she was executed by shooting? Said Eva: 'They shot her at Collorus and buried her there, a shallow grave I suppose.' (Ironically, as mentioned, Mrs Noble's mother came from Collorus, and there were probably relatives still living in the area.)

One wonders why her captors would have taken the prisoner on this extended journey to Collorus. If one assumes that this account is correct, Mrs Noble's captors, after navigating around Collorus Point, could have landed at a very secluded stony beach, just below the Ardgroom-Lauragh road – the beach cannot be seen from the road. In times past, a footpath led through the heather from the beach up the steep hillside to a stone arch underneath a bridge on the above-mentioned road. The bridge has been replaced by a modern overpass, one of the road improvements some locals have attributed to the Healy-Rae political dynasty. However, the subterranean arch is still there, as is one of the original parapets (on the landward side), and some believe that the arch is where Mrs Noble was put to death, although the arch itself is not mentioned by Eva O'Sullivan.

One version of events has Mrs Noble being hanged or strangled at the arch, while of course Eva's IRA informant says she was shot. It is noteworthy that, as will be shown, Bridget Noble's husband Alexander would also state, in an *In Memoriam* notice, that his wife was 'shot in Lauragh' – Collorus is in the vicinity of Lauragh. After locating the overpass with the aid of local information, I moved down from the road to take a closer look at the arch as I tried to follow in what may have been the final footsteps in the *via dolorosa* of Bridget Noble. The arch is in a very scenic area overlooking Collorus point and

Kilmakilloge Harbour. It was a bright day, but pondering what might have occurred here back in 1921, and the possibility that the arch had been used as a death chamber, or place of execution, the place in my imagination seemed to take on a sinister air of gloom and melancholy.

On the recording featuring Eva O'Sullivan's comments, a man who took part in the conversation mentions that he heard Mrs Noble's body was disposed of at sea. 'I heard she was taken out in the boat and thrown overboard.' He does not indicate if the IRA's purpose was to drown the victim or simply to dispose of a body at sea. Eva is insistent that she was told Mrs Noble was buried in a grave after being shot at Collorus.

After the first edition of this book was published, new leads emerged about various aspects of the story of Bridget Noble, including the issue of how the IRA disposed of her remains. One report that came to light could potentially resolve apparent contradictions between those who believed her remains were thrown in the sea, and those who maintained that the remains were placed in a grave, on land. A Beara man relayed an extraordinary account that came down in his own family from his grandfather, who had known Mrs Noble. According to this version of events, Bridget's body was disposed of at sea, in the Kenmare River. The body was reportedly tied to a cartwheel and thrown into the sea, but did not remain submerged, and was caught in the nets of a trawler operated by a fisherman from Kilmakilloge. He brought the body ashore and the IRA had it thrown again into the sea, only for it to be caught again in the fisherman's nets some time later. He brought in the body once again and this time the IRA decided to bury the remains on land. While the Beara man who provided this information obviously gave an honest account of what his grandfather related, there is no independent way of confirming this version of events. Relatives of the fisherman say they never heard of him finding the body of a woman at sea, although one speculated that if it happened, it was the kind of experience he may not have wanted to talk about.

As regards drowning as a means of execution, in a few cases during the War of Independence the IRA decided to use this method rather than shooting. This involved the victim being tied up, attached to a weight, and thrown live into a river or lake to sink below the surface. There were cases in County Roscommon where this method of inflicting death was used – the proximity of the mighty River Shannon was probably a factor. The victims included an RIC man, Constable Michael Dennehy, who was said to have been taken prisoner while cycling with a woman friend in November 1920. It was reported that he was later taken out in a boat and, while tied to a heavy stone, thrown into the Shannon.

In other cases during the conflict, men were shot and their bodies then disposed of in a lake or river. It could be an effective way of disappearing a person, but there was always a risk that a body could surface again, causing complications for the IRA. In County Kilkenny, an ex-soldier called William Kenny, who lived with his blind father, was said to have been gagged, blindfolded and tied to a 56 lb weight before being dropped into a deep section of the River Barrow. (It appears that the IRA feared that if they shot him, the sound could alert the crown forces.) Some weeks later, Kenny's decomposed body drifted to the surface further down the Barrow, and the remains had to be weighted down again by IRA members, and returned to the river. Another ex-soldier, 'Slickfoot' Maher, was shot by the IRA after being accused of informing and his body dumped in the Shannon. However, his wooden leg kept the body afloat, and it had to be hauled in and buried on the banks of the river.[6]

IRA members in County Cork were more likely to use the traditional method of shooting as a means of execution. In an unusual development, in August 1921 members of the Cork No 1 Brigade threw into the sea the weighted-down body of John Coughlan, from Cobh, County Cork who had allegedly hanged himself in IRA custody – the body was later washed up ashore.[7]

Among those who believed that the remains of Mrs Noble were buried on land, rather than given a permanent watery grave in the Kenmare River, the general consensus seemed to be that the place of burial was in the Lauragh area. One must give due consideration to the testimony of a Beara man who had a close relative who was an active officer of the IRA at the time Mrs Noble was put to death. This man, probably relying on information from his own IRA relative who would have been well-informed, is known to have identified the approximate area where Bridget is said to have been buried as Lauragh. This version of events would tally with what Eva O'Sullivan was told by her own IRA contact, that Mrs Noble was buried after being shot at Collorus – as mentioned, Collorus is close to Lauragh. The IRA had a Company at Lauragh, which had been organised by Liam O'Dwyer some years previously.[8]

One man whose father was a boy when Mrs Noble was disappeared heard that she was buried secretly at Kilmakilloge graveyard, near Lauragh, as the IRA men involved, being religious, wanted to bury the remains in consecrated ground. Another person heard that she was buried at Knockatee mountain, to the north of Lauragh. An elderly woman heard, on the other hand, that Mrs Noble was buried near a small inlet or creek called Goleenastacha (phonetic spelling), also in the Lauragh area, and close to Doorus Point. At Goleenastacha there is a small pier, Reenakilla pier, and in former times people from Collorus would come in by boat to the pier to attend Mass in nearby Lauragh church.

There is another school of thought which holds that Mrs Noble is buried in Doorus woods. The woods are on a promontory that juts out into the sea in sheltered Kilmakilloge Harbour, a prominent feature being Doorus Point. A path leading into the woods lies about two miles further east along the R571 from the afore-mentioned Collorus overpass, on the left-hand side. In the area to the right, there are ancient standing stones and a stone circle. A little further along the R571 is a minor road to the left leading to Reenakilla pier and Goleenastacha, also a supposed burial site for Mrs Noble, as mentioned.

One man who had relatives in the IRA and Cumann na mBan, heard that Mrs Noble was buried near the ruins of a house in Doorus woods. As I walked in the shaded woods towards Doorus Point with the sunlight filtering through the tall, spectral trees, it was easy to imagine that harrowing scenes may have been enacted here back in 1921. However, there is yet another version of the Bridget Noble story as it relates to Doorus woods. An elderly man whose father lived in the Lauragh area at the time of her disappearance heard that Bridget was shot at Doorus but not buried there – he heard that her body was taken by boat out to sea and dumped overboard. In the midst of so many conflicting reports, there are a couple of basic details that one can be absolutely certain about – Bridget Noble was put to death in 1921 and her remains are missing to this day.

Logistical Challenges

It is noteworthy that Mrs Noble was held prisoner for approximately one and a half weeks before being killed. From accounts that have emerged, it would appear that during the War of Independence, male captives who faced the death penalty were usually executed by the IRA far more swiftly after being taken prisoner. One wonders if Beara Battalion members were hesitant about inflicting the extreme penalty on a female and if this could partly explain the reason why she was held prisoner for such a comparatively long period before she was killed.

Since Mrs Noble was detained for eleven nights, and appears to have been moved from place to place, by land and sea, there were considerable logistical challenges involved for members of the Beara Battalion. Probably at least 20 members of the movement, IRA officers, Volunteers and Cumann na mBan activists, were involved, directly or indirectly, in the action taken against Mrs Noble in the period February – March 1921. This would include the punishment attack; the investigation into her complaint to the RIC about the 'bobbing' assault; the capture on the road to Eyeries; the guarding of her as a prisoner, both in places of detention and in transit from place to place; the conduct of her trial; the decision on her fate, and the subsequent execution and disposal of remains. All these matters had to be dealt with covertly, so as not to attract the unwanted attention of the RIC. While doubtless local republicans had learned how to keep sensitive matters quiet, word probably spread quickly in republican circles about the execution of the woman from Reenavaude. Local civilians would also gradually learn through word of mouth that Mrs Noble had been disappeared, and one local source suggested that this would have suited the purposes of the IRA as her fate would deter others from talking to the crown forces.

Alleged Executioner

In her remarkable taped testimony, Eva O'Sullivan states that her IRA contact told her the name of the man who executed Mrs Noble. 'It was a man from Glenbeg who shot her,' she says on the recording. A male voice on the tape seems to anticipate what Eva is about to say next and he says: 'Crowley'. She replies: 'Patsy Dan.' So, according to Eva, her IRA informant identified Patsy Dan Crowley as the man who killed Bridget Noble.[9] Patsy Dan Crowley, a very active member of Ardgroom Company, and a close associate of Liam O'Dwyer, was one of the Beara Battalion men who remained with O'Dwyer in Beara when other active fighters went off to join up with the Flying Column under Tom Barry in March 1921. One could speculate that extra responsibilities devolved onto Patsy Dan in light of information that has emerged indicating that the Captain of Ardgroom Company, John Sheehan, was one of those away from Beara with the Flying Column at the period in question.

As will be explained in more detail, these column men would have been away from Beara when Mrs Noble was put on trial, found guilty and put to death. John Sheehan was wounded in the Crossbarry engagement on 19 March, and the injuries he sustained may have been a factor when he later relinquished the post of Ardgroom Company Captain, with Patsy Dan Crowley succeeding him, although Sheehan would remain an officer, with the rank of 1st Lieutenant. In light of Patsy Dan's active role in Ardgroom Company, and his presence in Beara at the time Mrs Noble was killed, the suggestion that he was involved in her execution could be seen as having a certain plausibility, although his involvement cannot be confirmed. It is, however, apparent that Patsy Dan Crowley had certain connections with the Noble saga. According to the internal IRA report on Mrs Noble's execution, he was one of the men [all members of Ardgroom Company] said to have quizzed Nora Sullivan about Mrs Noble's role in complaining to the RIC about the men who forcibly cut her hair. As will be explained, it was also claimed in the IRA report that Crowley was one of the individuals named by Mrs Noble to the police as having been involved in the shooting of William Lehane. (As mentioned, the former Cumann na mBan member from Kilcatherine who guarded Mrs Noble also talked of hearing that Crowley was one of those involved in the shooting of her relative, Lehane.)

While the finger of suspicion has been pointed at Patsy Dan Crowley, it should be stated that at least one knowledgeable source in the Beara region believes that Crowley was not the man who executed Mrs Noble and, moreover, was not the man who shot William Lehane. This person has privately named two other members of the IRA, both from the Ardgroom area, suspected of being responsible for the killings. One of the IRA men was said to have shot Lehane, while the other, a close associate, is said to have executed Mrs Noble. Another source familiar with the republican families of Beara of that era speculated that when Eva's IRA informant identified Patsy Dan Crowley as the executioner of Mrs Noble there may have been disinformation involved. Crowley was dead at this stage, and the source suggested that the intention may have been to shift the blame onto a man who was deceased, and thus divert attention from the real killer, who was probably still alive.

In a report on Mrs Noble's disappearance and death, a unionist newspaper in Northern Ireland, the *Londonderry Sentinel* claimed, some months after her death, that there were rumours that Mrs Noble was tortured before being killed. The newspaper stated: 'Persistent rumours received from many different sources, some of them since the truce, state that a pig-ring was put through her tongue before she died. Proof is very hard to obtain but the local inhabitants, at any rate, regard this as a fact.'[10] While it appears that there were indeed rumours at the time of physical torture being used, these rumours cannot be confirmed and have to be treated with caution, although Mrs Noble must have suffered intense psychological torture as her time of execution approached. As regards the insertion into the flesh of pig-rings as a means of torture, there was an incident in County Roscommon during the War of Independence when a woman was punished in this way for her disobedient attitude – she had ignored an instruction not to supply milk to the RIC. The punishment was noteworthy in another way, in that it also involved indecent assault. It was reported that four men came to her home and that she was held down by the hands and feet and and that one man held his hand over her mouth [presumably to prevent her screams being heard], while three pig-rings were inserted into her buttocks with pincers.[11]

One of the male voices on the Eva O'Sullivan recording makes a comment that seems to suggest that after Mrs Noble's execution, a ballad was written to celebrate her death, with the lyrics including the words 'where did Mrs Noble go?' Apparently, the ballad was based on the song, *The Blarney Roses*, the first line of which goes: 'Can anybody tell me where the Blarney Roses grow?' The words were apparently amended to: 'Can anybody tell me where did Mrs Noble go?' This would suggest a rather sick attempt to mock the woman who had been abducted and killed. Incidentally, *The Blarney Roses* was also adapted to mark the capture by the IRA in 1920 of a senior British Army officer, Brigadier General Lucas. According to the republican Ernie O'Malley, the words were re-written thus: 'Can anybody tell me where did General Lucas go? He may be down in Mitchelstown or over in Mayo?'[12] While it is alleged that some republicans tried to mock Mrs Noble in death, it is noteworthy that a source also told of a man who had a role in the action taken against her, whose conscience greatly troubled him afterwards and who deeply regretted his involvement.

The Lehane Shooting Allegations

The internal IRA report on the execution of Bridget Noble claimed, as indicated above, that they heard from the RIC that she had given information to the force about the shooting of William Lehane leading to two men being pursued by the authorities although, as will be explained, there is a striking anomaly in regard to an aspect of this allegation. The IRA report stated: 'Information reached us from the RIC that Mrs Noble told them that Liam Dwyer and Pat Crowley were the men who shot William Lehane. This man was shot for land grabbing in Febr. 1920 [*recte* May 1920].' The report obviously refers to two of the leading members of the IRA in the Ardgroom area - Pat Crowley, also known as Patsy Dan Crowley, who as previously indicated, was an officer of the Ardgroom company and Liam O'Dwyer, who became Commandant of the Beara Battalion. The IRA report continued: 'What resulted from the information that Mrs Noble gave to the police was not too serious as any of the "murderers" were not caught, but were kept on the run. The district was constantly raided for them till the truce.'

It was not unknown for some members of the RIC to provide information to the IRA. An RIC man might do so because he had a friendly relationship or family ties with an IRA member, or he might act out of nationalist sympathies – as already indicated, most members of the force were Irish Catholics. In some cases there may also have been self-interest involved – the IRA was less likely to assassinate a policeman if he was considered 'friendly' or 'helpful'. In addition, depending on local circumstances, RIC men drank in local pubs, and there was the possibility of sensitive information leaking out through 'loose talk'. Young women, members of Cumann na mBan, could also make use of their contacts with RIC men to elicit information, and female republicans seem to have been an important source of intelligence for the Beara Battalion. It appears that information about RIC activities could also be gleaned, indirectly, through friendly contact with members of the military, who had dealings with the police.

Liam O'Dwyer had a potential source in the RIC although there is no indication that this was the conduit through which information was allegedly conveyed about the assistance claimed to have been given by Mrs Noble to the police about the Lehane shooting. Sergeant John Mulligan, from Oldcastle, County Meath, who at one time was based in the RIC station in Castletownbere, married a woman from the town, Hanna Dwyer, a cousin of Liam O'Dwyer.[13] The latter, in his memoir, relates how in November 1919, Mulligan, now based in King Street RIC barracks in Cork, had given a warning, via a third party, that two RIC constables from Castletownbere had spotted O'Dwyer in Cork and had rushed into the barracks to get a warrant for his arrest. O'Dwyer got on his bicycle and managed to make his getaway.

O'Dwyer also had a cousin in the RIC, Johnny Sullivan from Gortnabulliga, but his service in the force took him far from home and it is highly unlikely that he was a source. There is no reason to believe that he was anything other than a loyal member of the RIC – it seems unlikely he would have betrayed a police source to the IRA. Sullivan came from one of the big families mentioned earlier – he was one of 17 children of Jeremiah and Mary Sullivan. The constable was serving in Belfast from June 1920, and it appears his superiors were impressed by his performance, as his service record shows he received two 'First Class Favourable Records' that year. During the 1916 rebellion, while stationed at Oylegate, County Wexford, he was involved in the capture of two insurgents who had tried to disrupt a railway line, for which he had received a 'Third Class Favourable Record' and a monetary award.[14] It is not known if he returned to Gortnabulliga on holiday during the War of Independence. Policemen had reason to be cautious about returning to visit the family home, if it was located in an area of particular tension. There were a number of cases where policemen were kidnapped or shot dead after returning on leave to visit relatives.

As outlined above, Mrs Hannah Hanley, one of the Cumann na mBan members who guarded Bridget Noble as a prisoner, told in her application for a Military Service Pension how, as a single woman, she 'did a line' with an RIC man who had been stationed in Eyeries, and from whom she received information, but there is no indication that he was the source of the intelligence regarding Mrs Noble. Another woman who was in Cumann na mBan, Nora O'Sullivan (1894 – 1972), née O'Neill, from Castletownbere, told how she got information from an RIC man with whom she kept in constant touch. However, her contacts with the policeman seem primarily to have been in relation to ascertaining the needs of republican prisoners and sending in items that were required. 'If the prisoners wanted clothes and anything else they told this man and I would send it in.'[15]

Louise O'Connell, sister of Bella O'Connell, was also an active member of Cumann na mBan, and cultivated her own contacts among the crown forces. In her application for a Military Service Pension, she gave details of her various sources of intelligence, but there is no indication that she received information about Mrs Noble.[16] Ms O'Connell told how, in August 1919, her family home in Eyeries was taken over by the King's Own Yorkshire Light Infantry (KOYLI), and she got information about raids from a soldier, Corporal Dunne, from Harty Place, Dublin. (This seems to be a reference to William Dunne, who had been in the Royal Dublin Fusiliers, serving in the Great War, before becoming an Acting Corporal with the KOYLI.[17]) Ms O'Connell told of also getting assistance from an officer, Lieutenant Churchouse, 'who gave me every information supplied to him by RIC'.

It has not been possible to identify the Lieutenant Churchouse said to have been so helpful to Ms O'Connell. There were a number of Englishmen named Churchouse who had the rank of Lieutenant or 2nd Lieutenant in the British Army during the Great War or its aftermath. Records show that at least one of them, Reginald Rufus Churchouse from the Birmingham area, served in Ireland in 1918 but he was based in Dublin at Marlborough Barracks, now McKee Barracks, with the King Edward's Horse regiment. There is no indication that this unit was ever deployed to Beara. He can be ruled out as a source concerning the Lehane shooting as he emigrated to Australia where he married in Queensland in May 1920. His brother Harold Percy Churchouse was a Lieutenant in the Royal Warwickshire Regiment during the Great War. Elements of the regiment were based in Ireland during the Troubles but there is no record to show that this officer served in Beara. Among other men called Churchouse who attained officer rank was Lieutenant Montague Churchouse, from St Albans,

Hertfordshire, who served with the Lincolnshire Regiment in the Great War but once again, no link with Beara could be established.

Ms O'Connell also told of receiving information from an RIC man, Constable Shanahan. She stated: 'The military were withdrawn from our house in March 1919 and it was immediately occupied by RIC for a whole year. I managed to get in touch with Constable Shanahan and so was able to get valuable information. The force later became suspicious of him, he then resigned and left for USA.' Ms O'Connell was obviously referring to Constable Bernard Shanahan, a native of Ballinahow, Thurles, County Tipperary, who had joined the RIC in 1912 and who had served in Ballinrobe, County Mayo and Peter's Lane, Waterford before being sent to Eyeries.[18] RIC records show that he was a Catholic and that he resigned from the force on 30 April 1920. The stated reason for his resignation was that he had 'secured a better job'.[19]

In fact, as the force came under pressure from the IRA, there were many resignations around this period, and some of these departures were reported in the newspapers. In a report in the *Freeman's Journal* under the headline: 'More RIC Men Resign', Constable Shanahan's name was included in a list of men who had left the force. Shanahan's neighbour from Ballinahow, Constable [Thomas] Tynan, who had also joined the RIC in 1912, was included in the same list as having resigned.[20] Later in 1920, records show that Bernard Shanahan, aged 27 years, sailed from Queenstown [Cobh] on board the *Baltic*, bound for New York. Even though he was stationed in Eyeries, close to Bridget Noble's area of Ardgroom, it is noteworthy that the date of his resignation from the force was a week before the shooting of William Lehane, and this would suggest he was not the source of the claim that Mrs Noble gave the RIC the names of the men alleged to have killed the farmer.

While the IRA, with the assistance of Cumann na mBan, clearly had various sources of information among the crown forces in Beara, there is no way of independently confirming the claim that the IRA heard from the RIC that Bridget Noble gave the police the names of the men said to have shot William Lehane. If the IRA had an RIC source who gave them a tip-off about Mrs Noble's alleged informing, there would have been an obvious reluctance to identify him in a report such as the one written about her execution. One has also to consider the possibility that the case against Mrs Noble in regard to allegedly informing on suspects in the Lehane shooting was based on hearsay, and that, for reasons that will be outlined, it was embellished or exaggerated.

Chapter 10: A Curious Anomaly

In his report on Bridget Noble's execution, Liam O'Dwyer seems to portray himself and his comrade Patsy Dan Crowley as victims of the woman from Reenavaude. As indicated above, he refers to information that she told the RIC that Liam Dwyer and Pat Crowley were the men who shot William Lehane. O'Dwyer seems to imply that the RIC took her seriously and tried to arrest himself and Crowley in connection with killing Lehane, although the two managed to evade capture. In a seemingly magnanimous comment, O'Dwyer remarks that what resulted from Mrs Noble's information to the police was 'not too serious' as any of the 'murderers' [i.e. himself and Crowley] were 'not caught, but were kept on the run'. As mentioned, he goes on then to maintain that the district was 'constantly raided' for himself and Crowley 'until the Truce'.

There is a curious anomaly in O'Dwyer's report, and the issue of credibility arises. O'Dwyer omits the vital information that he was a deportee in England when Lehane was shot on 7 May 1920, could never have been a suspect for the Lehane killing. The crown forces would have known he was one of the republican prisoners that they themselves deported to England in 1920 for internment at Wormwood Scrubs prison, and that he had a cast-iron alibi. O'Dwyer himself, in his 1967 letter to a Department of Defence official cited above, mentions that he was 'in jail' at the time of the Lehane shooting. Contrary to the impression given in his report which was sent to GHQ, O'Dwyer could never have been 'kept on the run' over the Lehane killing, regardless of what Bridget Noble told the police, or was alleged to have told them, about those who shot Lehane. The dice seem to have been heavily loaded against Mrs Noble in this section of the report explaining why she was executed.

O'Dwyer did indeed go on the run, not as a wanted man for the Lehane shooting, but for an entirely different reason. Having been released by the British from internment in England, he was back in Beara in June 1920. He recalls in a statement in his Military Service Pension (MSP) file that he set up temporary headquarters in T. T.

Harrington's house in Eyeries and resumed activities as trainer and organiser. He would not have been wanted by the authorities at this stage. The crown forces only began pursuing him again the following month, after the IRA raid on Ballycrovane coastguard station, in which he played a major role. As he explains in his MSP application, he became a fugitive following the 25 July attack on the coastguard base, during which he shot dead two coastguards. O'Dwyer says in a statement in his MSP file: 'My house was raided for me on the night after the raid [on the coastguard station]. I was on the run again.' He also states that he was a 'much wanted man' for the rest of the period (i.e. until the Truce). In another statement in the MSP file he states that he was 'on the run from 25th July'.

Patsy Dan Crowley also took part in the attack on the coastguard station, and this could help explain why he also was a fugitive. According to O'Dwyer, in the period after the raids on Ballycrovane and Castletownbere coastguard stations, 'many men were on the run'.[1] From O'Dwyer's own accounts, and from British archival records, the sequence of events can be established as to O'Dwyer's incarceration in England, his treatment in hospital for the effects of a hunger strike, and the timing of his subsequent return to Ireland. In his MSP file, O'Dwyer says he was captured 'at the end of January 1920' – he was held in prison in Cork.

British military records show that Brigadier General J. Brind signed an order on 26 February 1920 for the internment of a number of men under Defence of the Realm Regulations, including 'William Dwyer' [Liam O'Dwyer] and Michael Crowley.[2] (The latter, from Castletownbere, became Adjutant of the Beara Battalion, and held that position when Bridget Noble was kidnapped.) On 2 March a deportation order for 'William Dwyer of Ballycrovane, Castletown Bere' was handed to Captain C.J. O'C. Kelly.[3] This would have cleared the way for O'Dwyer to be sent from prison in Cork to Wormwood Scrubs. (Captain Campbell Joseph O'Connor Kelly was an Irish Catholic, born in the Ballyhaunis district of County Mayo in 1893, who served in the Great War and became a key intelligence officer with the British Army's 6th Division, based at Victoria Barracks in Cork city. He was involved in the interrogation of prisoners, developed a notorious reputation among republicans and became a major target for the IRA, which made attempts to assassinate him.[4])

It appears that O'Dwyer was interned at Wormwood Scrubs from around mid-March 1920. A British record lists 'William Dwyer' as among a number of internees who arrived at Wormwood Scrubs on 16 March. On the same list is Mark Sullivan, who would become Intelligence Officer of the Beara Battalion. (A British military record indicates that both Dwyer and Sullivan had been arrested on information from the RIC Inspector General.[5]) The deportees were taken to the prison by an escort headed by Lt. R.C. Woodbridge, RFA [Royal Field Artillery] who had served internment orders on the prisoners the previous day and who was duly given a receipt for the handover of the men into prison custody.[6] More than 100 Irish internees staged a mass protest by going on hunger strike, which received much publicity in the British and Irish newspapers. At the end of April the prison medical officer, Dr Richard Le-Geyt Worsley, became concerned about the condition of O'Dwyer and other internees who were refusing food. He alerted the prison authorities, and arranged to have the men transferred to hospital. (Worsley, aged 45 years, had served in the Great War and seems to have been quite a humane medical officer. One of his more unpleasant duties as a Home Office medic was to attend executions, and to certify the death of the person hanged.)

O'Dwyer was among 13 internees who were transferred on stretchers by ambulance, under escort, to St James' Infirmary, Wandsworth on one particular day. According to O'Dwyer, in a statement in his MSP file, the transfer occurred in mid-May, but his memory may have been faulty on this point. British Home Office archives show that O'Dwyer (referred to as '3918' in a prison record) and a dozen other internees were moved to St James' Infirmary on 30 April. According to a memorandum drawn up by Dr Worsley, the condition of the men on removal was 'very weak'. Dr Worsley, who along with warder S. Wheeler accompanied the men to hospital, noted: 'The men refused all food and stimulants before arrival at the hospital.'[7] Men taken to hospital gradually recovered, and were ultimately released. Some did sight-seeing in London before returning to Ireland.

A number of the former prisoners, including a future TD, Martin Corry, took part in a religious procession through London in honour of the beatification of Oliver Plunkett, the Irish Archbishop who was executed by the English in 1681, and revered as a martyr for the Catholic faith.[8] In his MSP file, O'Dwyer states that after release from prison through the hunger strike, he spent the 'rest of the month' [May] in St James' Infirmary. In his BMH statement, he says he was released under a general amnesty 'towards the end of May'. He indicates in statements in his MSP file that he returned from prison to Berehaven at 'the end of May', or in June. In his activities for June he states: 'Returned to Berehaven and took up reorganization of the Batt. [Battalion] under Comdt Peter Neill...'

It could be argued that the apparent discrepancy in O'Dwyer's report on Mrs Noble's execution may possibly be explained by a lack of precision in the way that he worded the report, thus creating ambiguity. Maybe he meant to convey that he was kept on the run *after* Mrs Noble's alleged informing, but not *as a result* of the alleged informing. Nevertheless, a misleading impression could have been created in the minds of those further up the IRA chain of command who read the report. Senior IRA officers, and officials in the Dáil Government's Defence Department, may have concluded that the consequences of Mrs Noble's alleged informing were a lot more serious than they could ever have been, in that a senior IRA officer, who went on to become Commandant of the Beara Battalion, was forced to go on the run. It would have been helpful to GHQ in assessing the case against Mrs Noble if O'Dwyer had made it clear that he could not have been put in jeopardy as a result of information she allegedly provided to the RIC about the shooting of William Lehane. RIC personnel, in targeting Liam O'Dwyer, did not need information from Mrs Noble or anyone else to identify him as an active republican rebel – he was well known to them for a considerable period of time. Information in O'Dwyer's MSP file indicates that crown forces had begun raiding for him as early as March 1918, and he was first arrested and jailed in January 1920.

As regards the crown forces' pursuit of Liam O'Dwyer and Patsy Dan Crowley, they were both very active members of the IRA and had taken part in one of the most successful IRA actions on the Beara peninsula during the period of conflict – the attack on Ballycrovane coastguard station, as mentioned. The authorities would have been most eager to apprehend the perpetrators – and also to recover the sizeable quantity of arms and ammunition that the IRA party had seized as a result of the raid. While the crown forces would, no doubt, have sought to arrest the men involved in the shooting of William Lehane, it was, after all, a case of violence within the Catholic community, 'local on local' violence. While there seems to have been a rumour in circulation that Patsy Dan Crowley was involved in the Lehane shooting, there is no indication that there was hard evidence against him. One could speculate that the authorities were placing a higher priority on arresting those involved in the raid on the coastguard station which cost two lives and resulted in the rebels' seizure of war materiel that now posed an enhanced security threat to the crown forces.

Let us assume, for a moment, that Bridget Noble did give information to the RIC about the alleged killers of Lehane, either deliberately because she was angry over the vicious killing of a neighbour, or because she was sympathetic to the RIC and abhorred IRA violence, or inadvertently, because of her naivety. The police are unlikely to have been impressed by the quality of the information supplied. If Mrs Noble did indeed tell the RIC, as alleged in O'Dwyer's IRA report, that O'Dwyer was one of those who shot William Lehane, it is unlikely she would have been taken seriously as an informant by the police, for the reasons outlined. Any such allegation had to be based on wild rumour or groundless gossip rather than on verifiable facts. And if Bridget Noble also named Patsy Dan Crowley as having been involved in the Lehane killing, her unreliability in regard to the O'Dwyer involvement may also have raised doubts in police minds about the credibility of any allegation she might have made regarding Patsy Dan. While information based on rumour or gossip could, in certain circumstances, prove useful to the RIC from an intelligence point of view, it seems unlikely that Mrs Noble actually witnessed the shooting of Lehane, or that she would have been able to provide credible evidence to assist a prosecution in court.

While questions can be raised about issues arising out of the IRA report on Mrs Noble's execution, the report does seem reliable in one particular aspect. The report presents quite a credible case to back up the allegation that Mrs Noble provided the RIC with the names of the men she accused of 'bobbing' her. The use of the phrase 'not too serious' in relation to the Lehane case seems to imply that the offence considered 'serious' by the local IRA was the complaint to the RIC about the alleged culprits in the hair-shearing incident. The IRA report written by Liam O'Dwyer names the 'girl', or young woman, Nora Sullivan, who is said to have accompanied Bridget to the RIC station and to have seen Bridget hand in a letter containing the names of the alleged assailants. The report claims that Mrs Noble named seven Volunteers as having 'bobbed' her, and this figure for the number of named alleged assailants tallies with the story published in the *Londonderry Sentinel*, probably based on RIC or Dublin Castle sources, that she 'was able to identify seven of her eight assailants'. The names of the IRA men who questioned Nora Sullivan about Mrs Noble's letter to the RIC are also given in the IRA report. Then there are the details about the arrests of two of the alleged assailants – their names are provided in the IRA document and British records tally with the detail in the IRA statement, although as previously indicated, the British records do not provide detailed reasons for the incarceration of the two men concerned – there is no mention of any involvement in a 'bobbing' attack.

Suspected Spies and Informers

It was a period when the IRA in County Cork was particularly vigorous in hunting down anyone suspected of being a spy or an informer. The organisation had suffered a number of setbacks and local units could be ruthless in efforts to tighten security. The Dripsey ambush setback occurred, as indicated above, in January 1921 – this was a disaster for the IRA, and Mrs Lindsay and her servant, James Clarke, would pay dearly for the tip-off she had provided to the authorities about the IRA ambush plans. Another serious reverse occurred on the following 20 February at Clonmult, about five miles north of Midleton. Crown forces surrounded a house and twelve IRA members were killed, four wounded and four captured. The historian Michael Hopkinson commented that such setbacks 'emphasised the need to root out informers and led to a big rise in the execution of so-called spies'. He went on: 'Loyalists, masons, ex-servicemen and tramps became particular targets. The war in Cork, far more than elsewhere apart from the North, took on the nature of a vendetta.'[9] It has also been suggested that civilian 'spies' were singled out, 'largely on the basis that they were soft targets as the IRA found it increasingly difficult to confront Crown forces'.[10]

Cork city and county was a region noted for the number of civilians executed by the IRA in 1920-21 as suspected spies or informers. A study by the academics Dr Andy Bielenberg and Professor Emeritus James S. Donnelly Jr has listed 78 civilians put to death during this period.[11] The authors comment: 'While IRA leaders argued they were all spies and informers, some British sources claimed they were mostly innocent; the truth is likely to fall somewhere between these extreme positions on the spectrum.' In the Cork No. 1 Brigade area, the IRA had a prison, an underground vault in Kilquane graveyard at Knockraha, near Glanmire, where some prisoners, including alleged spies, were held before execution. It was a very grim place, a dark, rat-infested dungeon with no windows or facilities, designed for accommodating coffins rather than humans, and must have been a terrifying place in which to be held captive.

Martin Corry, as mentioned, was connected to the prison as Captain of Knockraha Company. He recalled in the 1930s how, in 1919, he appointed local blacksmith Edward Moloney as 'O/C' of the prison, known with a touch of black humour as Sing Sing, after the American penitentiary. Corry explained that at first it was the 4th Battalion prison, but afterwards became the Brigade prison. According to Corry, 'the vast majority' of Tans, British military, 'spies etc' captured in both Brigade and 4th Battalion areas were sent on there. Corry was exaggerating when he used the term 'vast majority', but prisoners were undoubtedly sent to Knockraha, and it seems that for many captives these were one-way trips. Corry boasted that 'not one prisoner' ever escaped from Moloney's custody.[12]

I remember Martin Corry from the Dáil Bar in the late 1960s when, as a reporter with the *Irish Press*, I would occasionally be sent to Leinster House to cover the Dáil or Seanad. A colleague pointed him out to me one evening in the bar – Corry was having a friendly drink with a legendary journalist, Ned Murphy of the *Irish Independent*. Ned, a tough old newspaper veteran, was a renowned Free State supporter who, it would later emerge, kept an old gun, possibly a relic from the Civil War, hidden in his desk at the newspaper offices on Middle Abbey Street. His politics would have been anathema to Corry. Nevertheless, here were two elderly men from different sides of the Treaty divide having a friendly chat. My colleague, who had republican sympathies, was impressed by the rapport between them. He had considerable regard for Corry, describing him as a 'great republican' and I probably also formed a positive image of the long-serving TD.

I had no inkling then of the chilling accounts that would later emerge of Corry's role in the revolutionary period. He was described as the 'chief executioner' around Knockraha by East Cork IRA officer Mick Leahy in an interview with Ernie O'Malley. Recordings of Corry chuckling over executions and secret burials were played during a documentary shown on the Irish channel TV3. Corry seemed to have a macabre sense of humour and could see the 'funny' side of executions, so long as it was the 'right' people who were being put to death. The old cliché comes to mind: 'He knew where the bodies were buried', although one wonders if he could recall who was in what grave.

It seems that bodies of persons executed in Corry's territory were buried haphazardly, some in a boggy area called The Rea, near Knockraha, with no record kept as to who was buried where. There would thus have been little hope of exhuming remains for proper post-conflict burial or for a funeral that might provide some consolation to relatives. The local Volunteers might not necessarily have known the identity of a person being executed and secretly buried. Martin Corry told Ernie O'Malley of British soldiers coming into the area dressed in 'civvies', like tramps. One night they picked up a 'tall fellow', who had a khaki shirt and a pair of old boots. He had silk underwear, with a monogramme, under his shirt, a cigarette case also with a monogramme on it, and a Webley revolver with 14 rounds of ammunition. 'We never found out who he was.' At the Truce, a British Army captain asked about him, but not by name. 'I said we had shot him as a spy.'[13]

In some cases, it would appear that individuals were executed in the Cork No. 1 Brigade area as suspected 'spies' despite doubts that may have arisen as to whether they were really guilty, to judge by a statement made to the BMH by Sean Healy, Captain of 'A' Company,

1st Battalion. Describing how 'spies and informers' were dealt with generally, Healy said that Sean O'Hegarty, the Brigade O/C, 'took no chances'. 'If there was a doubt in his mind about such people, he gave his men the benefit of that doubt.' This would suggest, of course, that suspected 'spies' were *not* given the benefit of the doubt by O'Hegarty. (Martin Corry remarked to Ernie O'Malley: 'Sean Hegarty was a great man. He never asked awkward questions.'[14]) Healy added: 'No spies or informers were executed without the sanction and specific orders of our Brigade staff, and it was not necessary to obtain confirmation from our Headquarters in Dublin.'[15]

Ernie O'Malley referred to Sean O'Hegarty and the question of 'spies' in his classic account of the War of Independence, *On Another Man's Wound*: 'East Cork had shot many spies. Hegarty had the name of not being very particular about evidence, but that might be talk.' In the book, O'Malley went on to make the surprising claim that 'all information connected with an espionage case had first to be sent to Dublin and the sentence confirmed by our HQ before an execution took place.'[16] O'Malley's claim lacks credibility – it does not tally with other information that has come to light about the execution of persons accused of spying or informing, and is contradicted by Sean Healy's account of procedures in the Cork No. 1 Brigade area, which carried out more executions than any other IRA Brigade. In cases involving women, where IRA rules did provide for HQ to be consulted, there is no indication that this procedure was followed in the case of the three females known to have been executed in 1921, Mrs Lindsay, Mrs Noble and Kate Carroll, as will be shown in more detail.

It appears that when O'Malley himself, in 1921, was personally involved in sentencing to death a Church of Ireland clergyman at an IRA court martial held in County Kilkenny in the accused man's absence, the matter was not referred to GHQ in Dublin.[17] In another of his books, O'Malley makes the assertion: 'The IRA stood over their activities. If a civilian was shot as a spy, he had previously been court-martialled, and a label placed on his body stated that he had been executed by the IRA.'[18] This statement also lacks credibility, and fails to address the issue of the Disappeared, the scores of individuals who, like Mrs Noble, were taken away, put to death, and their bodies disposed of in secret locations.

Sean O'Hegarty's brother, Patrick Sarsfield O'Hegarty did not share his sibling's zeal for eliminating 'spies'. P.S. O'Hegarty had been active in Sinn Féin, had been a member of the Supreme Council of the Irish Republican Brotherhood and was a dedicated supporter of Irish independence and of the Irish language. However, he was horrified by some actions of republicans during the War of Independence. A tolerant and humane man, he also opposed any attempt to force Northern Ireland into a union with the Free State, enunciating a doctrine of northern consent that would have been anathema to militant republicans at the time, but which anticipated the Good Friday Agreement signed in 1998. O'Hegarty, who became a senior civil servant in the new Free State, showed considerable moral courage in 1924 by writing a book that challenged some core republican beliefs.[19] He expressed concern over what he saw as the assumption by the Irish Volunteers 'of the power of life and death in the country, without reference to the civil side of the movement...' He recalled how the first shootings started, developing into a 'guerrilla war' and considered that the 'public conscience as a whole was never easy about it...' He saw a 'moral collapse' occurring, with 'gun law' operating, and the gunman becoming 'supreme'.

O'Hegarty wrote: 'When it was open to any Volunteer Commandant to order the shooting of any civilian, and to cover himself with the laconic legend "Spy" on the dead man's breast, personal security vanished and no man was safe. And when it was possible for the same Commandant to steal goods and legalise it by calling it "commandeering", and to burn and destroy goods and legalise that by saying they were Belfast or English goods, social security vanished.' He deplored that 'we placed gunmen, mostly half-educated and totally inexperienced, as dictators with powers of life and death over large areas...'

P.S. O'Hegarty's brother Sean was, of course, in charge of the IRA's Cork No. 1 Brigade when Mrs Mary Lindsay was abducted and later shot. From the account of author Sean O'Callaghan, it appears that Sean O'Hegarty had instructed Frank Busteed to do all that was necessary to track down the informer responsible for the Dripsey ambush debacle, and that Busteed duly informed O'Hegarty of the execution of Mrs Lindsay. Mary Lindsay and Bridget Noble are the only two females who appear on the list of executed 'spies' in Cork city and county compiled by Bielenberg and Donnelly. The authors of the study state that Mrs Noble's disappearance 'caused embarrassment to the IRA HQ in Dublin, as there was an unwritten but fairly rigid IRA rule against killing women'. In fact, as will be shown, there was more than an 'unwritten rule' against executing females – General Order No. 13, introduced in late 1920, specified various punishments, but not the death penalty, for a woman found guilty of spying. As regards the Beara Battalion, this was certainly not a unit noted for the number of alleged spies or informers it put to death – it appears to have been responsible for just one execution. However, the fact that the person put to death was a woman, Mrs Noble, meant that the killing acquired special significance.

Chapter 11: 'Fortified with the Rites of the Church'

B ridget Noble's captors got a priest for her before she was put to death. The IRA report notes that 'she was fortified with the rites of the church before being executed'. While local members of the IRA had decided to take Mrs Noble's life, clearly they were willing to help her save her soul. One could speculate that getting a priest for Bridget made it a little easier for them to be involved in the unpleasant task of killing her. While they were going to end her life, perhaps they were reassured by the consideration that they were enhancing her chances of getting into Heaven, her chances of achieving eternal salvation.

Mrs Noble was a member of Eyeries parish, known formally in the church as Kilcatherine parish. It is likely that individuals involved in kidnapping her, keeping her captive and ultimately putting her to death were also members of the parish. There were two churches in the parish, at Eyeries and Ardgroom; the former was, of course, the church where she was married and the latter, the Church of the Resurrection, was where she would have attended Mass. Although the parish was located in County Cork it was part of the Diocese of Kerry, overseen by a Bishop based in Killarney. Other areas of West Cork at this period were part of the Diocese of Ross, under Bishop Denis Kelly, based in Skibbereen, who had been a strong supporter of Home Rule. In the Diocese of Cork, Bishop Daniel Cohalan was particularly outspoken in his condemnation of IRA violence. He had issued a decree of excommunication upon anyone 'who in this diocese of Cork, shall organise or take part in ambushes or kidnapping, or shall otherwise be guilty of murder or attempted murder'. This decree would not have applied to those who kidnapped and killed Bridget Noble as these actions took place in Kerry Diocese rather than Cork Diocese.

Anecdotal evidence suggests that the priest who attended Mrs Noble was the Parish Priest of Eyeries, Rev. Michael Daly. It is unclear exactly when or where the priest attended Mrs Noble. There were a number of possible locations where the priest might have visited the prisoner. According to one account, he was brought to Mrs Noble while she was being held in a cowshed in Eyeries, and on emerging, is said to have remarked to the men guarding her, that she was 'innocent'. On the other hand, a local man heard from his own family that the priest was brought to her at Collorus. If this is correct, one could speculate that the priest ministered to the prisoner at the arch under the bridge at Collorus.

Father Daly was a relative newcomer to the parish, having replaced the previous incumbent the previous year. There had been turmoil among the clergy in Eyeries parish in the years prior to Bridget Noble's death. The parish priest for a considerable period was the elderly Father James O'Callaghan. He was in charge of the parish when Bridget married Alexander, having been appointed parish priest in 1904. He may have had a role in the preliminary arrangements for the wedding, as it involved one of his parishioners marrying a man from a different religious background. The priest was said to have been distantly related to James Callaghan, the Labour Party leader who served as British Prime Minister in the 1970s. In his younger days as a curate, in 1887, Father O'Callaghan was reported to have organised 300 pikemen to block a road and thus successfully prevented a ruthless landlord evicting tenants in Ballyferriter, County Kerry. Like many other priests, he would go on to become a strong supporter of Home Rule.

In old age, it appears that Father O'Callaghan had become eccentric and difficult and was having disputes with his curates, Rev. Gerald Dennehy and the latter's successor, Rev. Robert O'Reilly, over issues such as financial matters and accommodation. In an unusual move, the Bishop of Kerry, Dr Charles O'Sullivan removed the parish priest from his post. Father O'Callaghan did not take kindly to being sacked. He sued the bishop in the civil courts of the new Free State, going all the way to the Supreme Court, but without success. The case raised interesting issues to do with canon law and civil law. He tried to bring an appeal to the English Privy Council but was rejected. He took his case to Rome and failed there also.[1]

In moving to dismiss the turbulent Father O'Callaghan, the Bishop chose as his replacement Rev. Michael Daly, whom he clearly considered to be a safe pair of hands. Previously a curate in Kenmare, Father Daly took up his post in March 1920, serving initially as Administrator for some months before becoming Parish Priest. Some weeks after moving to Eyeries, according to local anecdotal evidence, he dealt with the aftermath of the shooting of one of his parishioners,

William Lehane, and visited the family to comfort them. Then, the following year, there was another disturbing incident when another of his parishioners, Mrs Noble, was kidnapped, and he was reportedly called on to give her spiritual consolation prior to her execution.

Father Daly was a native of Rathmore, located in the Sliabh Luachra region of County Kerry, a region noted for its tradition of Irish music and culture. Ordained at Maynooth around the turn of the century, he seemed to exercise considerable authority in his bailiwick, as parish priests did in that era. But he also appears to have been a caring pastor in the tradition of the 'Saggart Aroon', concerned not only with the spiritual needs of his flock but with their temporal welfare as well. Father Daly may have had some sympathy with those of his parishioners who were in the IRA. As previously indicated, on 4 March 1921, which happens to be the day that the republican John Dwyer was arrested and Mrs Noble was taken prisoner by the IRA, Father Daly became aware of a major roundup by crown forces in Ballycrovane and Eyeries, and passed on this information when he met James McCarthy, an officer of Eyeries Company of the IRA, who would also be arrested.

It has also emerged that during the Troubles the attic of the church at Eyeries was used by the IRA as a hideout for men who were on the run or wounded, and also for storing arms. Bella O'Connell and her sister Louise told how, as members of Cumann na mBan, they looked after men hiding in the attic.[2] Hannah O'Neill, who guarded Mrs Noble as a prisoner, told later how an arms dump was kept in the attic, and how she helped men get away from the church hideout, evading the military who were billeted in the village.[3] Presuming that these activities took place after Father Daly took up duties in Eyeries, one cannot rule out the possibility that he was unaware of the IRA's use of church facilities for purposes other than devotional, although it seems more likely that he turned a blind eye or co-operated.

Aged in his late forties, Father Daly was assisted by a curate, the Rev. James O'Connor, a native of Killarney who had been ordained at Maynooth in 1911.[4] He had been appointed to Eyeries parish in February 1921, the month before the abduction of Mrs Noble. No doubt he would also learn of the fate of the woman from Reenavaude. The Rev. O'Connor had experience of ministering to people in times of crisis and conflict. He served as a priest in Scotland for a period and then, during the First World War, served as Chaplain to the Munster Fusiliers on the Western Front. In May 1920 he was based in Listowel when he was told of an IRA ambush outside the town. He motored to the scene and attended three RIC men who had been shot. Sergeant Francis J. McKenna was dead and Constables Colgan and Rabbit were wounded. It was reported that Sergeant McKenna had been involved in the arrest of Roger Casement.[5]

Catholic Priests and IRA Executions

Details have emerged of cases during the revolutionary period in which the IRA arranged for a priest to minister to a person accused of spying or informing and who was about to be executed. The historian Brian Heffernan comments in his book on Catholic priests and political violence during the revolutionary period: 'It appears to have been standard procedure to call a priest before the execution took place.' He also states that there is some evidence that priests called in to hear prisoners' confessions sometimes tried to persuade their captors to reprieve them. However, on the whole, he observes that priests simply heard the victim's confession and then left again. 'There is every appearance that they accepted the legitimacy of proceedings and simply played their part, thus at least tacitly giving moral sanction to the affair.'[6]

In County Roscommon in June 1921, a priest was summoned to minister to a prisoner about to be put to death by the IRA even though the condemned man had no religion. The man agreed to be baptised and then, having been tied up, he was thrown live into the River Suck to drown.[7] In at least one case that has come to light, a Protestant prisoner was allowed to see a clergyman before being put to death by the IRA. Former soldier William Gordon was given spiritual assistance by a Presbyterian Minister, Mr Irwin, before being executed at Dunboyne, County Meath in June 1920. Gordon was accused, not of spying, but of murdering a farmer Mark Clinton (who was also a Volunteer) in a land dispute.[8]

The IRA did not always comply with a condemned prisoner's request to see a minister of religion. A man called Denis Lehane, who was about to be executed at Knockraha, where the IRA's underground prison was located, asked for a priest. Mick Leahy, a senior officer in the IRA's Cork No. 1 Brigade, said it was too late for a priest, but then seemed to take on a rather macabre priestly role himself. According to Mick Leahy's later account, he said an Act of Contrition and had the prisoner repeat it after him. 'Then we all knelt down and said the Rosary before we shot him,' Leahy told Ernie O'Malley.[9] In July 1921, just two days before the Truce, the IRA in King's County [Offaly] captured and condemned as a 'spy' an English ex-soldier called Neil Steadman who was apparently living as a vagrant. It appears that Steadman was not a Catholic and one of his captors explained Catholic doctrine to him and 'how nice it would be if he could die in the state of grace'. They sent to Tullamore for a priest but nobody came out. One of the IRA men recalled later: 'So begob Seamus then got the water and we had him baptized. Then he was shot afterwards.'[10]

It must have been a very difficult situation for the priest who was called to attend to Mrs Noble under such harrowing conditions. Catholic churchmen had condemned the excesses and brutality of Black and Tans and Auxiliaries, and some priests had republican sympathies. Nevertheless, churchmen had also condemned the methods of the IRA, and there was particular concern over attacks on the RIC, many of whose members were devout Catholics. In 1920, the titular head of the Catholic Church in Ireland, Cardinal Logue, railed against the IRA, saying that 'no hearts unless hardened and steeled against pity, would tolerate their cruelty'[11].

On the Beara peninsula, a priest also condemned the IRA. Father John Godley (1854 – 1938), parish priest of Adrigole, was a native of Ballyheigue, County Kerry, and had been ordained at the Irish College, Paris in 1885 – the college had a particular link with Kerry diocese. One of his parishioners was Mícheál Óg O'Sullivan. The elderly priest was said to have been very interested in the Irish language and to have been a collector of books in Irish. This interest in Gaelic culture would doubtless have impressed Mícheál Óg. Nevertheless, the priest suffered retaliation for the anti-IRA remarks he made from the pulpit. It was reported in late 1920 that his motor car was stolen and set on fire.[12] This was an unusual act of vengeance against a Catholic cleric. Despite church condemnations of IRA violence, there was a strongly Catholic ethos among 'physical force' republicans in West Cork, to judge from Tom Barry's account in his memoir. Barry wrote: 'Every Volunteer in the West Cork Brigade was a Catholic and, with few exceptions, deeply religious.'[13]

Regardless of their views on political violence, some priests clearly considered that it was part of their duty to minister to a prisoner facing death at the hands of the IRA, even at the risk of appearing to be an accessory to murder. Had the priest who attended Bridget Noble refused to hear her Confession and give absolution, a Catholic woman would have gone unshriven to the grave, and from the point of view of Catholic doctrine, her eternal salvation might have been put at risk. However, on the other hand, Brian Heffernan notes that there are examples of unsympathetic priests who disapproved of the IRA and refused to attend prisoners, such as John Canon Doherty, the elderly parish priest of Ardara, County Donegal. In June 1921, he refused to accompany a Volunteer who had come to collect him to hear the confession of a 'spy'.[14]

As regards the provision of spiritual assistance to Bridget Noble, the IRA report gives no clue as to the identity of the priest involved, although, as mentioned anecdotal evidence indicates it was Father Daly. The rites of the church would at the very least have involved the Sacrament of Penance, with the priest hearing Mrs Noble's confession of her sins. Then, probably wearing the traditional purple stole, he would have recited the ancient Latin words of absolution: *Ego te absolvo a peccatis tuis, in nomine Patris, et Filii et Spiritus Sancti, Amen.* While the rites of the church must have been a consolation for a believing Catholic, on the other hand they may have involved considerable mental torture for Mrs Noble, a confirmation that the end of her life was at hand, that all hope was gone and that there would be no reprieve.

It seems that after Mrs Noble was kidnapped, word gradually spread in Ardgroom that she was missing. It is not recorded if Father Daly made any comment at Mass about the disappearance of one of his parishioners. Just days after the execution of Mrs Noble, Father Daly experienced the aftermath of a violent firefight while travelling by train in his native County Kerry. At Headford Junction, near Killarney, the IRA ambushed a train carrying British soldiers as well as civilians. The priest rendered spiritual aid to the wounded.[15] The British Army reported that seven soldiers were killed and two more died of injuries. The IRA lost two men, and three civilians died.

Subsequent events in County Kerry illustrate the severity of the IRA's drive against suspected or alleged spies at this period. Among those targeted were men on the margins of society. In March, IRA officer and future Fianna Fáil TD Tom McEllistrim executed a tramp, Sardy Nagle, who was being held by the IRA as a suspected spy. His body was found near Kenmare – he had been shot three times in the head and twice in the heart. In April, the IRA seized another vagrant, 80-year-old Tom O'Sullivan, known as Old Tom. He had apparently been seen in the company of the crown forces, and two British Army deserters who were being held by the IRA as suspected spies allegedly claimed that Old Tom was a frequent visitor to the Black and Tans. The Black and Tans were well-paid, and one wonders if the visits were for the purpose of soliciting alms. Old Tom was not given the benefit of the doubt and was sentenced to death by an IRA courtmartial. A local priest was summoned to give him 'spiritual consolation' the night before execution. Early the following morning the elderly man was taken to a location near Rathmore, County Kerry where he was shot three times and his body left on the road as 'bait' for the crown forces. The ploy worked, RIC men and Black and Tans were lured into an ambush, in which eight policemen died. Subsequently the two British Army men who apparently sealed Old Tom's fate were themselves executed by the IRA.[16] Tom O'Sullivan who, as a young boy, would have survived the ravages of the Famine was one of the oldest of those shot as suspected or alleged spies by the IRA during the revolutionary period. He was described in an RIC report as 'a harmless ballad singer'.[17]

Friction with Republicans

Father Daly ran foul of local republicans over difficulties that arose from the Civil War. He protested at the use of Eyeries church to hold two rosary and hymn singing events in October 1923 in support of IRA men, taken prisoner during the Civil War, who were on hunger strike. In a letter to a newspaper, Father Daly maintained that the events were held without church permission and were in breach of canon law.[18] He also removed posters advertising the devotions. He recalled that certain individuals, some months previously, had rung the church bell at Eyeries to warn of the approach of the [Free State] military, and in their zeal had pulled down the rope. The rope was replaced, only to be used again on the occasion of the unauthorised devotions. (It appears that Cumann na mBan activist Hannah O'Neill, mentioned above in the context of the Bridget Noble narrative, was involved in ringing the bell. She said that she rang the bell to warn 'that the military were arriving'. She said she had 'no other means of warning' and was 'excommunicated' from the Catholic church for ringing the bell.[19] However, when O'Neill went on to marry John Hanley in 1926, the ceremony was in the Catholic church at Eyeries, and the officiating priest was Father Daly himself. The couple went on to have nine children, and two sons became Catholic missionary priests.)

As one might expect, the priest who attended Mrs Noble never made any comment in the public domain about her execution or his own involvement in providing spiritual assistance in her final moments. From time immemorial, a Catholic priest has been under a strict obligation to maintain absolute secrecy about anything a person confesses to him as part of the Sacrament of Penance. Breaking the seal of the confessional is considered one of the most serious offences a priest can commit, and is punished by excommunication. The priest may have felt obliged, for various reasons, to keep confidential the identity of those involved in the kidnapping, detention and execution of Mrs Noble. But the need to observe the secrecy of the confessional may also have discouraged him from revealing details about her death. It was not unknown for a priest to acknowledge that he had ministered to a person who was then executed by the IRA. But a priest also needed to be careful that he did not let slip something he had learned in the course of hearing a confession. Mrs Noble's confessor may thus have been absorbed all the more deeply into the web of secrecy surrounding her death.

Chapter 12: Noble to de Valera: 'It Is Not Clean Work...'

On 19 August 1921, the Chief Secretary for Ireland, Sir Hamar Greenwood, gave a list in the House of Commons of soldiers, police and civilians who had been kidnapped or captured by the IRA and who were still missing.[1] Bridget Noble's name was included in the list, as was that of Mrs Lindsay. To the latter's name a note was added: 'Now believed to be dead.' A third woman was also mentioned, Bridget Burke [*recte* Bourke], of Kilrush, County Clare – it was indicated she had been kidnapped on 9 July 1921 but released the following 21 July. It appears that she was home on holiday from her job as a typist in the British Army's Victoria Barracks, Cork when she was taken away by a number of IRA men. (According to an IRA intelligence report, Ms Bourke was 'confidential typist' for the afore-mentioned Captain Kelly, the Cork-based British military intelligence officer who was a particular target for the IRA.[2]) Greenwood's list was reproduced in the *Irish Times*, although Mrs Noble's name was spelt incorrectly as 'Nogle'. The list was also printed in the *Freeman's Journal* and in a few provincial newspapers.[3] Apart from these reports, there seems to have been little publicity in Ireland given to the publication of the list, and Bridget Noble's abduction seemed to receive little public attention. As mentioned above, she did figure in a story published in a local newspaper in Northern Ireland, the *Londonderry Sentinel*, in August 1921. The story stated: 'Reliable information stated that she was murdered in the mountains south of Ardgroom and her body thrown into the bog.'

Meanwhile, Alexander Noble was still trying to find out what happened his wife. Weeks after receiving his initial reply from de Valera in July, just after the Truce, Alexander had still not heard anything about Bridget's fate. While the case of Mrs Lindsay had been 'fast-tracked', there seemed little movement on the Bridget Noble case. It appears that Alexander was living in lodgings at this stage at a terraced house in Grimsby, and that the landlady was an Irish widow in her fifties, Mrs Mary Ann Mulligan, née Brooke, originally from the Esker area of Lucan, County Dublin. Her husband, James Mulligan, originally from Carlingford, County Louth, had died in 1919. The couple had two children, and James had operated a shoe and boot making and repair business from the family home at 30 Railway Street. The couple took in boarders at their modest home to supplement their income – the 1911 Census shows that in addition to Mr and Mrs Mulligan and their son James junior, and daughter Catherine, an Irish dock labourer, John Casey, was in residence as a boarder. With the passing of Mr Mulligan, there was probably an even greater incentive for his widow to accommodate a lodger. On 8 September 1921, from his address at 30 Railway Street, Alexander wrote again to de Valera, pointing out that he was 'longing to hear' the result of any investigation that had been carried out. The letter to one of the leaders of Irish republicanism is respectful in tone, but Alexander cannot resist an embittered comment condemning the abduction of his 'lone defenceless wife'.[4]

The letter from Alexander Noble to 'Eamonn De Valera, Esq.' reads:

Dear Sir,

I wrote to you last July at the Grosvenor Hotel, London, wanting to ascertain the fate of my wife, Bridget Noble, who was kidnapped between the village of Ardgroom and Castletown-Bere on the 4th day of March last. You answered my letter on the 18th July, stating you had sent my letter to the proper authorities in Ireland for enquiry and investigation. Well, Sir, I am longing to hear the result of the same. It is not clean work to take away my lone defenceless wife. I am obliged to come over here and provide a living for her as it is not to be got in Ireland.

Hoping you will make an inquiry and do your best to restore my wife to me again that that you will have peace in Ireland soon and lasting.

Yours respectfully,
Alexander Noble.

This second letter from Noble to de Valera appears to have sparked some action. On 21 September 1921 the Chief of Staff [Richard Mulcahy] of Óglaigh na hÉireann [IRA] wrote from GHQ in Dublin to the O/C, 1st Southern Division. (This position was held by Liam Lynch, who would later lead the anti-Treaty forces during the Civil War, and who would himself be shot and fatally wounded during that conflict.) The letter stated:

126

Bridget Noble, kidnapped near Ardgroom, 4th March 1921.
Will you let me have a report as to the whereabouts of this woman.

By 13 October the Chief of Staff still had not received a report and he wrote again to the O/C, 1st Southern Division:

I await the report asked for in my communication of 21st September.

It would appear that the request for information was passed further down the chain of command to Gibbs Ross, Commander of Cork No. 5 Brigade. (The Cork No. 5 Brigade had come into operation just after the Truce of July 1921, and the Beara Battalion formed part of the new brigade, which was set up as a result of the sub-division of Cork No. 3 Brigade, into No. 3 and No. 5 Brigades.[5] The designation of the Beara Battalion was changed from 6th Battalion, Cork No. 3 Brigade to 5th Battalion, Cork No. 5 Brigade.) Gibbs Ross, in turn, secured a report from the Commandant of the Beara Battalion [Liam O'Dwyer]. The latter wrote the report referred to above – it was dated 21 October 1921. He began his report thus: 'I received your despatch re Mrs Noble asking for further particulars. I have been looking up these particulars for the past three or four days which accounts for delay. The following details are all that are available…' The memorandum was addressed to the Adjutant of the Brigade. (According to records in Irish Military Archives, the Adjutant of the Brigade on 1 July 1922 was Michael Crowley of Castletownbere.[6] This is the Michael Crowley who was a staff officer of the Beara Battalion at the time of Mrs Noble's disappearance.)

Ross forwarded the report from the Battalion Commandant to the Adjutant, 1st Southern Division on 22 October. He stated: 'As these reports were sent in to the old Cork No. 3 Brigade some time ago I had some difficulty in getting them again. I have nothing to add to the information contained in the reports from the Battalion concerned.' The internal IRA report on the case of Bridget Noble confirmed that she had been 'arrested', 'put on trial' and 'executed', but there seems to have been a delay in Alexander Noble being updated on the contents of this report. As will be explained, his quest for answers would continue.

Commandant and Staff of the Beara Battalion, and the Execution of Bridget Noble

According to Liam O'Dwyer's report on the fate of Bridget Noble, the 'officers responsible for the execution of Mrs Noble' were the staff of the 5th Battalion 'at that time'. Apart from the Commandant, the staff officers of the Beara Battalion were the Vice-Commandant, Mícheál Óg O'Sullivan; Michael Crowley, Adjutant and Daniel T. Sullivan, Quartermaster.[7] It is unclear if O'Dwyer meant that the staff officers were personally involved, or if they were responsible in a purely legalistic or collective sense. As indicated below, it would appear that at least two of the staff officers, Mícheál Óg O'Sullivan and Daniel T. Sullivan, were away from the Beara region, operating with the Brigade Column [led by Tom Barry], when Mrs Noble was put on trial on 13 March and when she was put to death two days later. The report adds: 'The then Batt. Comdt. was of course responsible for anything that happened in the Battn. Area.'

O'Dwyer does not state specifically that he himself was the Battalion Commandant at the time, or refer to himself in the first person. O'Dwyer's use of the phrase, 'the then Batt. Comdt.' might suggest that a person other than himself was Commandant at the period in question – his predecessor in the post was Peter Neill. It is noteworthy that O'Dwyer himself indicated in later life that he was Battalion Commandant from 'the end of March' or early April 1921, which would indicate he was *not* O/C when Mrs Noble was abducted and put to death, effectively excluding him from responsibility for these actions. It would mean that his predecessor was in charge of the battalion during the crucial period when Bridget was 'bobbed' and then disappeared. (The 'end of March' date is given in O'Dwyer's 1956 statement to the BMH, while the early April date appears in his 1977 memoir.[8]) In his report on the execution of Mrs Noble, as indicated above, he explained that he had been 'looking up the particulars for the past three or four days' which might suggest that he lacked first-hand knowledge of the case, and had to carry out research to establish what actually happened. When he states that the details in the report 'are all that are available' this could also suggest a lack of personal knowledge of what occurred, and might indicate that there were facts in the case that he was unable to ascertain or verify. Questions arise – was he trying to distance himself from the killing of Bridget Noble? And who exactly was in command of the Battalion at the time of the action taken against Mrs Noble?

The latter issue was cleared up by O'Dwyer himself, when statements that he made in 1935 came to light more than eight decades later, when his Military Service Pension file was finally made available online in late 2019. O'Dwyer states that he became O/C of the battalion on 8 February 1921. This would tally with information in a document in Ted O'Sullivan's papers, which also appears in the Irish Military Archives, that O'Dwyer was Battalion Commandant on 8 February.[9] This means that 25-year-old O'Dwyer was in charge on the day the punishment attack on Mrs Noble was said to have been carried out (23 February), and when she was abducted on 4 March and executed later that month. As Commandant, O'Dwyer bore responsibility for these actions as, to quote himself, the Commandant was 'responsible for anything that happened' in the Battalion area. In drawing up the report on the Noble execution, O'Dwyer does not mention his own family connection to the case. He omits the information that John Dwyer, the man he said was jailed for 'bobbing' Mrs Noble, was his own brother. The blaming of Mrs Noble for John's jailing seems to have been the major factor in the decision to abduct and execute her.

In his pension application, O'Dwyer seems quite definite about 8 February as the date he became Battalion Commandant. He gives the date when filling in a form outlining his military service, and also in a typed 'Supplementary Statement of Service'. He also mentions the date verbally in a sworn interview with an Advisory Committee, the transcript of which is included in the pension file. (O'Dwyer's afore-mentioned statements made in 1956 and 1977, that he became Commandant in late March or early April 1921, may have been based on faulty memory, as they were made decades after the events in question.) In his pension file, O'Dwyer indicates that as Commandant of the Battalion, his superior officers at Brigade level were Charlie Hurley and later Liam Deasy. O'Dwyer had command experience, and may have had the role of assistant Commandant prior to taking over as Battalion O/C. The previous Battalion Commandant, Peter Neill had lung cancer and as a result, left 'most of the Battalion work' to Liam O'Dwyer, according to O'Dwyer's own account in his memoir. It was thus left to O'Dwyer, for instance, to organise a section of men to join up with the Brigade Column in November 1920.[10] Neill, from Knockane, Eyeries, would die while quite a young man.

Following his internal IRA report on the execution of Bridget Noble, O'Dwyer never elaborated on any role he might have played in the drama. It would appear that just a couple of weeks after becoming Commandant, the punishment attack was carried out on Mrs Noble. To quote O'Dwyer's own report, she was 'bobbed by order of Battalion', which presumably meant that O'Dwyer himself was involved in ordering the punishment to be inflicted.

O'Dwyer seems to have played a personal role in arranging for the guarding of Mrs Noble after she was taken prisoner. As previously indicated, former Cumann na mBan activist Hannah Hanley described how she was 'called on by the Commandant' to attend to the prisoner. On the basis of afore-mentioned information that came to light in 2019, the Commandant she was referring to was obviously O'Dwyer.

Although, as O'Dwyer said himself, the Battalion Commandant 'was responsible for anything that happened in the Battalion area' it is not known if he was involved in the actual trial of Mrs Noble or in passing sentence, or if he recused himself from the proceedings because of his own personal interest in the case – as mentioned, a major accusation against Bridget was, of course, that her actions had led to his own brother John being jailed for six months. In his Military Service Pension file, he records his activities for March 1921, the month that Mrs Noble was disappeared, thus: 'Set about perfecting the organisation of the Batt. in capacity of O/C. No fighting was possible in the area at this time as almost all the Batt. Arms were in the Brig. Column.' While 'no fighting was possible' during the month, O'Dwyer's organisation obviously had enough resources and capabilities to deal with the detention, execution and disposal of remains of the woman from Reenavaude. As regards the other men who were Beara Battalion staff officers at the time of the action taken against Mrs Noble, details of their respective backgrounds are outlined below.

Mícheál Óg O'Sullivan

Mícheál Óg O'Sullivan, Vice-Commandant of the Beara Battalion, was one of the more remarkable of the IRA leaders to emerge on the Beara peninsula. His home area of Inchintaglin, Adrigole was close to a spectacular route through the hills, the serpentine road now known as the Healy Pass, that winds up high through the wild, dramatic scenery of the Caha Mountains and descends into Lauragh on the northern side of the peninsula. He was one of nine children of Eugene Sullivan, a farmer and cattle dealer, and his wife Nora. The fact that Eugene was able to send Mícheál Óg to County Dublin to attend Pádraic Pearse's innovative St Enda's College might suggest he had attained a certain level of affluence. It is also possible that Mícheál Óg's older brother Pronnséas O'Sullivan, through his income as a national teacher in Dublin, helped to finance the boy's studies at St Enda's, where there was a particular emphasis on Irish language and culture. Eugene O'Sullivan spoke only English and could not read, according to the 1911 Census returns, although his wife Nora had both Irish and English and could read and write.

While at St Enda's, Mícheál Óg seems to have taken a full part in the Gaelic cultural life of the school, located in an 18th century mansion set in almost 50 acres of idyllic parkland in Rathfarnham. In May 1915 a boy called Michael O'Sullivan (almost certainly a reference to Mícheál Óg) played the lead role of Dunlaing Óg in a play by Pearse himself, *The Master*, staged at the Irish Theatre on Hardwicke Street, Dublin. Pearse, who would face execution over his leadership role in the 1916 Easter Rising, gave a talk during the interval on the Irish Style of Dramatic Speaking. One of the actors in the play was his brother Willie Pearse, who would also face the firing squad after the rebellion.

In July 2019 a school report for a boy called Mícheál Ó Súilleabháin, and signed by Pádraic Pearse as headmaster of St Enda's, came to light. The report, which once again almost certainly relates to Mícheál Óg, is dated 1 July 1915, and was highlighted in an RTE TV news report after being found in County Kerry.[11] Commenting on the youth's performance during the previous year, Pearse writes: *Do bhí Mícheál lag go leor i dtosach na bliana, ach tá mianach maith ann, agus tháinig sé chun cinn go maith. Níor mhór do cúpla bliain eile ar scoil, nó bliain ar a laghad.* ['Michael was quite weak at the start of the year, but he has ability, and he improved well. It would benefit him to have a couple more years at the school, or one year at least.'] Pearse describes the boy's ability with the Irish language as: *Go han-mhaith* ['Very good'].

No record has emerged to indicate that Mícheál Óg took part in the Rising – he was aged 17 years at the time. But his brother Pronnséas seems to have been caught up in the drama of Easter Week in Dublin city centre. Pronnséas was deeply involved in the Gaelic cultural revival. He was a very active member of the Irish language organisation Conradh na Gaeilge and had become a notable exponent of Irish step dancing – he was something of a 'Michael Flatley' figure of his day. On Easter Monday, 26 April, the 26-year-old teacher from Adrigole was due to act as an adjudicator in the 'Irish dancing solo reel' competition at the Father Mathew Feis on Church Street, when attendees were shocked by the sound of gunfire – the rebellion had broken out. The dancing abruptly ended and frightened children hid under the stage until they could be brought home. There was a shocking development when a distraught young woman, Mrs Katie Foster, came into the hall carrying the body of her two-year-old son Sean who had been shot. As Joe Duffy notes in his book on the young people who lost their lives in Dublin during that Easter Week, Sean was the first of 40 children aged 16 years and under who died as a result of the Rising.[12]

Pronnséas O'Sullivan, who taught at the Central Model School on Marlborough Street, had friends and contacts in the independence movement. On 18 May 1916, from his south Dublin city home address, 28 New Bride Street, near St Patrick's Cathedral, he wrote a letter of sympathy to Nancy O'Rahilly, widow of one of the prominent rebels killed in the Rising, Michael O'Rahilly, known as The O'Rahilly.[13] He indicated that he had contacts in America who could raise funds to assist the dependants of men 'who lately died in the fight'. Pronnséas's brother Mícheál Óg worked as a clerk in Dublin after leaving St Enda's, and resided with Pronnséas at the latter's lodgings on New Bride Street. Mícheál Óg became active in the Irish Volunteers, and in October 1917 he was one of a number of young men arrested by the Dublin Metropolitan Police for illegal drilling in a field at Whitehall, Rathfarnham. They were jailed for two months but went on hunger strike and, it appears, were released after just one or two weeks.

There was a dramatic development when, on 29 April 1918, detectives raided the lodging house at New Bride Street where the O'Sullivan brothers resided, and Mícheál Óg was arrested. The following month he was brought before a British Army courtmartial in Ship Street Barracks at Dublin Castle, charged with having bought a revolver from a British soldier called Lewis Hynd, aged 20 years, a Private in the Cameron Highlanders, who was constantly in trouble with the army authorities. Mícheál Óg had a highly effective barrister, George Gavan Duffy, later one of the signatories of the Anglo-Irish Treaty. A newspaper reported that a number of ladies, 'including Miss Alice Milligan', were present in court.[14] Milligan, a poet, writer and feminist, was a County Tyrone Protestant who had broken with her family's unionist ethos and become an ardent nationalist. Despite evidence of ammunition being discovered in his room, the British officers who formed the court gave Mícheál Óg the benefit of the doubt, and he was found 'not guity'.

Pronnséas pursued further studies in Modern Irish at University College Dublin and in 1920 he moved to Germany, where he gained a Ph.D at Freiburg University, and became a lecturer in Irish and English. Pronnséas and another Irishman, Daniel Binchy, are thought to have been the first Irishmen to see Adolf Hitler speaking in public – that was when the future German dictator gave a fiery, rabble-rousing speech at a Munich beer hall in November 1921, which led to a melee.[15] Binchy, uncle of the writer Maeve Binchy, would go on to become a distinguished Irish diplomat and a firm opponent of Nazism while O'Sullivan, like some other Irish republicans and nationalists, would go on to develop pro-Nazi sympathies. Pronnséas, noted for his Irish dancing skills, would, during the 1930s, dance to Hitler's tune, so to speak. Public comments he made during that era in support of the Hitler regime were, of course, made before details of the Holocaust emerged. His pro-German sentiments pre-dated the Nazis, and went back to the start of the First World War in 1914, when he wrote a poem in Irish for the magazine *An Claidheamh Soluis*, expressing the hope that the Germans would vanquish the 'crooked Saxons'.

Meanwhile, Mícheál Óg returned home to the Beara peninsula. He joined the Adrigole Company of the Volunteers and became increasingly active in republican activities. There were various factors that may have facilitated his rise through the ranks of the Beara Volunteers – his commitment to the cause; his training with the Volunteers in Dublin; his sojourn, albeit brief, in prison for illegal drilling; his trial before a British courtmartial over allegedly buying a gun from a soldier, and his links to the revered Pádraic Pearse. He also, as mentioned, became active in local politics.

Mícheál Óg went on to operate with Tom Barry's Flying Column and took part in some notable engagements. As mentioned, because of his involvement in the Flying Column, it is unlikely that he was in the Beara region when Mrs Noble was put on trial on 13 March 1921, or when she was put to death two days later. He was probably part of the contingent from the Beara Battalion that assembled in the vicinity of Coppeen, Enniskeane on 12 March for service in the Flying Column.[16] He took part in the column's engagement at Crossbarry some days later, on 19 March, and in the column's attack on Rosscarbery RIC barracks on 31 March.[17] One wonders if the execution of Pearse, his former teacher, was one of the factors that reinforced his decision to take the road of republican militancy, a road that would ultimately take him to the position of Vice Commandant of the Beara Battalion during a period when Bridget Noble was subjected to a punishment attack and later put to death.

Michael Crowley

Michael Crowley, Adjutant of the Beara Battalion, was another very active staff officer. He took part in a number of IRA operations, including an armed raid on Castletownbere coastguard station in 1920. While held at Wormwood Scrubs Prison in London he went on hunger strike, like Liam O'Dwyer and other prisoners. His release from detention in England in May 1920 must have greatly displeased Brigadier General J.E.S. Brind, a member of the General Staff at British Army GHQ in Ireland. In a memo marked 'secret', dated 19 May 1920, and signed 'J. B.', the officer lists the names of eight men who had been deported, and inquires if they have been released. Michael Crowley, Castletownbere, is one of the men listed. In his memo to the 'Under-Secretary', Brind opposes any move to release the men, stating: 'These are dangerous men and their release would involve risk to the Military Intelligence Officers and RIC.' He points out that in a previous letter, dated 28 March 1920, 'it was recommended that for the reasons given above, that none of these men should be released.' Crowley had already left Wormwood Scrubs by the time Brind wrote his memo. It is unclear why Crowley was singled out by Brind as being 'dangerous', in comparison with other members of the Beara Battalion.

Like Mícheál Óg O'Sullivan, Crowley served on the local Rural District Council and the Board of Guardians. Records show that on Wednesday, 9 March 1921, just a few days after the abduction of Bridget Noble, Michael Crowley [M. Ó Cruadhlaoich] chaired a meeting of the Board of Guardians in Castletownbere. (Mrs Noble was probably a prisoner in the isolated farmhouse at Feith Bhui at this stage.) The minutes show that business proceeded as usual, despite the drama being played out at the secret prison housing a female captive some miles away. Among the mundane items discussed by the Guardians was a request from the master of the workhouse for a 'half dozen sweeping brushes' and 'one ton of coal'. The board agreed to instruct the storekeeper to provide these items. It was also recorded that on 5 March, following admissions and departures, the workhouse was accommodating 20 aged or infirm adults, consisting of ten males and ten females. In addition, there was one girl aged over nine years; one child [gender unspecified] under nine years, and three infants – a total of 25.

Shortly after this date, as will be shown, Bridget Noble's father, John Neill, may himself have become an inmate at the workhouse. Mícheál Óg O'Sullivan seems to have been absent from the 9 March meeting of the Board of Guardians.[18] Michael Crowley was on the anti-Treaty side in the Civil War. He was described as a 'fine footballer' who played for Castletownbere in his youth, and continued to be active in the Gaelic Athletic Association (GAA). He became manager of the Labour Exchange when it was set up in Castletownbere in 1933. He died in December 1948 at age 55 years, having been ill for six months. The cause of death was recorded as 'myocardial degeneration, hepatitis'. He was unmarried.[19]

Daniel T. Sullivan

Daniel T. Sullivan, from Gorth, Urhan in the Eyeries area, the long-serving Quartermaster of the Beara Battalion, was from the Seer branch of the Sullivan clan. He took part in the attack on Allihies RIC barracks and in the raid on Castletownbere coastguard station. He was also probably one of the contingent from the Beara Battalion that joined up with Tom Barry's Flying Column at Coppeen on 12 March 1921, prior to the Crossbarry engagement, in which he took part, as mentioned.[20] Thus, as in the case of Mícheál Óg O'Sullivan, it seems unlikely he was in the Beara region when Bridget Noble was put on trial on 13 March and killed two days later. At one stage during the War of Independence, Sullivan was injured, sustaining a bullet wound to a finger. Margaret O'Neill (1896 – 1985), a member of Cumann na mBan in Castletownbere, told later how she provided first aid, and then found a bed for him in a house near her own home. She arranged for Dr [Patrick V.] Murphy to visit Sullivan nightly and she herself looked after him, cooking for him for a few weeks, and also supplying him with clothes.[21] Like other staff officers of the Beara Battalion, Dan Sullivan was on the anti-Treaty side in the Civil War. He emigrated to America after that conflict.

The Crossbarry Engagement

At least two members of the Beara Battalion were wounded in the Crossbarry engagement in March 1921, when the Flying Column fought an enemy force that sought to track down the column. John Sheehan from Ardgroom Company was one of the wounded. (In Liam Deasy's book *Towards Ireland Free*, which includes a list of those who took part in the battle, it is stated that the wounded man was John Sheehan, from Barrakilla, Ardgroom. A man of this name, from this address, was 1st Lieutenant in Ardgroom Company – he later emigrated to America. However, an official's handwritten note in the Military Service Pension file of Mrs Julia Sheehan, released in 2018, indicates that the man who was wounded at Crossbarry was her husband John Sheehan, who was Captain of Ardgroom Company.[22] As indicated above, the Captain was linked to the story of Bridget Noble.) The other Beara man wounded at Crossbarry was Richard Spencer from Rossmacowen. Another member of the Beara contingent that joined up with the Barry column, Christopher O'Connell from Eyeries, was a section leader during the Crossbarry engagement. Yet another participant was Liam O'Dwyer's brother, Tim O'Dwyer. Apart from Beara Battalion staff officers Mícheál Óg O'Sullivan and Quartermaster Dan T. Sullivan, among the others from the battalion who fought at Crossbarry were Sean O'Driscoll, Jackie McCarthy, Matt Sullivan, Murt McCarthy, Jerry McAuliffe, Tim O'Shea and John O'Sullivan. As a commander in the field, Flying Column leader Tom Barry showed much tactical skill and resolve by ambushing one of the military convoys and then leading his column to safety from an encircling military force, inflicting more casualties on the enemy (ten reported killed) than he suffered himself (three killed), and destroying three military lorries.

Meanwhile, back on the Beara peninsula, in early May 1921, Mícheál Óg O'Sullivan was one of seven men arrested in a big roundup by crown forces in the areas of Collorus, Ardgroom and Eyeries.[23] The drama began when a British gunboat was spotted in the Kenmare River one evening and a horn was sounded to warn the Volunteers. An IRA party under Liam O'Dwyer quickly assembled and lay in ambush overnight to attack any of the crown forces who landed – it was expected they might come ashore at Collorus but they failed to show. The gunboat, it appears, lay hidden overnight behind an island, and then dropped off a party of troops who caught some of the Volunteers unawares, as they were taking refreshments in local houses.[24] Perhaps for lack of evidence, some of the prisoners were released within days while Mícheál Óg O'Sullivan was detained for longer, but ultimately he was also freed within a short period.

Destruction of Homes

One of the operations in which Mícheál Óg subsequently participated took place on 14 May, shortly after being released by the British. He led an IRA party in an attack on British soldiers near the military camp at Furious Pier.[25] An order had been received to 'shoot up' soldiers and police following the execution of IRA members in Cork. According to an account by former IRA member Jerry O'Neill, four unarmed soldiers were captured, placed against a fence at Thornhill Cross, and shot.[26] Three died and one survived. O'Neill claimed that the military had been warned to stop sending out unarmed groups of soldiers 'to spy'. According to a Dublin Castle statement, three girls had 'encouraged' the soldiers to follow them along the road.[27] The soldiers who died were John Hunter, aged 20 years; Robert McMillen, aged 18 years and Donald Chalmers, aged 21 years. As a reprisal for this attack, later in May crown forces burned the homes of Liam O'Dwyer and Jeremiah O'Connor (a name also rendered as Connor) in the Ardgroom district. (Jerh O'Connor was one of the Ardgroom Company members said to have questioned Nora Sullivan about Bridget Noble's action in giving the RIC the names of the men who had allegedly 'bobbed' her.) According to an unconfirmed story told locally, O'Dwyer observed the burning of his home from a nearby hillside, and the experience engendered much bitterness in him, and boosted his determination to fight the 'ancient enemy'.

Referring to the destruction of houses by the crown forces, Jerry O'Neill wrote: 'The IRA decided to introduce its own form of reprisal for this conduct, and for every IRA house destroyed the houses of two loyalists (of whom there were a good number at that time) mostly big Protestant farmers in the Bandon area, were burned to the ground.'[28]

136

In one significant operation, on 23 June 1921, the IRA burned five 'Unionist' houses in Inishannon.[29] (An elderly man living in England told the author how his Church of Ireland grandmother, who resided in a fine house in West Cork at this period, and who had a son serving abroad with the British Army, lived in constant fear that she would also be targeted as a 'loyalist' and her home destroyed.) Reflecting on the number of 'Loyalist' houses that were burned as part of what he described as 'IRA counter-terror', Tom Barry reflected in his memoir: 'Our only fear was that, as time went on, there would be no more Loyalists' homes to destroy.'[30]

Destroying a family home was a particularly severe punishment inflicted by both sides in the conflict. When crown forces destroyed the home of an IRA member, it obviously impacted not only on the person who was being targeted but on family members as well. Liam O'Dwyer's sister Annie, who had been a member of Cumann na mBan before becoming a nun, had left religious life and returned to look after the younger members of the family after the death of both parents. With the older members of the family in the IRA, the children had been minded by neighbours. Annie O'Dwyer had been a member of the Sisters of Charity of St Vincent de Paul, and was based at the order's convent at Mill Hill, London. After the burning of the family home, she created an improvised shelter, building a lean-to against one of the walls of a ruined outhouse and covered it with branches and rushes.[31] A new house was later built, close to the dwelling that was destroyed.

In addition to burning the O'Dwyer and O'Connor houses, crown forces destroyed the homes of Mícheál Óg O'Sullivan (at Inchintaglin) and Tim Spillane in the Rossmacowen area.[32] The O'Sullivan family's thatched house was blown up. (The internal British Army report on the reprisals refers to the latter dwelling as the house of 'Frank Sullivan'. Eugene Sullivan, father of Mícheál Óg was also known as 'Frank', as indeed was Eugene's other son, Pronnséas.) The report also mentions a fifth home destroyed – that of Tim Murphy, Rossmacowen.[33] The report states that the destruction of the houses was carried out on 24 May 'as a reprisal for the murders of three unarmed soldiers...' Other information suggests that the destruction was carried out over two or three days.)

The senior IRA officer Ted O'Sullivan recalled that he had been at the O'Sullivan home [at Inchintaglin] and then went over to Kilmakilloge Harbour where, it was hoped, arms from the Continent were to be landed. When he returned, there was 'no trace' of the O'Sullivan house. In an interview with Ernie O'Malley, he wondered what kind of explosives the British used.[34] Nora Mary Crowley who, as previously indicated, came from Glenbeg, was a very active member of Cumann na mBan. In later years (under her married name Healy) she told how, after the destruction of the homes of Liam O'Dwyer and others, she had to 'collect clothes for them and also provide homes for them'. She said she also assisted others who had been threatened that their homes would be burned, by having their furniture moved to neighbours' homes.[35]

After the destruction of the houses, Bella O'Connell, head of Cumann na mBan in Beara, wrote to her brother Henry in America. Like many other Beara natives, he had emigrated to Butte, Montana – he also served in the US Army in the Great War. The letter was subsequently published in a Butte newspaper, *The Anaconda Standard*, which explained that another brother, Christy O'Connell, 'a youth of 21 or 22 years', is now 'a soldier of the Irish republic and on the run'.[36] Bella O'Connell stated in her letter: 'The state of the country is beyond description. The times are desperate, with executions, shootings and burnings. It is indeed a state of war, but we are not disheartened. The home of the Dwyers of Cailroe and the home of Jerry Connors [Jerh O'Connor], of Ardgroom, formerly a miner in Butte, were burned to the ground with their entire contents. We are expecting the same kind of treatment ourselves. Let it come, if it does.' She went on: 'Christy got into the clutches of the Black and Tans a short time ago and made a dash for freedom, under fire, and got away.'

Amid increasing tension, there was a tragic and very shocking incident in the remote Clogherane area of Lauragh in the County Kerry part of Beara on 19 June 1921 when a 13-year-old boy, Jerry Healy, was shot dead by crown forces. The boy was a first cousin of Patsy Dan Crowley – his mother, the former Margaret Crowley came from Glenbeg, and was a sister of Patsy's father Dan Crowley. The boy and his father were said to have been out before dawn, tending cattle, when soldiers from the King's Own Scottish Borderers (KOSB) came into the area. It appears the troops were moving on foot along a mountain track then called 'Bealach Scairt' which now forms the route of the steep, winding road known as the Healy Pass. It was reported that scouts sounded horns to give a warning to members of the IRA's Lauragh and Ardea Companies. According to Lauragh-born historian Gerard Lyne, the boy took fright and 'ran for his house'. In the half-light, the soldiers did not fire on him directly but apparently 'laid it on the fence' immediately before him. 'He was badly wounded but apparently survived for four or five hours. They carried him, apparently in a military greatcoat, into his parents' house. Presumably they would have been accompanied by medical orderlies, who no doubt did their best to save him, but would have had to move on with the regiment.'[37]

Apparently crown forces later claimed they thought the boy was somebody on the run. According to a subsequent report by the Adjutant of the IRA's Kerry No. 2 Brigade, the boy's father also had 'a very narrow escape', adding: 'They also shot some cows.'[38] According to the death certificate, there was no inquest, and the cause of death was recorded as 'gun shot wounds inflicted by Crown Forces KOSB'. As indicated above, three soldiers from the KOSB based at Furious Pier were shot dead by Mícheál Óg O'Sullivan and his men the previous month, the incident that led to the reprisal destruction of homes, including that of Mícheál Óg.

Search for Pronnséas O'Sullivan

Shortly after the destruction of Mícheál Óg O'Sullivan's family home at Inchintaglin, the British military and Auxiliaries in Dublin were targeting Mícheál Óg's brother Pronnséas. On 14 June 1921 Captain L. Hodson, acting on behalf of the Brigade Major, 24th Provisional Brigade, Kilmainham, Dublin issued a written order to the O/C, 'C' Company, Auxiliary Division, RIC, to search two specified addresses between the hours of 3 am and 6 am and, if he was found, to arrest Frank Sullivan [Pronnséas O'Sullivan], described as a 'Lieutenant in the IRA'.[39] It is unclear why the British concluded that dancing enthusiast Pronnséas was an IRA officer, or why they deemed it necessary to detain him at this particular time. One raid was carried out at 28 New Bride Street, where Pronnséas had resided with Mícheál Óg. The other address raided was 40 Herbert Park in the affluent Ballsbridge district. This was the impressive residence of Mrs Nancy O'Rahilly and her family – as mentioned, she was the widow of The O'Rahilly who had been killed in the 1916 Rising. (There was a controversy over the demolition, in late September 2020, of the spacious detached house with historic links.) This raid was led by Lieutenant Archibald N. Glover MC, Intelligence Officer of 'C' Company of the Auxiliaries, who had the rank of 3rd D.I. There was no trace of Pronnséas at either address. At some stage in 1920 Pronnséas moved to Germany, the start of a remarkable new phase in his life.

Chapter 13: Relatives of Disappeared Seek Help from IRA Liaison Officers

Although Liam O'Dwyer had drawn up a report in late 1921 on the execution of Bridget Noble and passed it up the line to GHQ in Dublin, there was still a delay in her husband getting a reply to his queries about her fate. Alexander Noble would not get clear confirmation of Bridget's fate until March 1922, more than a year after she was abducted. He was not the only person seeking information about a loved one who had been taken away by armed men during the War of Independence, put to death, and then the body secretly buried or otherwise disposed of. As letters in the Military Archives show, relatives of the Disappeared went through torment as they struggled to find out what happened the family member who had gone missing. They had a very human need to know the fate of their loved ones. Some also sought to retrieve the remains for a Christian burial.

Like other relatives of the Disappeared, Alexander's hopes of a breakthrough in the wall of silence seem to have been raised by developments following the Truce. A system was set up whereby the IRA would liaise with the British authorities on observance of the Truce. The IRA appointed a Chief Liaison Officer who oversaw the work of local Liaison Officers around the country. For their part, senior figures in the British military and in the British civil administration in Dublin Castle took on the role of liaising with the IRA. The appointment of IRA Liaison Officers meant that members of the IRA were now emerging from the shadows and setting up public offices from which to conduct their business. The names and office addresses of these officers were published in the newspapers. IRA representatives were now officially contactable and some relatives of the Disappeared saw an opportunity to get information from the IRA about those who were missing.

From late 1921 Commandant Emmet Dalton was the IRA's Chief Liaison Officer, based at the exclusive Gresham Hotel in Dublin, having succeeded Eamonn Duggan in the post. Born in the Massachusetts town of Fall River (where, incidentally, many Beara migrants settled) he was raised in the Dublin suburb of Drumcondra. Dalton had been awarded the Military Cross for bravery while serving as a junior officer with the Royal Dublin Fusiliers during the Battle of the Somme but after being demobilised would change sides, and serve as Director of Training in the IRA General Headquarters staff during the War of Independence. He was particularly close to the Irish leader Michael Collins and he had accompanied Collins to the Anglo-Irish Treaty talks in London as an adviser on defence matters and observance of the Truce.

Alexander Noble was one of the relatives of the Disappeared who sought information through the new liaison system. He wrote initially to a Liaison Officer covering County Cork to inquire about Bridget but got no reply.[1] The officer in question was probably Tom Barry, commander of the formidable IRA flying column in West Cork during the War of Independence, and who, at the time of the Truce in July 1921, was appointed Liaison Officer for martial law territory, including West Cork.[2] The work would have required certain administrative and diplomatic skills, whereas Barry's forte was as a soldier and fighting man. He said later he did not want the job. After taking on the post, the combative Barry was soon at loggerheads with the senior British military officers with whom he was required to liaise, and who were part of the British Army's 6th Divisional Area. A British intelligence report referred to him sarcastically: 'Suffers from "swollen head"'.[3] (Not a man for false modesty, Barry would remain proud of the number of casualties he inflicted on members of the crown forces during the War of Independence. In 1940, in the course of an appeal for a better Military Service Pension, he declared that he 'personally led, organised and commanded IRA Columns during the fight with the British, which killed more of the English soldiers, Auxiliaries, Black and Tans and RIC that any of those led by any other six senior officers combined in all Ireland'.[4])

Jasper Travers Wolfe

Alexander Noble, in his ongoing quest for information about Bridget, clearly felt the need for expert assistance and in late 1921 he enlisted the aid of a prominent County Cork legal firm Travers Wolfe, headed by a well-known solicitor, Jasper Travers Wolfe, who, as will be recalled, had previously represented Bridget in a case in the courts. Wolfe was a liberal Protestant, a Methodist who was not a unionist but a prominent campaigner for Home Rule. An advocate of inter-denominational harmony, in December 1912 he had made an eloquent speech in London advocating Home Rule, at a meeting organised by the Irish Protestant Home Rule Committee. The Skibbereen-based solicitor described how he himself had been shown tolerance as a Nonconformist in southern Ireland. Jasper and his brother Willie joined the All-for-Ireland League, a Home Rule party headed by the charismatic William O'Brien who advocated a reinvigorated transfer of land from landlords to tenants, and who sought reconciliation with all Protestants.

While Jasper Wolfe believed in reform of the political and land-owning system, he also believed that reforms should be carried out peacefully, in compliance with the common law. He believed in parliamentary democracy and was opposed to violent insurgency. Because of his work as a crown prosecutor, he was marked down for assassination by the IRA, and had some close shaves. He would have been particularly unpopular among members of the Beara Battalion, having acted as prosecutor when Charlie Hurley of the Castletownbere Company was jailed by a military court in Cork in December 1918. In another move that would not have endeared him to republicans, he represented the Crown at the inquest into the murder in March 1920 of the Lord Mayor of Cork, Tomás Mac Curtain, who was also Commandant of the 1st Cork Brigade of the IRA – the jury found that the murder was carried out by the RIC, 'officially directed by the British Government...' (The RIC reported that on the night of April 11-12 1920, Wolfe's office was broken into, 'and a number of books, legal documents, etc, torn or destroyed for which a claim for £2,000 has been lodged'. The report pointed out that the solicitor represented the crown 'in the inquest of the late Lord Mayor of Cork'.[5])

Wolfe was a Freemason, having joined in December 1905, and was Master of the Skibbereen Lodge in 1908 and again in 1924.[6] This would also have been viewed in a negative light by some republicans. Members of the IRA in the Cork region were particularly suspicious of the Freemasons. Florence O'Donoghue, intelligence officer with the IRA's Cork No. 1 Brigade, compiled lists of Freemasons in the Brigade area as part of his intelligence work.[7] (In 1935 there was a remarkable example of republican hostility towards Freemasons when Tom Barry and a group of IRA gunmen disrupted a dinner at the Masonic Hall in Tuckey Street, Cork, holding up attendees at gunpoint, and smashing plates and furniture.[8])

Wolfe was a most astute West Corkman, with well-honed instincts for survival who enjoyed amazing good fortune in avoiding the assassin's bullet. In October 1921, Wolfe had been abducted by the

IRA, despite the Truce, but his execution was apparently averted by the intervention of a local Catholic priest, Rev. Florence McCarthy. According to a biography written by his grandson, Jasper Ungoed-Thomas, Wolfe had been targeted on this occasion after winning sizeable damages from Judge John W. Hynes KC at Bandon Quarter Sessions for victims of republican violence.[9] Damages awarded for malicious personal injuries had to be paid by local councils, and Sinn Féin councillors did not appreciate paying compensation for acts carried out by the IRA. To overcome this difficulty, Wolfe had also secured garnishee orders from the court to enable him to compel banks that held council funds to extract compensation money from these funds and hand it over.

Wolfe was a man of great charm who would later reconcile with his republican enemies and after the Civil War would act as a defence lawyer for republicans in Free State courts. He would also be elected to the Dáil as an Independent TD. But in the meantime, he was a thorn in the side of the republicans. Despite this close brush with death, it would appear that the feisty solicitor was not deterred in pursuing further cases for compensation for victims of IRA actions. As will be explained, one of these claims for compensation would be in relation to the killing of Bridget Noble.

Later in October, among the cases Wolfe brought to Skibbereen court was a claim for compensation by three children of Chief Officer Philip Snewin for the murder of their father. As already indicated, Snewin was one of the two men shot dead by Liam O'Dwyer in the raid on Ballycrovane coastguard station on 25 July 1920. Elsie, Ethel and John Snewin, all minors, suing by their brother-in-law, sought £8,000 in compensation. It was stated that the claimants resided at Aylesworth, Middlesex. Wolfe, as the claimants' solicitor, instructed barrister Mr J.F. Bourke BL in the case. (As will be explained, Bourke would also act in a compensation case arising out of the death of Bridget Noble.) Judge Hynes awarded £2,500 - £500 to Elsie and £1,000 to each of the other children. He said that their little home had been broken up and the children had been deprived of their father at a time of their lives when he would be a great advantage to them, and they had been 'thrown on the world as poor orphans'. Judge Hynes (1864-1930), a Catholic who was educated by the Jesuits at the exclusive Clongowes Wood College and later at Trinity College Dublin, was one of Ireland's leading cricketers in his younger days. He was Captain of the Dublin University XI in 1887 and was Captain of the Gentlemen of Ireland on a number of occasions, twice visiting Canada and America in that capacity. A kind-hearted man, he had much sympathy for victims of the insurgent violence that had now erupted in his area of West Cork.

Following reforms that were introduced in the late 1890s by the British government, the power of the landed gentry in local government in Ireland had been removed, grand juries were abolished and elected councils took their place. Men from the Beara Battalion were now serving as Sinn Féin members of the Castletownbere Rural District Council (RDC), and one can only speculate as to their reaction to the award of compensation arising out of actions carried out by the battalion. The *Cork Examiner* reported in May 1920 that there were only seven candidates for the seats on the RDC and that there was no contest. Two candidates had withdrawn their names to bring about this situation – one was Michael Sullivan, Gurteen, who had figured in the story of Bridget Noble, as mentioned. One of the more prominent of the members of the new council was Mícheál Óg O'Sullivan, Vice O/C of the Beara Battalion. Two others had been on hunger strike in prison in England prior to their election. The newspaper reported that Michael Crowley, Castletownbere (mentioned above in the context of the Bridget Noble narrative), and J. [Joseph] Foley, Coulagh, were 'at present in hospital after release from Wormwood Scrubs, but are expected to be sufficiently recovered to take part in the first meeting'.[10] As mentioned, Joe Foley had been interned at Frongoch following the 1916 Easter Rising.

Captain Thomas Healy

Jasper Wolfe took up Alexander Noble's case, and towards the end of November his firm wrote to Captain Thomas Healy, the local IRA Liaison Officer, who had an office at South Main Street, Bandon, seeking information about Bridget.[11] Captain Healy had only been appointed Liaison Officer for Cork West Riding in early November, and records show that he sought advice from the Liaison Office in Dublin on how to handle particular issues. Healy had replaced Tom Barry in this area of West Cork after the latter stepped down from the liaison post. Barry had been invited to go to London by Michael Collins to act as adviser on military matters during the talks with the British on an Anglo-Irish Treaty.

Healy faced challenges in taking over from Barry. On 10 November Healy had written to the Chief Liaison Office in Dublin pointing out that he had received a number of complaints from the C.I. [County Inspector] of the RIC [C.I. George R.W. Patrick] 'relating to alleged breaches of the truce by a number of our men which occurred as far back as the 9th September 1921'. Healy went on: 'I suggested to him that these events happened during Commandant Barry's time in charge

144

and being probably dealt with by him it would be improper for me to now deal with.'[12] Healy was informed by the Dublin office that he was indeed responsible for dealing with events that occurred since the Truce, and was advised that the Cork [liaison] office should be able to supply him with the necessary information regarding matters dealt with by the 'previous officer'.

Jasper Wolfe knew Healy well, as Healy himself was also a solicitor and came from a family prominent in the legal profession in Skibbereen. His father was solicitor Joseph J. Healy, who had a large number of clients, including Cork County Council, and he also served as a director of the *Southern Star* newspaper. Like Judge Hynes, Tom Healy was educated by the Jesuits at Clongowes Wood College. He was an ally of Michael Collins, one of the most iconic of Irish leaders during the revolutionary period, and would serve as election agent for him. According to a record in the Military Archives, Healy had also been Intelligence Officer with the 4th Battalion of the IRA's Cork No. 3 Brigade during the War of Independence, under Battalion Commandant Neilus Connolly, who was also from the Skibbereen area. In his Service (1917-1921) Medal file, Healy also mentions serving under Liam Deasy.[13] Healy would later serve as a captain with the pro-Treaty National Army during the Civil War, and in early 1923 the Free State government appointed him State Solicitor for Cork West Riding – in effect, he was successor to Jasper Travers Wolfe who had a similar role under the crown. In later life Healy was a prominent yachtsman.

Wolfe's letter to Healy pointed out that Mrs Bridget Noble had been taken away by the IRA earlier in the year and that her husband was anxious to ascertain her fate.[14] (As outlined in the letter below, Wolfe states Mrs Noble was 'taken away from her home'. However, as previously mentioned, the internal IRA report on the Noble execution, and the account given by Eva O'Sullivan, both state that she was taken prisoner on the road to Castletownbere. In the afore-mentioned letter to de Valera, Alexander also states that Bridget was kidnapped 'between the village of Ardgroom and Castletown-Bere'.)

Captain Thomas Healy,
Liaison Officer,
South Main Street,
Bandon
28 Nov 1921

Dear Sir,

Mrs Bridget Noble, Ardgroom

The above was taken away from her home by the IRA in February last [*recte* March], and since then she has not been heard of. Her husband is most anxious to know whether she is alive or not. He wrote your predecessor but had no reply. It does not appear unreasonable that this man should receive the information which he seeks, and perhaps you could let me know, if she is dead, the date of her death?'

Yours faithfully,

J. Travers Wolfe

As regards the date of Bridget's death, Alexander probably would have needed this information for various legal purposes, such as the disposal of the house and land, and an application to the courts for compensation. He may also have been anxious to have the date so that he would have an anniversary on which to commemorate her. He would ultimately be given the date of her execution, and, as already mentioned, he would go on to place *In Memoriam* notices in his local newspaper in Scotland in 'loving remembrance' of Bridget on the approximate anniversaries of her death. But in the meantime, he would be left in the dark about this and other matters to do with Bridget's disappearance. Unfortunately for Alexander and other relatives of persons who had been disappeared before the Truce, he would find that these matters did not come within the remit of the IRA Liaison staff – they were only authorised to deal with matters that happened after the Truce.

Healy duly forwarded Wolfe's letter to the Chief Liaison Officer in the Gresham Hotel in the capital on 6 December, with a hand-written covering letter. Commandant Dalton considered that this was not a matter that they could deal with. Dalton wrote back to Healy to advise him on how he should reply in regard to the query regarding Mrs Noble: 'Your reply should be on the lines that the incident happened before the truce, and as you only deal with events which happened subsequent to that period, you regret that you cannot reply [sic] the desired information'.[15] Despite the assistance of Travers Wolfe, Alexander Noble had once again hit a brick wall in his quest for answers.

Captain Healy also sought advice from Dalton regarding an embarrassing situation that had arisen concerning Wolfe himself, his fellow-solicitor. It was a time when the IRA police, known as Irish Republican Police (IR Police or IRP), were exerting their authority, but the RIC was still in operation – the latter force would not be formally disbanded until August 1922, although most personnel were demobilised in the April/May period. Healy explained that Wolfe was

146

fined 2/6 for being found 'after hours' in a public house by the IR Police.[16] (Wolfe enjoyed the conviviality of pub social life, and sometimes the whiskey and the conversation would go on into the early hours.) The Dáil Minister for Home Affairs had given an order that 'the decree should be executed', and a warrant was given. 'IR Police called on him for the amount. He sent word to RIC and kept the former talking until the latter called when he denounced them and turned them out.' Later the RIC District Inspector (D.I.) called on the IR Police D.I. in Skibbereen stating that he would regard any further interference with Mr Wolfe who is one of the Crown Forces [sic] as "a breach of the Truce". 'Our D.I. desires to know if he is to enforce warrant or not.' Dalton kicked to touch, stating in his reply: 'This is a matter entirely for the police.'[17]

Intimidation of Mrs Maria Sweetnam

While Dalton felt unable to take up the case of Bridget Noble, he indicated that he would pursue another matter that Wolfe had raised with Captain Healy – the matter had arisen after the Truce and was thus something that would come within his remit. An attempt had been made to intimidate an elderly Church of Ireland widow, Mrs Maria Sweetnam, off her property. Wolfe had written a letter outlining the woman's concerns and Healy had passed it on to Dalton along with the letter covering the Bridget Noble case. Healy explained that Mrs Sweetnam's farm 'is on the same basis as the other confiscated farms'. At the time of the Truce the IRA, especially in the Cork No. 3 Brigade area, was in possession of a number of properties, known as 'spy farms', that had been confiscated during the War of Independence from the families of alleged 'spies' or 'informers' who had been executed.[18]

Wolfe outlined how Mrs Sweetnam, from Lissanoohig, near Skibbereen, had received a letter purporting to come from the Commander of Cork No. 5 Brigade of the IRA [Gibbs Ross] with an apparent eviction threat. Wolfe wrote: 'I shall feel obliged if you will let me know if this letter is genuine. The letter contains a statement that the lands and house "were confiscated by the old Cork No 3 Brigade IRA".'[19] The woman's husband Mathew Sweetnam had been shot dead by the IRA in February 1921. It was reported that a group of men called to the house and taken him a short distance away, telling his wife he would be 'back soon to you'. His wife heard shots and Sweetnam came running back into the house, where he collapsed in the kitchen. One of the gunmen followed him into the house and, in front of a horrified Mrs Sweetnam, delivered the *coup de grace* by shooting her husband in the neck. A Church of Ireland neighbour, William Connell, was shot dead in bed the same night, while his wife Elizabeth was held outside the house by one of the gunmen.[20] It emerged that the two farmers had given evidence in court against an IRA arms fund collector, who received a six months sentence.[21] A former IRA officer, Patrick O'Sullivan told the BMH that orders were received from brigade headquarters that the men 'should be executed and their lands forfeited'. (According to a Dublin Castle report, a third man gave evidence in this case in a military court, and 'all three have been murdered'.[22])

Connell was a client of Jasper Wolfe's legal firm, and after receiving a letter warning him that he was in danger, asked advice from solicitor Willie Kingston, who worked in Wolfe's firm. Kingston, a cousin of Jasper, advised Connell to take the warning seriously and leave the country, but Connell decided to stay – with tragic consequences.[23] William Connell's brother Thomas Connell, who resided at Bridge Street, Skibbereen, figured in a list of civilians accused or suspected of giving information to the crown forces, drawn up in early 1922 by the 2nd Battalion of the Cork No. 5 Brigade. The report described him as 'member of Orange & Freemason societies. Very Black.' (The word 'black' was a pejorative term used to describe Protestants seen as prejudiced against Catholics.) The report goes on: 'Would have no hesitation in transmitting information'. However, the only evidence for this assertion is stated to be: 'Evidence of suspicion'.[24]

Patrick O'Sullivan added in his statement to the BMH that a Flying Column under Tom Barry had at one stage moved into the area to carry out the Brigade order to execute Sweetnam and Connell, and also to ambush any crown forces arriving to investigate the shooting of the farmers, but the column withdrew after an IRA man was shot accidentally. (The task of killing the farmers was then apparently left to the local battalion of the IRA.) O'Sullivan said that about 20 Protestant farmers had refused to pay the levy, and stock to the value of the levy was seized from each defaulter.[25] Dalton wrote back to Healy saying that the Mrs Sweetnam issue was 'receiving attention'. In the context of the Bridget Noble disappearance, the Sweetnam/Connell case illustrates the draconian punishment that could be imposed on those who gave information to the authorities about an IRA member, even if that information led to a comparatively short prison sentence rather than a more severe penalty.

Mrs Juliana Lynch

Mrs Juliana Lynch was one of those who sought information from the IRA Liaison authorities about a loved one who had gone missing. Like Alexander Noble, Mrs Lynch enlisted the aid of solicitor Jasper Travers

148

Wolfe after failing to get information from the local Liaison Officer about her missing spouse. Juliana had been married only six months to former soldier John Sullivan Lynch when he was abducted by two men from their home at Carrigrohane, County Cork on the afternoon of 29 May 1921. It would later emerge that he had been seen making visits to Ballincollig military barracks and was suspected of passing information. He was shot as a spy by the IRA and his remains secretly buried. (Ex-servicemen were disproportionately targeted by the IRA as 'spies', especially by the Cork No. 1 Brigade.) Meanwhile, a distraught Mrs Lynch fled from County Cork to her native Cavan after getting a threatening letter, but made arduous efforts to find out what happened her husband.

In a letter to the Dáil Department of Defence she seemed to imply that her husband had been targeted because of a personal grudge by IRA member Patrick Sullivan. She claimed that Sullivan, following a dispute with her husband, threatened to have him killed by the IRA. London-born Sullivan was a brother of Joseph Sullivan, one of two men who would be hanged in 1922 for the murder of Field Marshal Sir Henry Wilson. Ultimately, in March 1922, she would receive a letter from the Department stating: 'I am directed by the Minister for Defence to say that he regrets to have to inform you that records go to show that your husband was executed on 5th June 1921, having been court-martialled on a charge of espionage and sentenced to death by a duly authorised authority.'[26] Alexander Noble would get a similar reply to his own quest for information about the fate of his wife.

Constable Joseph Daly

Another case of the Disappeared that was raised with the IRA liaison authorities concerned a young RIC man who had vanished in County Tipperary. The policeman's father, John Daly, a postman from Enfield, County Meath wrote to the local IRA Liaison Officer in Nenagh, north Tipperary, seeking any news of his son, Joseph Daly, a constable who had been based at Silvermines and had gone missing on 14 May 1921. Just a couple of months before the policeman disappeared, John Daly senior and his family suffered a heavy blow when masked men ordered them out of their house and then set it on fire – apparently because a family member was in the RIC. The Liaison Officer, Commandant Quinlan, declined to take on the case as the disappearance had happened before the Truce. It later emerged that Constable Daly and a colleague, Constable Thomas Gallivan, from Milltown, County Kerry, were in plain clothes and off-duty when they went out cycling to visit two young women at Ballymackey. On the return journey they were taken prisoner by the IRA. The IRA men were unsure what to do with the captives and consulted local IRA brigadier Sean Gaynor. He ordered that the policemen were to be 'shot and buried'. In 1925 the local council, on public health grounds, arranged for the remains to be exhumed from a bog at Lower Graigue. It could be said that these two young Catholic men were in the wrong job, in the wrong place, at the wrong time, and ended up on the wrong side of history. But at least their remains were ultimately recovered and given a proper burial. In the case of others of the Disappeared, such as Bridget Noble, there would be no recovery of remains.[27]

Chapter 14: Alexander Noble

Returns to County Cork

Alexander Noble pressed ahead with his quest for information about the fate of his wife and at some stage returned to West Cork to pursue matters arising out of her disappearance. Presumably he made contact with his father-in-law John Neill. At some stage, after Bridget disappeared, the aged John Neill was said to have been removed to the workhouse. It seems that Bridget had been his carer and after she was taken away there was nobody to look after him.[1] The Board of Guardians records show, as previously indicated, that the workhouse at Castletownbere was still admitting aged and infirm persons at this period and a place may have been found for him at this facility. (There was also an arrangement whereby inmates could be transferred from Castletownbere to Kenmare workhouse.[2] Castletownbere inmates could also be transferred to Bantry workhouse.) Alexander may also have consulted with District Inspector Oates of the RIC – certainly, as explained below, Oates would give evidence in a court hearing arising out of Bridget's disappearance. One wonders if Alexander also spoke to Nora Sullivan, who is said to have accompanied Bridget on her fateful visit to the police station to complain about the men who had carried out the hair shearing attack.

Court Compensation Claim

With the assistance of Jasper Travers Wolfe, Alexander brought a case to court in Skibbereen on 23 January 1922, claiming compensation for the kidnapping of his wife on 4 March, and her subsequent murder.[3] Wolfe had particular expertise in such cases. The barrister J.F. Bourke BL represented Alexander at the Skibbereen Quarter Sessions. The instructing solicitors were Travers Wolfe. (Jack Bourke, a noted orator with a distinguished academic record at King's Inns, was a son of a prominent judicial office holder, Matthew Bourke, who served as

Recorder of Cork, but he also defended IRA members at British military tribunals. He appeared as counsel on behalf of three of the IRA men who went on trial following the disastrous Dripsey ambush, the event which ultimately led to the death of Mrs Lindsay at the hands of the IRA. He also represented the relatives of the Auxiliaries killed in the Kilmichael ambush in November 1920 when they sought compensation at Macroom court the following January. On that occasion, J.F. Bourke told Judge Hynes that counsel had agreed that relatives of the deceased men should withdraw from the court while medical evidence [about the state of the remains of the deceased] was being given because 'the details are very distressing'.[4]

The local newspaper, the *Cork County Eagle* [popularly known as the *Skibbereen Eagle*], carried a brief report of the proceedings in the Noble case before Judge Hynes. The introduction to the report stated: 'Alex. Noble, Ardgroom claimed compensation for the kidnapping and shooting of his wife on the 4th March.' In light of the speculation as to how Mrs Noble was put to death, it is noteworthy that the newspaper used the word 'shooting'. It is unclear if the reporter simply assumed that Mrs Noble was shot, or if this information emerged during the court hearing. It is also possible he gained some intelligence informally from a source, possibly a police source.

Alexander gave sworn testimony that he was aged 48 years, a cooper by trade, and a Scotchman by birth. He married in 1907 and his wife was aged 38 years. (This was incorrect – Bridget was, in fact, aged 45 years at the time of her disappearance – either Alexander was confused or the newspaper reported incorrectly what was said in court.) On 4 March she went to visit her father, who was aged 80 years, but she was not seen or heard of since. (The use of the term 'she went to visit her father', attributed to Alexander, suggests that Bridget was living apart from her father. All the indications are that she remained in residence with her father in the family home at Reenavaude after Alexander moved to England. However, there was also a local rumour, unconfirmed, that she went 'on the run' after falling foul of the IRA, possibly hiding out in the locality, which could explain the term 'she went to visit her father' but this is all in the realm of speculation. If she had attempted to go into hiding, it is unlikely she would have remained undetected for very long, in light of the detailed local knowledge of the Volunteers.)

According to Alexander, before her disappearance on 4 March, his wife had gone a number of times to the police barracks, and therefore she must have been suspected of giving information. He said that after a long number of letters written, he received only one answer, which was handed to the judge. (This may have been a letter from Captain

Healy, stating that the Liaison authorities could not take on the case as Mrs Noble had been abducted before the Truce.) Alexander said that for a long time he hoped that she was spared, but now he had nearly abandoned hope. He had suffered a severe loss by the death of his wife. 'He then wept bitterly,' the court report in the *Cork County Eagle* noted.

District Inspector Oates of the RIC, stationed in Castletownbere, also gave evidence. Inspector Oates said that he knew the applicant's wife. She had been at the police barracks. He understood she was taken away on 4 March, but he was not in the district at the time. [In February 1921 he was transferred to Bantry but the following August he was stationed once again in Castletownbere.] Oates, who probably had his own means of getting local intelligence, said he was almost certain Mrs Noble was murdered, as he had 'certain authority' for saying it. Judge Hynes commented that it was 'a most appalling case', and it was most appalling to read the documents that he had seen. According to the newspaper report, Judge Hynes awarded the sum of £1,500. It would appear that Inspector Oates did not provide details to the court as to the reasons Mrs Noble was visiting the RIC station in Castletownbere. Her final visit was probably the one in which she complained about the IRA members whom she accused of the hair-cutting attack. Oates may have been reticent about revealing such information in open court.

Other compensation cases heard on the same day and reported in the *Cork County Eagle* illustrate the unsettled nature of life in West Cork at the period. John Driscoll, a Civil Bill Officer, aged 75 years, from Schull, claimed £400 for injuries and shock as a result of being kidnapped on 8 October. He was held for six days and nights in different houses. In one house he heard the word 'shoot' being used, and was in great suspense. The judge awarded £300. Henry Alcock, North Street, Skibbereen, who had served in the British Army during the First World War and was the son of a retired RIC sergeant, claimed £5,000 as a result of being 'savagely beaten' by groups of men on 30 September, being rendered unconscious. The judge awarded him £1,000 – which seems generous in comparison with the £1,500 awarded to Alexander Noble for the death of his wife.

Compensation Register

In the British National Archives at Kew, there are records of compensation paid to 'private persons' as a result of injuries suffered during the revolutionary period in Ireland. One item is of particular interest – a big ledger with a cover bearing the inscription: 'Ireland, Criminal Injuries to Private Persons'.[5] The ledger forms part of the records of the Compensation (Ireland) Commission and related bodies, and is so big in terms of its width and length that it has to be inspected in the map room, where outsize items are made available to researchers, rather than in the reading room. The ledger contains a register listing compensation claims arising out of injuries suffered during the Anglo-Irish war, between 21 January 1919 and 11 July 1921, and Bridget Noble figures in the list.

Following the signing of the Anglo-Irish Treaty, arrangements were put in place whereby representatives of the British and Irish Free State governments would decide which state was liable for particular injuries suffered in the above-mentioned conflict. In many of the cases listed in the register, the British accepted liability for paying compensation. Among the claimants listed in the section dealing with County Cork is Alexander Noble, whose address is given as 30 Railway Street, Grimsby. It is noted in the hand-written register that he was paid compensation in respect of 'Bridget Noble', described as a 'married woman', now 'deceased'. In the column under the heading 'Date of Injury', the date is given as '4.3.21', the day that Bridget was abducted.

As in the case of many of the other pre-Truce claims listed in the register, the letter 'L' for Liability is entered on the record regarding Mrs Noble, indicating that the British Government accepted liability, and was prepared to pay the compensation awarded by Judge Hynes at the court in Skibbereen. It is noted that a 'Copy of Award' [given by the court] was received on 6 April 1922. As in a considerable number of other cases outlined in the register, the term 'British Supporter' is also written alongside the entry concerning Mrs Noble. If the term is meant to refer to Mrs Noble rather than Alexander, various thoughts occur. The perception of a person as a 'British Supporter' could be bolstered by the fact that compensation was awarded by a judge who was presiding in a court operating under the auspices of the crown and who had the legal authority to award compensation in cases where death or injury had been inflicted by an 'unlawful association'.

As previously indicated, it may be the situation that the very fact that an individual had been targeted by the IRA for punishment and/or execution could have been seen, in certain cases, as *prima facie* evidence that the person was a 'British Supporter', unless other information emerged to the contrary. Doubtless, Alexander Noble's legal team, comprising solicitor Jasper Travers Wolfe and barrister J.F. Bourke, would have been eager to talk up Mrs Noble's contacts with the RIC to bolster the view of her as a loyal citizen, in the interests of securing a compensation award from the court. The lawyers called District Inspector Oates as a witness to state that Mrs Noble had made visits to the police station in Castletownbere, prior to her abduction and disappearance, no doubt to portray her to the judge as a citizen who was in good standing with the RIC. (In March 1924 the House of Lords was informed that the British Government 'is under an obligation to pay in full to its own supporters all decrees for compensation for personal injury prior to the Truce, awarded by the Courts, and this obligation has been fulfilled at a cost of about £3 million. A small number of cases have not come to the Courts or have not been completed, and the compensation for these is being assessed by two members of the Wood-Renton Commission.'[6])

The description of a person as a 'British Supporter' in the compensation register would not, in itself, constitute conclusive proof that the person was a spy or an informer. There is no indication that, following the Treaty, officials deciding liability for compensation consulted with the disbanding RIC, or examined records of the disbanded force, so as to establish who was, or was not, a police informant. (Many police records were destroyed at the time of disbandment, as mentioned.) Despite the use of the term 'British Supporter' in the register entry relating to Mrs Noble, one wonders, once again, if she had strong political views of any type.

The two governments split the cost where the person injured was seen as neutral in the conflict, and the term '50/50' is entered alongside various names in the register. It probably suited the impecunious Irish Free State side for the British to designate individuals as 'British Supporters' as it meant that the British would pay the compensation from their own considerable Treasury resources. In a number of cases the term 'agreed to accept as British liability' is entered, which might suggest that the British had to be persuaded to accept liability.

On the same page of the register with details of the Noble case, it is noteworthy that details are also given of compensation awarded for the deaths of James Blemens and his son Frederick. These men were disappeared by the IRA, accused of being members of an alleged spy ring operating in the Protestant organisation, the YMCA, in Cork city. The British accepted liability for a Commission award of £3,000 to James's daughter Matilda. However, compensation to family members for the killing by the Cork IRA of James Blemens's English-born son-in-law James Charles Beal, as an alleged YMCA spy, is recorded as a 50/50 Liability case. It is unclear how this difference in the allocation of liability arose. (The deaths of the Blemenses will be discussed in more detail in the context of the IRA's execution of a Protestant youth, William Edward Parsons.)

The register records that £5,000 was sought in compensation for the death of Bridget Noble, and that the sum of £1,500 was awarded. Deductions were made to cover costs of £44.7s, and tax of £92.13s.5d, indicating that the amount payable to Alexander was approximately £1,363 (more precisely, £1,362.19s.7d). It is recorded that the compensation was paid by the Government on 5 March 1923. The records also show that the British accepted liability for the payment of £600 compensation for the death of one of the other women executed by the IRA in 1921 – Catherine [Kate] Carroll, the claimants being her mother Susan and brother Patrick.

Requests to the Irish Authorities for Information about the Disappeared

While the IRA Liaison authorities usually felt unable to supply information about those who had been disappeared before the Truce, there were other ways whereby relatives could get information. Following the Truce, relatives of those who had gone missing could ask for clarification about the fate of their loved ones from the Dáil government, or from the Provisional Government that came to power in early 1922 by agreement with the British. This followed the approval, by a narrow Dáil majority, of the Anglo-Irish Treaty.

As indicated above, Mrs Juliana Lynch had received information about the fate of her missing husband through the Dáil government. Alexander Noble pressed ahead with his quest and efforts were now made to clarify matters with the new Provisional Government. On 16 March 1922 Jasper Travers Wolfe wrote to the 'Minister of Defence, Provisional Government, Dublin'.[7] In fact the Provisional Government did not have a Defence Minister – General Richard Mulcahy fulfilled that role as a member of the Dáil government, having taken up the post on 10 January, replacing Cathal Brugha who objected strongly to the Treaty. At this stage in March there was a dual authority – the Dáil government headed by Arthur Griffith would stay in existence for some months, and acted in parallel with the new Provisional Government headed by Michael Collins. Griffith had the position of President of Dáil Éireann while Collins was Chairman of the Provisional Government. There was close liaison between the two authorities, with some Ministers occupying the same posts in both administrations. In addition, Mulcahy attended Provisional Government meetings, so perhaps he could be seen as the *de facto* Defence Minister in the Provisional Government. While Alexander Noble seems to have accepted that his wife was dead, the fact that he had not received official clarification as to her fate seems to have weighed heavily on him. Jasper Wolfe states in the letter to the Minister of Defence:

156

Sir,

Mrs Bridget Noble of Ardgroom, Castletownbere, was taken from her home on 14th March [*recte* 4 March] 1921 by armed men, believed to be members of the I.R.A. Her husband, Alexander Noble, for whom I am acting is anxious to learn definitely his wife's fate. Some months since, I applied to Capt. Thomas Healy, Liaison Officer, Bandon, but he replied, informing me that he had been directed to notify me that as this was a matter that occurred before the Truce, it could not be dealt with. I am afraid there is no reason to believe that this woman is alive, but I would feel obliged if you could let me have definite information that would remove from this woman's husband the state of suspense which he is in.

I am, Sir,

Your Obedient Servant,

J. Travers Wolfe

It appears that some official now located the IRA report drawn up by Liam O'Dwyer in October 1921. The Secretary at the Department of Defence replied on 22 March 1922, withholding most of the detail, and only giving the salient points:

I am directed by the Minister for Defence to say in reply to your letter of the 16th inst., regarding Mrs Bridget Noble of Ardgroom, Castletownbere, that he regrets to have to inform you that records go to show that this woman was arrested on the 4th Mar. 1921, on a charge of espionage, courtmartialled by a duly authorised authority, found guilty and executed on the 15th Mar. 1921.[8]

At long last, Alexander now had official confirmation from a Dublin government source about Bridget's fate, and the reasons being advanced for her execution. By now, he had no reason to hope for good news, and one can only speculate as to his emotional reaction on being informed that his wife had been put on trial, 'found guilty' of 'espionage', and her life brought to an end. There was, of course, no indication in the letter as to where her remains were located, but at least he was given the date of her death.

Wolfe, always courteous, replied on 24 March 1922 to 'The Secretary, Department of Defence, Provisional Government, Dublin' as follows:

Dear Sir,

Re Mrs Bridget Noble, Ardgroom

I am in receipt of your letter of the 22nd inst (A. 2111) and am obliged for your prompt attention to my letter hereon.

Yours faithfully,
J. Travers Wolfe.[9]

The Department of Defence used a similar formula, involving the legalistic language of due process, in replying to other persons inquiring about loved ones who had been disappeared by the IRA during the conflict. As already mentioned, a reply along these lines had been sent to Mrs Juliana Lynch in reply to a query about her husband's fate. Mrs Mary Nagle, from Waterfall, near Cork city, was another person who contacted the Dáil Government about the fate of her missing husband David Nagle after an IRA Liaison Officer declined to take on the case, as the former RIC constable had been disappeared in March 1921, before the Truce. Ultimately, in February 1922, the Dáil Department of Defence sent her a letter with the usual form of words stating that a death sentence had been carried out on her husband for espionage after he had been 'courtmartialled by a duly authorised authority'.[10] As for Bridget Noble, the Department's claim that she had been courtmartialled by 'a duly authorised authority' is unconvincing, for reasons that will be outlined.

Bandon Valley Atrocity

Jasper Wolfe was himself facing into another challenging period in his eventful career. If Alexander Noble wanted to tie up any loose ends with Wolfe personally at this stage there might have been a problem. It appears that Wolfe's work for his clients was disrupted towards the end of April 1922 when, according to his biographer, he felt obliged to flee the country for several weeks, following an outbreak of violence which struck fear into the local Protestant community.[11] Even though the Truce was still in place, the RIC had effectively disbanded and British forces were leaving Ireland, gunmen went on a killing spree in County Cork, shooting dead Protestants in their homes. The IRA had split on the issue of the Anglo-Irish Treaty, and the gunmen were believed to be republicans, members of the anti-Treaty IRA, acting without the authority of their leaders.

Once again, Wolfe's astonishing luck held out – he was away on court business in Cork when gunmen called to his house. His wife Minnie frantically rushed by train to Bandon and managed to locate him when his train stopped at that location on his way home. Jasper turned back and, like other frightened Protestants, is said to have fled the country, taking the ferry from Rosslare to Fishguard.[12] (It seems he made an appearance in court in Cork city on 2 May before fleeing.) Gunmen also visited the Skibbereen home of Wolfe's cousin, William Good Wood, who reportedly fled in his slippers out the back door, took refuge with a neighbour and made his way to England, not returning until July 1923, when the Civil War was over. A business associate of Wolfe's, fellow-solicitor Francis FitzMaurice, aged 72 years, was not so fortunate – he was shot twelve times in front of his wife at the door of his home on Main Street, Dunmanway.

The killing of the Protestants may have been sparked by the fatal shooting of an IRA officer, Michael O'Neill when, along with two colleagues, he broke into the house of a Protestant, loyalist family at Ovens in the early hours of the morning after they refused to open the door. An inquest would later hear that he had gone there 'on business'. One historian has quoted two local people as having heard that O'Neill had been drinking in Killumney and had gone to the Hornibrook home to borrow their car, to get to Bandon.[13] The Hornibrook family had suffered harassment and one of the occupants, Captain Herbert Woods may have panicked when faced with the intimidating sight of intruders, or considered that he was acting in legitimate defence of himself and the others in the house. In a High Court case in Dublin in 1928, it would be claimed by a family member, Mrs Matilda Woods, that in the period 1919-22 the property of Thomas H. Hornibrook JP 'was maliciously injured on numerous occasions, his crops destroyed, farm implements broken and stolen, a motor car badly disabled and from time to time he was severely boycotted. His corn rotted because no one would thrash it.'[14]

Following the death of Michael O'Neill, the three male occupants of Ballygroman House, Thomas Hornibrook, his son Samuel and son-in-law Captain Woods, were taken away, killed and their bodies secretly buried. The house was destroyed by fire. Over the following nights ten Protestants were murdered in their homes in West Cork, the victims ranging in age from 16 to 81 years. One of two 16-year-old youths shot dead was Robert Nagle from Clonakilty. His father was secretary and caretaker of the local Masonic Lodge, which was burned down – one of a number of Masonic halls damaged or vandalised or forcibly occupied in Ireland during the revolutionary period. (Two men who had been in the IRA gave accounts to the BMH of their role in burning the Masonic hall in Ballinamore, County Leitrim in October 1919.[15]) A republican who acted as an escort to Tom Barry during the Civil War would later be charged by the Free State authorities with Nagle's murder – the charges were dropped as witnesses were unwilling to testify. Barry himself was away from County Cork when the murders occurred.[16] In addition to the murders of Protestants, the Rev Ralph Harbord was shot and seriously wounded at Murragh Church of Ireland rectory.

There has been speculation that the killers may have been influenced by resentment over the persecution of Catholic nationalists by Protestant Loyalist extremists in Northern Ireland. During the revolutionary period, it is doubtful if anybody on either side of the religious divide was killed primarily because of doctrinal or theological differences. One historian has suggested that many protagonists on both republican and Ulster unionist sides identified those of alien religious affiliation as 'potential collaborators and rebels respectively', while 'most influential organisers on both sides construed their struggle as a patriotic rather than a religious enterprise...'[17]

The Bandon Valley atrocity was condemned by both pro- and anti-Treaty sides, and a local IRA leader, Tom Hales, moved to restore order, threatened punishment on anyone not observing military discipline, while armed protection was provided to some Protestants. However, despite the condemnations, there is no indication that any of the killers were disciplined by the IRA, and it is unclear to what extent the atrocity was investigated by the IRA's policing wing, the Irish Republican Police (IRP). The IRP Superintendent for Bandon and Clonakilty would later emerge as one of the suspects for the murders, and he would take a very active role on the anti-Treaty side in the Civil War.[18]

In later years some commentators have sought to focus attention on the alleged guilt of some of the victims. Arguments have been advanced that those who were murdered were 'loyalists' or 'informers' or 'suspected informers' or the relatives of such people. The modern term 'victim blaming' comes to mind. It was even suggested that the British, acting as *agents provocateurs*, carried out the killings – a most imaginative but rather implausible theory. It is difficult to see the atrocity as anything other than a 'hate crime' against members of a vulnerable minority community.

In condemning the murders, the journal *An t-Óglach*, under Free State military control, blamed a 'militarist dictatorship' for these 'cowardly crimes' and claimed also that the homes of Protestants had been entered by 'armed parties of the irregular forces' and the residents 'forced to leave'. Around this period, William Salter and his family hurriedly left their Dunmanway farm to flee to England in fear of the IRA after being ordered to get out. William's son, Irish-speaking Church of Ireland clergyman Canon George Salter told the family's remarkable story in recent years in the RTE TV documentary, *An Tost Fada* ['The Long Silence'], presented by Eoghan Harris. The clergyman said that if his father had not gone, he would have been 'shot dead'.[19] William Salter later returned to County Cork, settling in

Castletownshend. His six sisters and two brothers, who had all left Ireland by the end of 1922, did not return to live in Ireland.

It is noteworthy, in the context of the Bridget Noble execution, that all those who died were male – no females were shot. Even though the killers were extremely callous, showing no mercy to the very young or the very old, women were spared. In the village of Ballineen, a middle-aged woman, Frances Peyton, asked one of the raiders who came to her home if he was going to shoot her. He said: 'No, I don't shoot women.'[20] However, the woman's 16-year-old nephew Alexander McKinley was killed with three bullets to the head as he lay in bed. In the afore-mentioned raid in Clonakilty, it is noticeable that when the gunmen's primary quarry, Thomas Nagle, eluded them, and the two raiders sought another victim, they refrained from shooting Nagle's wife who was present, and instead killed the couple's son Robert, even though he was a minor. In Dunmanway, an elderly Methodist couple, James and Clarina Buttimer, were roused from their bed by shouting and banging at the door. Mrs Buttimer lit a candle and as they went to the door she held her husband's hand as he had been unwell. The gunmen made it clear that they were not targeting Mrs Buttimer, telling her: 'We don't want you.' James Buttimer, an 81-years-old retired draper, pleaded with the gunmen: 'Surely, boys, you would not harm an old man like me?' But they fired five shots at him, killing him instantly.[21] Even while carrying out acts of great inhumanity, the gunmen abided by the unwritten rule that women were not to be shot.

It is not known if Alexander Noble was still in Ireland when the Bandon Valley murders took place. Beara was one of the areas unaffected by the murder campaign against the Protestants. Nevertheless, if he was still in West Cork, one could speculate that the atrocity might not have encouraged him to linger in a region where gunmen had murdered Protestants with such impunity. He was, after all, of Scots Presbyterian background and was the husband of a woman who had been put to death after being accused of informing – he himself could have been suspected of loyalist or pro-British sympathies, or worse. He would not have been reassured by the fact that his own solicitor was among the West Cork Protestants who fled their homes after the atrocity, returning only when it was deemed safe to do so. At some stage Alexander resumed his life in Grimsby. As will be shown, the fallout from Bridget's horrendous fate would have dire personal consequences for him, and he would encounter much further misfortune.

Chapter 15: Death Sentence In Breach of IRA Rules

From Liam O'Dwyer's report, it would appear that when Mrs Noble was put on trial for her life, the matter was not referred to senior figures further up the chain of command. There is no indication in his report that there was liaison with the Brigade Commandant or GHQ. As a result, it is apparent that the execution was not in accordance with the IRA's own rules, specifically General Order No. 13, titled 'Women Spies', introduced in November 1920. The most important way in which the Order was violated was, of course, by the actual execution of Mrs Noble. As outlined below, the Order prescribes various punishments, but not the death penalty, for women found guilty of 'spying'. The order states:

Where there is evidence that a woman is a spy or is doing petty spy work, the Bde. Comdt. whose area is involved will set up a court of inquiry to examine the evidence against her. If the court finds her guilty of the charge, she shall then be advised accordingly, and, except in the case of an Irishwoman, be ordered to leave the country within seven days. It shall be intimated to her that only consideration of her sex prevents the infliction of the statutory punishment of death. A formal public statement of the fact of the conviction shall be issued in poster or leaflet form or both, according to the local circumstances, as a warning and a preventative. Ordinarily, it is not proposed to deport Irishwomen, it being hoped that the bringing of publicity on the actions of such will neutralize them. In dangerous and insistant [sic] cases of this kind, however, full particulars should be placed before GHQ and instructions sought. By order, Adjutant General.[1]

Instead of the Brigade Commandant setting up a court of inquiry into the allegations against Bridget Noble, as would have been required by the terms of General Order No. 13, the court seems to have been organised by members of the Beara Battalion. And while such a breach of the Order might be considered a simple technicality, a more significant breach was the lack of consultation with GHQ. Those responsible for the trial of Mrs Noble obviously considered the charges against her to be sufficiently serious for a death sentence to be imposed. In that situation, there is a clear implication in General Order No. 13 that the case should be referred to GHQ, with 'full particulars' being supplied and 'instructions sought' before any drastic action was taken, and this did not happen. It is unclear why the local IRA on the Beara peninsula failed to follow the procedures set out in the order. A possible reason was that it was a remote area, and communications were difficult. Also, while there was in theory a chain of command going up to the GHQ in Dublin, the IRA was not a regular, conventional army, control by GHQ was loose, and local units seem to have operated with a considerable degree of independence and autonomy. Ernie O'Malley, who was in command of the IRA's 2nd Southern Division during the War of Independence, observed that whatever GHQ did or did not do, 'there was a great deal of decentralisation in Ireland and we carried on independently...'[2]

A complicating factor may have been that Charlie Hurley, Commandant of the Cork No. 3 Brigade, of which the Beara Battalion formed part, had been wounded in the Upton railway station ambush on 15 February 1921, although he managed to escape. (One of the civilians who died in the crossfire was a young woman from Castletownere, Mary Hall, who worked as a cook in Cork city.) Hurley was recuperating in a safe house but was shot dead on 19 March while trying to get away from a British Army raid on his hide-out, as the Crossbarry engagement was about to start. However, he did have a Deputy, the Vice O/C, Ted O'Sullivan, from Bantry. There is no indication in the internal IRA report on Mrs Noble that O'Sullivan was consulted regarding the Noble case, although he was in Beara in early March, liaising with IRA officers about the deployment of local Volunteers with the flying column.[3]

The question arises – even if the Beara Battalion had put up posters or handed out leaflets labelling Mrs Noble as an informer, could this have caused embarrassment to the battalion? Members of the public would be bound to speculate as to why Mrs Noble was being branded an informer. In the event of background details emerging, some people may even have privately sympathised with the fact that she had stood up for herself and objected to the humiliating punishment of having her hair sheared off. They may have considered that in complaining about her alleged attackers to the police, she had been seriously provoked into doing so, that she had been forced into becoming an 'informer'. And if she did give information about the Lehane shooting, this might have been considered 'not too serious', to quote the IRA report, as nobody was ever arrested for the killing. Also, there may well have been those who would have privately considered that assistance to the RIC in this matter was a less heinous crime than the killing itself, in which a defenceless farmer was hit at close range by two shotgun blasts. It is unlikely that any local person harbouring such dangerous thoughts would have expressed them in public, given the conditions that prevailed at the time. One wonders also if the Beara Battalion leadership was even aware of General Order No. 13, and if it was aware, would the order have been seen as merely a guideline, rather than an instruction that had to be obeyed to the letter?

As regards punishments for women specified in General Order No. 13, it is unclear if any element of the IRA did, in fact, produce posters or leaflets during the revolutionary period to shame a woman accused of informing, although banishment was used in certain cases. The question can be asked – could Bridget Noble not have been given the option of leaving the area covered by the Beara Battalion or the area covered by the Brigade that encompassed the battalion, or perhaps leaving Ireland? The story in the *Londonderry Sentinel* referred to above, suggests that after the hair-cutting punishment attack she was in fear of her life and planned to flee the country. As indicated below, banishment was a punishment imposed by members of the Beara Battalion on a medical doctor who gave offence to the movement, although he was not accused of being a spy or an informer, and the banishment was not from Ireland but from the area covered by the local IRA brigade. Two former RIC sergeants who came to live in the Castletownbere area, having married local women, were also banished from Beara by the IRA just after the start of the Civil War – apparently because they had served in the crown forces. (During the War of Independence, a local journalist living in the Kilbrittain district of West Cork was, according to a BMH statement, courtmartialled by the IRA and banished from the area after he reported on sermons denouncing the IRA given by the local Parish Priest.[4] The priest himself was not banished by the Catholic republicans.)

In the case of Mrs Noble, a possible argument against banishment or other non-lethal punishment was that there might still be a risk that she could complain about her captors to the RIC, naming individuals who had kidnapped her and held her prisoner. After all, she had shown courage and defiance by complaining to the police about the men she accused of the 'bobbing' attack. Execution would ensure her silence this time. 'Dead women tell no tales.' It is not known if this was a factor in the IRA decision to execute Mrs Noble.

Letter from the Department of Defence

The afore-mentioned letter from General Richard Mulcahy's Department of Defence confirming Mrs Noble's execution failed to clarify important issues. The Department's letter to Alexander Noble's solicitor claiming that she had been arrested 'on a charge of espionage' and 'courtmartialled by a duly authorised authority' omitted to explain how those who passed judgement on Mrs Noble had been 'duly authorised' to do so. There was no indication as to what person, or what entity, might have 'duly authorised' the court martial session that resulted in a death sentence on a female. The letter implied that those responsible for the court martial had the authority to sentence Mrs Noble to death, whereas, as outlined above, under IRA rules, the so-called 'duly authorised authority' was not 'authorised' to condemn any female to be executed.

Mrs Noble had been put to death before the Truce, during a period when there was unity in the IRA. Even though differences were now emerging over the Treaty, the Department (pro-Treaty) failed to acknowledge that personnel in Beara (who would emerge as anti-Treaty) had neglected to follow proper procedures in the Noble case. In reply to the query about Mrs Noble, the Department simply supplied the stock answer used to answer queries about persons who had been put to death, ignoring the fact that the Noble case was particularly unusual, in that it involved the execution of a woman, an execution that was in violation of the IRA's General Order No. 13, as outlined above.

It must have been obvious to the Department that there was no consultation with GHQ, as specified by the Order, before drastic action was taken against Mrs Noble. At GHQ, IRA Chief of Staff Richard Mulcahy had no knowledge of Mrs Noble when inquiries were made about her fate, and in September-October 1921 requests for information about her whereabouts had to be sent down the chain of command to the Beara Battalion. While Mulcahy had verbally admonished Dan Breen for the unauthorised shooting of two RIC men at Soloheadbeg in 1919, there is no evidence in available records that he rebuked the staff of the Beara Battalion for the unauthorised execution of Mrs Noble. While General Order No. 13 had been violated by those involved in the execution, there is no indication that the perpetrators were disciplined or admonished in any way by General Headquarters in Dublin. (Neither is there any indication that those who executed Mary Lindsay and Kate Carroll were disciplined for a breach of the Order.)

In its reply to the solicitor, the Department was using a form of words that was probably convenient from a bureaucratic point of view, but that in this case was economical with the truth. It was unlikely that anyone would have questioned the department's claim that the trial of Mrs Noble had been carried out by the afore-mentioned 'duly authorised authority', with the clear implication that it had the 'authority' to sentence her to death. It was an era when people were more deferential to those in authority, and were more likely to accept a pronouncement from a government department than might be the case today. There also seems to be a strong element of hyperbole in the Department's use of the elaborate term 'espionage' in relation to Mrs Noble. The indications are that the major factor that led to her execution was her complaint to the police about the men she accused of the punishment attack on her, and such a complaint cannot be described as 'espionage'. The term 'espionage' seems more applicable to the exotic world of Mata Hari, or a John le Carré-style spy novel dealing with international intrigue, rather than the actions, or alleged actions, of a simple, unsophisticated woman living in a thatched cottage in Reenavaude.

Banishment of Women

As Bridget Noble suffered execution rather than exile from her native place, it is noteworthy that in another part of West Cork, in June 1921, banishment was the method used by the IRA to deal with an elderly Protestant woman, Beatrice Whitley, aged about 60 years, who was accused of giving information to the crown forces. As a result of her alleged activities, an IRA report recorded that she was 'ordered to leave the country'. As outlined above, a GHQ Order had stated that 'ordinarily, it is not proposed to deport Irishwomen...' In light of her religion and probable English descent, Beatrice Whitley may have been regarded as Anglo-Irish. It has been suggested that she may have been seen as 'not quite an Irishwoman' in west Cork IRA eyes, and that this may have been a factor in the decision to banish her from Ireland.[5]

Beatrice Whitley's fine residence in Rosscarbery, Merton House, where she resided with her sister, Emily Louisa Whitley, aged 54 years, was burned down, and the ruins later demolished. The unmarried sisters, daughters of a Church of Ireland clergyman, moved to England. A Catholic man who had worked as a steward for the Whitleys for more than 20 years, Frank Sullivan, paid a heavier penalty after he was accused of giving information – he was executed. An IRA intelligence report on Beatrice Whitley, drawn up in early 1922 by the 2nd Battalion of the Cork No. 3 Brigade, included a description which stated that she had 'bright complexion', 'dark hair' and 'bad feet'.[6] Her present whereabouts were 'not known'. Beatrice Whitley died in London at age 78 years in June 1939 and was buried at Ealing and Old Brentford Cemetery. Her sister Emily also died in exile in London at age 90 years in 1957 and was buried in the same plot.

In yet another area of West Cork, a female accused of trying to give information on the IRA to the crown forces was exiled rather than shot. Liam Deasy describes in his book *Towards Ireland Free* how a letter was intercepted from a 17-year-old girl to the British commander at Bandon Barracks, giving the names of 16 officers and men of the local IRA companies. Officers of the battalion staff questioned the girl and she admitted writing the letter. She was angry because a local Volunteer, whose bicycle had broken down, had commandeered her bicycle and left her the broken one. According to Deasy, the officers of the IRA's Bandon Battalion felt that in the circumstances 'drastic action should not be taken but instead they ordered the girl and her family to leave the country within 24 hours'.[7]

In Dublin, a 'woman spy' said to have been masquerading as a member of Cumann na mBan was captured by members of that organisation and was given 24 hours to leave the country rather than facing a death sentence. An account of this incident was given in a statement to the BMH by Brighid O'Mullane, who was a prominent activist in Cumann na mBan during the War of Independence. In a chilling passage in the same statement Ms O'Mullane told how she herself was almost shot by the IRA after being mistaken for the same female spy while on a visit to Naas, County Kildare to organise local branches of Cumann na mBan. She told how she was 'shocked' to discover that local Volunteers had planned to summarily execute her without a trial, and had even prepared a label 'Spy' to attach to her body.

A woman posing as the mother of well-known IRA combatant Dan Breen tried to infiltrate republican circles in County Armagh. The would-be spy was accompanied by a young man who, she said, was her son, Dan's brother. The IRA concluded she was really a Mrs Rafferty, and suspected that an RIC officer had arranged for her to get early release from prison to do intelligence work. According to a statement given to the BMH, 'Mrs Breen' wanted to meet regional IRA leader Frank Aiken. When Aiken was informed of the matter, he gave orders 'that the lady and her young man companion should be chased from the area'.[8]

Some time before the Truce in 1921, a woman identified only as 'Miss Kennedy' was detained by the IRA in Cork city, and expelled from Ireland. It appears that the she had been sent over from London to tighten security at the Cork Telephone Exchange, after the British had become concerned about leaks of information. Jennie Golden and three other female telephone operators were collecting intelligence from military calls and passing it on to the IRA.[9] It emerges that Miss Kennedy was sent back to London within 24 hours of being detained by the IRA. Despite the Cork No. 1 Brigade's reputation for ruthlessness, it is noteworthy that the 'lady watcher' was allowed to leave the country rather than face a more drastic penalty.

In Cork city, a woman identified in a police report as 'Miss McGrath' was kidnapped by three masked and armed men who forced her into a car on 1 December 1920. According to a police report, Miss McGrath had been accosted by a man while travelling on a train from Cork to Queenstown. He brought her to Mullally's public house, Cork, where she was abducted. She was freed after a week and, it seems, unlike Bridget Noble, did not give any information about the culprits to the RIC. A police report commented that Miss McGrath 'is unable to give any information of value'. The police believed she had been kidnapped because she had been summoned previously to a Sinn Féin court and was 'suspected of giving information to the military in connection with it…'[10]

Sean Healy, who was the Captain of 'A' Company, 1st Battalion, Cork No. 1 Brigade, told the BMH how he and his comrades received an order to deal with a 'woman informer' in Cork. 'This fiend resided on the Old Youghal Road and her activities as an informer were well known to most of the people who lived in her vicinity,' he wrote.[11] As the shooting of women was 'abhorrent to soldiers generally', they decided to take her prisoner in the first instance. They knew she was in the habit of attending a 'house of worship' on a Sunday and they kept watch, equipped with a bottle of chloroform and a horse-drawn covered car, but she failed to show up, and was not seen in the district again for a long time. Healy did not indicate what they proposed to do with the woman after being taken prisoner. It was reported that the IRA in Cork sentenced to death a Mrs Marshall who was accused of being a spy, and who was described as 'a woman of easy virtue'. She was rescued from detention as a result of a search by the British military, and wisely left the country.[12] As regards various other cases, cited above, where women had come to the adverse attention of the IRA, it is noteworthy that, in contrast with the draconian punishment imposed on Bridget Noble, none of them faced the extreme penalty.

Ernie O'Malley and Female Spies

Even if the IRA had never introduced a rule excluding women from the death penalty, it seems likely that many local units would have spared females from the ultimate sanction, in light of traditional considerations of chivalry towards women in that era. However, Ernie O'Malley was one senior IRA officer who wanted a tougher approach towards women accused of spying or informing, and he lobbied for the death penalty to be imposed on females. O'Malley, a former medical student, was one of the most remarkable of the IRA leaders – intelligent, cultured, dedicated and with much physical bravery. Some considered him arrogant and aloof, and he was undoubtedly ruthless. In County Tipperary, in retaliation for the execution by the British of IRA Volunteers, he ordered the execution of three British officers who had been taken prisoner. His books about the revolutionary period have been hailed as literary masterpieces. However, archivist Catriona Crowe has expressed horror at his apparent lack of concern for the security of Ireland's precious national archives which were destroyed in explosions at the Four Courts in Dublin at the start of the Civil War. Grieving over the loss of archives dating back to the 13th century, Ms Crowe admitted she gets 'into a state of incoherent rage' about O'Malley's 'cultural disconnect' when she reads his account of his activities at the IRA garrison at the courts complex.[13]

O'Malley showed he was prepared to break taboos, notably in regard to shooting women. In early July 1921, just before the Truce, he wrote to IRA Chief of Staff, Richard Mulcahy, urging that 'women spies' should be shot, arguing that some were 'only hiding behind their skirts'.[14] Mulcahy demurred, and in his reply stated that women must not be executed without the matter being reported to GHQ first. It appears that O'Malley made his call for a tougher line against female offenders in the wake of a British court martial in Cork. A young woman from Listowel, County Kerry, Kathleen Burke, gave crucial evidence for the prosecution in the trial of four men accused of the murder of District Inspector Tobias O'Sullivan in the town in January 1921. The assassination of the District Inspector received much public attention, as he was shot while walking along the street with his five-year-old son Bernard.

At the court martial, under cross-examination by defence counsel, Ms Burke (who was identified only as a 'lady witness' in newspaper reports) acknowledged that she had served with the Women's [Army] Auxiliary Corps in the Great War. The counsel then apparently sought to discredit or embarrass her by stating: 'When you returned from service, I think you had the misfortune to have an illegitimate child?'

The prosecutor objected, but the question was allowed, and Ms Burke answered in the affirmative.[15] Two defendants were cleared and two others, who protested their innocence, were found guilty and sentenced to death. Due to peace talks that were in progress in the run-up to the Truce of 11 July 1921, the sentences were not carried out, and early the following year, the two men were released.

Ms Burke may have had to leave Ireland as a result of giving evidence. An IRA intelligence report on Kathleen Burke, 'servant girl', compiled in early 1922 by the 6th Battalion, Kerry No. 1 Brigade stated that there was 'no trace of her since she left Listowel'. The report, which was sent to the 1st Southern Division, claimed that none of the men accused of the killing of District Inspector O'Sullivan had actually taken part in the shooting. The writer of the report seemed to indicate that he was still interested in identifying Ms Burke's whereabouts by making the comment: 'I will forward further particulars after inquiries.'[16] In the minds of some, Kathleen Burke, daughter of an ex-soldier, would have become the ultimate outsider - a person who bore the stigma of 'informer', and who was also stigmatised in another important way, as mother of an 'illegitimate child'.

The RIC and the Abduction of Bridget Noble

The abduction of Bridget Noble occurred at a time when the RIC in West Cork was under extreme pressure by the IRA. The RIC learned of her abduction at some stage but it is unclear to what extent a search was mounted for her, although, as previously mentioned, Hannah Hanley states in her Military Service Pension file that Mrs Noble's arrest [by the IRA] 'caused considerable excitement by the British military'. The RIC in the Beara peninsula was under particular stress, and as a result of IRA pressure it no longer had full control of some outlying areas that came under the jurisdiction of the district headquarters in Castletownbere. The annual 'Constabulary List' for 1921 includes details of stations closed since the previous issue. For Cork West Riding there are 18 stations listed as having been 'discontinued' in the previous year, including the Beara stations of Allihies, Eyeries and Adrigole, an indication of how the RIC was gradually losing its presence and authority in areas outside the main towns.[17] The force still maintained its base in Castletownbere, but according to an internal RIC report, the Castletownbere district was 'practically isolated', as were the districts of Macroom and Clonakilty.[18]

On Wednesday, 9 March, five days after Mrs Noble disappeared, a force of military and police carried out raids in the Ardgroom area, with two men being arrested and taken to the army camp at Furious Pier. It is not known if these raids were as a result of Mrs Noble going missing, or if the RIC knew at this stage that she had been taken away by the IRA.[19] The two men detained were named as Patrick Sullivan and Michael Sheehan. They were released after three days.[20] They may have been members of Ardgroom Company, but this cannot be confirmed with absolute certainty – the names were quite common in Beara. Two men called Patrick Sullivan were listed as members of the company, one from Ardgroom and the other from the townland of Ardgroom Inward; in addition, there was a company member called Patie Sullivan, also from Ardgroom Inward. Also listed as a member was Michael Sheehan, from Barrakilla.[21] Crown forces also detained a number of men in the Adrigole area but they were also released after a few days. In another development, it was reported that Tim Shea, Cleandra and J. Murphy, Eyeries, who had also been taken prisoner, were released from Furious Pier camp on 29 March.[22]

In the third week of March, as mentioned, crown forces suffered casualties in an engagement with Tom Barry's flying column at Crossbarry – according to an internal RIC report, an RIC constable was among the ten members of the crown forces killed. (According to a statement made in 1940 by Tom Barry in his appeal for a better military service pension, his column killed 47 of the enemy at Crossbarry, including six officers.[23] However, a recent study by academics has concluded that there were ten fatalities among the crown forces, which would tally with the RIC report.[24]) District Inspector Oates was not in Castletownbere district when Mrs Noble was kidnapped, but as previously indicated, it appears that he later acquired intelligence indicating that she was dead.

County Inspector George R.W. Patrick

The RIC County Inspector at Bandon, covering Cork West Riding (Cork WR), was George Richard William Patrick, son of a Church of Ireland clergyman. George Patrick had joined the force in 1898, not as an ordinary constable but as an officer cadet. He was born in 1873 at Clonbeg, in the Glen of Aherlow, County Tipperary, where his father, Rev. Thomas Patrick, was Rector – he would later become Canon in Lismore cathedral in County Waterford. Canon Patrick officiated when son George married Eleanor Anne Harvey in the Church of Ireland church at Marmullane, Passage West, County Cork in June 1911. The bride's father, William Watson Harvey was a Justice of the Peace who, during the 19th century became Consul in Cork for various foreign countries. George Patrick had served as a District Inspector (D.I.) in various parts of Ireland before being transferred to West Cork. He would eventually be notified of the kidnapping of Mrs Noble, but there were many other events occurring in a turbulent period that may have

171

diverted his attention from the disappearance of the woman from Reenavaude.

Having previously served at Wexford, Patrick was transferred to Bandon as a D.I. and on 1 November 1920, at age 47 years, he had been promoted to the demanding post of County Inspector (C.I.) at that location. Later that month, the Kilmichael ambush occurred, when Tom Barry's Flying Column wiped out a patrol of Auxiliary police, a major blow to the crown forces in County Cork. Just days later, on 2 December, C.I. Patrick was travelling in a police convoy in the area of Brinny, near Bandon, when they were ambushed by the IRA, according to newspaper reports at the time. An RIC report stated that there were 'about 50 ambushers' and that 'police returned fire and dispersed the attackers.'[25] Patrick's RIC record shows that he was given a 'First Class Favourable Record' for 'Courageous Conduct in Brinny Ambush'.[26]

Patrick's area continued to be turbulent, as illustrated by his County Inspector's report for March 1921, the month that saw the abduction of Mrs Noble. Patrick listed the more serious offences committed during that month in Cork WR. They included seven murders, two attempted murders, 20 robberies, five cases of arson, and 'one kidnapping'. It is unclear is this is a reference to the abduction of Bridget Noble – no further details are given. (It was not until a few weeks later that the name of the Ardgroom woman would figure in one of Patrick's reports.)

C.I. Patrick's report for March 1921 begins thus:

I beg to state that this county could not be much worse than it is at the present time. Intimidation of loyalists is more prevalent and ranges from murder downwards. The Protestant section of the county is specially marked out for persecution by the IRA [with] no less than four [Protestants] being murdered in cold blood during the month. Other forms of intimidation, such as the destruction of houses and property, robberies and threatening letters have brought things to such a pass that loyalists are selling their farms and leaving the country, at very great sacrifice.[27]

The RIC Inspector General, in his own report for March 1921 to senior officials in Dublin Castle, using data from C.I. Patrick, outlined 'some of the most serious outrages committed during the month', in Cork WR, although an incident from late February, out of chronological sequence, is also included:

On 3/3/21 Thomas Cotter Protestant farmer, murdered at Curraclough, Macroom.

On 28/2/21 Const Brock murdered at Rosscarbery.

On 10/3/21 John Good, Protestant farmer, Timoleague, murdered.

On 19/3/21 eight soldiers and one military officer and an RIC Constable killed and fatally wounded at Crossbarry.

On 26/3/21 William Good, son of the abovementioned John Good, was murdered. He was an ex-Army Captain.

On 29/3/21 Denis Donovan, ex-Naval man, murdered at Bandon.

On 31/3/21 Sergeant Shea and Const. Bowles murdered at Rosscarbery, on the occasion of the destruction of the barracks.

The Inspector General comments in regard to Cork WR:

> In all 67 outrages were committed in the month of March. The only political activity is that of the IRA assassins who hold the community under their heel. The most active measures, supported by the strongest forces of the Crown are now urgent and necessary if the county is to be saved from the present flood of anarchy.

There is a belated and very brief mention of Mrs Noble in the 'summary of outrages' in the Cork WR report for the following month, April 1921, compiled by C.I. Patrick.[28] Among the 56 crimes referred to, there is just one case of kidnapping, and there is a handwritten note in the margin, explaining that the victim was 'Mrs Noble, Ardgroom', and that the kidnapping 'took place March 1921'. This rather cursory reference seems to be the extent of the attention given in the monthly RIC county reports to the disappearance of Mrs Noble. C.I. Patrick's report is dated 4 May 1921, a full two months after Mrs Noble was abducted – there may have been a delay in the RIC establishing that she had been taken away by the IRA. At this stage in early May, Mrs Noble's disappearance was still being treated officially by the police as a kidnapping, rather than a murder, although D.I. Oates at some stage would apparently acquire intelligence that she had been killed. The abduction of Mrs Noble did not make it into the monthly summary submitted by the Inspector General to officials in Dublin Castle.[29]

Protestants and Loyalists

It is noteworthy that RIC reports on West Cork at this period emphasise the extent of the fears and concerns of Protestants and Loyalists. Although Protestants were a minority in West Cork, they accounted for a disproportionately high number of persons shot by the IRA during the War of Independence after being accused of being spies or informers – a study has shown that in the area of the Cork No. 3 Brigade, 11 out of 19 civilians shot were Protestants.[30]

As regards Bridget Noble, her marriage to a man of Scots Presbyterian background would not, of itself, have made her a target for the IRA, although it may not have been regarded as a positive factor in her favour when she came to the adverse attention of the Volunteers, and may have heightened the suspicion that she was a 'British sympathiser'.

Another person in Ardgroom Inward who was apparently targeted by the IRA was an ex-service man, George P. Sullivan. He was one of a small minority of Protestants living in the townland. According to the 1911 Census, Ardgroom Inland and the neighbouring townland of Ardgroom Outward had a population of 647, and 98 per cent of the residents were Catholic. George belonged to the afore-mentioned Church of Ireland family that resided at Carrigaphrechane. There is no indication that he was suspected of being a spy or an informer – he does not figure on a list of suspects drawn up by the Beara Battalion in early 1922. But it may be the case that he was seen as having loyalist views, and suffered harassment as a result. As will be outlined in more detail, he would later seek compensation for losses he said he suffered because of 'allegiance to the UK government'. The other Church of Ireland family in Ardgroom Inward townland would have been in good standing with the IRA in light of Eva O'Sullivan and her sister Nell being members of Cumann na mBan, and the role of other family members in sheltering Roger Casement's colleague Captain Monteith in 1916, as mentioned.

It is noticeable, from archival records, that the only two individuals who were apparently targeted by republicans in Ardgroom Inward in 1921 both had Protestant connections. Bridget Noble had married a man who was probably the only Presbyterian in Ardgroom Inward at the time, and in 1921 George P. Sullivan was probably the only Church of Ireland adherent left in the townland as church numbers dwindled – apart from Eva O'Sullivan's family that had nationalist/republican connections. (In the 1911 census returns, George was residing with his widowed mother Abigail [Abbey] and sister Mary on the family farm. Mary moved away in 1913, having married a Protestant farmer in Dunmanway, and Abigail passed away in 1918, so it appears that George, a bachelor, was the sole member of his family residing in the townland by 1921.)

In another part of the peninsula, another person who could be regarded as an 'outsider' came under suspicion by the IRA but with a different outcome. Albert Thomas was an English ex-soldier who had served in South Africa during the Boer War. In 1921 he came to work with his wife Rose as caretaker of the Puxley mansion at Dunboy. Soon after arrival he provided hospitality to a couple of British naval officers.

Despite the initial suspicions of the Volunteers, he managed to win their trust, assuring them that he had no intention of doing them any harm. To further mollify the republicans, he gave a job to the daughter of one of the Volunteers, and paid her handsomely. It is noteworthy that the IRA decided not to seize binoculars from the mansion when they learned they were Thomas's personal property.

Thomas had worked as a footman for the Duke of Norfolk, and later as a steward at a Dublin club. One wonders if he developed diplomacy skills that helped him in a time of tension, skills that Mrs Noble and indeed George P. Sullivan may have lacked. Nevertheless, despite the rapport that Thomas established with local republicans, the IRA did go on to burn the mansion in June 1921. In his MSP file, Liam O'Dwyer said he ordered the burning of what he termed 'Dunboy Castle' as it was 'about to be occupied by British military'. (Thomas had failed to persuade local republicans that the British had no intention of occupying the mansion.) A different explanation for the destruction of the big house was given by O'Dwyer's comrade Christy O'Connell. In his BMH statement, O'Connell said he took part in the burning of the mansion 'as a reprisal for the destruction of the homes of IRA men or sympathisers in the area' – a reference to the destruction by the British, in May, of houses in Beara, including that of Liam O'Dwyer. Thomas, who had been taken to Bere Island along with his wife by the British military, saw the glow in the sky and reflected sadly on 'all the lovely old silver, the beautiful glass and splendid linen all being burnt, all those gorgeous statues and pictures, the wonderful drawing room all burning, for what?'[31]

Little Publicity

It is noteworthy that Bridget Noble's disappearance seems to have received no publicity at the time in local newspapers, and only minimal coverage subsequently. As previously indicated, her name was included in a list of the 'missing' given in the House of Commons in August 1921, and later that month her disappearance was mentioned in an article in the *Londonderry Sentinel* but that was a local newspaper based in Northern Ireland. In early 1922, the *Cork County Eagle* carried a brief account of the court proceedings in Skibbereen when Alexander Noble claimed compensation for the murder of his wife. While the newspaper report referred to him as 'Alex. Noble' it did not mention Bridget's name at all.

The punishment attack on Mrs Noble received a brief mention in a pamphlet produced in England in 1921 to highlight the plight of victims of what the publication described as 'Sinn Fein Terrorism'. However, her name was not mentioned in the pamphlet and there was no reference to Mrs Noble being subsequently abducted and killed. The writers of the pamphlet had relied on press reports to compile a long list of incidents in which individuals were killed, injured or punished in some other way, in the first four months of 1921. The abduction of Mrs Noble had not received any coverage in the newspapers in the immediate aftermath of her disappearance, and this can explain how the kidnapping was omitted from the pamphlet. The reference to Mrs Noble stated: 'Woman ill-treated in Castletownbere; hair cut off, and robbed of £35; supposed to have given information to police.'

The pamphlet was titled *Plight of Southern Loyalists*, and the writers seemed to assume that any attack on an individual by republicans meant that the victim was a Loyalist. The pamphlet was produced by the Publicity Office of the Duke of Northumberland's Fund and declared that the position of southern Irish Loyalists in many districts was 'almost intolerable' and in parts of County Cork especially, 'life is one long nightmare'. The writers of the pamphlet commented that a 'disquieting feature' of the position was the 'increasing number of Protestants who have been murdered since the beginning of the year'.[32] The pamphlet referred to 'mysterious disappearances' of men whose fate has never been discovered, and stated that 'many Catholics' have been shot by the IRA, 'particularly ex-Service men, whose lot in the South is truly deplorable'. The pamphlet listed more than 100 incidents in which individuals were shot dead or wounded or suffered intimidation, or had their houses destroyed. The pamphlet alleged that 'Sinn Feiners' were responsible for desecrating Meenglas Protestant Church, County Donegal, on 25 April: 'Communion Table used for meals. Wine drunk. Prayer books, Bibles and surplices torn up and Font defiled.'

None of those involved in the abduction and killing of Mrs Noble made any public statement about the matter. As will be outlined in more detail, there is no reference to her in any of the statements made by former members of the IRA to the Bureau of Military History, nor is there any reference to her in any of the books about the conflict in West Cork written by former participants. There is no record of any inquest, or military court of inquiry in lieu of an inquest. Bridget Noble became one of the largely forgotten Disappeared of that era.

Ted O'Sullivan was a leading IRA officer in West Cork and became Deputy or Acting O/C of the Cork No. 3 Brigade during the period when it encompassed the Beara Battalion. In later life he was a Fianna Fáil TD and Senator. A native of Bantry, he lived for a period in Ardgroom after the Civil War, as mentioned. In his papers at the National Library, one can find no mention of the Bridget Noble case.

In the papers, there is a typewritten document titled 'Activities, Cork III and V Brigades Area'.[33] It covers operations and killings carried out by the IRA in this region between April 1918 and the date of the Truce, 11 July 1921. It includes details of cases where male civilians were shot by the IRA, apparently after being accused of being spies or informers. (Details of killings carried out by the crown forces are also covered.) There is a noticeable omission – there is not a single reference to Bridget Noble. It is possible that O'Sullivan was relying, in part, on press reports to compile his list, and since Mrs Noble's death was not reported in the newspapers at the time, and later received little coverage, this could help explain the omission.

There is no reference in O'Sullivan's list either to the shooting of William Lehane on 7 May 1920, even thought that killing was widely reported in the press and, according to Liam O'Dwyer, the shooting was carried out by members of the IRA. (As mentioned above, O'Dwyer referred to the Lehane shooting in a 1967 letter to an official in the Department of Defence, and stated that he himself was 'in prison' at the time of the incident.) A possible explanation for the omission of the Lehane shooting from Ted O'Sullivan's list is that this was not an operation officially authorised by the IRA. Another possibility is that it was authorised at some level but the IRA did not want to acknowledge responsibility.

In the Ted O'Sullivan file, the list of activities for March 1921, the month in which Mrs Noble was kidnapped, reads:

1/3/21: Attack on RIC patrol, Rosscarberry.

10/3/21: John Good shot at his home, Barry's Hall, Timoleague.

17/3/21: Shippool. [IRA flying column took up positions at this location on the Innishannon-Kinsale road, but military convoy failed to show.]

19/3/21: Crossbarry. [This clash between Tom Barry's Flying Column and crown forces was one of the biggest engagements in the War of Independence.]

23/3/21: Tim Whooley, IRA, accidentally shot Shannonvale, Clonakilty. Dan Lyons, ex-soldier, shot dead Castle Bernard Park, Bandon.

26/3/21: Wm. Good, ex BF [British Forces] officer, found shot near home, Barry's Hall, Timoleague.

29/3/21: Denis Donovan, Naval pensioner, shot dead in home Watergate St., Bandon.

30/3/21: Fred C. Stenning shot at home in Inishannon.

31/3/21: Capture of Rosscarberry RIC barracks; 2 D. [dead], 9 W. [wounded]; bks [barracks] demolished.

The final item recorded in the document is dated the day of the Truce, 11 July 1921, and states: 'RIC man shot dead Townsend St., Skibbereen, 8.30 am.' The insertion of the time of the shooting is particularly significant – the Truce formally came into operation at noon. Constable Alexander Clarke was particularly unfortunate to meet his death just hours before offensive operations were supposed to cease.

In a file of papers at the Irish Military Archives dealing with executions by the IRA during the War of Independence, there are handwritten lists of persons, both civilians and members of the crown forces, who were put to death in 1920 and 1921.[34] In many cases, details of the date of death and approximate location of death are also included. Only two of the women known to have been executed in 1921 by the IRA feature on the list – Kate Carroll and Mrs Lindsay. It is recorded that 'Kathleen Carroll' was executed on 18 April [recte 16-17 April], while no date is given for the death of Mrs Lindsay. Once again, there is no mention of the third woman known to have been put to death by the IRA that year, Bridget Noble.

Secret Disposal of Remains

The decision by members of the Beara Battalion to secretly dispose of the remains of Mrs Noble was probably a crucial factor in the lack of publicity about her death. It could also help to explain her exclusion even from internal IRA lists of those executed during the revolutionary period. Beara Battalion personnel could have decided to leave her body on a roadside with the usual written notice declaring that the dead person had been shot by the organisation as an 'informer' or 'spy'. However, killing a woman could generate adverse publicity for the IRA. In the event of a victim's body being found, there would have been, at this period, a military court of inquiry in lieu of an inquest. This, in turn, could mean coverage in the newspapers. The RIC could testify that she had complained to the police about the alleged culprits in the humiliating 'bobbing' attack, and present this as the likely reason why she had been kidnapped and killed. She could be portrayed as a brave woman who objected to being degraded and who had been put to death by the IRA because, under the IRA's exteme provocation, she had the temerity to report her alleged attackers to the authorities. Officials in Dublin Castle would have been eager to ensure that available details were publicised in order to discredit the IRA. The matter might even be raised in the House of Commons.

Considerations of security may also have been a factor in the decision to hide the remains. Leaving a corpse on the roadside could have attracted the unwelcome attention of crown forces to the locality, and pressure on those living nearby. Local people could find themselves suspected of complicity in the killing, and face the threat of reprisals. It could also be argued that there might have been a benign motive behind the decision to disappear the body. There was a stigma about being labelled a spy or an informer, and it was a stigma that could have a serious adverse effect on relatives of the victim, and Mrs Noble's aged father would be spared embarrassment and shame. Having an 'informer' in the family would have been considered shameful, perhaps like the shame that would arise from the pregnancy of an unmarried daughter. In the Ireland of that era, the prospects for neither were very bright.

The pregnant single woman could face exile from her native place, either on a temporary or permanent basis or even being consigned by her family to the misery of a Magdalen asylum, and forced to give up her child for adoption, while the informer's fate could be execution and disposal of the body in a secret location. But while the secrecy surrounding Bridget Noble's fate might have saved her father some public embarrassment, he would have to suffer the agony of his daughter going missing and not knowing for a considerable period what had happened to her. As her remains would never be found, he would die without ever having had a chance to mourn at his daughter's grave.

In another case of an executed person whose remains were disappeared by the IRA, the excuse of seeking to spare the feelings of the man's children was put forward by an IRA officer, although the secret disposal of the body probably only increased the agony of suspense suffered by family members. In April 1921 John McNamee, from Drumlish, County Longford was secretly executed by the IRA after being accused of being a spy. His body was thrown into the River Shannon. After McNamee's disappearance, his distraught wife made strenuous efforts to find out if her husband was alive or dead, stating in one of her letters to the Dáil government's Minister for Defence that her health 'is in a bad way owing to suspense'.[35] Ultimately, the O/C of the Longford Brigade of the IRA, Brigadier General Redington, wrote to the O/C of the 1st Midland Division on 1 June 1922 stating that after John McNamee was executed, 'his body was thrown into the Shannon with the object of saving his children from any disgrace that might arise'. Mrs McNamee later received a letter dated 1 June 1922 from the Department of Defence with the usual form of words employed at this period, stating that her husband 'was arrested on a charge of espionage, courtmartialled by a duly authorised authority, found guilty and executed...' The letter omitted to mention that her husband's body had been thrown into the Shannon.

Returning to the case of Bridget Noble, it could be argued that by secretly disposing of the body, IRA members were saving themselves from embarrassment. While there was a stigma about being labelled a spy or an informer, there was also a stigma about killing a woman, as it conflicted with traditional ideas of chivalry towards females. The vast majority of individuals killed by the IRA for alleged or suspected spying or informing activities were male, with only three women known for certain to have been executed for these reasons. While women could undoubtedly prove useful to the crown forces as sources of information, the IRA generally treated women who came under suspicion differently from men. The action of the Beara IRA in executing Mrs Noble was unusual, and republicans may have been concerned about a negative reaction from members of the local community. Abducting a middle-aged woman, keeping her captive and then putting her to death might not have been seen by some members of the public as a heroic act, or something to be celebrated in the annals of republican bravery. It might even have been viewed as a shameful act of barbarity and inhumanity.

Chapter 16: Witnesses In Other Hair-Shearing Attacks Not Targeted as Informers

The War of Independence took place in what some might term a more patriarchal era, when some Irishmen, imbued with patriotic fervour, felt entitled, or perhaps even obliged out of a sense of duty, to monitor the behaviour of women, to admonish them if they were failing to live up to the standards expected of Irish womanhood, and in some cases to inflict punishment on females who had offended in some way. One way of punishing a woman during the Troubles of the 1920s was to shame her by forcibly shearing off her hair. As regards the female victims, it was not unknown for women who suffered a hair-cutting punishment attack, or who had witnessed such an attack, to hit back at the perpetrators by cooperating with the RIC and agreeing to appear in court when alleged assailants were charged. In at least two cases, men (apparently Volunteers) were jailed as a result of this cooperation, but none of the women concerned seemed to suffer the retribution visited upon Bridget Noble.

Mrs Noble was unfortunate in that she fell foul of the IRA in West Cork, a region where the War of Independence was fought with considerable intensity, and at a time when elements of the crown forces were retaliating with particular ruthlessness against the IRA. In other parts of Ireland, the local IRA units seemed to take a more restrained attitude towards women who complained to the RIC about hair-cutting assaults, or who testified as witnesses about such assaults, as illustrated by two cases that have come to light.

Margaret Cooney and Bridget Faulkner

In the year prior to Mrs Noble's abduction, two young women from County Meath gave evidence in a military court in Dublin, in August 1920, against two men who, they said, had cut off their hair at gunpoint after they were found in the company of two British soldiers in Navan. The resulting court case was reported in the newspapers at the time, and the military file on the prosecution has survived in Britain's National Archives at Kew - there appears to be no trace of any similarly detailed file on a prosecution arising out of the Bridget Noble case.[1]

After the hair-shearing incident at Navan on the evening of 31 July 1920, Margaret Cooney (aged 25 years) and Bridget Faulkner (aged 21 years) both gave information to the RIC identifying two alleged assailants who were then arrested and given bail. Patrick Kane and James Dalton were each charged, not with forcibly cutting the women's hair but with possession of a revolver without a permit. It appears that they were members of local IRA companies in County Meath.[2] The two women gave evidence at the court hearing in Marlborough Barracks (now the Defence Forces' McKee Barracks). The soldiers who were with the women at at the time of the attack, Private Noel Thompson and Corporal H. Evans of the South Wales Borderers, also testified. The young women said they were held down on the ground while their hair was being cut. Margaret Cooney said that she became unconscious during the attack. They both identified the defendants present in court, Kane and Dalton, as being among the assailants. During the hearing, the two women were cross-examined by Kane and Dalton, and also by the defendants' solicitor, Mr Steen.

Margaret Cooney said that on 31 July she met Private Thompson on the Moate road about 8 pm and they went to the railway line, about 30 yards from the road. She saw some civilians coming and she left the soldier and ran into a field. Asked why she ran away from the soldier, she said she thought it was the priest who was approaching. (It was an era when some Catholic clergymen would patrol secluded areas to disrupt the amorous activities of courting couples.) She said Kane followed her and called out to the others, 'Here she is.' Bridget Faulkner said that she went for a walk along the railway line with Corporal Evans. Four men, two of whom were the accused, approached. One of them, called Keogan, grabbed her by the arm and said she should be 'ashamed' of herself, 'going with soldiers'.

The defendants' solicitor, Mr Steen, called witnesses who gave alibi and character evidence. The complexity of social and political life at this period is shown by the fact that one of the witnesses for Dalton was his brother Private J. Dalton, a member of the British Army's Leinster Regiment. Private Dalton said the two girls, Cooney and Faulkner, seemed to be against him and his family and when he was home on leave they 'sneered' at him. He said that Faulkner, while she might 'go with soldiers', was 'in sympathy with the Sinn Féin movement'. The defendants were ultimately sentenced to a year in prison – Kane was also given 'hard labour'. (Incidentally, records show that one of the officers dealing with administrative matters in connection with the court hearing was Captain G.T. Baggallay, based at Dublin Castle, who was one of the British officers assassinated by the IRA on 21 November 1920, the day known as 'Bloody Sunday'.) In contrast with the draconian punishment meted out to Bridget Noble on the Beara peninsula, there is no indication that the IRA in County Meath pursued the two young women as 'informers' to be executed for giving testimony that resulted in the jailing of two men.

Bridget Keegan

There was another hair-cutting punishment attack carried out in Tuam, County Galway, also in 1920, which resulted in a court case, with five local men going on trial. The young woman who was the victim of the attack did not give evidence – the court heard that she had fainted during the assault, was receiving medical treatment for shock, and was 'delicate'. However her sister, brother and niece all testified in court, and there is no indication that they were subsequently targeted by the IRA as 'informers' to be executed. The court heard how, on 30 April, a group of seven masked men, one of whom was armed with a revolver, broke into the home of the Keegan family near Tuam, County Galway. According to the evidence, Bridget Keegan, who was in her night clothes, fainted as the raiders burst into her bedroom in the house at Cloondarona at 12.45 am. They put her sitting in a chair and carried her outside, where they cut her hair off with a shears. One of them told her sister Margaret: 'That is what she got for going with Tommies.'

The court heard that Bridget and Margaret and their niece had been to a carnival and had gone for a couple of rides on the hobby horses with a Corporal Simpson. Later, a number of men followed them, calling them 'soldiers' girls' and saying they were 'bringing disgrace on the country'. Margaret Keegan, a brother Thomas Keegan and a niece, Madge Keegan all gave identification evidence at the trial in May 1920. Peter Joyce, a married man, was acquitted and four other local men were convicted and sentenced to six months hard labour. On appeal, Frank and William Jordan were cleared but the convictions of Michael Leonard and Jack Jordan were upheld.[3]

Other Women Targeted

In Arklow, County Wicklow, a young woman named Kennedy was walking near the town with a soldier, Private Coker, on the night of 21 April 1920 when they were confronted by 12 masked men, according to an RIC report.[4] 'The leader pointed a revolver at Coker's face, and ordered him to put up his hands. Coker was then searched but no arms were found on him. The girl was asked her name and ordered to a gateway. They intended to cut off her hair but she ran and was pursued by the crowd. She reached the Military Barracks and made a complaint, and some of the soldiers turned out. Some shots were fired but no other injury was done.' Despite the fact that Ms Kennedy had alerted the crown forces who then, apparently, confronted the masked men with shots being fired, there is no indication that she was subsequently targeted as an informer. It appears that she had also defied a warning by going out walking with her soldier friend. According to the police report, the young woman had received a letter earlier on the day of the incident 'telling her to look out if she spoke to soldiers or police' after Wednesday, 21 April. Technically she was still within the deadline but to go out with the soldier after receiving such a warning must have seemed particularly provocative to local republicans.

In another case, also in 1920, James Hynes of Midleton, County Cork was arrested after a young woman who was out walking with a soldier was taken away by men who cut her hair off. It appears that the woman complained to the crown forces about the assault. Hynes appeared before a District Court Martial in Cork on 6 October and denied he had anything to do with the attack. The victim failed to identify him as one of her assailants, and Hynes was cleared of 'unlawful assembly' and released.[5] Unlike the witnesses in the court cases outlined above, Bridget Noble would face horrendous consequences after it was found that she had given the names of her alleged assailants to the police.

The Forcible Shearing of Women's Hair During the War of Independence

The forcible shearing or 'bobbing' of women's hair was a punishment imposed not only by the IRA but by the Black and Tans and Auxiliaries during the War of Independence. In a study of violence against women during the conflict, the academic Marie Coleman noted that in September 1920 five members of Cumann na mBan in Galway were subjected to this unofficial punishment by crown forces 'in reprisal for a similar attack carried out on a woman who had given evidence to a military court'.[6] In a statement to the BMH, Margaret Broderick Nicholson described how, as a member of Cumann na mBan in Galway, her hair was cut 'to the scalp' by members of the crown forces.[7] Limerick-born Agnes Daly, whose sister Kathleen was married to 1916 leader Tom Clarke, also suffered a hair-shearing assault, carried out by Auxiliaries. In County Clare, masked men, believed to be police acting as an 'Anti-Sinn Féin Gang', entered the Kilmihil home of a young dressmaker, Delia Browne, and forcibly cut her hair. In April 1921 she sought compensation in the county court in Ennis. Judge Bodkin, operating under the auspices of the crown, was sympathetic and awarded her the sizeable sum of £400. The judge, an outspoken critic of crown forces' ill-discipline, took the view that the money should be paid from public funds rather than levied on ratepayers.[8]

Ms Coleman said that the IRA was equally liable to commit hair-shearing attacks 'and there are many instances of women who were friendly with the police or who worked for them' being treated in this way. She described this type of assault as 'gender violence', which occurs as a result of the victim's gender, 'without the kinds of sexual contact included in sexual violence'. She says that the use of such a form of violence by the IRA against Irish women conforms to the idea of 'insider violence', deployed as a method of disciplining women, 'including those who were, or were expected to be, on the same side as the perpetrators'.

In a 2020 article, Professor Linda Connolly commented: 'Hair-taking both in Ireland and in other wars throughout time served other functions as a weapon of war – policing of women's sexuality, social control of women's intimate or personal relationships, in particular with "enemy" men, a symbolic attack on women's sexuality/sexual reputation by removing their hair, thereby marking or labelling them sexual transgressors/whores/"horizontal collaborators" etc, and as a war trophy.'[9]

Some attacks were carried out late at night or in the early morning, after the women being targeted had retired to bed. It was reported in May 1920, for instance, that men entered the bedroom of a young woman called Annie Devine near Tuam, County Galway and challenged her about a letter written to her by an RIC constable. She had known the policeman, Edward Daly, a neighbour, before he joined the force. The letter was taken in the capture of mail bags between Bantry and Bandon. One man held her while her hair was cut off with shears; a hair-cutting machine was then used to cut the hair almost to the skin. The raiders told her: 'We will make Irish girls have nothing to do with Ireland's sworn enemies.'[10] (RIC records show that Edward Daly was appointed Constable at age 19 years on 2 January 1919, just before the start of the War of Independence. He was based at Schull in Cork West Riding, and resigned from the police in August 1920, citing 'personal affairs'.[11])

As in the case of Bridget Noble, associating with members of the RIC was a particular reason for women being punished. In RIC files there are details of various reprisal attacks on females over connections to members of the force. In one case it was reported that in the Mallow area of County Cork, armed men called to the home of the widow of an RIC Head Constable. They were looking for her daughter, who was due to marry an RIC constable the next day. 'She was at her cousin's house and on being so informed, the raiders took her to her mother's place. In reply to a raider she said she was going to marry a policeman. A raider then went to cut off her hair; she asked that her mother be allowed to cut it. The mother cut some, but the raiders cut what remained.'[12] (Despite the ordeal suffered by the bride, records show that the marriage did go ahead in the local Catholic church at Ballyclough.)

In another case it was reported by the RIC that twenty armed men visited a man's home in County Fermanagh at midnight looking for his two daughters. The young women were in bed and were taken from the house in their night attire and put in the centre of a crowd. 'They were brought some distance from the house, put on their knees and gagged. A "court martial" was held on them for "walking and associating with Peelers". Their hair was cut off with a scissors.'[13] In another case reported by the RIC, a young woman who had brothers in the police force was reported to have been taken from her home near Tralee, County Kerry at 12.30 am by a group of armed and masked men who 'cut off her hair and tarred her head'.[14]

In yet another case in County Kerry, an intelligence report drawn up by the 5th Battalion of the Kerry No. 2 Brigade on a woman from the Headford area who was punished for 'going with enemy' described her thus: 'Middle age, good looking, wore yellow wig as she was bobbed in January 1920.'[15] In a case in County Roscommon in 1920, it appears that a young woman was particularly brave and defiant when confronted at her home by a dozen men, who were said to have been disguised and armed. She confirmed that she was 'keeping company' with an RIC man, and when told that her hair would be cut, retorted: 'Cut away, that will not alter my mind.' According to a newspaper story based on a Dublin Castle report, the raiders forced her onto a chair and one man held her while another cut off her hair.[16]

Leo Buckley, who served as an Intelligence Officer with the Cork No. 1 Brigade IRA, in his statement to the BMH, recalled 'young girls' from Cork going out to Ballincollig 'to meet the British soldiers'. 'We curbed this by bobbing the hair of persistent offenders. Short hair was completely out of fashion at the period, and the appearance of a girl with "bobbed" hair clearly denoted her way of life.'[17] Professor Connolly has commented that Buckley's 'way of life' remark indicated that the 'policing of women's sexuality' was a motive behind such shearing.[18] James Maloney, who was an IRA company captain and Battalion adjutant in Bruff, County Limerick told the BMH that 'some young girls created a problem'. He went on: 'The British uniform was an attraction to them, as indeed would any uniform. They could be a real danger to the movement and gave bad example by consorting with the enemy. They were warned repeatedly and stronger measures had to be resorted to. No Volunteer liked the job, but on occasions these girls' hair had to be cut. Years later Dame Fashion was to dictate bobbed hair but at this period of revolution it was deemed shameful.'[19]

While Maloney stated that Volunteers were reluctant to forcibly cut the hair of females, it has also been claimed, as will be outlined, that in some cases the perpetrators wielding the shears were cheered on by male accomplices. Apart from the 'danger to the movement' motive for hair shearing punishment attacks, one has to consider the possibility that in some cases male jealousy may have been a factor, and that the assailants were resentful that young Irish women were conferring their affections on outsiders rather than on Irishmen. In 1917, during the Great War, young Irish women seen in the company of American sailors in Cork also attracted considerable hostility, and some were physically assaulted, apparently by vigilantes enforcing 'morality'.[20]

It was not just younger women who were 'bobbed' – older women could also be subjected to the punishment. It was reported that a woman aged 60 years who worked as a servant in an RIC barracks in County Donegal was taken from her lodgings by armed and masked men, gagged, and taken to a field 'where she was kicked to the body and had her hair cut off'.[21] A woman in her fifties was 'bobbed' in County Donegal apparently because she complained to the military about a neighbour who, she alleged, had poisoned her dog.[22] In another incident in the same county, the RIC reported that a woman in Falcarragh called Logue 'had her hair cut off by armed and masked men'. According to the RIC, the woman was attacked because she 'placed wreath on coffin of murdered policeman'.[23]

Punishment Attacks During Truce

In a case in Kings County [County Offaly] in September 1921, during the Truce period, a group of men seemed to be operating as 'morality police' when they attacked two young women. It was reported that Jennie Green and Margaret Byrne were chained to telegraph poles by eight men. According to an RIC report, 'over each girl's head was a paper with printed word: "Immorality" on it. The girls were taken to a shed and their hair cut off.' Historian Diarmaid Ferriter commented: 'One wonders if the irony of it all ever dawned on the eight men.'[24]

In another incident that occurred during the Truce, two teenaged girls were abducted at night from their homes in the Portumna area of County Galway, in October 1921, by a group of masked men who were said to have been armed. The young women were taken blindfolded by motor car to a location where their hair was 'cut to the bone'. One young woman, Julia Goonan, aged 17 years, told a court compensation hearing how she was 'slapped across the face' in the car. She said she was 'hung up' by the hair by one man, and another shaved her hair. Nonie Ryan, aged 16 years, gave similar evidence. Goonan said that the men told her they would take her to Athlone barracks and get 'two nice Black and Tans' for herself and her companion. She said she had to give up her job in service. She intended to go to America, but did not think her hair would be fully grown before twelve months. At Loughrea Quarter Sessions, Julia Goonan was awarded £75 compensation while Nonie Ryan was awarded £70.[25]

'Public Humiliation'

In an academic study of paramilitary violence in Ireland and Poland after the First World War, Dr Julia Eichenberg states that the shearing of women in Ireland took place predominantly in secluded spaces.[26] 'The female victim was either visited at night in her home or trapped while wandering alone or in a small group. Often she was led or chased into the fields where the actual shearing took place, under the observation and cheering of the male companions of the perpetrator(s).' According to Dr Eichenberg women were sheared on suspicion of spying or passing on information, and it was sufficient to be seen with the 'wrong men'. Dr Eichenberg also notes that during the War of Independence, Black and Tans had shorn Irish women 'for taking part in IRA activities, or for witholding information on the IRA'. She comments: 'The hair shearing in Poland and in Ireland display striking similarities. The assault implies public humiliation of the victims and carries a message and a warning to their own community.' She also suggests that this form of violence was 'a public shaming to warn, to maintain conservative values within the community and to enforce communal boundaries'.

In an academic thesis, Gabrielle Machnik-Kékesi posed a question: Since the IRA considered themselves as the 'chivalrous, clean, sober, well-disciplined and pious' protectors of the community, how did they justify violence against civilian women?[27] She states that as an extension of their own 'conservative nationalist values', and given the nature of the 'particular brand of masculinity' espoused by the organisation, the IRA was 'unforgiving of women who negated these values'. She argues that for the IRA, 'preserving the integrity of the

188

Irish Republic necessitated the punishment of those who deviated from the national ideal, especially women, who were seen to have a unique moral role to play'. She went on: 'The IRA's self-perception as protectors of the people depended on expelling people who undermined communal support, including women who consorted with the enemy.' Women who 'misrepresented Ireland' needed to be 'singled out' in their communities, in a way that denoted they 'were not the kind of women worthy of IRA protection'.

Associating with members of the crown forces could entail more severe consequences than hair shearing, as illustrated by an incident in another area of County Cork, in March 1921. A 19-year-old woman, Nellie Carey, was out walking in her native Fermoy with two off-duty British soldiers, one of whom was her fiancé. They came under fire and she was fatally wounded.[28] In another incident in Limerick on 26 December 1920, Elizabeth Scales, also aged 19 years, was also shot and fatally injured. It was reported that she had thrown herself in front of her friend, an Auxiliary policeman, Constable George Richardson, when a gunman tried to shoot him.[29]

Chapter 17: Fate of Mary Lindsay and Kate Carroll

Shortly after Bridget Noble was abducted, in another part of County Cork, Mrs Lindsay and her chauffeur, James Clarke, were shot by their IRA captors. (In Cathal Brugha's letter to Mrs Lindsay's sister, Mrs Benson, revealing the fate of the abducted woman, he stated that Mrs Lindsay was shot five days after the execution of the five Volunteers – this would indicate she died on 5 March, the day after Mrs Noble was taken prisoner. Probate records also give 5 March as the date of death.[1] However, it appears she was alive some days later, and sources cite other dates in March – Sean O'Callaghan indicates 11 March as date of death.) It seems that while being interrogated by 22-year-old IRA officer Frank Busteed, a Catholic of partly Protestant descent, the diminutive Mrs Lindsay infuriated him by treating him with disdain and refusing to answer his questions. Busteed's response, as reported in Sean O'Callaghan's book, *Execution*, does not suggest a courteous attitude to the elderly female prisoner over whom he wielded the power of life and death. Apparently, in the course of insisting his campaign had nothing to do with religion, he verbally abused her, declaring his own Protestant background, insisting he was not fighting a 'religious war', and calling her an 'old bitch'.[2]

As the time approached for her execution, author Tim Sheehan quotes Mrs Lindsay as telling Frank Busteed: 'I am no spy. I acted to save lives.' Sheehan describes how she upbraided Busteed for failing to heed the priest's warning, saying that if he and his men had left the ambush site when told to do so, those who died would be alive today. Apparently stung by the veracity of her comment, Busteed retorted that they would be alive today 'if you minded your own business'.[3] According to Sean O'Callaghan, Mrs Lindsay, who had lost over a stone in weight during her captivity, and who was physically exhausted, was brave and defiant to the end.[4] On a dark night, as she went out from the house where she had been kept captive to meet her death, she took her small round hat from the dresser and placed it firmly on her head. As she stood in front of the firing squad, beside the open grave that had been dug and that was lit by paraffin lamps, she refused a blindfold, saying, 'I am not afraid to die.' Tim Sheehan also reported that Mrs Lindsay rejected a blindfold, and described how the elderly woman 'emaciated but unbent', told her executioners that she had a 'clear conscience' and was 'not afraid to face her murderers'.[5]

Mrs Lindsay's chauffeur, James Clarke apparently found it more difficult to face death. Perhaps he felt he had done nothing to deserve execution. According to O'Callaghan's account, Clarke had been plied with poteen and was dragged to the execution spot, with excrement streaming down his legs. He was then propped up by two spades driven into the ground. Supervised by Frank Busteed, the gunmen opened fire and the hostages died. According to O'Callaghan, Mrs Lindsay tumbled backwards into the shallow grave and Clarke's body was pitched in on top of her.

In contrast with the apparent reluctance of men who had served with the Beara Battalion to make any public comment on the execution of Mrs Noble, Frank Busteed cooperated with two journalists who were researching the Dripsey ambush and the execution of Mrs Lindsay. In the period 1970 to 1971, Busteed and other former members of the IRA gave interviews to Dripsey-based reporter Tim Sheehan. He used these interviews as part of research for his 1990 book, *Lady Hostage* and for a subsequent newspaper article. Busteed also cooperated with journalist Sean O'Callaghan for the latter's book *Execution*, published in 1974, the year that Busteed died at age 76 years. The authors of both books were very sympathetic to the role of the IRA in the events covered. There were inaccuracies in both books,[6] and as will be shown, doubt has been cast on some of the claims made by Busteed in O'Callaghan's book. Nevertheless the books are a useful addition to the store of knowledge about the events surrounding the execution of Mrs Lindsay, while gaps remain in the story of the execution of Mrs Noble.

Kate Carroll

In the month after the shooting of Mrs Lindsay, in another part of Ireland, another woman was shot as an 'informer' by the IRA. Kate Carroll was put to death in County Monaghan in mid-April after reportedly writing letters to the RIC giving information about the poteen trade and making hostile comments about the IRA. (One IRA man also alleged that she gave information about IRA members.) Unlike the case of Bridget Noble, there was no effort by the local IRA to hide the fact that they had killed a woman. Although described as a

Protestant in some reports, the 1911 Census returns show that she was a Catholic. As the body of Kate Carroll was recovered, the British held a military court of inquiry in lieu of an inquest, and there was publicity in the newspapers.

Information provided to the Bureau of Military History (BMH) points to a medical doctor as the person who uncovered the intelligence that doomed Kate Carroll. Dr Con Ward was a republican who served as an IRA Intelligence Officer – he went on to support the anti-Treaty side in the Civil War and would later become a prominent Fianna Fáil politician and a Parliamentary Secretary [junior minister] for Health in the 1930s and 1940s.[7] Information that emerged through the BMH suggests that senior IRA officer Eoin O'Duffy, later a key figure on the pro-Treaty side in the Civil War, and who later held important positions in the Free State, was the local commander who decided that Kate Carroll should die, on the basis of intelligence supplied by Dr Ward.[8] O'Duffy (1890 – 1944), who developed fascist sympathies and maintained a pro-German attitude during the Second World War, had become first President of Fine Gael in 1933, but was forced to resign after a short period, and would become an embarrassment to members of that party. (O'Duffy seems to have been particularly opposed to the making of poteen. An internal RIC report in July 1920 identified him as the leader of a group of Volunteers who carried out an early morning raid on a house in County Fermanagh where, apparently, the raiders suspected that poteen was being made.[9])

Kate Carroll, also known as 'Kitty', was a 40-year-old single woman who lived at Aghnameena, near Scotstown. She was shot on the night of 16/17 April. Impoverished and slow-witted, she was the sole provider for her 80-year-old mother Susan and her 53-year-old brother Patrick who was an invalid. Kate scratched a precarious living from the family's small farm consisting of about ten acres of mountain land, and sought to earn some extra money by crochet work – and by making illegal spirits known as poteen. Because of the latter activity, she had come to the adverse attention of the IRA, which disapproved of the poteen trade, and also of the RIC. It was reported that she wrote anonymous letters to the RIC about the illicit drink traffic, and that these were intercepted by the IRA.[10] A possible motive was that she felt she was being unfairly singled out for her own poteen making activities and was pointing the finger at others. According to another account, she wrote 'chaotic letters to the RIC in Scotstown denouncing their inaction against the IRA and rival illicit distillers'.[11] A member of the local IRA claimed that she gave information about an arms dump and where IRA men stayed at night, although it is unclear if any action was taken by the RIC on the basis of this alleged informing.[12]

Kate Carroll's brother told a military court of inquiry at Monaghan of what happened the night his sister was taken away.[13] It was about midnight, and he and Kate were sitting beside the fire. The dogs began to bark and she opened the door. A man wearing a white mask walked into the kitchen. He asked Kate: 'Are you making any drink now?' She replied that she was not, and would not pay any more fines. She had been raided 'many times' by the IRA for making whisky, and had also been fined by the Government for illicit whisky. The masked man told Kate she would have to go with him. Her mother begged the man not to take Kate away. His sister refused to go and the man pulled her towards the door. Another masked man then appeared and the two of them tied Kate's wrists together and dragged her out of the house. As she was being taken away, Kate screamed and cried: 'I will never come back.' Her dead body was found about a half mile away in a lane at Drumscor the following morning. She had been shot five times. A neighbour said that pinned to her shoulder was a paper bearing the words, written in blue pencil, 'Spies and Informers beware. Convicted – IRA.'

The matter was raised in the House of Commons on 19 April. Replying to Sir W. Davison, Mr Denis Henry said that recently Miss Carroll wrote some letters to the police concerning illicit drink traffic in the neighbourhood. 'These letters were captured from the local postman by members of the Irish Republican Army, and this capture was the cause of her death.' He added: 'The murder has caused a feeling of terror in the district, and every effort is being made, and will be made, to bring the murderers to justice.'[14]

In a statement in 1954 to the BMH, James McKenna, who was at that time a Garda Superintendent in Bandon, County Cork, recalled events in 1921, when he was O/C, North Monaghan Brigade of the IRA.[15] He stated: 'Dr Con Ward was Brigade I/O [Intelligence Officer] and it was as a result of the information received by him that a direction was given by Gen. O'Duffy for the execution of spies. Two were executed in my area by this procedure, Arthur Treanor in Bragan Company area and Kitty Carroll, Knockatallon area. The proof against the latter was very strong. She was scarcely normal and was not sufficiently intelligent to cloak her activities. On the other hand, Arthur Treanor was intelligent and shrewd and more difficult to involve.'

Superintendent McKenna's description of Kate Carroll as being 'scarcely normal' and 'not sufficiently intelligent to cloak her activities' indicates that, remindful of the accounts that have emerged of Bridget Noble, she was a rather simple, naive person. As Ms Carroll was engaged in the production of illicit spirits, she may have been seen as involved in anti-social behaviour, and thus an 'outsider' in the world of

Catholic nationalist respectability. As in the case of Mrs Noble and Mrs Lindsay, there is no indication that the decision to execute Kate Carroll was referred to IRA GHQ. While Bridget Noble had the benefit of the rites of the church before being put to death, it is not known if the IRA men who shot Kate Carroll had a priest on stand-by in the lane at Drumscor to minister to her in her final moments.

Charlie O'Neill, a Volunteer who was in prison when Kate Carroll was executed, said later that it was now thought 'that one of the Volunteers himself was an informer but deliberately shifted the blame on to Kate Carroll who was condemned by a secret court martial'. He said the killing brought a wave of revulsion against the IRA. O'Neill's own family blamed him for the sudden death of his father the following year, believing that this was 'a judgement on them' for allowing a family member to be in an organisation that had killed a hapless neighbour.[16]

Dublin Castle and Bridget Noble

Close on twelve weeks after the abduction of Bridget Noble, the press publicity department at Dublin Castle drew up a statement or briefing note for the newspapers headlined 'Sinn Fein War Against Women'.[17] Mrs Noble figured briefly in the statement, but it is unclear to what extent the material was actually used by the press. The disappearance of Bridget Noble still seemed to attract little publicity. The archives of many newspapers in Ireland and Britain have become available online, and a search of digitised files for 1921 gives no indication that the brief paragraph about the missing Beara woman figured in these publications. There were many other incidents at this period to grab the attention of newspapers. The statement in which Mrs Noble is mentioned is in a folder marked 'Dublin Castle Statements, May 1921' and there is a handwritten note on the document, 'File issued May 26, 1921.'

The statement was drawn up by the Public Information Department at Dublin Castle, headed by an extremely skilled publicist, Basil Clarke. A native of the Manchester area, he had been a notable war correspondent during the Great War, and became one of the pioneers of the public relations industry. Short, bespectacled, energetic and feisty, he was pro-active in seeking to promote the British government's viewpoint on Irish issues. According to his obituary in *The Times*, during the period he worked at Dublin Castle, 'several attempts were made on his life but he remained at his post'.[18] The Anglo-Irish War was being fought not just with guns but with words. Each side sought to publicise the misdeeds of the other. The Irish nationalist/republican side was well served by skilled publicists such as

194

Desmond Fitzgerald, who served as Dáil director of publicity, and by Erskine Childers who succeeded him in that post. (Sons of both men would later gain prominence in Irish life – Desmond's son Garret became Taoiseach and Erskine's son, Erskine junior, became President of Ireland.)

During the War of Independence, Fitzgerald and Childers had plenty of issues to highlight, thanks to the more nefarious activities of Auxiliaries and Black and Tans. (In November 1920, there were two notorious incidents in which women died as a result of gunfire from crown forces. In County Galway, a pregnant mother-of-three, Ellen Quinn, was fatally injured by a shot fired from a police convoy as it drove by. A military court of inquiry recorded a verdict of 'death by misadventure' concluding that Mrs Quinn was hit by one of a number of shots fired as 'a precautionary measure'. Local Parish Priest, Rev John Considine concluded that the killing was either 'murder or manslaughter'.[19] In Dublin, Jane [Jennie] Boyle, aged 26 years, was one of 14 civilians who died after crown forces opened fire during a football match at Croke Park on Bloody Sunday.)

The Dublin Castle statement referred to a number of recent controversial incidents, including the shooting by the IRA of Mrs Lindsay and Kate Carroll. It also mentioned the deaths of two other women, Winifred Barrington and Lily Blake, who were fatally injured in separate incidents when the IRA launched attacks on members of the crown forces. In Youghal, County Cork a young woman, Essie Sheehan suffered serious gunshot wounds and one of her male companions, a young man called Tom Collins, was killed when gunmen opened fire on a group who had attended a dance in the town's military barracks. In Kilgarvan, near Kenmare, County Kerry, a young woman, Susan Sullivan, was taken from her aunt's home at night and paraded by torchlight through the town, after which her hair was shorn off and shots fired around her. It was alleged she had been talking to the police.

There were also references in the statement to livestock being taken from the West Cork farms of widows whose husbands had been shot by the IRA. It was stated that armed men had driven off all the livestock of Mrs Good whose husband John had been killed – her son William, a student in Trinity College Dublin and former British Army officer, returned home from Dublin for the funeral and then he, too, was killed as a 'spy' by the IRA. It was also stated that the livestock had been taken from the land of Mrs Sweetnam, referred to above, and a ban imposed on her selling or leasing the land. According to the statement, intruders had taken the furniture from the home of Mrs Connell, whose husband had also been shot, as mentioned above.

In regard to Mrs Noble, the statement said:

Mrs Bridget Noble of Ardgroom, County Cork, lived with her father who was 80 years of age. On March 4th she was kidnapped by Sinn Feiners and the police have not received any information as to her fate. The outrage was committed because Mrs Noble was a loyalist. Her father has been removed to the workhouse as there was no one left to look after him.

As already outlined, Mrs Noble had dealings with the RIC and the indications are that she gave the police the names of seven IRA Volunteers whom she accused of the 'bobbing' attack on her. These factors could explain the rather simplistic description of 'loyalist' applied to her, although once again one wonders if she really had any strong political views or an understanding of the politics of the period. The possibility also arises that the writer of the statement assumed, from her surname, that she was a Protestant – it was an era when 'Protestant' and 'loyalist' were virtually synonymous in the minds of some. The 1911 Census shows that the overwhelming majority of people with the name Noble in Ireland were Protestant.[20] To the extent that Bridget Noble's Catholic family had political leanings, they were probably nationalist, to judge by her sister Dora's activities in America. It is noteworthy that Dora, as explained above, was a member of the Ladies auxiliary of the Ancient Order of Hibernians (AOH) in New Hampshire and, in 1919, donated money to a fund organised by the Friends of Irish Freedom in support of Irish independence. Many Irish-Americans involved in the Democratic Party were also members of the AOH. Meanwhile, the IRA's war with the crown forces ended with a Truce in July 1921, but Ireland would later be torn apart by internecine strife, and the Beara peninsula would not escape the violence.

Chapter 18: Release of Prisoners

There was a period of calm on the Beara peninsula following the July 1921 Truce in the War of Independence. There was, however, trouble on the horizon and some of those linked to the Bridget Noble drama would experience some very turbulent times. But at least for a while, members of the Beara Battalion could afford to unwind, although, like IRA units around the country, the Battalion maintained its organisational structure and continued to train its members, so that Volunteers would be in a state of readiness if hostilities resumed. Around the time of the Truce, the IRA brigade structure in West Cork was re-organised, with the brigade being split into the Cork No. 3 and Cork No. 5 Brigades, as mentioned. The No. 5 Brigade, encompassing the Beara Battalion, or 5th Battalion, covered the western section of what was formerly the No. 3 Brigade, and included Castletownbere, Bantry, Skibbereen, Schull and Drimoleague. Mícheál Óg O'Sullivan joined the staff of the No. 5 Brigade and held the post of Operations Officer.

In contrast with the drama and challenges of the recent guerrilla campaign, IRA men on the Beara peninsula who were members of public bodies such as the local Rural District Council (RDC) were now concentrating on rather more mundane matters. At a meeting of the Castletownbere RDC in September 1921, the attendance included Mícheál Óg O'Sullivan, Sean O'Driscoll, Mark Sullivan and Christopher O'Connell, all active members of the republican army. One of the items they discussed was the employment of two local men on the steamrolling of a road in the Rossmacowen district. They also heard that Mr Kelly, the cottage rent collector, had reported that two of the tenants had not paid their rent.[1] It was all routine, non-sensational stuff – but also a clear sign that normality was prevailing.

After the Truce, there was also time for social events. Mícheál Óg O'Sullivan, in particular, liked to socialise and to take on the role of entertainer. Like his brother Pronnséas, an academic in Germany who was himself an accomplished Irish dancer, Mícheál Óg seemed to have an artistic temperament. His speciality was the recitation, a popular art form at the time, which could involve considerable feats of memory and acting skills, as the performer recited a long poem, that was either humorous or told a story full of melodrama, and in which the lines always rhymed. His public speaking skills had probably been enhanced during his time at St Enda's by taking part in at least one drama production overseen by Pearse. Mícheál Óg was one of the performers when an aeríocht (open-air concert) was held in a scenic valley known as Coomhola, in an Irish-speaking area between Glengarriff and Bantry, on Sunday, 21 August 1921. Songs, recitations, Irish dancing, all formed part of the festivities on the day, and it was recorded that Mícheál Óg gave a recitation.[2]

The following Sunday, Mícheál Óg attended another concert, this time in Bantry, in aid of republicans who were still being held prisoner by the British. The event in the local Town Hall was organised by Cumann na mBan and once again Mícheál Óg's contribution to the merriment was to give a recitation.[3] He also seems to have had some sporting prowess and skill with the hurley, and at the Castletownbere Sports held on Sunday 18 September, it was recorded that Mícheál Óg O'Sullivan came second in the 'Hurley Puck'.[4] This was a contest designed to test the skill and strength of a hurler, and how far he could hit the hurling ball known as a sliotar.

The RIC Disbands

It was a period when the IRA moved to set up its own police force, the Irish Republican Police, and there are indications that Patrick Malvey from Ardgroom became the Beara Battalion's Chief of Police, and that part of his role was the maintenance of order at Sinn Féin court hearings.[5] He was a member of Ardgroom Company, as was his brother James Malvey who, as previously indicated, was one of the Volunteers said to have questioned Nora Sullivan about Bridget Noble's complaint to the police about the 'bobbing' attack. As for the RIC, the Truce of July 1921 meant that District Inspector Oates, who gave evidence at the compensation hearing arising out of Mrs Noble's death, had some respite from the stress engendered by IRA offensive operations. However, the end was near for the force in which he made his career – the RIC would be effectively disbanded by April 1922, with the process being formally completed the following August. Even before disbandment, in West Cork in particular, the force had lost control of large areas outside the main towns. A minority of former policemen would go on to join the Civic Guard, some pursued other career options in Ireland or decided to live off their pensions, while there were also those who decided to leave the country.

The RIC authorities sent out various circulars informing the men of opportunities to emigrate to Canada, Australia, New Zealand, South Africa or Rhodesia, and also of the possibility of joining the RUC in Northern Ireland or the Palestine Gendarmerie, or the Royal Air Force. In the latter case, it was stated that service would be 'anywhere in the world, probably in Palestine or Mesopotamia'. As the RIC men prepared to move out of their stations for the last time, they received an instruction from the RIC Office in Dublin Castle, dated 27 March 1922, to destroy their files, except for certain records to be sent to headquarters. Among the items to be destroyed were 'Register of Evicted Farms', 'Crime and Offence Registers', 'Patrol Diaries (Confidential)', and 'All Correspondence'.[6] It may be the case that among the correspondence destroyed at Castletownbere was a letter from Mrs Noble naming the men she accused of the punishment attack on her.

Meanwhile, a few months before he was pensioned off from the disbanding RIC, District Inspector Oates suffered the indignity of having his bicycle stolen. According to an internal RIC report, the bicycle was taken on the night of 23/24 October 1921 from an outhouse attached to his lodgings in Castletownbere. The report added: 'It is believed that the machine was taken by members of IRA.'[7] It could be seen as a breach of the Truce, as it had been agreed there would be 'no interference with government or private property', but at least nobody died. More serious breaches of the Truce would occur in various parts of Ireland. There would be a series of murders of men who had served in the RIC, and police families and retired policemen would face intimidation, and threats designed to force them from their homes.[8]

To give one example, according to an internal police report, on 31 October 1921 a number of armed men tried to force their way into the West Cork home of Mrs [Amelia] Johnston, widow of an RIC sergeant, who resided at the house with her four daughters. The report claimed that the motive for the attack was to force Mrs Johnston to clear out of her home at Kilbrittain. The family were Protestant, and Mrs Johnston's son William had been shot dead by the IRA the previous February as an alleged spy – he was found with a bullet in the back of his head. The RIC report noted that police removed Mrs Johnston to Bandon on 1 November.[9]

Claims for Compensation

As the power and authority of the RIC declined, and as the force was ultimately disbanded and the British Army withdrew, those considered Loyalists were left without their traditional means of protection. In

West Cork hundreds of such people, mostly Protestant, would later tell of distress or losses they suffered as part of claims for compensation to the Irish Grants Committee (IGC), set up in London to assist persons such as refugees, Loyalists and former servants of the crown.[10]

One of those who claimed compensation from the IGC was George P. Sullivan who, as previously indicated, came from a Church of Ireland family in Carrigaphrechane, and was probably the last Protestant Loyalist remaining in Ardgroom Inward in 1921. He was the son of Paddy 'Sylvie' Sullivan and his wife Abigail also known as Gobnait who married in 1869 and were native speakers of Irish. Paddy seems to have been a dedicated church activist. He was a teacher of scripture in various parts of Ireland and was also a teacher in the Church of Ireland school at Reenavaude.[11] Apparently Paddy's own father Sylvester had converted from Catholicism to the Church of Ireland around 1848. (A few years earlier, in 1843, a minister of the church had a scary experience after conducting a service in Ardgroom. The Rev. Charles Henry Seymour was returning to Castletownbere when he was attacked by a stone-throwing mob, but managed to escape on his horse. Seven men were later jailed. It appears that they objected to the presence of a Protestant minister in the Ardgroom area.)

One of the sons of Paddy Sylvie and Gobnait was called Patrick. Like another man from Ardgroom Inward, the afore-mentioned James Bartley Shea, Patrick went on to study at Trinity College Dublin and was awarded an honours BA degree. Like Shea, Patrick became a Church of Ireland minister, often making use of Irish language skills. The Rev. Patrick Sullivan [Pádraig Ó Súilleabháin] wrote articles and poetry in Irish and died during the 1918 influenza epidemic. When he was being laid to rest in a County Antrim cemetery, one of his clerical confreres, Rev. Frederick O'Connell [Feardorcha Ó Conaill], a native Irish speaker from County Galway, said prayers in Irish over the grave.[12]

Three other sons of Paddy Sylvie joined the Royal Navy, including George, who served as a stoker. George purchased his discharge from the navy in 1908, and returned to Beara to run the family farm. George stated in his IGC application that in 1921 he refused an invitation to 'join the rebels'. He implied that this refusal was the catalyst for the harassment that would follow. He attributed the losses that he suffered to his 'allegiance to the UK government'. (This declaration was a requirement in order to qualify for compensation.) He also referred to his membership of the Church of Ireland, but his handwriting is partly illegible and it is unclear if he is arguing that this was a factor in the losses that he suffered. From his own account his problems began in

February-March 1921, with the seizure of two bicycles and a raincoat, and the incurring of other losses. (This was, of course, the same period when Bridget Noble was 'bobbed' at her home in the same townland and then abducted and executed.)

George's testimony suggests he was a victim of 'forced billeting'. A member of the Cork No. 3 Brigade's Active Service Unit told of a policy of billeting men, when possible, on 'wealthy loyalists'.[13] (It appears that not all the 'loyalists' were wealthy. Alice Bevan, a Church of Ireland spinster who lived near Dunmanway and worked as a domestic servant, told in her IGC compensation claim how 13 men arrived at her home in September 1921 and, 'under threat' demanded supper and bed overnight.[14]) George Sullivan, in his IGC application, referred to 'extortion of food, drink, firing & light' over a period of more than a year, from 21 March 1921 to the end of April 1922. He also claimed for the loss of five sheep and loss of fowl, the destruction of doors, windows and furniture, as well as the destruction of gate pillars; the loss of £75 on 30 September 1921 and other losses, including the robbery of £5 in April 1922. He claimed for 'destruction of fences in meadow land' on 14 July 1921, and claimed that this [destruction] 'continued up to July 8th 1923'. He stated that he received compensation of £7 from the Irish [Free State] Government and £20 from the Southern Irish Loyalists Relief Association.

At the time of George Sullivan's application to the IGC in December 1924, he stated that his income from all sources was only £1 a week, and that he was 'engaged among the Romanists [Catholics] in the circulation and teaching of God's Holy Word, the Holy Scriptures'. Such missionary activities may not have gone down well with some elements in a strongly Catholic community and may have made him unpopular. His application to the IGC was for £472.18.6 and was ultimately awarded, in 1927, the sum of £50.[15] Unlike other co-religionists who left Ireland as a result of their experiences during the revolutionary period, George P. Sullivan continued to reside in the Ardgroom area and died in a Cork hospital in January 1946 aged 66 years – he was unmarried.

The Report

Meanwhile, in the latter part of 1921, the spectre of Bridget Noble still hung over the leadership of the Beara Battalion and in October that year, as mentioned, battalion commandant Liam O'Dwyer was asked by IRA GHQ in Dublin for information about the whereabouts of the missing woman. O'Dwyer presumably consulted with other members of the Beara Battalion during the few days it took to write the report, which explained that the woman from Reenavaude had been executed seven months previously. (The report is very brief, less than 500 words.) One could speculate that O'Dwyer talked to the two men who became officers of Ardgroom Company and who were mentioned in his report – the Company O/C [John Sheehan] and Pat [Patsy Dan] Crowley, who was to succeed Sheehan as O/C, or Captain. This report to IRA GHQ was, of course, kept private and did not enter the public domain at that time. A copy was preserved in the Military Archives and has become available to researchers in more recent times.

In the more relaxed atmosphere that prevailed among republicans during the Truce, the afore-mentioned John Sheehan found time to get married to a fellow activist. Sheehan and Julia O'Sullivan, Secretary of Ardgroom Cumann na mBan, were wed at the Catholic church in Ardgroom on Friday, 10 November 1921, with the parish priest, Father Daly officiating. In the marriage registration certificate, the bride is described as a shopkeeper, residing at Ardgroom, daughter of Mortimer Sullivan, also a shopkeeper, while the groom is stated to be a farmer resident at Canfie, Ardgroom, son of Jeremiah Sheehan, also a farmer.

Internees Return Home

There was an important development when, just before Christmas 1921, men from the Beara Battalion who had been interned were released by the British. Among them, according to a local newspaper report, were John Dwyer of Kaelroe [Cailroe] and Michael Sullivan, Ardgroom. (As mentioned previously, in the IRA report on the fate of Bridget Noble, it was outlined how John Dwyer and Michael Sullivan had been incarcerated following the 'bobbing' of Mrs Noble.) Dwyer and Sullivan were among 32 former captives who received a warm welcome from relatives and well-wishers when they arrived aboard the steamer *Princess Beara* in Castletownbere on Saturday, 17 December.[16] As well as Michael Sullivan, his two brothers Eugene and Peter were also among the released prisoners. Also on the ship were the four men taken prisoner along with John Dwyer in the roundup on 4 March, the same day that Bridget Noble was abducted – Michael Sullivan, Eyeries; Mortimer McCarthy, Ballycrovane; John Shea, Ardgroom and James McCarthy, Boffickil, Eyeries. Of these four, Shea would apparently stay in Ireland while the other three would later emigrate to America.[17]

Another former prisoner on the vessel was James Malvey, mentioned previously in connection with Bridget Noble. Another man who was released from prison was Eugene Dunne, from Adrigole, who had himself worked for the steamship company operating the ferry. He was not with the other released prisoners who arrived in port – it was stated that he had broken his journey to meet friends, and would arrive home later. He was a cousin of Mícheál Óg O'Sullivan and had been released from Maryborough Prison (now Portlaoise Prison) on 8 December.[18] Dunne (1888 – 1968) had a sister, Margaret Dunne, who was a member of Cumann na mBan – as will be explained, she would later be shot dead during the Civil War. Henry Wills from Allihies, son of an RIC pensioner, was another internee who was released and who sailed into Castletownbere on the *Princess Beara*. The atmosphere in the port was relaxed, and it was said that even some of the crown forces joined in the festive spirit as the ship docked. The *Cork Examiner* reported that some imperial troops, leaving the pier in a military motor boat, 'joined in the welcome'.[19]

The British had begun releasing internees following the signing of the Anglo-Irish Treaty between the British and an Irish delegation in December. On the Beara peninsula, a correspondent for the *Cork Examiner* reported, in early January 1922, that he had interviewed 'people representing every interest in the town of Castletown and the surrounding country', and that there 'appears to be an overwhelming majority in favour of the ratification of the Treaty...' He went on: 'Very Rev. Canon Hayes has expressed himself warmly in favour of the Treaty and so has every other one of the clergy of the Deanery.'[20] (The Beara Deanery comprised the parishes of Castletownbere, Eyeries, Adrigole and Allihies.) The following March, Canon Hayes presided at a public meeting in Castletownbere in support of the Treaty.[21]

As crown forces evacuated their bases following the signing of the Treaty, IRA personnel moved in to occupy the vacated buildings. The process of taking over the facilities was overseen at national level by Commandant Emmet Dalton, who had become Evacuations Officer, in addition to his duties as Chief Liaison Officer. In Castletownbere, the IRA occupied the police station and coastguard station. The police station had been vacated by the RIC in February 1922. The coastguard station, which had been in charge of a British Admiralty caretaker since the signing of the Treaty, was formally handed over by Commander May (Royal Navy) to Captain Hughes, acting on behalf of the Provisional Government, in mid-April 1922. Hughes, who would have been an emissary of Emmet Dalton, then handed over the coastguard buildings to Liam O'Dwyer, Commandant of the Beara Battalion.[22] The local Volunteers had few resources at the time, and received assistance from Cumann na mBan. A local member of that organisation, Margaret O'Neill, would recall later the situation in the earlier part of 1922: 'At this time, IRA were quartered in town, awaiting taking over of barracks. I provided food and clothes for them as they had no money.' She kept some men in her own home 'and from time to time cooked food for men when in barracks before it was properly in order.'[23]

Tension over the Anglo-Irish Treaty

While the Treaty was producing tangible results, such as the release of prisoners and the withdrawal of British forces, tension was mounting between pro- and anti-Treaty elements of a formerly united republican movement. Under the Treaty, Ireland would become a self-governing dominion within the British Empire or Commonwealth. The six-county state of Northern Ireland which had been set up prior to the Treaty talks under Westminster's Government of Ireland Act, 1920, could opt to join up with the south. If not, the boundaries of Northern Ireland would be decided by a Boundary Commission. The northern state, with its Protestant Unionist majority, was destined to remain part of the United Kingdom.

A major focus of the debate on the Treaty was on the oath of allegiance, which members of the Dáil and Senate were required to take. The first part declared allegiance to the Irish Free State. The second part declared that the person taking the oath would be 'faithful' to the King and his heirs. (This was often described inaccurately as an 'oath of allegiance to the King' – that phrase does not occur in the oath. Pro-Treaty leader W.T. Cosgrave took the view that one can be 'faithful' to an equal, and that this did not equate to having 'allegiance' to that person. Liam Lynch, who would lead anti-Treaty forces in the Civil War, was initially equivocal towards the Treaty, remarking in a letter to his brother Tom: 'There is no allegiance asked to the British empire, only to be faithful to it.'[24])

The King remained as head of state and while some may have seen this as a mere formality, it was anathema to militant republicans. The Treaty also had a provision that allowed British forces to maintain a presence in three 'Treaty ports' – Berehaven, Queenstown [Cobh] and Lough Swilly. Anti-Treaty republicans considered that the deal fell short of the 32-country republic that had been declared in 1916. Free State leader Michael Collins argued that it was the best deal that could be achieved, and was a 'stepping stone' to the republic.

After a heated and highly emotional debate, the Dáil approved the Treaty by a narrow majority of seven votes on 7 January 1922. Éamon de Valera, who had led the political opposition to the Treaty, resigned as Dáil President. Subsequently, in June 1922, a general election was held following a pact between de Valera and Collins. The result was a landslide vote against the anti-Treaty candidates – they won only 36 out of 128 seats. The historian Ronan Fanning has observed that without the pact the anti-Treaty side would have done even worse – it enabled 17 of them to be elected unopposed; no anti-Treaty candidate topped the poll in any contested constituency.[25] The result indicated strong public support for the parties and candidates that were pro-Treaty or were at least prepared to take their seats in the 'Free State' Dáil, and bolstered the sense of legitimacy of the 'Free Staters', as they became known.

Gathering Intelligence

In January 1922 the Beara Battalion (now, as mentioned, designated as the 5th Battalion of the Cork No. 5 Brigade), in common with other IRA battalions in counties Cork, Kerry and Waterford and in West Limerick, drew up intelligence reports on suspect civilians for the 1st Southern Division headquarters.[26] The Division sought the information amid concerns that hostilities could resume. Officers of the various battalions filled in forms giving information about persons considered guilty of assisting the British forces during the War of Independence, or suspected of having assisted the enemy. Photographs of suspects were rarely available and so descriptions of physical features of suspects were included. It was not unusual for the male writers of the reports from the various battalions, when describing female suspects, to include comments on their looks. Some women were described as 'good looking' or 'not bad looking' and in one case the writer ungallantly described a woman as 'ugly'.

A person did not have to be suspected of being a spy or an informer to be the subject of an intelligence report. Lizzie Sullivan from Glengarriff made it into a report drawn up by the 4th Battalion of the Cork No. 5 Brigade because of a disparaging remark she made about IRA members and their low social status, comparing them unfavourably with the status of the Auxiliaries [former British Army officers] who had been based in Glengarriff. She made the comment privately in a letter to a friend, and it appears that the letter was intercepted by the IRA. Listed under the heading 'offence' was her remark that though the Auxiliaries had left, they couldn't be compared with their successors, the IRA, 'who were no class'. The report described her as 'good looking, dreamy eyes'. Another woman named O'Sullivan, who was apparently a priest's housekeeper from Adrigole, was the subject of a Beara Battalion report because it appeared that she was friendly towards Auxiliaries in Glengarriff while making a two-day visit to the town in February 1921. Once again, the evidence seemed to be based on a letter that had been intercepted. As regards her appearance, the writer described her in unflattering terms as having 'thin features' and a 'long crooked nose'.

In the case of one young woman from the Castletownbere area, Ms O'Halloran, the report by the Beara Battalion alleged: 'This girl was always in company of the police, especially in the past two years. She was always hostile to the Volunteers.' As regards evidence of any offence [i.e. spying or informing], the report stated: 'We have no evidence in this case, except the evidence of suspicion.' One of the witnesses was named as William O'Neill of Castletownbere (an apparent reference to the man who was Captain of the IRA's Company in the town, and who became known as 'Billy the Kid', as mentioned.) The other witness was Michael Sullivan, also of Castletownbere. (It is unclear if this is the Michael Sullivan who was a member of Castletownbere Company and was wounded in the IRA attack on the local coastguard station in 1921.) The comments made about this suspect were stated to apply to two other young women from the Castletownbere area named in separate reports, Ms Neill, aged about 30 years (described as 'good looking' and Ms Mahony, aged 18 years (also said to be 'good looking' with 'fair curly hair'). William O'Neill was also a witness in the case of Ms Mahony. Unlike the case of Bridget Noble, there is no indication that these three females were subjected to a punishment attack for their contacts with the RIC and their hostility towards the Volunteers.

A fourth young woman from the Castletownbere district, Ms Sullivan, aged 20 years, who was the subject of an intelligence report, was said to have been 'always in company with Lt. Hatton-Hall while he was stationed at Furious Pier'. The report went on: 'The only evidence in this case is that it looked very suspicious that this girl would be always in the company of the above-named officer, who was Intelligence Officer for this district.' The witnesses in this case were Jerh Barry, Derrymihan and John Lowney, Castletownbere. The officer in question was obviously Lieutenant Hubert Christopher Hatton-Hall of the King's Own Scottish Borderers (KOSB) – as mentioned, three soldiers from this regiment based at Furious Pier had been shot dead by the IRA in May 1921, leading to the reprisal destruction of a number of houses in Beara.

Once again, it is noteworthy that while Bridget Noble was targeted after various developments, especially her visits to the RIC station in Castletownbere and conversations with a police sergeant on two occasions in a private house in the town, no action seems to have been taken against the young woman who was said to have been constantly 'in the company' of a British Army intelligence officer. Let us assume for a moment that Mrs Noble was subjected to a hair-shearing punishment attack due to her contacts with members of the crown forces, while the death sentence was attributable primarily to the accusation of informing on the alleged culprits who 'bobbed' her, and perhaps to a lesser extent, to the accusation that she informed on the alleged killers of William Lehane. In this scenario, it is unclear why republicans responsible for the punishment attack apparently felt far more provoked by Mrs Noble's activities than those of Ms Sullivan who seems to have been the constant companion of Lt. Hatton-Hall. Was Bridget Noble considered more of a threat? Or was there something about Bridget, in terms of her personality, background or marital status, that singled her out for particular attention?

Other questions arise. Ms Sullivan and the other 'errant' young single women who figured in the Beara Battalion intelligence reports, and who apparently escaped IRA punishment, were all from the Castletownbere area, on the southern side of the Beara peninsula. On the other hand, the older woman, Bridget Noble, who suffered a 'bobbing' attack, the prelude to her death, came from the northern side of Beara. Were senior members of the Beara Battalion based on the northern side of the peninsula, around Eyeries and Ardgroom, particularly offended by the idea of a woman from their own locality mixing with the crown forces? Were they more aggressive in pursuing a woman from their own area who had offended, while a softer approach was taken to the younger female 'offenders' from the Castletowbere area?

(From a territorial point of view, the Beara Battalion was organised partly on the basis of northern and southern elements, and the appointment of staff officers seems to have been based partly on territorial considerations. At the time of Mrs Noble's disappearance, major elements of the battalion leadership, comprising the Commandant and the Quartermaster, were based on the northern side of the peninsula, while the Adjutant was located in Castletownbere on the southern side, and the Vice Commandant was based in Adrigole, to the east.)

Returning to the subject of the above-mentioned British intelligence officer, Hubert Christopher Hatton-Hall, records show that he was was born in 1892, the only son of an army officer who lived in Devon. Hatton-Hall won the Military Cross for bravery in the Great War, during which he became Intelligence Officer of 4 Tank Brigade.[27] His military record indicates that he was based in Ireland in 1921.[28] He was, apparently, a handsome, dashing young officer who, unfortunately, figured in a widely-reported court case in England in that same year of 1921. He had won the heart of a young woman with Irish connections residing in the seaside town of Teignmouth, Devon with the memorable name of Honoria Mary Maud O'Shaughnessy. They met at a dance in Torquay in 1919 while he was home on leave from Germany and became engaged. Then, to her dismay, he decided that it would be unwise for them to marry. She brought a case to the High Court for breach of promise of marriage and Mr Justice Avory ordered Hatton-Hall to pay her £300 damages.[29] After this bruising and costly experience with the feisty Ms O'Shaughnessy, it seems the officer sought the consolation of other female company while based in Castletownbere, causing concern to members of the Beara Battalion.

Hatton-Hall returned to England in 1922 and married a young English woman. Once again, there were difficulties in his private life, and the union ended in divorce. Hatton-Hall, now a Lieutenant-Colonel, would die while undergoing an operation in a London hospital in 1945. His son Nigel, also a KOSB officer, became a Catholic convert and in 1955, at Brompton Oratory, London, married devout fellow-Catholic Chiara Kendall, a socialite with Anglo-Irish connections whose father Charles had been a Royal Artillery officer on Bere Island in the late 1920s. Chiara ran a riding school in Kent, and Princess Anne was one of her pupils. After Nigel died, Chiara became a Franciscan nun and travelled the world teaching instructors how to train disabled adults and children to ride. She told her remarkable story in a 2013 memoir, *The Galloping Nun* (Paragon Publishing).

Turning again to the situation in Beara in early 1922, trouble was brewing once again, this time between Irish people who differed over the Anglo-Irish Treaty, and it would have serious consequences for some of those linked to the Bridget Noble affair.

Chapter 19: Rejecting the Treaty

L iam O'Dwyer was one of those republicans who totally rejected the Anglo-Irish Treaty and he was less than impressed by the outcome of the 1922 general election. The fact that it had gone heavily against the anti-Treaty side did not come as any surprise to him. As mentioned, he believed that during the War of Independence only a 'minority' were 'wholeheartedly behind us', and that most always favoured peace 'at any price'.[1] As regards the election result, he wrote: 'Most of the IRA members, who were now in intensive training for a resumption of hostilities, ignored the plebiscite. All these men knew from experience of the people's attitude during the struggle years that the pro-Treaty Party would win, and win they did.'[2] He seemed to have little confidence in the ability of the Irish people to make the correct decision, and appeared convinced that a patriotic, brave and wise elite, the IRA, would have to press forward with the fight, regardless of whether or not their campaign or their methods had public support.

He believed that the IRA should never have given its allegiance to the Sinn Féin political party 'who were depending on the votes of the people'. He certainly did not feel himself bound by the vote in the June 1922 election, or the 'plebiscite' as he described it, with a note of disdain. Liam Deasy, a prominent figure in the anti-Treaty IRA in West Cork, took a similarly dismissive view of the election result. In his book *Brother Against Brother*, Deasy remarked that 'from the first by-election of 1917 we were never unduly influenced by election results'.[3] O'Dwyer and Deasy came from a physical force tradition, rather than a tradition dominated by constitutional and parliamentary procedures, or by reverence for the ballot box. The historian Richard English commented on IRA thinking at this period: 'Many in the IRA saw their role as that of a vanguard protecting the prior rights of the Irish nation, an army that led rather than followed popular opinion.'[4]

The Truce was still in force, but O'Dwyer was one of those hardline republicans who urged that hostilities be resumed against British forces 'wherever they remained in any part of Ireland'. This meant attacking British naval and other forces which, under the terms of the Treaty, maintained a presence in Berehaven. O'Dwyer described in his memoir how he sent a dispatch to anti-Treaty IRA headquarters urging that hostilities be resumed against the British.[5] The matter was apparently then referred to the 1st Southern Division, of which the Beara Battalion formed part. Meanwhile, he decided to mount an attack anyway, showing that as a local commander, he tended to make up his own mind about such matters, rather than waiting for, or heeding, a decision from further up the chain of command. If those from the Beara Battalion who decided the fate of Bridget Noble followed a similar tendency, it could help to explain why her case was not referred to a higher authority in the IRA, as required by IRA rules.

O'Dwyer described how he and Christy O'Connell spotted a British sloop in the Kenmare River that, he said, had shelled an IRA training post a few days earlier. On their own initiative, they opened fire on the vessel, and the following day they learned that they had killed two men and wounded five, one of whom died after being taken into Bere Island Camp. In his statement to the BMH he says that this incident happened 'after the attack on the Four Courts' – the courts assault began on 28 June 1922 and is generally seen as the start of the Civil War. However, he states in his memoir that the incident in which they fired on the naval vessel occurred on 18 June, before the start of the Civil War. In his Military Service Pension application, he gives the date as 23 September. O'Dwyer observed in his memoir that the proposal to attack the British was defeated in a ballot at an IRA convention. [The convention was held in Dublin on 18 June]. Nevertheless, O'Dwyer decided to continue with his attacks on the British. He had the belief, which may be seen as unrealistic, that such attacks would heal the rift between the pro- and anti-Treaty sides and unite them against a common foe. He stated that 'we were determined to continue our attacks on the British military and navy at every opportunity, in the hope that the Army Council would change their attitude and prevent Civil War'.[6] O'Dwyer's over-ambitious attempt to re-unite the divided IRA through a localised attack on the British forces proved fruitless.

As indicated above, it was on 28 June that the Civil War started in earnest and would continue for close on a year. On that date, the National Army of Michael Collins's Provisional Government opened artillery fire on the Four Courts complex in Dublin. Republican forces had set up their headquarters at the Four Courts in April in defiance of the government's authority, and had rejected an ultimatum to evacuate the buildings. The British had put pressure on the Provisional Government to act against the Four Courts garrison. But even without British pressure, it may only have been a matter of time before the two sides engaged in serious conflict – republicans had been robbing banks, procuring arms and engaging in sporadic acts of violence. Liam O'Dwyer observed in his book: 'They [the Free State forces] got plenty war material from England and army officers to train their recruits. They got very few of the IRA into their army. Of the Beara Battalion less than thirty men, out of 644, joined the Treaty army.'[7]

Some members of the Battalion, it is unclear how many, took a neutral stance and did not participate in the hostilities that arose as a result of discord over the Treaty. Others may have had only nominal membership of the battalion. None of the battalion staff officers who were in place at the time of Bridget Noble's disappearance took the Free State side, nor did the officers of Ardgroom Company, the unit that covered Mrs Noble's home area. Around the start of the Civil War, the men now in place as officers of Ardgroom Company had all been linked to the Bridget Noble case. According to a record in the Military Archives, the Captain on 1 July 1922 was now Pat [Patsy Dan] Crowley, Glenbeg; the previous Captain, John Sheehan of Canfie, who had been wounded at Crossbarry, was now 1st Lieutenant, and the 2nd Lieutenant was Michael Sullivan, Gurteen, who according to an internal IRA report, had been interned following the 'bobbing' of Mrs Noble – he had resumed IRA activities after his release.[8]

Joining the National Army

While a minority of the Beara Battalion personnel joined the Free State forces, they included some significant fighters, a number of whom had been active with the Flying Column under Tom Barry. Some joined the Provisional Government's new National Army at Skibbereen on 1 May 1922, after the split in the movement. Sean O'Driscoll from Eyeries, who had played a key role in setting up the Volunteers in the Beara peninsula, was one of those who joined the Free State army, becoming an officer and serving until May 1923, according to a former comrade.[9] O'Driscoll had operated with the Flying Column and had taken part in the Crossbarry engagement. His brothers Tim [Tadhg] and Jeremiah [Diarmuid] who had also been active in the IRA as members of Eyeries Company, also joined the Free State army, Tim enrolling at Skibbereen as a Private on 1 May 1922 and Jeremiah joining at Bantry on 19 August. (Sean and Jeremiah, as well as another brother, James, who had likewise been in Eyeries Company, and who had also been with the Flying Column, would go on to serve in the police force, An Garda Síochána, while Tim would emigrate to America.[10])

Another member of the Beara Battalion who joined the Free State forces, becoming an officer, was Patrick Joseph Murphy from Gour, Castletownbere. A member of Castletownbere Company during the War of Independence, he told in his Military Service Pension application how he took part in a number of engagements, and served with the Flying Column at Crossbarry.[11] Yet another battalion member who became an officer in the National Army was Sean T. O'Sullivan, from Croumhane, Eyeries. He wrote later: 'I took the side of law and order, and acted under General Michael Collins, my chief in the IRB [Irish Republican Brotherhood].'[12] Henry Wills, who was listed as an NCO (Non-Commissioned Officer) of Allihies Company of the IRA, and who was one of the released internees who sailed into Castletowbere in December 1921, as indicated above, was one of the Beara Battalion personnel to join the Free State forces. He joined at Skibbereen on 1 May 1922, and was appointed a Company Captain, based in Bantry.

Another of the new Free State officers was 21-year-old Captain Tim Spillane, from the Waterfall area near Castletownbere. He had been a member of the Rossmacowen Company of the Beara Battalion during the War of Independence and, as previously indicated, his family home at Waterfall was destroyed by crown forces after the IRA shot dead three British soldiers in May 1921 – his father, Michael Spillane, would receive compensation of £750 in 1924.[13]

John 'Jackie' McCarthy (aged 20 years), from West End, Castletownbere, was another former Beara Battalion member who went with the Free State, joining the National Army at Skibbereen on 1 May. He was appointed a 2nd Lieutenant. McCarthy had taken a very active role in the War of Independence and had been with the Flying Column at Crossbarry. In local republican circles he was renowned for his narrow escape after being wounded in the attack on Castletownbere coastguard station in 1920. He took refuge in the local hospital and it was reported that the nuns dressed him in bed like a member of their order, and he escaped detection by the British forces who raided the hospital in search of him. A member of the local Cumann na mBan, Margaret O'Neill told later how she arranged for Dr Hayes to provide treatment to McCarthy.[14] As previously indicated, Dr Michael Hayes, Medical Officer of the local Workhouse, had served as a Justice of the Peace – it is unlikely that he would have sympathised with the IRA campaign. Nevertheless, it appears that he wisely maintained confidentiality regarding the medical care he provided to McCarthy. (This Crossbarry veteran would later join Eoin O'Duffy's Irish brigade and fight on the pro-Franco side in the Spanish Civil War. McCarthy was apparently motivated by loyalty to the Catholic church. Both sides committed terrible atrocities but there was much concern in strongly Catholic Ireland about the persecution of the church by left-wing militias. It is estimated that militants executed more than 6,800 priests and religious, as well as nuns and many lay people, with many churches desecrated or destroyed.)

After Tim Spillane joined the Provisional Government forces, he was placed in charge of a small National Army garrison in Castletownbere, and there was soon friction between army personnel and anti-Treaty republicans. (According to a National Army document, an 'Irregular garrison' operated in Berehaven [Castletownbere] 'from March 1st 1922 until Aug. 23rd 1922'.[15] The term 'irregular' was commonly used by the Free State to describe members of the anti-Treaty IRA.) The National Army post was situated in a private house belonging to a Mrs O'Regan. At this stage, before the start of the Civil War, Spillane had the temporary rank of Acting Commandant. According to a National Army statement, the house was raided at 2 o'clock on the morning of 14 May [1922] by armed men 'numbering about twenty of the irregular army'. The raiders demanded at gunpoint an electric exploder. The officers decided to let the raiders take off the exploder 'as they were not in a position to defend the buildings'.[16]

Following the start of the Civil War, it was reported that on the evening of Wednesday, 5 July, a republican force surrounded a house that had been occupied by Free State officers for about a fortnight, outside the East End of Castletownbere. Republican officers entered the house and after discussions that lasted about a half hour, the Free State officers left the building, which was then put under armed guard by the republicans.[17] At this early stage in the Civil War, elements on both sides were often reluctant to inflict casualties on each other. In a statement in his MSP file, Liam O'Dwyer recorded that he 'disarmed Free State section in their billets in Castletownbere, and expelled them from the area'. He also stated that he held up, near Castletownbere, a car occupied by Free State officers from Skibbereen. He 'disarmed and expelled the officers from the area, and held the car'. Liam O'Dwyer's anti-Treaty Beara Battalion seemed now to be in full control of the town and that part of the peninsula covered by the battalion. It was reported that on the night of 4 August, most of the buildings at Furious Pier, the military camp and former naval facility east of Castletownbere that had been evacuated by the British some months previously, were destroyed by fire.[18] From a reference in his afore-mentioned MSP statement, it appears that Liam O'Dwyer was involved in burning the buildings.

Banishment of Former RIC Men

While the Beara Battalion leadership decided that execution rather than banishment would be the fate of Bridget Noble, it is noteworthy that banishment was used in other cases, as mentioned. Two men, Michael

Flynn and John Twomey, who had been sergeants in the RIC, were demobilised from the force at the time of disbandment. The two Catholic men had married Beara women and had settled in the Castletownbere area. They were both forced out of the area by the IRA after the start of the Civil War. As will be shown, during that conflict a prominent local citizen was also banished after giving offence to republicans. The fact that at least three men were ordered to leave raises the question as to why Bridget Noble was not allowed to depart under a similar 'banishment' arrangement, rather than face execution.

Michael Flynn and his wife Annie and family had previously been forced out of their home in Liscannor, County Clare by armed and masked men who gave the former policeman 48 hours to depart. Flynn told later how his wife was extremely upset.[19] There was further trauma in store after the family settled in Castletownbere. Flynn, a native of Castleisland, County Kerry who had served for a period at Adrigole, was handed a typed banishment order, dated 9 July 1922, signed 'L. DWYER, Commandant, 5th Battalion'. The order stated: 'A Chara, You are hereby noticed [sic] that you are to leave this Area within TWENTY-FOUR Hours from receipt of this Order. Failure to comply with above Order will warrant a severe penalty.' (The original document still survives in Britain's National Archives at Kew.) Flynn immediately left Castletownbere, and later crossed to England on 16 July, his distraught wife joining him in Dover, Kent, a few days later.

John Twomey, a native of Ballinhassig, County Cork, was serving at Kenmare when he was demobilised from the RIC. He lived with his wife Mary and family at Derrymihan West, near Castletownbere. In an application for compensation to the Irish Grants Committee (IGC), Twomey said that on 11 July 1922 he 'got a notice from the IRA to clear out within 24 hours'. He left home the following morning and went via Dublin to London, where he stayed in lodgings in Clapham.[20] Before the banishment order was issued, he said that on 29 June the IRA came to his home and told his wife and children to get out of the house 'as they intended burning it'. He said the men 'threw out the best of the furniture', and the eldest child, who was unwell, they brought down in a blanket and 'laid him out in the field'. Because the child was ill, the IRA men changed their minds about burning the house and instead smashed furniture, and damaged other items, including a baby's pram.

Commandeering Supplies

Since the Beara republicans did not have a government to supply them with materiel during the Civil War, they commandeered items they required, and this caused resentment locally. In July, the *Freeman's*

214

Journal reported that a local Catholic woman had two motor cars commandeered by the IRA and that she had a confrontation with a local republican leader when she and her son tried to recover one of the cars after they found it outside the church when they were going to Sunday Mass in Castletownbere. It was also alleged that this leader rounded up all the young men in the town who were supposed to be favourable to the Treaty, including young men who had been in the flying column prior to the Truce. The *Freeman's Journal* reported: 'The Irregulars took all these to the Coastguard Station, where they beat them savagely.'[21]

Daniel T. Sullivan, who was Battalion Quartermaster at the time of Bridget Noble's disappearance, still held that position and one of his roles now was to collect duty on spirits. After the Civil War, Anna Regan Harrington claimed compensation from the state for licence duty 'demanded by Daniel Sullivan, Quartermaster Irish Republican Army at Castletownbere on 25 November 1922'.[22] Henry Harrington of Allihies also claimed compensation, stating he was 'forced to pay licence duty to Irregular forces'. Timothy 'Tade' Kelly, a publican residing in Bridget Noble's area of Ardgroom, claimed compensation for 'spirit duty and fee seized by Irregular forces on 25 November 1923'. (Kelly ran a popular pub, the Holly Bar, in Ardgroom village.)

Other business people sought compensation for having to supply a range of goods, including cigarettes, drink, boots and foodstuffs to 'Irregulars'. John P. Breen of the Millbrook Hotel, Castletownbere, made a claim in relation to the 'commandeering of food and goods' by Irregular forces between 10 October and 13 Dec 1922. People also claimed for bicycles and at least one motor cycle that were commandeered. Jeremiah O'Connor of The Terrace, Castletownbere, claimed for 'a mare commandeered at Eyeries by armed Irregulars', in January 1923. Arthur Cecil Carey of the Munster & Leinster Bank in Castletownbere sought compensation for 'seizure of cash by unidentified armed men on 28 August 1922'. He also claimed in relation to the seizure of cash by 'uniformed men' on 23 October 1923.

The Landings

The anti-Treaty forces in Munster suffered a devastating blow in August 1922. Their nemesis was 24-year-old Emmet Dalton who, as previously indicated, had functioned as the IRA's Chief Liaison Officer, and in that role had been notified of Bridget Noble's disappearance. Now he was a Major General in the Provisional Government's National Army, or the 'Free State Army' as it was colloquially known. In early August he led a four-ship seaborne invasion of Cork city and county, ousting the anti-Treaty forces from their last major stronghold, sometimes dubbed 'The Munster Republic'. Ultimately, the Free State forces would penetrate even into the remote territory of the Beara Battalion.

As Dalton sailed into Cork Harbour, he availed of the advice and local knowledge of his orderly officer, Captain Frank O'Friel, from Howth, County Dublin. O'Friel had spent part of his youth in the Cork Harbour area, where his father was a lighthouse keeper. Dalton had considered landing at Cobh, but O'Friel advised him that Cobh was on an island, Great Island, and that the enemy could easily block their advance across Belvelly bridge to the mainland with a few machine guns.[23] O'Friel was one of the first of Dalton's officers to go ashore when two of the ships tied up at Passage West. During the troops' advance from Passage West towards Cork city, Dalton was impressed by the bravery shown by O'Friel and another officer Peadar Conlon, as they led their men in heavy fighting against strong republican resistance at Rochestown and Douglas.

One of the prominent republican fighters who resisted the Free State forces at these locations was Frank Busteed, who had executed Mrs Lindsay and her chauffeur, James Clarke. Busteed told later how he was operating with a column of 60 men, and they were forced to retreat to Cork city. At this stage, republicans were burning the bases they occupied before retreating further west. 'We retired from Douglas back to Union Quay Barracks – it was burning when we got in there.'[24]

Dalton gave promotions in the field to O'Friel and Conlon, elevating them from Captain to Commandant. O'Friel would later lead Free State forces in the Beara peninsula, as will be outlined in more detail, and he would have a fraught encounter with one of the figures in the Bridget Noble saga. Another officer who took a prominent part in the advance on Cork was Tom Kilcoyne, who had been a member of Michael Collins's special unit, The Squad, and who would also command forces in Beara.

Later in August, the Commander-in-Chief of the National Army, the charismatic Michael Collins, paid a surprise visit to Dalton in his headquarters at the Imperial Hotel, Cork. Collins was planning a tour of his home area of West Cork, and Dalton considered this was unwise, recalling later that he told Collins that being in the region was an 'unnecessary risk'. Collins replied: 'Nobody will shoot me in my own county.' Collins was travelling with Dalton in a touring car when their convoy was ambushed at Bealnablath, near Bandon, on the evening of 22 August, and Collins was killed. After the demoralised National Army party reached their HQ in the Imperial Hotel in Cork in the early hours of the morning, it reportedly fell to Commandant Frank O'Friel, and another officer, Commandant Sean O'Connell, to accompany Collins's body in an ambulance to Shanakiel Hospital.[25] There was shock, grief and anger among National Army personnel following the shooting of Collins, and the death of the 'Big Fellow' seemed to usher in a more bitter phase of the Civil War.

Later in the year, the Provisional Government would introduce draconian punishments for a range of offences, and 77 republican prisoners would face the firing squad before the conflict ended. Undisciplined elements in the Free State forces also carried out 'unofficial' reprisals such as the notorious Ballyseedy massacre in County Kerry, when IRA prisoners were tied to a mine and blown up. This seems to have been retaliation for a 'trap-mine' that killed five Free State soldiers at Knocknagoshel. In Dublin, there was a series of extra-judicial executions, often attributed to shadowy elements in Military Intelligence and the Criminal Investigation Department at Oriel House. Such killings caused great embarrassment to members of the Provisional Government. Most members of the National Army probably did exercise restraint, in light of the fact that about 12,000 prisoners survived the war. Nevertheless, events such as Ballyseedy left a legacy of bitterness. Republicans were also ruthless in carrying out their own executions – it has been estimated by one historian that the anti-Treaty forces executed 53 persons during the conflict.[26]

One Beara native seems to have had a lucky escape from anti-Treaty executioners – the afore-mentioned Timothy R. Harrington, editor of the *Irish Independent*. In response to the Provisional Government's executions policy, the anti-Treaty IRA leader Liam Lynch had issued orders that those who had voted for the 'Murder Bill' should be shot at sight; other Treatyite supporters would also face reprisals. Ernie O'Malley recalled that he was instructed by Lynch 'to capture and execute' the editors of the *Irish Independent* and *Irish Times*.[27] It was one way of dealing with unsympathetic newspaper coverage, and may have seemed like a good idea at the time, although it would surely have been unwise from the point of view of press relations, as it was bound to alienate members of the Fourth Estate and lead to negative publicity. O'Malley did not carry out Lynch's order, deciding that he had a more pressing priority – he wanted to execute the members of Free State Cabinet. O'Malley did send a letter to the *Irish Times*, threatening the editor, John Edward Healy. As for Harrington, he armed himself with a licenced .32 Webley & Scott automatic pistol after receiving death threats. The pistol, which came with holster, two magazines and 30 rounds of ammunition, was provided by the National Army's Quartermaster General with the approval of the army's Intelligence Department and the Minister for Defence.[28]

Two young men who had served in the Beara Battalion would die during the Civil War – ironically they had both been members of Inches Company. John Cadogan, from Croumhane, Eyeries, was fatally injured in an ambush near Killarney on 24 October 1922 while serving with the Dublin Guard element of the National Army – he had landed at Fenit, County Kerry with Free State forces the previous August. His mother, Mrs Julia Cadogan, embarked on a long, difficult journey to bring the body back to Eyeries – John was the eldest of her ten surviving children. Concerned that her private correspondence might be intercepted by republicans, she asked her son's superior officer, Captain Robert Walsh, to ensure that any letters sent to her be addressed to the Eyeries Parish Priest, Rev. Michael Daly.[29] The other casualty, John Dwyer, from Inches East, Eyeries, was killed while fighting with the anti-Treaty forces at Kealkil, Bantry, on 8 December.

Liam O'Dwyer, who took part in the fighting at Kealkil, described in a document in his MSP file how he volunteered to 'draw fire' on horseback in an effort to locate the Free State line 'for our Armoured Car, which trailed me'. It is unclear if this is a reference to a Whippet armoured car known as the *Slievenamon* which was part of Michael Collins's convoy when he was killed in the Bealnablath ambush. The car had been handed over on 2 December to the anti-Treaty forces by the vehicle's Scots-born machine gunner, John McPeak, when he defected to the IRA. The fighting at Kealkil occurred as National Army troops mounted a big comb-out operation to recover the *Slievenamon*. Meanwhile, after the start of the Civil War between different elements of Irish nationalism, Liam O'Dwyer would also engage in a fight with the 'ancient enemy' – the British.

Chapter 20: Firefight at Castletownbere

For Liam O'Dwyer, the sight of uniformed British military personnel on the street in Castletownbere must have been like the proverbial red rag to a bull. It was 25 August, just three days after the Bealnablath ambush, and a British military party had sailed over from Bere Island to collect money from a bank in Castletownbere. In line with his personal policy of confronting crown forces who still remained in Ireland, O'Dwyer assembled a group of his men and, according to his memoir, went into the Berehaven Hotel and told the British officer there to 'get his men out of the town and never come back'.[1] Angry words developed into a firefight and men on both sides were wounded. A stray shot wounded the local parish priest, Canon Hayes. It was reported that the British ran to their boat and steamed out of the harbour, still under fire.

Mícheál Óg O'Sullivan was one of those injured, and British archives at Kew indicate that the British wounded were Lieutenant E.N.C. Symonds, Royal Garrison Artillery (RGA), who suffered 'gunshot wound to left shoulder'; Mate James Kennedy, War Department Fleet, who sustained 'gunshot wounds left arm, hand and thigh', and Bombardier James Archibald Stonehouse RGA, who suffered 'gunshot wounds left thigh and right hip'.[2] Mícheál Óg O'Sullivan's wounds were serious, and he was taken into hiding at Bella O'Connell's house in Eyeries, where he received medical treatment from the local dispensary doctor, Dr Patrick V. Murphy who, as previously mentioned, treated farmer William Lehane after he was shot. O'Sullivan was also nursed by Bella O'Connell herself and other members of Cumann na mBan. Among the latter were O'Sullivan's sister Nora O'Sullivan, who visited him 'every second day for a few weeks'.[3]

Hannah O'Neill, who had guarded Bridget Noble as a prisoner, was another CnB activist who looked after Mícheál Óg. She told later how she went to Miss O'Connell's house every night to attend to O'Sullivan, and that Miss O'Connell helped her in this work. She said she 'often stayed up all night watching, fearing the house may be surrounded as he was a critical case and not fit to be removed; this treatment and keeping watch carried on for several weeks'.[4] Dr Murphy would later provide medical treatment to Mícheál Óg O'Sullivan at the latter's home in Inchintaglin, Adrigole. It appears that another prominent IRA officer, Mark Sullivan, was also wounded in the gun fight, and that he also received medical treatment from Dr Murphy.[5]

General Macready, commander of British military forces in Ireland, considered the firefight at Castletownbere significant enough to include details in one of his regular weekly reports to the War Office, which were routinely circulated to the Cabinet. The report shows that the activities of Liam O'Dwyer had been brought to his attention. In his report Macready stated that 'one of the attackers – Commandant Dwyer – is believed seriously wounded'.[6] O'Dwyer, in fact, escaped injury, and the wounded man the British had in mind was probably Mícheál Óg O'Sullivan. Condemning the Castletownbere attack and other attacks on the British forces, the head of the Provisional Government, William T. Cosgrave said the Truce entered into by the English and Irish had never been called off, and was still in force. He talked of the importance of an Irishman's 'word of honour'. He said the attacks were a breach of the Truce and 'a stain on the national honour'.[7]

In attacking the British party at Castletownbere, Liam O'Dwyer may have come closer than he realised to provoking a response from the British that would have been to their detriment. It would later emerge that the British C/O on Bere Island was planning a shore raid to 'round up' members of the local IRA when a destroyer arrived, and the navy intervened, raising issues about the military and diplomatic repercussions were such an operation to be launched.[8] The British wisely did not proceed with the raid. A British incursion that would have netted IRA prisoners or resulted in IRA casualties may not have resulted in uniting republican and pro-Treaty forces against the British, as Liam O'Dwyer would have desired, but it would surely have embarrassed the Provisional Government, and given a propaganda coup to the republicans who would doubtless have been eager to highlight an example of the Free Staters receiving support from imperial forces. During the revolutionary period, and in the more recent Troubles, republicans were able to provoke the British to react with aggressive or oppressive measures that made them unpopular and that caused serious problems for them in Ireland. In retrospect, in light of the information that has emerged, Hannah O'Neill was justified in her concerns, while looking after Mícheál Óg O'Sullivan, that the house might be surrounded, requiring her to stay up all night, while 'keeping watch'.

There was a tragic sequel for the family of the soldier who was wounded, Bombardier Stonehouse. The former farm labourer from Cove, Farnborough, Hampshire was treated for his injuries in hospital at Devonport, Plymouth. Apparently he became depressed as he felt he was not getting better. On 6 March 1923 Stonehouse, aged 29 years, hanged himself from a hot water pipe in a scullery at the hospital.[9] The case was reviewed by the Compensation (Ireland) Commission. The Commission members involved were the Free State representative, Cork businessman James C. Dowdall, and the British representative, C.J. Howell Thomas, a senior Revenue official. The Commission recommended to the British Treasury that the sum of £750 be paid to the deceased man's parents, James Stonehouse and his wife, Anne Elizabeth Stonehouse.[10]

Banishment of Dr Patrick V. Murphy

By the latter part of September 1922, Free State forces had not yet taken control of the Beara peninsula, where Liam O'Dwyer and his men were poised to resist the government forces. During that month, a prominent local citizen was banished from the Beara region after giving offence to the republicans. The person in question was the young local dispensary doctor, Dr Patrick V. Murphy, who, it will be recalled, had treated shooting victim William Lehane, removing pellets from the farmer's mangled legs, and who also provided treatment to Beara Battalion staff officers Mícheál Óg O'Sullivan and Dan Sullivan when they were wounded. (It is possible that Bridget Noble was also a patient at the time she underwent treatment in hospital.)

Dr Murphy, a native of the town, had been educated by the Holy Ghost Fathers (now known as Spiritans) at Rockwell College in County Tipperary and had taken his M.D. degree at University College Cork, obtaining first place in Ireland. He was a dedicated and very popular medical practitioner, and, during the War of Independence, had treated IRA members who were wounded or ill, without charge. He also provided classes in first aid and hygiene to members of Cumann na mBan. When he applied for a Service (1917-1921) Medal in later life, he stated that he was Medical Officer (M/O) to the flying column sick and injured, 1918 to 1921.[11] He indicated that he was also M/O attending to injured IRA men in a covert 'sick bay' located over Wiseman's drapery shop in Castletownbere, following the 1920 attack on the town's coastguard station, in which Volunteers were wounded. In addition, he mentioned that he was M/O to various wounded men, including Danny Sullivan, Quartermaster; Michael Sullivan, who suffered a 'wound in leg'; Mark Sullivan and Mícheál Óg O'Sullivan. Dr Murphy told how he himself had come under the scrutiny of 'Hatton-Hall' – obviously a reference to a British Army intelligence officer based at Furious Pier, Lieutenant Hubert Christopher Hatton-Hall, of the King's Own Scottish Borderers. According to Dr Murphy, there was a search of his 'records and activities' by Hatton-Hall. Dr Murphy also referred to an attack on Brandy Hall Bridge – an apparent reference to an unsuccessful attempt by the IRA in April 1921 to blow up a bridge at Castletownbere. After this incident, he stated that he called to Breen's Mill 'to attend wounded', and there was 'further investigation' into his affairs by Hatton-Hall. (Despite Dr Murphy's considerable service, his application for a medal failed on a technicality – he was not actually a member of the Volunteers.)

In May 1921 Dr Murphy's own brother, John Murphy, a teacher in Ballinalee, County Longford, had been taken from his home at night by men believed to be Auxiliaries, and shot dead. It was suggested that he was murdered by crown forces in retaliation for an IRA ambush, and because he and his wife were friendly with a local IRA leader, Sean MacEoin.[12] Murphy was brother-in-law of Sean Connolly, an IRA organiser who was fatally wounded by crown forces in County Leitrim the previous March. The murder of John Murphy was raised in the House of Commons by Nationalist MP Joe Devlin, and he was informed that the Commander-in-Chief had been asked to inquire into the 'very grave allegations' that had been made.

A major factor that seems to have driven a wedge between Dr Murphy and the IRA was the Anglo-Irish Treaty. Dr Murphy, who was pro-Treaty, was angry at the actions of the anti-Treaty IRA, and expressed his views in a letter to a friend in Australia. He said that 'there is nothing but looting, incendiarism, murder and commandeering goods at the point of a revolver by these blackguards.' The letter was intercepted by members of the local IRA who were outraged at his comments, even though they were meant for private, rather than public consumption. Taking on the seemingly Orwellian role of a 'Thought Police', the republicans moved against Dr Murphy, returning a 'guilty' verdict at a trial without hearing any evidence for the defence – indeed Dr Murphy was not even aware of the accusations against him until he was informed that he had been convicted and a punishment decided upon. As previously indicated, some IRA courts martial were conducted in the absence of the accused person. In the case of Dr Murphy, one presumes he could have been approached and asked for comments in his own defence before a verdict was reached and a penalty imposed, as the IRA would have been in full control of

Castletownbere at the time. In light of the manner in which Dr Murphy was dealt with, one wonders about the quality of justice accorded by local republicans to Bridget Noble.

Dr Murphy told later of his experience in a statement published in the army magazine *An t-Óglach*, now under Free State military control.[13] He expressed the view that 'ninety-nine per cent' of the people of Berehaven supported the Treaty and said that the 'few Irregulars' were holding the district 'under armed terrorism'. He told how he was confronted at his home on 18 September by four men – Liam Dwyer [O'Dwyer], whom he described as the local leader of the Irregulars; the Irregulars' Quartermaster [presumably a reference to Dan Sullivan, whom he would have known from previously treating him], and two other men. Dr Murphy said that at least two of the men were armed. It was indicated to him that they had referred the matter of his intercepted letter to a higher authority and that an instruction had been received that he was to be courtmartialled and fined £100. He was now required to pay the £100. His remarks were considered to be 'destructive to the good name of the Irish Republican Army'.

As far as Dr Murphy could recall, his IRA visitors told him the instruction for him to be fined came from the GHQ of '1st Southern Brigade'. [This may have been a reference to the 1st Southern Division.] Dr Murphy refused to pay, telling his visitors he did not recognise their court or their authority in any way. 'They gave me 24 hours to consider whether I would pay the £100 fine or not. They told me that as far as they were concerned they would maintain strictest privacy. I told them that as far as I was concerned, I would make the matter as public as I could.' Subsequently O'Dwyer, as Commandant of the 5th Battalion, served him with a 'banishment order' instructing him to leave the 5th Cork Brigade area within 24 hours, after which his motor car would be confiscated.

In his statement, Dr Murphy said he was 'compelled' to attend an Irregular who had been wounded in an attack on British troops in Castletownbere – an obvious reference to Mícheál Óg O'Sullivan. Dr Murphy said that he was escorted by armed men every day to where the man was in hiding. 'At the interview to which I am referring, Dwyer told me that if I had refused to attend the man, I would have been shot, and he also added that he held me personally responsible for the welfare of the wounded man.' Ironically, in September 1921, it was Mícheál Óg O'Sullivan who seconded a proposal by Mark Sullivan at a meeting of the Castletownbere Board of Guardians that Dr Murphy be appointed medical officer of Kilcatherine dispensary – the previous incumbent, Dr Harrison, had died.[14] Dr Murphy wrote to the

Board thanking the members 'most sincerely' for electing him to the office.

It is unclear why officers of the Beara Battalion decided to refer the Murphy case to a higher authority but not, apparently, the case of Bridget Noble. One could speculate that it was because Dr Murphy was a figure of considerable standing and influence in the community, while Mrs Noble, being of more humble background, had a far less prominent position in society. Perhaps she was an easier target. It is noteworthy also that the battalion officers desired to maintain the 'strictest privacy' about the punishment of Dr Murphy, an echo perhaps of the secrecy surrounding the execution of Mrs Noble. One wonders if the battalion officers were seeking to avoid any adverse publicity that could give their enemies a propaganda advantage – any such hopes would prove to be in vain, as will be shown.

As regards the move to banish Dr Murphy, the fact that the local community was to be deprived of the vital services of a dispensary doctor does not seem to have been taken into account. Also, the confiscation of Dr Murphy's car meant that it would be unavailable to local medical personnel to bring seriously ill patients to hospital – it will be recalled that Dr Murphy had used his car to take the grievously wounded William Lehane to Castletownbere Hospital after he was shot. It is also likely that it was in Dr Murphy's car that the afore-mentioned Richard Newman was taken to the same hospital with serious injuries after being shot by crown forces.

According to Dr Murphy, the banishment order signed by O'Dwyer warned that any repetition of the offence would 'warrant the employment of the extreme penalty' – i.e. he would be executed. (One wonders if the IRA would have actually killed Dr Murphy for a 'repetition of the offence'. But then again, it would have been prudent for Dr Murphy to heed the warning.) Dr Murphy decided to leave the area, and his car was seized. Ironically, by banishing Dr Murphy the IRA had provided the enemy with a very useful recruit. Dr Murphy travelled to Dublin and joined the National Army as a medical officer with the rank of Captain. From a propaganda point of view, the move to banish Dr Murphy could be seen as an 'own goal' for Liam O'Dwyer. Dr Murphy's account in *An t-Óglach* was widely publicised – it was taken up by the *Cork Examiner*, the *Kilkenny People* and also by newspapers further afield, in Northern Ireland, Scotland and England.

While seeking to protect the 'good name' of the IRA, O'Dwyer had, in fact, generated considerable negative publicity for the organisation. Local IRA officers were portrayed as intolerant, authoritarian and oppressive figures who spied on people's private correspondence, who sought to suppress free speech and who used death threats and intimidation against a respected professional man supplying a vital service to the community. Members of the Beara Battalion had managed to avoid adverse publicity by maintaining strict secrecy around the execution of Bridget Noble, but when they sought to punish the feisty Dr Murphy, he emerged as a far more formidable adversary than the unfortunate woman from Reenavaude. It would have been wiser for the senior Beara IRA officers to have simply ignored the private derogatory comments made about the IRA by Dr Murphy to his friend in Australia. In October 1922, the month after being banished from Beara, Dr Murphy married his fiancée Nan Murphy in the more secure surroundings of Skreen Parish Church, Dunshaughlin, County Meath. They would go on to have eight children. He would serve in the National Army until 1924, by which time the Civil War was over.

Women 'Spies'

As the Civil War got under way, the anti-Treaty IRA observed the convention that women were not to be put to death. In an order issued on 4 September 1922 on the question of 'spies', Liam Lynch, IRA chief of staff, essentially renewed the IRA order that prevailed during the War of Independence, that the death penalty was not to be inflicted on women. In 'General Order No. 6' Lynch stated that persons charged with espionage 'must be tried by Military Court set up by the Brigade Commandant of the area where the crime was committed'.[15] Where the information provided led to the death of Volunteers, the sentence was to be Death. Death sentences had to be confirmed by General Headquarters (GHQ) before being carried out. Where the information conveyed led to the wounding or capture of Volunteers, the sentence was to be a fine, or confiscation of property to the value of the fine. In cases where the information given did not lead to injury of Volunteers or failure of military operations, the guilty person shall be paraded publicly as a 'spy' or deported. While the death penalty would not be imposed on women, they would be subject to the other penalties set out above.

By the standards of the time, some of these measures were relatively mild and had they been in force during the War of Independence and complied with, Bridget Noble and others who were put to death would surely have been spared. However, Lynch's order in regard to 'spies' seemed to make it easier to shoot certain former members of the RIC. Death sentences on ex-members of English forces 'with previous bad records' did not have to be confirmed by General Headquarters but by the Divisional Commandant, before being carried out.

The Army Executive seemed anxious to row back on some of the concessions made by Lynch in regard to punishments and to take a harder line on 'spies', although the ban on executing women still persisted. A few days after Lynch's edict, the Executive, which of course included Lynch, issued another notice, dated 8 September, stating that any citizens giving information to the enemy which led to the death, wounding or capture of republican troops 'will be regarded as spies and will be liable to the same penalties as those inflicted on Spies previous to the Truce July 1921'.[16] On 24 November as the conflict entered an even more bitter phase, Liam Lynch issued 'General Order No. 12: Spies' which formally cancelled General Order No. 6 and its measures laying down relatively mild penalties for spying that did not result in death. Under the new order, Lynch stated that a spy shall not be executed 'until convicted by a Brigade Court of Inquiry and sentence ratified by Divisional Commandant, who 'must feel satisfied that evidence submitted absolutely proves guilt of spy'. The order also made provision for the punishment of those who were suspected or rumoured to be engaged in espionage: 'Due consideration will be given to rumour cases of espionage when a less penalty than death will be inflicted.'[17] However, there was no deviation from the principle that women were not to be executed.

A question can be asked as to the extent that the procedures laid down by Headquarters in relation to dealing with 'spies' were actually followed by forces on the ground. General Order No. 12, in addition to banning the execution of women also stated that 'boys under 18 years' shall not be executed. There was a clear violation of the latter rule in West Cork on 17 March 1923 when IRA members took 17-year-old Benny McCarthy from his home at Ardagh, Bantry around 4 am – his body was later found by the roadside with a label: 'Convicted Spy. Shot as a reprisal for our comrades who were executed during the week.'[18] The use of the term 'convicted' implies that a 'trial' took place – one wonders what kind of 'trial' would result in such a draconian punishment being imposed on a minor.[19] (McCarthy's sister May married farmer Ger Johnny Sheehan, and their son P.J. Sheehan, noted for his affability and good humour, served for many years as the Fine Gael TD for Cork South West. He passed away in 2020.)

Also during that week in March 1923, there was a violent incident reminiscent of the kind of murderous attacks that took place during the afore-mentioned Bandon Valley atrocity. William G. Beale, a member of the Society of Friends, was shot and fatally injured in Cork, his assailants reportedly telling him it was a 'reprisal' for [Free State] executions.[20] He was one of several Protestant civilians shot by gunmen in Cork city and county during the Civil War or shortly afterwards.[21] It is unclear if such deaths are included in the afore-mentioned 53 executions estimated by one historian to have been carried out by anti-Treaty forces during the Civil War. Meanwhile, National Army forces would capture or come to grips with anti-Treaty fighters in Beara, including some whose names have been linked to the story of Bridget Noble.

Chapter 21: Free State Forces
Occupy Beara Peninsula

The Free State forces ultimately made inroads into the Beara peninsula, moving down the long, winding road by the coast and entering areas where the republicans had formerly held sway. The *Freeman's Journal* reported: 'A large column left Bantry on December 12 [1922] and proceeded towards Glengarriff and Castletownbere. Both towns were taken without opposition and garrisons were established in both towns.'[1] The incoming forces included men who were Beara natives, and doubtless their local knowledge proved useful as the National Army tightened its grip on the peninsula. In Castletownbere, the old workhouse, built in the 1850s, would become a base for the troops. Reporting on the entry of the Free State forces into Castletownbere, the *Cork Examiner* stated that 'the town was taken without a shot being fired, and the troops received a great welcome from the people'.[2]

The National Army troops based in Castletownbere carried out raids, picking up various men active, or alleged to be active, on the anti-Treaty side. On 6 January 1923, the *Cork Examiner* reported: 'Arrests and a big haul of munitions and equipment have taken place at Castletownbere.' According to another report, five men were arrested and the arms seized included ten rifles – three Lee Enfields and seven Mausers.[3] In the Adrigole area, Mícheál Óg O'Sullivan's territory, members of the local company of the Beara Battalion were among those picked up in the early swoops. On 6 January the Captain of Adrigole Company, Flor O'Sullivan of Droumlave, was arrested, as was the 1st Lieutenant, Matt Sullivan, Lackavane (who fought at Crossbarry), and Volunteer Patrick J. Sullivan, of Droumagoulane. (Flor O'Sullivan would later emigrate to America, while Patrick J. Sullivan went to Australia. Matt Sullivan also went to America for a period.[4]) Later, in April, another member of Adrigole Company, Tim T. Sullivan, would be taken prisoner.[5]

Meanwhile, on the Beara peninsula, the local anti-Treaty fighters pressed on with their guerrilla tactics, which included cutting roads and destroying bridges to disrupt the movements of National troops. The anti-Treaty forces had assistance from members of Cumann na mBan, especially in the area of intelligence gathering. Hannah O'Neill, who as already outlined, was linked to the story of Bridget Noble, told how she went daily to Castletownbere 'and got information of the military positions'.[6] Margaret O'Neill described how she kept in touch with a Free State lorry driver called Kelly, 'who told me beforehand about raids'. He also told her how the Free State military had mislaid a pan of ammunition while raiding at Kealroe [Cailroe – the home area of Liam O'Dwyer] and she walked four miles to Eyeries and informed B. O'Connell [Bella O'Connell], and Volunteers recovered the ammunition before Free State troops raided the next morning.[7] Bella O'Connell, head of Cumann na mBan in Beara, told how, in the latter stages of the Civil War and afterwards, from 1 April to 30 September 1923, she was 'made responsible for all IRA intelligence work at this period as all IRA servicemen were on the run'.[8]

Hannah O'Neill was also involved in providing treatment to three Beara Battalion men who were wounded in fighting at Ballineen, West Cork, and who were taken to Lauragh for recuperation. She later indicated in her application for a Military Service Pension that she was guided to the men's hiding place by Liam O'Dwyer. There were 'safe houses' in this region of mountains, woods and sea inlets, and also located here were reliable members of Cumann na mBan willing to assist. One of the wounded was the afore-mentioned Patrick Malvey.

Liam O'Dwyer told in his MSP file how he organised an ambush of Free State forces at Pollincha Bridge, about two miles from Castletownbere on the road to Eyeries. According to a National Army report, the Irregulars staged the ambush on 9 March 1923 at 600 yards range and numbered 20 men armed with rifles and one Thompson gun. The National Army unit under Captain E. Galvin had nine men, armed with rifles and a Lewis gun. The report comments: 'Irregulars maintained constant fire on troops for ½ an hour. One of the National Forces was slightly wounded.'[9]

The National Army troops operating in Beara were particularly wary of the danger posed by landmines, and exercised particular caution when seeking to dismantle barricades for fear they might be booby-trapped. 'Trap mine' incidents had caused carnage among Free State troops at Knocknagoshel, County Kerry and Carrigaphooca, near Macroom, County Cork. Captain Galvin, based in Castletownbere, in a report for 13 March 1923, records that he carried out a patrol with 'Lancia and crew', and goes on: 'Removed barricade on road to

Allihies, mines discovered, barricade with mines in it on Eyeries road fired at, without effect.'[10] On another day he reports: 'While patrolling Allihies mine road met two barricades and broken bridge, removed one. Left other alone as it was reported to be mined.'

National Army troops continued to round up suspects in Beara and in the latter part of April 1923 a number of arrests were made. Details of those detained, their alleged offences, and the names of the arresting personnel are among the details recorded in a National Army ledger for County Cork and still preserved at the Military Archives. Recorded alongside many names is the comment: 'A committee of officers recommended internment.'[11] Among those detained in Beara in late April were Patrick Murphy, Patrick Sheehan and Jerh Sullivan, of Rossmacowen; Richard Dwyer and Timothy O'Neill of Inches, Eyeries, and Timothy O'Leary and Michael Walsh, Eyeries. There was an ominous development on 5 May when John Murphy, Dunboy, was captured with a Lee Enfield rifle and ammunition, including 'a dum dum bullet'. It appears that he was sentenced to death by a military court but was spared.[12] He died in 1987 in his 85th year.

The Shooting of Margaret Dunne

Apart from the Bridget Noble case, during the revolutionary period there was another tragic incident of a woman suffering a violent death on the Beara peninsula. Margaret Dunne, a member of Cumann na mBan, was on the anti-Treaty side in the Civil War and was shot dead during an incident near Adrigole in the latter stages of the conflict. One newspaper report, apparently incorrect, stated: 'Two men and a girl were shot dead when National troops came into conflict with an armed party near Adrigole.'[13] Another newspaper simply reported that a woman was shot 'during an engagement between National troops and irregulars'.[14] According to one account, a Free State soldier was wounded in a gunfight with two IRA men at Adrigole, and ten minutes later Ms Dunne was seen talking to a third IRA Volunteer, and a Free State officer, Captain Hassett, opened fire, fatally wounding Ms Dunne.[15]

The death registration record shows that Margaret Dunne was aged 26 years, single, a goods clerk by occupation, and that she died on Sunday, 8 April 1923, at Droumlave, Adrigole. The record stated that her death was as a result of 'shock and haemorrhage' caused by a bullet wound, and that she 'died instantaneously'. In her application for a Military Service Pension, Nora O'Sullivan [Nóra Ní Shúilleabháin], who was Captain of Adrigole Company of Cumann na mBan, said that the Free Staters had come in to the village on a raid during Mass. She gave a despatch to Margaret Dunne to take to 'two of the boys' [IRA members] who were up on the side of the mountain, to warn them that the Free Staters were 'around the place', and Ms Dunne was carrying this despatch when she was shot. As mentioned, Nora O'Sullivan was a sister of Mícheál Óg O'Sullivan, Vice O/C of the Beara Battalion, and they were first cousins of Margaret Dunne. A newspaper reported that, during Ms Dunne's funeral, a party of National troops 'brought their arms to the salute' as the cortege passed.[16]

Taken Prisoner

Liam O'Dwyer would have been a prime target for the Free State forces but he managed to evade capture, even though a number of republicans were arrested in the Ardgroom area, including his brother Tim. A senior republican taken prisoner in Ardgroom in May 1923 was Morty Sullivan.[17] It is recorded that Sullivan, from Bantry, became a Special Services officer, in charge of Supplies, with the newly-formed Cork 5 Brigade – he held that post on 1 July 1922.[18] Tim Dwyer was taken prisoner on 20 May 1923 during a roundup in Ardgroom. Military records show that he was arrested by troops under the command of Captain Cashman. Dwyer was described at the time in a National Army record thus: 'Active Irregular known to have taken part in several attacks against the Nat. [National] forces.' The note added: 'A committee of officers recommended internment.'[19] (After the Civil War, Tim Dwyer was one of the many local republicans to emigrate. He settled at Butte, Montana, where he worked for the Anaconda Mining Company. He passed away in 1986.) Also arrested in Ardgroom when Tim Dwyer was detained were John Harrington and Michael Sullivan. It is unclear if this is the same Michael Sullivan, mentioned above, who was interned following the 'bobbing' of Bridget Noble.

After their expedition to Ardgroom, Free State troops were ambushed near the village while returning to Castletownbere. According to a statement from the National Army headquarters, they returned fire and suffered no casualties. The statement added: 'An Irregular named Joseph Sullivan, Ardgroom, who was badly wounded, was captured after the engagement.'[20] During the roundup in Ardgroom, it appears that John Dwyer, who figured in the story of Mrs Noble, came close to arrest and to another spell as an internee, this time courtesy of the Free State. But while his brother Tim was detained, John Dwyer somehow managed to get away from the clutches of the National Army troops and, under cover of darkness, sought refuge in the valley of Glenbeg. A member of Cumann na mBan, Nora Mary Crowley, according to her later account, helped John Dwyer 'to a safe hiding place, after he had escaped from the enemy'. She said that when he called to her house at 3 o'clock in the morning, he also informed her 'of the shooting of Joseph Sullivan'.[21] (Nora Mary Crowley's home in Glenbeg was a well-known 'safe house' and he may have gone into hiding here, or in a neighbouring house, or in one of the dug-outs constructed in Glenbeg.)

During research on the Beara peninsula, I interviewed a relative of Joseph O'Sullivan, who gave a different version of events. He said that Joseph, from Dreenacappra, was not a member of the IRA. He was walking along a road towards Ardgroom village with John Dwyer when the Free State military came on the scene. Dwyer ran off and managed to evade arrest. Joseph was told to walk on along the road and then somebody shot him in the leg. The soldier believed to be responsible covered Joseph with his coat and he was later taken to Ardgroom for treatment, and then by sea from Castletownbere to Cork where he underwent various operations for the injury. According to another local source, the treatment he received in Ardgroom was at the post office, run by Mrs Brigid McCarthy. This was also, of course, the post office that Bridget Noble had visited on her last day of freedom.

Ceasefire

In late April 1923, fighting in the Civil War was coming to an end. There was a crucial development when IRA Chief of Staff Liam Lynch was shot and fatally wounded on 10 April in the Knockmealdown Mountains in County Tipperary. He was succeeded by Frank Aiken who had little enthusiasm for the war. On 27 April Aiken issued an order suspending hostilities; this was followed the following month by a 'ceasefire' order, dated 23 May, which also stated that arms 'are to be dumped', and not given up to the enemy.

Liam O'Dwyer said in a statement in his MSP file: 'We did not dump our arms at all. We had to carry them for protection after the Dump Arms order was given.' (He also stated: 'We did not get the order to dump. There was a controversy about it. It was not generally accepted.') In line with his apparent tendency to make up his own mind about issues, rather than accept an order from a higher authority, O'Dwyer did not fully observe Aiken's ceasefire order. In his MSP file he tells how he carried out attacks in July and August on Free State forces. 'On July 16th I organized a large Column and made a night attack on the F.S. [Free State] billets in Castletownbere, but after an hour's fighting our General Reserve line was shelled by the British Navy from the harbour and we had to retreat under shell fire. In the end of August we attacked a F.S. Military boat in Bannaw [Bunaw] Harbour.'

Despite such sporadic attacks, the Civil War was effectively at an end but since there was no negotiated peace and the IRA still held arms, the Free State authorities continued to detain prisoners, and government forces would continue, for a period, to pursue IRA members and to carry out arrests. During the conflict, Liam O'Dwyer had operated not only in the Beara peninsula but in other parts of the Cork No 5 Brigade area, including Bantry and Skibbereen. O'Dwyer commented in his memoir: 'In all we took part in ten fights in the Brigade area during the Civil War period.' During one firefight, according to his account, O'Dwyer came close to being hit by a hail of machine gun bullets – one went through his right coat pocket and another through the left side of his coat collar.[22]

As will be outlined, one of those who would be taken prisoner by the Free State forces after the IRA ceasefire was a man with a particular link to the Bridget Noble narrative, and his capture would have serious personal consequences.

Chapter 22: The Capture of Patsy Dan Crowley

On the evening of Friday, 1 June 1923, a party of Free State troops under Commandant Frank O'Friel drove out from Ardgroom village along the narrow road towards the mountains, leading into the valley known as Glenbeg. This was the majestic valley with a fjiord-like lake that had so impressed Rudyard Kipling, as earlier outlined. O'Friel and his men were about to carry out a raid. There had been previous Free State raids into Glenbeg but on this occasion the National Army would make some significant arrests. The IRA had ceased hostilities but the Free State forces were still rounding up suspects, as mentioned. Glenbeg was the bailiwick of Patsy Dan Crowley, who, as previously noted, was linked to the saga of Bridget Noble, and was allegedly her executioner, although this cannot be confirmed.

Glenbeg had long been used by the IRA as a hiding place where Volunteers and more senior figures in the movement could be discreetly billeted. The narrow road leading into the valley could be kept under surveillance, and an early warning given of any enemy incursion. Men who were wounded or suffering from ailments such as scabies received treatment in Glenbeg. Of the four houses in the valley, the main 'safe house' was the family home of the afore-mentioned Con Crowley, largely because his sister Nora Mary Crowley (1904-2000) was the only young woman residing in Glenbeg at the time, and she was a trusted member of Cumann na mBan who supplied vital services to the Volunteers.

The teenaged Nora Mary did work that would have been regarded at the time as primarily 'women's work' – cooking, washing clothes and tending those who were sick or injured. But she also minded arms dumps, carried dispatches long distances across mountain paths and stood guard at night, armed with a rifle, ready to fire a shot in the air to warn of any danger. Liam O'Dwyer was one of those who had found refuge in the house. He greatly admired Nora Mary's work for the cause, and gladly backed her later application for a Military Service Pension. In minding the arms dumps, Nora Mary worked under her neighbour Patsy Dan Crowley, who was in charge of the dumps.[23] Glenbeg was an important area for hiding IRA stores, arms and other equipment. Some of the materiel taken in the raid on the coastguard station at Ballycrovane had been hidden in dumps in this secluded area. Glenbeg was the site of both Battalion and Brigade arms dumps.

At the time of Commandant O'Friel's raid into Glenbeg, Patsy Dan Crowley was lying low in the valley along with a couple of well-known anti-Treaty republicans from Bantry – Edward 'Ned' Cotter and Thaddeus 'Ted' O'Sullivan, both of whom would later become Fianna Fáil members of the Dáil. The two may have figured that a remote area like Glenbeg would provide a safe haven – any such hopes were about to be dashed. Brigade Commandant Ted O'Sullivan was the most senior republican of the three, and it has been suggested that his presence in Glenbeg was 'betrayed' to the Free State forces, although no indication has emerged into the public domain as to the identity of the suspected informant.[24]

According to an informed source, Cotter and O'Sullivan were working in the fields on a potato crop with Patsy Dan Crowley prior to the roundup. They were engaged in a process known as 'earthing' or 'earthing up'. It was said that Patsy Dan's brother Jer Dan discovered that the Free State forces were in the area, and urged the others to flee, but they stayed put, not considering themselves at risk. They may have been lulled into a false sense of security by the fact that hostilities had just ceased. Jer Dan got away to the mountains and thus avoided arrest. Like his brother Patsy Dan, Jer Dan was a member of the IRA's Ardgroom Company.[25]

Patsy Dan Crowley, Cotter and O'Sullivan, all aged in their twenties, were taken prisoner. The three were taken to Castletownbere, and were apparently held in the former RIC barracks. Even though the building had been set on fire by IRA members before withdrawal from the town, it appears that National Army personnel were still able to use the facilities. Commandant O'Friel, as already indicated, was one of the most resourceful of the officers who had accompanied Major General Dalton in the landings at Passage West. Following the landings, O'Friel lost comrades who were killed in fighting at Rochestown during the advance on Cork. O'Friel and his men had come under heavy fire from Lewis guns operated by the anti-Treaty forces. O'Friel would tell later how he himself came close to being killed, with a bullet putting a hole in his cap.[26]

The memory of comrades killed in action and the later shooting of Michael Collins may have weighed heavily on O'Friel – as mentioned earlier, O'Friel reportedly escorted the body of the Big Fellow to hospital the night after the Bealnablath ambush. An historic photograph shows O'Friel among the officers standing to attention at the quayside in Cork as Collins's tricolour-draped coffin was carried onto the ship *Classic* for transport back to Dublin for one of the biggest funerals the city had ever seen. O'Friel's role now on the Beara peninsula was to round up IRA men still perceived to pose a threat – and to seize the arms they still kept hidden away. (Commandant O'Friel was appointed O/C of the 30th Battalion – military records show he held that post on 1 February 1924.[27]) O'Friel may have had intelligence that there were arms dumps in Glenbeg, and that the man who had particular knowledge of them was Patsy Dan Crowley.

Details of the arrest by O'Friel of the three men in Glenbeg are outlined in records that were kept by the National Army's Cork Command. It was stated that Patrick Crowley, of Glenbeg, Ardgroom and Edward Cotter, of Market Street, Bantry, were arrested 'while on the run' at Ardgroom on 1 June by Commandant O'Friel. The two were also described as 'active Irregulars'. It was recorded that they were both taken to the County Jail.[28] As regards Ted O'Sullivan, the records show that 'Thaddeus Sullivan' of Bawngorm, Bantry, was also arrested on the same date at Ardgroom by O'Friel. O'Sullivan was described thus: 'Active Irregular, known to have taken part [sic] against the National forces.' It was noted that he was also taken to the County Jail. In the case of all three, the records note that 'a committee of officers recommended internment'. O'Sullivan's arrest was deemed sufficiently important to merit newspaper coverage. Under a headline 'Leading Irregular Arrested', the *Cork Examiner* reported that word had reached Cork of the arrest of 'Ted' O'Sullivan, 'leader of an irregular column'. The report said he had been arrested 'together with several other important irregulars'.[29]

Public Inquiry Sought

Complaints would later emerge that both Crowley and O'Sullivan were seriously assaulted after arrest. Liam O'Dwyer alleged that Crowley was badly beaten on the head by rifle butts, and that this would lead to his early death.[30] After being held in Cork, Crowley was transferred to an internment camp at Newbridge, Co Kildare, where Cotter was also detained. (Cotter would later become a member of Cork County Council and would serve 15 years as a Fianna Fáil TD, from 1954 to 1969. He died in 1972 at age 72 years.) Allegations about the beating of O'Sullivan were raised in the Dáil later in June 1923 by Labour TD

Tomás de Nógla. He asked the Minister for Defence if he was aware that a man called Ted O'Sullivan was arrested on 1 June and beaten with rifles in the barracks at Castletown Berehaven [Castletownbere]; that on the journey to Bantry he was further ill-treated by the escort and again on the Square, Bantry in the presence of about 50 persons. De Nógla asked that a public inquiry be held into the behaviour of the troops. The President of the Executive Council, Mr Cosgrave, replying on behalf of the Minister for Defence, said that when the men were being arrested they attempted to escape and were recaptured. 'The allegations of ill-treatment are denied. The matter was inquired into by a Committee of Investigation on the 5th inst., but Mr O'Sullivan declined to make any statement. It is not proposed to hold a public inquiry.'[31]

O'Sullivan himself, in his application for a Military Service Pension, states that after his arrest by Free State troops on 1 June 1923 he was 'assaulted in Castletownbere on that date by being struck on the head with a hammer and revolver and rifle, and beaten on the shoulders and arms with a rifle and stick.'[32] O'Sullivan alleged to Ernie O'Malley that he was beaten by Frank O'Friel in the guardroom at Castletownbere, in the presence of two other prisoners, Patrick [Patsy Dan] Crowley and Patrick Mahoney, both of Ardgroom.[33] O'Sullivan also alleged that Crowley and Mahoney were taken back from Bantry to Castletownbere where they were 'hammered with revolver butts' to get information as to 'where our [arms] dumps were'. He also alleged that the two men were made to 'dig their own graves'. (As mentioned above, IRA leader Frank Aiken had sent out an order to 'dump arms' rather than surrender weapons and ammunition. Clearly National Army forces were eager to recover arms that were deemed to still pose a threat.)

On the same day that Patsy Dan Crowley and his two companions were arrested in Glenbeg, another republican, Patrick Malvey, was taken prisoner in nearby Ardgroom. Malvey, who had presumably recovered from his wounds after treatment in the afore-mentioned hide-out at Lauragh, was arrested by Captain Murphy and taken to Cork County Gaol. As previously indicated, he was active in the Beara Battalion's police force after the Truce. A National Army record states that he was an 'active Irregular, arrested whilst on the run'.[34] It was not Malvey's first experience as a prisoner, and he must have had a sense of déjà vu when picked up by Free State forces – it will be recalled that in 1918 he was arrested in Ardgroom by the RIC and later given a 28-day sentence for refusing to answer police questions.

One of the raids carried out by Free State forces following the ceasefire was on the Eyeries home of the O'Connell family – the siblings Christy, Bella and Louise were, of course, particularly active on the anti-Treaty side. A military party under Captain Cashman carried out the surprise raid. Louise O'Connell told later how she pushed the door closed, allowing a wanted man, John O'Neill, to escape. It seems the door was damaged in the incident, Ms O'Connell stating that Cashman 'burst the door'.[35]

The Capture of Mícheál Óg O'Sullivan

In September 1923, Mícheál Óg O'Sullivan, Vice O/C of the Beara Battalion when Bridget Noble was disappeared, was taken prisoner by Free State forces. It appears that he was not 'on the run' but was arrested at his family home in Inchintaglin, Adrigole and interned at Cork Female Prison. From 1 July 1922 he was a Special Services Officer with the new Cork 5th Brigade, in charge of Operations, as previously indicated.[36] A newspaper report on his capture reported that he was a 'prominent irregular' and that he was 'a member of Berehaven R.D. [Rural District] Council and is the local council's representative on the County Council'.[37] The National Army regarded him as a particular threat and included him on a list of prisoners regarded as 'dangerous' who should be held 'until the very last'. (Also included on the list was Ted O'Sullivan, who was held at this period at Mountjoy Prison in Dublin.[38] O'Sullivan would later be held at Hare Park, one of the internment centres at the Curragh, County Kildare and was not released until 17 July 1924.[39] Ted O'Sullivan would go on to serve as a Fianna Fáil TD from 1937 to 1954, and was a member of the Senate from 1954 to 1969. He died in 1971 aged 81 years.)

Mícheál Óg O'Sullivan escaped from prison in Cork in late 1923. There was a mass break-out from Cork Female Prison in November and it is likely that O'Sullivan was one of the high-value prisoners who got away at this time. In the escape plan, priority was given to those prisoners who might face the death penalty or other severe punishment. On a moonlit night, prisoners used bed clothes to descend to the prison yard. Then they got across the exterior wall by means of a rope ladder. Some were re-captured soon afterwards. It is unclear how O'Sullivan, now a hunted fugitive, managed to make the long journey back safely to his native Beara district. He hid out with Liam O'Dwyer in a dug-out, and they were assisted by O'Sullivan's sister Nora O'Sullivan, who, as mentioned, was a member of Cumann na mBan.[40] The IRA had a number of dug-outs in the Eyeries/Ardgroom area at this period. Hannah O'Neill [Mrs Hanley] described how she delivered dispatches to dug-outs at Glenbeg, Ballycrovane, Boffickil, Urhan and Bawrs.[41]

With his background as an Irish-speaking former pupil of the iconic Pádraic Pearse, followed by his post-Rising training in Dublin with the

Volunteers, his active role in the IRA during the War of Independence and Civil War, and his election as a Sinn Féin local councillor as well as his role as a member of Castletown Board of Guardians, Mícheál Óg might have made a career in Irish politics, and would have fitted well into the ethos of Éamon de Valera's Fianna Fáil party. However, he was destined to emigrate to America and make his life there.

Aftermath of the Civil War

The anti-Treaty forces suffered defeat in the Civil War, and in Beara, the power of Liam O'Dwyer and the Beara Battalion was broken. During his time as battalion commandant, O'Dwyer had wielded considerable power in his bailiwick. A republican with utmost dedication to the cause, he had commanded a force that had fought crown forces, not simply in the War of Independence but also during the earlier part of the Civil War; he also commanded men in the fight against the Free State forces during the latter conflict. He had himself taken the lives of others – two members of the Coastguard and possibly other members of the crown forces – certainly he believed that he and Christy O'Connell killed three men after firing on a British naval vessel. (While the Coastguard men's deaths were registered locally in the Union of Castletown, there appears to be no record in the register of the three other reported deaths.) It was while O'Dwyer was Commandant that a taboo was broken with the execution by his organisation of a woman, Bridget Noble, contrary to IRA rules. When crown forces withdrew after the Treaty, he had been given control of the police barracks and the coastguard station in Castletownbere. He told in an account in his MSP file how he was 'personally responsible for the arbitration of all Civil disputes in Berehaven, and the handling of all Criminal and Mental cases'. (He did not elaborate on what handling 'mental cases' would have involved.)

During the Civil War, he had acted as *de facto* ruler of Beara, with his men commandeering motor cars and other items they required and his Quartermaster collecting licence duty on alcohol. They also intercepted and read people's private correspondence. O'Dwyer was prepared to punish those who made comments, even in private, which he considered damaging to the 'good name' of the IRA. He clearly considered he had the authority to impose fines on individuals, or to banish them from Beara, with the threat of severe punishment if they failed to comply with his instructions. He did not always comply with IRA rules, or instructions from the IRA leadership, and seemed inclined to make up his own mind about what should be done, or not done. As mentioned, he pressed on for a period with attacks on Free State forces after the Civil War, ignoring the ceasefire called by IRA leader Frank Aiken. With the ultimate defeat of the anti-Treaty forces, all the heady power he had wielded in Beara was gone, and he would never again exercise that kind of authority.

Eventually, men who had been interned by the Free State would return to their home areas. In 1924, after leaving the National Army, Dr Murphy also returned to his home town of Castletownbere to resume service as a dispensary doctor, and as Medical Officer of Health for Castletown Number Two district. The IRA banishment order against him could no longer be enforced. He resided at Churchgate, Castletownbere, and later moved to a three-storey house in the West End district of the town, diagonally across from the police station. Records show that he lodged a claim for compensation with the Department of Finance in regard to the 'seizure of motor car and accessories at Castletown, County Cork by Irregular forces on 21 September 1922'. He was awarded the sum of £91.[42]

John Twomey, the former RIC sergeant who had been banished from Beara, returned to his home near Castletownbere towards the end of April 1923, by which time the Civil War was effectively over, and Free State forces were in control. Around July 1924, former RIC sergeant Michael Flynn also returned to Castletownbere with his wife and family, following their involuntary exile in Dover, where they stayed in lodgings at various addresses. As in the case of Dr Murphy and John Twomey, the IRA banishment order against Flynn could now be ignored. Flynn later resided with his wife and six children in Bandon where, in 1930, he seemed to be in financial difficulty. In a letter to the Home Office asking that part of his police pension be commuted to a cash payment, he remarked: 'I have a big family and have no other means of getting the money as ex-RIC men won't get any employment on account of remaining in the force until disbandment.'[43]

Death of Patsy Dan Crowley

Patsy Dan Crowley was freed from internment a few months after the end of the Civil War. In November 1923 he was included on a list of prisoners who could be released 'without prejudice to the safety of the State'.[44] He returned home to Glenbeg before Christmas 1923. However, he was seriously unwell. He underwent an operation in hospital in Cork, but it was not a success – he died in hospital on 14 June 1924. He was one of eight children of Dan Crowley and his wife Mary O'Shea of Glenbeg. Patsy Dan and his brother Jer Dan were the youngest of the children – all the other siblings emigrated to Butte, Montana where, as mentioned, many Beara natives settled. Underground copper mining in Butte was a dangerous occupation. Toiling in the hot, airless tunnels took its toll, and there were accidents.

Patsy Dan was pre-deceased by two brothers, Con and Tim, who died in Butte. Con, the eldest, died in the Minnie Healey Mine in July 1905 at age 29 years. Tim died in the Anaconda Mine in May 1916, aged 25 years. According to a family history, at one stage Patsy Dan himself went to Butte 'seeking political asylum' but returned to Glenbeg.[45] It is unclear when he would have travelled to Butte.

According to Ted O'Sullivan, a beating received by Patsy Dan at the time of the Civil War had 'fractured a bone in his head, or in his nose'.[46] Crowley's father accompanied the tricolour-draped coffin back to the Beara peninsula via Kenmare, and it was met by many of his former IRA comrades. Reporting on his death, the *Southern Star* stated: 'During the Anglo-Irish War, and especially during the Black and Tan regime, deceased was one of the most ardent fighters. He was a "much wanted" man and eventually was arrested by troops of the National forces...' The *Kerry Reporter* described him as 'Lieutenant of Transport and Supply during the Black and Tan days', and commented that he was 'a true-hearted man and a good Irishman'. The newspaper reported that the people of Kenmare 'regretted very much that they were not notified of the arrival of the remains of Patsy Dan Crowley'.[47] Father Daly, parish priest, officiated at the funeral and Crowley was laid to rest in Kilcatherine graveyard.[48] He was aged 28 years. This burial ground occupies an ancient monastic site, and is dominated by the ruins of a 7th century church. It is located in an area of great natural beauty and tranquillity beside the sea, overlooking Coulagh Bay.

The immediate aftermath of the Civil War was a bleak period for those on the losing side, but there were also some brighter moments. In early 1924 the state publication *Iris Oifigiúil* published a list of persons who were awarded damages on foot of criminal injury claims. Among them were Liam Dwyer, Cailroe, Eyeries, who was awarded £700. Another name on the list was that of Jeremiah O'Connor, Ardgroom, who was awarded £725.[49] These awards were obviously compensation for the destruction of their houses by crown forces in May 1921, as mentioned. Following the Treaty, there was an agreement between the British Government and the Irish Free State whereby the British would contribute funds towards the payment of compensation for the destruction of property, or injury to property, by crown forces in Ireland (Northern Ireland excluded), between 21 January 1919 and 11 July 1921. The compensation would also cover destruction or injury resulting from action 'ordered by the military authorities under martial law'.[50] (Not every member of the British establishment was happy with this arrangement. In the House of Lords in June 1925, Lord Danesfort objected strenuously to the payment of compensation 'to men who were in active rebellion against us...'[51])

Despite attempts by the Free State forces to seize arms in the possession of anti-Treaty fighters, members of the IRA on the Beara peninsula still retained rifles after the Civil War. A photograph (See Picture Section) taken in the Ardgroom area after the cessation of hostilities shows Liam O'Dwyer with a female companion who is holding a Lee Enfield rifle. Such rifles could still be deployed after the conflict, when deemed necessary. This is illustrated by an incident in Ardgroom in early 1924. The previous year, on 15 January, members of the new police force, the unarmed Civic Guard [to be known as An Garda Síochána] had arrived in Castletownbere and gradually established a presence in Beara.[52] In March 1924, Civic Guard officers based at Eyeries went to Ardgroom and arrested a man called Sheehan who had been bound to the peace in Berehaven District Court but refused to sign the bails. It was reported that men with rifles held up the Civic Guard officers in Ardgroom and freed the prisoner.[53] It was also reported that some time later a man 'wearing a trench coat' called at Eyeries Civic Guard Station and told the Guards 'to desist from any further attempts to arrest Sheehan'. A trench coat would have signalled that the visitor was from the IRA. This item of apparel, perhaps worn with a certain degree of male pride, would have been a *de rigeur* garment in the wardrobe of any well-dressed IRA member during the revolutionary era, conferring a certain glamour and status on the wearer.

Moving To America

As Ireland moved towards a semblance of normality following a bitter, internecine conflict, the Free State declared, on 8 November 1924, a legal amnesty for all acts committed during the Civil War. The leadership body of the IRA, known as the IRA Executive, continued in operation, but essentially the organisation went deeper underground. Efforts were made to re-organise units and keep the 'secret army' functioning, although it would prove difficult to maintain strength and cohesion, as members dropped out or moved abroad. The leadership tried to stop IRA members emigrating without permission, but often the rule was honoured more in the breach than in the observance.

One of the IRA officers who argued for a relaxation of the policy restricting emigration was Liam O'Dwyer.[54] He himself resigned as Commandant of the Beara Battalion and emigrated, but he kept in touch with the leadership back in Ireland, during a period when Moss Twomey, from Fermoy, County Cork, operated as IRA Chief of Staff.[55] It was on 27 August 1926 that O'Dwyer sailed from Cobh on the liner *Scythia*, arriving in Boston some days later, on 3 September.

He was named on the passenger list as 'William Dwyer' and his occupation was given as 'motor mechanic'.

On arrival in Boston, the US immigration authorities recorded that O'Dwyer's nearest relative was Miss Annie Dwyer of Eyeries, County Cork – this was O'Dwyer's sister, who had been a nun but left the convent shortly before profession to look after her younger siblings after their widowed mother died. The immigration records show that O'Dwyer was in possession of fifty dollars, and that he planned to join his cousin, Eugene Sullivan, who lived at Cambridge, Mass.[56] He ultimately settled in Detroit. In his memoir he states that after moving to America he found that 'hundreds' of IRA men who had emigrated before him 'had lost their religion entirely' because of the attitude of the Irish Catholic hierarchy during the Civil War.[57] He says that he argued with those he met and brought many back to 'Church practices'. (In a strongly-worded pastoral letter on 22 October 1922, Cardinal Logue and the Catholic hierarchy had vehemently denounced the anti-Treaty Irregulars as waging an 'unjust war'; declared that the Provisional Government was supported by the 'vast majority', and branded the killing of National soldiers as 'murder before God'.)

Apart from Liam O'Dwyer, a considerable number of men who had been in the Beara Battalion emigrated to the USA after the Civil War. One of the more prominent members of the battalion to go to America was Christy O'Connell. Records indicate he travelled initially to Canada on the liner *Ausonia* in 1924 and crossed into the US at Buffalo, on 5 June 1926, his contact on arrival being given as his brother Henry.[58] US Census data indicates that in 1930 he was staying in San Francisco with former Beara Battalion Quartermaster, Daniel T. Sullivan, and working as a blacksmith. It appears that O'Connell went through some difficult times in America in the early 1930s, the time of the Great Depression. The Eyeries-born writer Diarmaid Ó Súilleabháin recalled a conversation with O'Connell in which he told how he was 'on the bread line' in New York in 1932.[59] O'Connell described looking along the bread line and asking himself a question: 'Why was I fighting?' Ó Súilleabháin had high praise for O'Connell as a fighter during the Troubles, stating he was 'as good as Tom Barry'. O'Connell was one of the former Beara Battalion migrants who would later return to live in Beara.

For former IRA men who became migrants in America, the lure of the old country was still strong. In New York City, some socialised together and kept in touch with developments back home – they were particularly interested in availing of the military service pensions which, as will be explained in more detail, became available in the 1930s for those on the anti-Treaty side in the Civil War. One of the exiles who remained active in the republican movement in Amercia was Mark Sullivan, the former Beara Battalion Intelligence Officer who became Adjutant of the Battalion, and who was on the anti-Treaty side in the Civil War. He emigrated to Canada and then moved to the US in 1927, settling in Somerville, near Boston, Massachusetts.[60] In Somerville, Sullivan was active in the republican organisation, Clan na Gael and was President of the Terence MacSwiney Club. He became ill and died in Somerville at age 45 years in 1938. His widow, the former Elsie Nagle, had been an active member of Castletownbere branch of Cumann na mBan, and according to her MSP file, had also engaged in intelligence work. There was a big attendance of republicans at his funeral, with volleys fired over the grave. The funeral director was Gene Sheehan, a legendary Irish undertaker in the Boston area who specialised in bringing the remains of Irish exiles back to Ireland for burial in the 'old sod'.[61]

Men Said To Have Guarded Mrs Noble Settle in America

As previously indicated, a number of the young men who were said to have guarded Mrs Noble as a prisoner also emigrated and were living in the United States in later life, including Mike Lynch and Mike Shea. Records indicate that Shea moved initially to Canada, residing at Montreal, before emigrating to the USA in 1925, taking up residence at Somerville and later at Medford in the state of Massachussets. He passed away in the late 1960s, as did Mike Lynch. The latter sailed from Cobh on 8 April 1923, in the latter phase of the Civil War, arriving in Boston, Massachussets just over a week later, ultimately settling in Chicago, as mentioned. Another man named as having guarded Mrs Noble, Dan Harrington from Droumard, who had been an officer in Ardgroom Company, also moved to America in the latter stages of the Civil War. Records show that he sailed from Queenstown [Cobh] on the *President Polk*, arriving in New York on 5 April 1923, later settling near Boston, Massachussets. He went on to marry and have a family, and worked as a pipefitter. From his address at Rogers Avenue, Somerville, Harrington applied for a Service (1917 – 1921) Medal, and it was issued in 1948.[62] In his application, there is no mention of guarding Mrs Noble as a prisoner.

As regards Tim Rahilly, otherwise Reilly, another one of the group said to have guarded Mrs Noble, records show that Timothy Reilly, aged 20 years, sailed on board the newly-built liner, *Athenia*, arriving in Quebec, Canada in July 1923.[63] (The *Athenia* was destined to become the first UK ship to be sunk by a German submarine in the Second

World War.) He stated on a form 'Declaration of Passenger to Canada' that his citizenship was 'British', that he was in possession of 75 dollars and planned to stay with a friend, Mick Driscoll, at 101 St Antoine Street, Montreal. He gave his occupation as 'labourer' and stated that his object in going to Canada was 'to earn a living'. He later moved to the USA, and, as mentioned, resided in The Bronx, New York City. He was still a resident of The Bronx when he died at age 87 years in January 1990.

A sizeable number of those who had been in the Ardgroom Company, which covered Bridget Noble's own area of Reenavaude, were recorded as being in America in 1935, according to Military Service Pension records compiled that year.[64] All of the company members said to have questioned Nora Sullivan about Bridget Noble's complaint to the RIC following the hair-shearing attack were among those listed as being in the USA, except, of course, for Patsy Dan Crowley who died in 1924. James Malvey, Ardgroom; Jerh Connor and the afore-mentioned Tim Reilly, both of Ardgroom Inward and Con Crowley, Glenbeg, were all stated to be in America.

James Malvey settled in New York City and was joined in the USA by his younger brother, the afore-mentioned Patrick. Like some other republicans moving to the United States, Patrick Malvey travelled first to Canada, before crossing over into the USA. It was apparently considered easier to get into Canada, a member of the Commonwealth. A US immigration file records that Patrick Malvey crossed into the USA in September 1926, and proposed to stay with his brother James Malvey.[65] Patrick went on to reside in The Bronx area of New York City. He had been through some turbulent times during the revolutionary period, and it appears that as a result of his experiences, he suffered mental health problems in later life – what might nowadays be described as Post-Traumatic Stress Disorder. A family history posted online states that in the 1940s he spent time in a mental hospital 'due to problems from British beating'.[66] He had also, of course, been wounded during the Civil War and later taken prisoner by Free State forces, as mentioned. He died in 1945, aged only 49 years. James Malvey died in New York in 1961, aged 61 years.

Con Crowley sailed from Cobh to New York on the liner *America*, arriving on 15 May 1925.[67] In 1930 he married another immigrant, a woman from the Ardgroom area, and they lived at East 102nd Street, in the East Harlem neighbourhood of Manhattan. He later married a woman from Ballyvourney, County Cork.[68] In his petition for US citizenship Con Crowley described his occupation as 'labourer'. In later life he lived in The Bronx, and in 1964 it was reported that he was helping to run Mike Reidy's café at 94th Street on Lexington Avenue, in Manhattan.[69] He died aged 88 years in August 1990.

John Sheehan

John Sheehan, who had been Captain of Ardgroom Company, emigrated to New York in 1927. As previously indicated, he was involved in the investigation into Bridget Noble. It will be recalled that, according to the internal IRA report on her execution, the Captain had ordered a search of her house, uncovering letters she had received from members of the RIC, and also two photographs of policemen. This would have been a major black mark against her, in the eyes of the IRA. He was also named as one of those involved in arrangements for the guarding of Mrs Noble as a prisoner. After Sheehan married Julia O'Sullivan, Secretary of Ardgroom Cumann na mBan, the couple took up residence at his family farm at Canfie East. Three children were born while the couple lived here, and then they moved to the wife's family place at Eskadour, Lauragh, where a fourth child was born.[70] It seems that the Sheehans faced financial challenges at this period, and John resolved to seek work in America while his wife and children (three daughters and a son) remained in Ireland – an echo perhaps of how Alexander Noble moved to England to find work while his wife Bridget remained in Reenavaude.

Tragedy was to engulf the Sheehan family. After only about six months in New York, Sheehan became seriously ill and died – according to his wife in her application for a Military Service Pension, the cause of death was 'spinal meningitis'. (US records show that John Sheehan, born 1890, died in Manhattan, New York City, on 20 May 1928, aged 38 years.[71]) Just like Patsy Dan Crowley, who had succeeded him as Captain of Ardgroom Company and who was also linked to the Bridget Noble case, John Sheehan's life was cut short while still a young man. Neither had the opportunity to claim a Military Service Pension, nor to give a statement to the Bureau of Military History. One presumes that any knowledge they had of the Bridget Noble story went to the grave with them.

Daniel T. Sullivan

Daniel T. Sullivan, one of the staff officers of the Beara Battalion when Bridget Noble was abducted, also made a new life in America. (On official forms, he now used the 'O'Sullivan' version of his name.) After the Civil War, like other migrants from Beara, the former Battalion Quartermaster travelled initially to Canada, arriving there in August 1923. He worked as a farm labourer in Bowden, Alberta before moving to the United States, landing from a ferry at Seattle, Washington state, in October 1926. The immigration record indicated that he planned to stay with a relative in Bellevue, Washington. He ultimately settled in San Francisco where, in 1927, he married a woman from Castletownbere and had a family. He worked as a shipping clerk and applied in 1941 to become a US citizen. The photo in the official file shows a well-groomed 45-year-old man with clean-cut good looks – he could have passed for a police detective or FBI agent. He was granted citizenship in 1944. Shipping records indicate that, following the death of his first wife, he made an extended visit back to Ireland in 1948, travelling by ship from New York to Cobh and making the return journey some weeks later. In 1949 he married again, in the Manhattan borough of New York City, his second wife also being from Beara. In the early 1960s, he was residing at North Alarcon Street, Prescott, a town set high in the Bradshaw Mountains of central Arizona. Occasionally Beara people seeking a Service (1917 – 1921) Medal arising out of activities during the revolutionary period, or an allowance under army pension legislation, would ask O'Sullivan for support and he would fill in a form or write a letter to assist. It is unclear when he passed away.

Katie Sullivan

Katie Sullivan, who was Captain of the Ardgroom branch (or company) of Cumann na mBan at the time of the action taken against her relative, Bridget Noble, sailed from Cobh to Boston in 1926, ultimately settling in Cincinnati, Ohio, where she lived at Mercer Street. She worked in Altman Brothers shoe factory. In later years she suffered ill health, and in October 1965 Liam O'Dwyer wrote to the Department of Defence in Dublin to inquire about the possibility of her getting a Disability Allowance. He stated that 'she is now living in very poor circumstances', adding: 'She is in receipt of Social Security benefit but it is not enough. For years she has been suffering from arthritis and three years ago she broke her back. Her medical treatment is taking away all her income. She was never married.'

Katie, under the name Catherine A. O'Sullivan, applied for a Service (1917-1921) Medal in 1974 and in a letter to the Department of Defence mentioned that she had been in hospital for over two weeks. 'I take pain pills. I'm very nervous, can't get on or off the bus.' She stated that she was Company Captain in Ardgroom Cumann na mBan from 1918 to 11 July 1921. The medal was duly awarded in 1974.[72] However, an application for a Special Allowance under the Army Pensions Act was rejected that same year on the grounds of means, in light of her US Social Security benefit.[73] She died at age 85 years in a Cincinnati hospital in October 1982, and was laid to rest at Gate of

Heaven Cemetery in Montgomery, Hamilton County, Ohio. It was noted in Ohio state records that she was 'single'. Ms O'Sullivan would have had particular knowledge of the Bridget Noble drama but there is no indication that she left a memoir dealing with this matter, or with her experiences as an officer of Cumann na mBan in Ardgroom during the revolutionary period. Only very limited details about her service are given in the Military Archives files relating to her applications for a medal and a special allowance.

Liam O'Dwyer Returns from America

During his own sojourn in America, Liam O'Dwyer remained committed to the cause. The militaristic 'physical force' tradition in Irish republicanism still had a major influence on his thinking. British forces were still in Northern Ireland, and in Detroit he made an unsuccessful attempt to start an organisation with other Irishmen that would 'resume the struggle for the freedom of Ulster'.[74] (A complicating factor was that the Protestant Unionist majority in Northern Ireland wanted to maintain the connection with Britain – they had no wish to be 'freed' from British rule. O'Dwyer would have had no tolerance for the 'Two Nations Theory' which emerged in some circles in Ireland – proponents argued that Ulster Protestants in the northeast part of the island of Ireland were a separate people, also entitled to self-determination.)

O'Dwyer told in his memoir how he had a disagreement with Robert Monteith on the new group – as indicated above, this was the man who had landed from a German submarine in County Kerry with Roger Casement in 1916. Monteith had settled in Detroit where he worked for Ford and other car manufacturing companies. O'Dwyer claimed that Monteith wanted the group to have a Communist ideology. O'Dwyer argued that Communism should be left out of this organisation, 'that our struggle was for the independence of Christian Ireland, and that when Ireland was free, the people should be the rulers of the country through their democratically elected representatives – but only when the country was free from foreign rule'.[75]

O'Dwyer returned to Ireland in 1935, and became very disillusioned with the Fianna Fáil government led by Éamon de Valera. Dev, the political figurehead of the anti-Treaty side during the Civil War, had founded the Fianna Fáil party in 1926, after splitting with abstentionist Sinn Féin. With his leadership qualities, his imposing presence, his background as a 1916 rebel leader, and his austere personal charisma, de Valera attracted the support of large numbers of those who had opposed the Treaty, including men who had been active in the Beara Battalion. Dev's mystique was probably enhanced by his exotic name, a combination of the Gaelic and the Spanish. The rather ordinary name, 'Eddie Coll' by which he was known as a boy in rural County Limerick, may not have had the same impact.

After the 1932 general election de Valera formed a government with the aid of Labour. He quickly embraced constitutional methods, and after a honeymoon period, outlawed the IRA. His government would go on to intern IRA members during the Second World War, or the Emergency as it was known in neutral Ireland, and some IRA men were executed for murder; others were allowed die on hunger strike. This caused great resentment among IRA members and supporters, although it may have enhanced support for de Valera among those who were strongly opposed to the IRA. Liam O'Dwyer did not consider Fianna Fáil a truly republican party. His sympathies still lay with the IRA, now outlawed, and he told in his memoir how he met a prominent former IRA commander and proposed a resumption of guerrilla tactics in Ulster, but clearly to the disappointment of O'Dwyer, the man did not consider that such tactics would work.[76]

Two murders carried out by the IRA in early 1936 caused widespread revulsion, and it was later that year that the de Valera government decided to ban the organisation. In County Waterford, a young man called John Egan was shot, apparently accused of giving information to An Garda Síochána. In West Cork, Vice Admiral Henry Boyle Somerville, a 72-year-old retired Royal Navy officer and member of the Church of Ireland, was shot at his Castletownshend home by an IRA gunman for a very trivial 'offence' – it appears he had given references to local youths who had approached him for help in joining the navy. The order for action to be taken against Somerville was given by IRA commandant in Cork, Tom Barry, who told writer Meda Ryan that he had given an order to 'get' Somerville. Barry seemed to distance himself from the actual killing, claiming that his intention was 'a kidnapping to be used in a type of deal with the government'.[77]

While de Valera decided he could not allow the IRA to arrogate to itself the right to execute Irish citizens and would go on to suppress the organisation, one particular action he took found favour with republicans. Under de Valera, the Military Service Pension (MSP) scheme was extended el to include suitably-qualified applicants who had operated on the anti-Treaty side in the Civil War. Shortly after he returned to Ireland, Liam O'Dwyer became one of many former members of the anti-Treaty IRA to apply for a pension. As a former Commandant of the Beara Battalion, and as Chairman of the Battalion Committee, he played an important role in the mid-1930s in supplying the MSP authorities at the Department of Defence with names of those who had served in the battalion. These records have since come into the public domain.

In giving an account of Ballycrovane company, he explains to the Department how Robert Dwyer [his brother] was Captain of the company in February 1917; in 1918, after Robert's death, he himself, Liam, was elected Captain; when Liam was made Battalion Adjutant, John Dwyer [another brother] was elected Captain and held the position until February 1923 – John would also apply for a pension. This, of course, was the brother who was given a prison term in March 1921 and was later interned, and who has been mentioned in the context of Bridget Noble. It appears that John Dwyer maintained his rank as Captain of Ballycrovane Company while incarcerated. Liam O'Dwyer comments in his notes accompanying the lists he supplied to the Department: 'While Capt [Captain John Dwyer] was interned the Coy [Company] was managed by the Lieutenants.'

It emerges that Liam O'Dwyer was in severe financial difficulties at this period in the mid-1930s when he was dealing with MSP matters. In a communication with the Department of Defence, which has been released online, he stated that he was unable to supply a map of the battalion area that had been requested, as he regretted he was not financially able to buy one. 'I have been living for the past twelve months on borrowed money and I would be very grateful if you would expedite the disposition of my claim which was heard seven weeks ago. My wife and children are often hungry.'[78]

O'Dwyer was a man of considerable enterprise and energy and his situation gradually improved. He built a house in Ardgroom for his growing family, set up a shop, built a dance hall behind his house, and later had a farm near the town. (In building the dance hall in the late 1930s, O'Dwyer installed iron-framed windows salvaged from the ruins of the afore-mentioned Church of Ireland church in Reenavaude. The windows, with small diamond-shaped panes of glass, were a quaint feature of the hall where locals enjoyed the innocent pleasures of céilí dancing and old-time waltzes.)

No doubt it must have pleased O'Dwyer considerably when, in 1938, the British withdrew from Berehaven and the other Treaty ports. During the Second World War, there was an unusual development. Liam O'Dwyer's youngest brother James became a member of the force that Liam and other members of the family had once fought strenuously against – the British Army. Apparently, Jim was conscripted after emigrating to London, and served with the British forces in the Sahara Desert and North Africa.[79] Some other siblings of Liam O'Dwyer moved to America, including younger brother Michael. After emigrating in 1928, Michael pursued a military career, enlisting in the US Army. Records show that in October 1939, just after the start of the Second World War, he was serving with the 13th Infantry Regiment at Fort Adams, an historic coastal fort in Newport, Rhode Island.[80] Later during the war he was a training officer with the US Army in Texas.[81] He died at age 79 years in New York City in December 1985.

Liam O'Dwyer Assists Woman Who Helped Him Evade Arrest

Liam O'Dwyer was often called on to assist individuals seeking a Military Service Pension by writing letters testifying to their role during the revolutionary period. He was particularly diligent in assisting those former members of the movement who had fallen on hard times. In the early 1940s, one particular request for a testimonial clearly had particular resonance for him, and he gave unstinted support to the claimant. Mrs Julia Sheehan was in poor health and, apparently, in poor financial circumstances when she decided to seek a pension.

The former Julia O'Sullivan, who had been Secretary of Ardgroom Cumann na mBan, was the widow of John Sheehan, who had served as Captain of Ardgroom Company. As previously outlined, both had figured in the Bridget Noble saga, and John had died as a young man in New York in 1928. As will be recalled, it was Julia who helped Liam O'Dwyer evade capture in 1921 by slamming the door in the faces of a military raiding party who tried to arrest him during his mother's wake. Mrs Sheehan was too ill to attend an interview in Dublin in connection with her pension claim, and she provided only basic details in the form she was required to fill in. (Although Mrs Sheehan would have had particular knowledge of the Noble case, there is no reference to Mrs Noble in the pension file which has been released online.) As previously indicated, an official observed in a handwritten note in her pension file that the man she married, Sheehan, had been a Company Captain; there is also a reference to Sheehan being 'wounded at Crossbarry'.[82]

From her home at Eskadour, Lauragh, Mrs Sheehan told the pension authorities in a letter dated 14 October 1940 that her husband went to America 'to make money for us' and he died 'when my eldest child was only six years and the youngest was only six months'. She hoped they would award her something 'to help me rear my four orphans after my years of work for my country'. In her application she wrote of how her house was used as a billet during 'both fights' – a reference to the War of Independence and the Civil War. She claimed that when the 'fight was over', she was deeply in debt and had to sell her house. 'My shop faded out during the second fight [Civil War] as I could not replace the stock.' She recalled her assistance to Liam O'Dwyer in his hour of need: 'I saved my Commandant's life when the billet was surrounded by blocking the door and holding it so, till he was safe in a hide-out.'

Mrs Sheehan's original application was rejected, and Liam O'Dwyer wrote to the Pensions Board on 12 October 1940 warning that if services such as Mrs Sheehan's are not recognised, 'it will cause a hell of a kick amongst her Army and Cumann na mBan friends when taken in comparison with awards made to even men of less service.' He pleaded: 'Give her something and you will do what is right.' In a further letter dated 14 January 1942, O'Dwyer stated: 'I would very earnestly recommend that this woman be awarded something in consideration of her outstanding services which, amongst continuous routine work, included the saving of my life by holding the door of my house against "Tans" with fixed bayonets till I got into safety.' Ultimately, Mrs Sheehan was awarded a pension in 1943 based on her service during the War of Independence and the Civil War. She died in 1973, aged 81 years. As in the case of her fellow officer in Ardgroom Cumann na mBan, Katie Sullivan, it appears Mrs Sheehan did not leave any record outlining what she knew of the Bridget Noble disappearance.

In the 1948 general election Liam O'Dwyer made a rare foray into electoral politics by running as a candidate in West Cork constituency for the new republican party, Clann na Poblachta, headed by Sean MacBride, former IRA Chief of Staff. O'Dwyer's aim was to get the de Valera government 'out of office' and free IRA prisoners.[83] O'Dwyer's former IRA comrade Ted O'Sullivan of Fianna Fáil topped the poll and O'Dwyer came in last. A collection was organised to re-imburse him for the loss of his deposit. Tom Barry also lost his deposit when he came last in the Cork Borough by-election in 1946 – he had stood as an Independent. The experience of Barry and O'Dwyer would suggest that having a notable record as an IRA commander did not necessarily guarantee success at the polls.

Chapter 23: Bridget Noble

Excluded from Accounts of Conflict

in Beara

In later life Liam O'Dwyer wrote up memories of his own role in the IRA. He contributed a lengthy statement to the Bureau of Military History (BMH) in 1956 and in the 1970s he wrote a book, *Beara in Irish History*, which included a personal memoir giving a detailed account of his activities during the revolutionary period. Both the statement and the book commemorate the bravery of the Volunteers during the time of conflict and are an important contribution to the history of those turbulent times. However, even though he was Commandant of the Battalion when his men abducted and later executed Bridget Noble, and even though he had written an internal IRA report on the execution, there is no mention of Bridget in either the statement or the book, or indeed any reference to a woman being put to death by battalion personnel. As previously indicated, neither is there any reference to the Noble case in O'Dwyer's Military Service Pension (MSP) file which has been released into the public domain.

Other men who had been in the Beara Battalion, including Christopher O'Connell who became Vice O/C around the time of the Truce, also gave statements to the Bureau of Military History but none of them mentions Mrs Noble. It appears that in preparing statements for the Bureau, Liam O'Dwyer called 'several meetings of the surviving officers in the area' to help visiting Bureau investigators get 'as compete a record as possible', according to investigators' notes. One historian has suggested, in the context of the Bridget Noble case, that this may have been partly an attempt 'to control the narrative'.[1]

Liam Deasy's book, *Towards Ireland Free*, about the Cork No. 3 Brigade of the IRA, includes a considerable amount of material on the Beara Battalion, but there is no reference to Bridget Noble. Sean T. O'Sullivan wrote a series of newspaper articles in the 1970s about the activities of the Beara Battalion during the War of Independence – once again, there is no mention of a woman being executed.[2] As previously stated, Mrs Noble is mentioned in the MSP file of Mrs Hannah Hanley. However, the Noble case does not appear to figure in other MSP files relating to prominent Beara republicans that have been released to the public via the Military Archives website. Mrs Hanley's superior officer in Cumann na mBan, Bella O'Connell, who was the head ['District Secretary'] of the organisation in Beara and who organised local branches in Ardgroom and elsewhere, sought a Military Service Pension. Liam O'Dwyer wrote in support of her application. In her pension file, which has become available, she stated that she organised a 'special intelligence system in cooperation with the IRA Battalion intelligence department'.[3] However, there is no mention of Bridget Noble or of a female being executed.

Another prominent Beara republican who applied for a pension and whose file is available is Michael Crowley, Castletownbere, who was a staff officer of the Beara Battalion, serving as Adjutant, at the time of Mrs Noble's abduction – once again, there is no reference in the file to a woman being taken prisoner and put to death, although Liam O'Dwyer asserted that the officers responsible for her execution were the staff of the battalion 'at that time'.[4]

There was one man from Beara, from a younger generation than Liam O'Dwyer, who followed in the militant republican footsteps of O'Dwyer, and who made a rare public comment about hair-cutting attacks on women. This was Eyeries-born Diarmaid Ó Súilleabháin (1932 – 1985), a teacher and Irish language novelist who was proud to declare himself a cousin [col ceathar] of O'Dwyer. Both men were involved in the 1971 unveiling of a memorial tablet at the Beara grave of Gaelic scholar and teacher Pádraig Ó Laoire, with a wreath being laid from Joe Cahill of the Provisional IRA (PIRA) in Belfast. In the 1970s Ó Súilleabháin was a member of the Ardchomhairle [supreme council] of Sinn Féin and editor of the party newspaper *An Phoblacht*. It emerged after his death that he was also a member of the PIRA, acting as an intelligence officer and Director of Publicity.[5] In 1972 he became the first person to be given a prison sentence by the new Special Criminal Court in Dublin after evidence that he had incited a crowd to join the PIRA.

In an Irish-language interview published after his death, Ó Súilleabháin expressed admiration for the Old IRA and said it would be wrong to think the IRA men of a former era were 'soft'. [… *ná ceap go rabhadar bog.*][6] He went on to relate how they shot men as informers and were right to do so, and how 'the hair was cut from girls that time as well, believe it'. One wonders if he was referring to Mrs Noble, who

254

seems to have been the only recorded victim of such an attack in Beara. Ó Súilleabháin had particular knowledge of the War of Independence in Beara – it forms the backdrop for his award-winning 1964 novel *Dianmhuilte Dé*.

Ó Súilleabháin was the son of the afore-mentioned Johnny Sullivan, and his wife Mary Ann. Sullivan was one of the demobilised RIC men who decided to join the Royal Ulster Constabulary (RUC) in the new state of Northern Ireland – a third of the force's membership had been reserved for Catholics. His first wife, Margaret, died tragically in Belfast in 1925 at age 27 years from a pulmonary embolism while expecting their first child, and he later returned to Eyeries. In 1930 he married a widow, Mary Ann Murphy at Glengarriff. She was a teacher, and sister of Sean O'Driscoll who, as mentioned, was a leading IRA figure in Beara, and was on the Free State side in the Civil War, later serving in An Garda Síochána.

In MSP files currently available, there are cases where 'bobbing' operations were mentioned as part of a claim for a pension. Timothy O'Donoghue, who was a member of Kilmeen Company in West Cork, part of Cork No 3 Brigade, stated that he 'carried out special operation against a woman spy in another Company area, the lady subsequently awarded £300 for the loss of her hair'. In another pension file, Patrick M. Ahern stated that he led a section of Volunteers in Templeglantine, County Limerick and that they 'broke into houses of people who were giving information to the RIC'. Some of these were 'young girls' and after they ignored warnings their hair was cut off. In regard to the hair cutting, he said they 'made a good job of it'. He claimed it was also a 'good job' for the 'young girls' as they were 'very well paid for it' [i.e. giving information]. In his pension application, James Gannon stated that as a member of the Fianna boy scouts in Dublin in 1919, he was involved with others in the punishment of the daughter of an 'Orangeman' in the Donnybrook area of the city. They received information that she was 'keeping company' with a British 'secret service agent'. They tied up the girl, 'cut her hair and tarred her'. In another application for a pension, Maurice Quinn, of Rathkeale Company in County Limerick, told how his family home was wrecked by British military, and he himself wounded, as a reprisal for his brothers 'docking' [cutting] the hair of women who associated with British soldiers. He did not personally take part in the 'docking' but he 'sharpened the scissors'.[7]

Frank Busteed's Pension Claim

As regards the shooting of Mrs Lindsay and her driver, James Clarke, the former IRA officer Frank Busteed cited his own involvement in these killings as part of a claim in the 1930s for a military service pension. Details of his application emerged when the file was released in 2014. Clarke, whose body was said to have been buried in the same secret grave as Mrs Lindsay in the Flagmount district of Rylane, was particularly unfortunate. There is no indication that this Presbyterian from County Down was a spy or an informer. He was the chauffeur who just happened to be driving Mrs Lindsay on the day she decided to inform the British about the planned IRA ambush. When Mrs Lindsay was abducted, the IRA officer Jackie O'Leary abducted Clarke as well.

Tim Sheehan states in his book that Busteed and other officers considered it was a mistake for O'Leary to abduct Clarke. Instead of being of any practical use to them he was an added burden. 'Frank Busteed desired nothing better than to release him, if he was convinced it would be safe to do so.'[8] (This would suggest that Busteed, who was interviewed by Sheehan, did not see Clarke as a spy or an informer. It is unlikely Busteed would have contemplated releasing Clarke if any suspicion attached to the prisoner. According to Sheehan, Busteed had a particularly unforgiving attitude towards suspected spies, and told of how Jackie O'Leary intervened just in time to stop Busteed executing a Donoughmore man as a 'spy' – O'Leary believed the man was the victim of viciously-spread half-truths. The man apparently lost his 'mental balance' after his terrifying experience of coming close to death by being placed in front of Busteed's firing squad, with Busteed measuring the range for the rifles, and was committed to an institution.[9])

Unfortunately for James Clarke, it seems local IRA men considered that he knew too much about the abductors of Mrs Lindsay and their hiding places, and feared that, if released, he could give information to the crown forces. It seems he was shot, not because he was an informer but in case he might become an informer. The academic authors of the study of 'suspected spies' killed by the IRA in County Cork, comment: 'It is unlikely that James Clarke was a spy or an informer. His execution was attributable primarily to his association with Mrs Lindsay at the time of her abduction and then to the knowledge he must have acquired about her captors and the location of their hiding places.'[10]

The perception of Clarke as an Ulster Protestant Loyalist may not have helped him, and may have added to the concern that he could not be trusted to stay quiet about what he had seen. In his book *Execution*, Sean O'Callaghan claimed that Clarke, on his monthly visit to Cork, got very drunk 'and picked up young soldiers'. Then he would return on the last train to Coachford, and 'weave his way to Leemount House' singing the Loyalist ballad, *The Sash My Father Wore*.[11] Nowadays, Clarke's sexual orientation is unlikely to be an issue, but in an era rife with homophobia, the suggestion, even though unproven, that Clarke was a homosexual, especially one who allegedly consorted with British soldiers, and who had Loyalist or Orange Order sympathies, would have had very negative connotations among republicans of that period. The unfortunate Ulsterman seemed to tick all the wrong boxes. (Tim Sheehan, in his own book, gives no indication that the butler/chauffeur was homosexual or bi-sexual, stating that Clarke was 'courting' Alice Conway who, along with her sister Grace, were servants employed by Mrs Lindsay. [12] The sisters were Catholics from County Mayo.)

While Frank Busteed apparently accepted that Clarke was not a spy, he referred to both Clarke and Mrs Lindsay as 'spies' when he cited his role in their execution as part of his successful application for a pension. Maybe Busteed meant to convey that Clarke was a 'potential' spy. In his pension application, Busteed also recalled his role in burning Mrs Lindsay's house. He also mentioned that they took a British Intelligence Officer off a train at Blarney 'and executed him'.[13] It was easy to put the label of 'spy' on a person like James Clarke who had been shot – the victim could not answer back. The sad case of Mr Clarke would suggest that not everyone labelled a 'spy' during the revolutionary era was actually involved in spying.

In his pension application Busteed also made the surprising claim that in the Dripsey ambush, 'the British must have lost about 20 men'. No other reports of any casualties on the British side have come to light. Sean O'Callaghan's book *Execution*, written with the cooperation of Busteed, states there were 'no casualties' among the British.[14] IRA participants in the ambush, in statements made to the BMH, do not mention any casualties sustained by the crown forces in this engagement, while the British unit involved, the 1st Battalion, Manchester Regiment, recorded its own casualties as 'nil'.[15]

In his book, author Sean O'Callaghan depicts Busteed as having considerable contempt for James Clarke. Busteed is, for instance, quoted as describing the chauffeur as a 'worthless specimen' during a confrontation with Mrs Lindsay. The idea of 'manliness' was part of IRA culture, and perhaps Busteed saw Clarke as being deficient in this area. Clarke was obviously in fear of his life, a fear that would prove well-grounded, and it appears that he did not manage to conceal his sense of anxiety and apprehension. By diminishing Clarke's dignity as a person and describing him as 'worthless', one wonders if Busteed was seeking to make his own action in executing a rather harmless individual appear more acceptable.

In contrast with the allegedly 'worthless' Clarke, Busteed is portrayed as a courageous man of action in O'Callaghan's book. An account is given of how Busteed tracked down and killed three British officers after two of them, a year earlier, had thrown his mother [aged 50 years] down the stairs during a raid, resulting in her death.[16] Busteed is quoted in the book as stating: 'They must have had some suspicion that I was responsible for the death of Mrs Lindsay. I haven't any doubt about that. That is why they killed my mother. It was revenge all right.'[17] (Three British officers, two of whom had an intelligence background, were abducted along with their army driver, in late April 1922 in Macroom, despite the Truce. According to statements made to the BMH, the four were executed on orders from the leadership of the Cork No. 1 Brigade. The bodies were secretly buried in a shallow grave.[18])

The authors of an academic study of the Bandon Valley atrocity, which happened around the same period, have cast doubt on the account of Busteed's reported role in the capture and killing of the officers. They say that accounts by Macroom IRA veterans do not mention Busteed's involvement, and that Irish Republican Police records place him at a court hearing in Blarney, 28 kms from Macroom, on the day of the abduction. The authors also point out that the death certificate for Busteed's mother states that she died of 'chronic pneumonia and heart disease', and that the informant was Busteed himself. The authors conclude that 'it seems unlikely that he had directly participated in the officers' arrest or their execution'.[19]

After the Civil War, Frank Busteed lived for a period in America, before returning to reside in Cork. He became active in Fianna Fáil and served as a Lieutenant in the Irish Defence Forces during the Emergency. His son, Frank junior, born in Massachusetts in 1927, was ordained a Catholic priest in Waterford Cathedral in 1951 by Bishop Daniel Cohalan, ironically a nephew of his namesake, the Bishop of Cork, Dr Daniel Cohalan, who had strongly condemned the IRA during the War of Independence, and who was still in office. It was a great honour to have a son a priest, and Frank senior and his family posed proudly for photos with the newly-ordained cleric. The Rev. Busteed served in San Antonio diocese, Texas, and died there in 1998. Frank senior died at the South Infirmary, Cork, on 9 November 1974 and after Requiem Mass at St. Patrick's Church was buried at St. Finbarr's Cemetery. A vote of sympathy to Busteed's relatives was passed at a meeting of the Southern Committee of Cork County Council. The proposer was a man who was no stranger himself to the murky world of IRA executions, former Fianna Fáil TD, Martin Corry.

Liam O'Dwyer's Later Life in Beara, and the Ulster Troubles

On the Beara peninsula, as the years passed, Liam O'Dwyer and other former members of the Beara Battalion gathered from time to time for reunions or commemoration ceremonies or to attend the funerals of comrades who had died. At the funerals, it was usually O'Dwyer who led the graveside recital of a decade of the Rosary in Irish for the deceased. Firing parties were arranged, and they included men like Connie Healy, but with the passage of time the firing of volleys was replaced by having a tricolour on the coffin. In April 1966, on the 50th anniversary of the Easter Rising, large crowds gathered in Castletownbere for the Beara 1916-21 commemoration ceremonies. Members of the local Catholic clergy were on the platform, and Liam O'Dwyer had pride of place as the main speaker. In his oration, he said he was happy to speak on a platform 'on which there are representatives of the church'. O'Dwyer said that the main object of the Rising was not to win freedom then and there, 'it was to awaken and inspire the then dormant soul of Ireland'. He urged young people to learn the Irish language, through which 'your Christianity was brought down to you intact through centuries of trouble and adversity'. Among the dwindling number of former combatants present was Christy O'Connell, who laid a wreath at the Republican Monument.

In old age, Liam O'Dwyer continued to be a man of strong views, and would write letters to the newspapers on various contentious issues. During the War of Independence and Civil War, the IRA had burned down many big houses belonging to the former landed gentry, while other houses later fell grandually into decay. In one letter, O'Dwyer scorned efforts to conserve such mansions, arguing that they were not part of 'Irish Heritage', and were built with rents 'extracted from the downtrodden Irish'. He looked forward to the day when they would all be 'without roofs, windows or doors...'[20]

In 1973 a controversy generated by another letter led to him becoming the first person to successfully sue the newly-launched *Sunday World* for libel.[21] The newspaper had published an interview with the colourful hypnotist and showman, Paul Goldin and his then-wife Maeve. The couple supplied a handout photo of Mrs Goldin, taken by Mr Goldin in sunny Hawaii, in which she was in holiday attire, wearing shorts and a summery blouse. Mr O'Dwyer was a newsagent and, according to him, he received complaints from female customers about the photo. He wrote a strongly-worded letter of protest for publication in the newspaper, objecting to Mrs Goldin's attire, finding her top with its plunging neckline too revealing, and condemning the publication of the photo. He demanded that the person responsible be sacked. Subsequent comments on the letters page were critical of Mr O'Dwyer. He sued for libel for £2,000 over certain comments that he deemed defamatory and in February 1974 was awarded £500 damages at Cork Circuit Court.

It was not generally known at the time that the man who objected to the photo of Mrs Goldin was, in a previous era, the IRA commandant who had written an internal IRA report explaining why his organisation 'bobbed' and then executed Mrs Noble. It is noteworthy that the legal firm that represented him in the libel action was J. Travers Wolfe & Co. This is the Skibbereen firm founded by Jasper Travers Wolfe who was once targeted for assassination by the IRA and who also, of course, figures in the story of Bridget Noble. The solicitor dealing with the case was Jim O'Keeffe, a partner in the firm, who would not have shared O'Dwyer's political views – the lawyer would later become a long-serving TD with Fine Gael, successor party to Cumann na nGaedheal which was founded in 1923 and was supported by those on the Free State side in the Civil War.

Mandate from the People

When the Troubles in Northern Ireland escalated in the early 1970s, Liam O'Dwyer was in full sympathy with the insurgency campaign launched by the Provisional IRA (PIRA). The PIRA aimed to undermine the Northern Ireland state and, in effect, to force northern Protestant Unionists into a united Ireland against their will. A civil rights campaign by Catholic nationalists had sparked a vicious reaction by Loyalist extremists, who attacked Catholic districts forcing some residents to flee to the republic. Reforms were introduced to make the northern state a 'warmer house' for Catholic nationalists, but in the meantime the PIRA went on the offensive.

The PIRA strategy, as outlined in its internal 80-page handbook, *The Green Book* (probably compiled in 1977), was to carry out a war of attrition against enemy personnel 'aimed at causing as many casualties and deaths as possible'.[22] The PIRA was to become a highly efficient killing machine and would become the biggest single source of deaths during the Troubles, responsible for the deaths not just of men and women in uniform but of many civilians, Catholic and Protestant. PIRA violence brought a ruthless reaction from loyalist paramilitaries, who committed many atrocities and murdered many Catholics as part of their own terror campaign. Victims were often chosen at random and in some cases were brutally tortured before death. In targeting women specifically, there were times when loyalist paramilitaries seemed far more ruthless than their PIRA counterparts.

260

PIRA atrocities against civilians were widely condemned and in the republic, critics of the organisation assailed it for carrying out acts of terrorism in the name of the Irish people, while having no such mandate. Liam O'Dwyer had no patience for the argument that the PIRA had no mandate. He took the view that the PIRA did not need a mandate from the people. Writing in his 1977 memoir, he said it was 'sickening' to hear 'the politicians of today' shouting that the present IRA 'have no mandate from the people'. He went on: 'Did the Easter Week patriots have a mandate from the people? Did the Fenians or any previous patriots have such a mandate? Any Movement for freedom operating on a mandate from the people is doomed to failure.'[23] PIRA leaders did not seem unduly concerned about a 'mandate from the people'. PIRA doctrine, as outlined in *The Green Book*, states that the PIRA leadership is 'the lawful government of the Irish Republic' – a most remarkable claim, as PIRA bosses had never put themselves before the people in an election.

The idea of a 'mandate from the people' was a sensitive issue for some republicans. Stung by suggestions that the PIRA of the modern era was engaged in acts of terrorism, with no mandate from the people, while the Old IRA of the early 1920s fought a morally superior, clean war for freedom, a pamphlet was issued in 1985 by Sinn Féin, political wing of the PIRA, to hit back at the critics.[24] The pamphlet lambasted the attitude of Catholic clerics and constitutional nationalists, and assailed the 'hypocrisy' of those who revered the Old IRA while 'deriding their more effective and arguably less bloody successors'. The pamphlet claimed that when the people returned a Sinn Féin majority in the 1918 election, they had not voted for war. 'Nobody was asked to vote for war.' It stated that Michael Collins did not have a mandate from the ballot box 'to carry out his bloody guerrilla war'.

The pamphlet went on to list acts of violence carried out by the Old IRA during the War of Independence, with particular emphasis on the shooting of civilians and policemen. Many harrowing details were included in the narrative, to illustrate the ruthlessness of republicans of that era. Details of women who were wounded or who died as a result of Old IRA actions were provided. It was recalled how an elderly woman, Mrs Ellen Morris, was shot dead at point-blank range – she had tried to stop six men entering her County Wexford home to search for arms. There was also an account of the execution of Kate Carroll. There was no mention of the execution of Bridget Noble – understandable, perhaps, in light of the fact that little had emerged into the public domain at the time about the disappearance and killing of the woman from Beara.

Despite the focus on the victims of Old IRA violence, including female victims, the PIRA was, in fact, responsible for the deaths of a considerable number of women during the more recent Troubles. The versions of the Old IRA that operated during the revolutionary period either excluded measures allowing the execution of women, or specifically banned such executions, as previously indicated. The PIRA, by contrast, did not include in its *Green Book* any measure outlawing the execution of females. While Jean McConville eventually became the most high-profile female victim of PIRA executioners, PIRA members did, in fact, execute or deliberately kill other women during the 'armed struggle'. Examples include Catherine Mahon, shot with her husband Gerard as alleged informers and mother of three Caroline Moreland, also shot as an alleged informer. Young mother Joanne Mathers was shot while collecting census forms in Derry – republicans had boycotted the census, and forensic tests showed that the gun had been used in PIRA punishment attacks. Heather Thompson (17 years) was one of two Protestants shot dead in 1974 at the Belfast filling station where they worked – Ms Thompson was made to kneel and then shot five times. One of the teenaged gunmen convicted of the murders said they were in retaliation for the assassination of Catholics. In 1984 the PIRA went after its highest-profile female target when it narrowly failed in its bomb attempt to assassinate Britain's first female Prime Minister, Margaret Thatcher. Five people died, including three women.

There were many incidents in which women died as 'collateral damage' or as a result of indiscriminate bomb or gunfire attacks carried out by the PIRA. Examples include Linda Boyle (19 years) and Joanne McDowell (29 years) two of five Protestants killed or fatally injured when the PIRA attacked the Bayardo Bar in Belfast. Mother of three, Ruby Kidd (28 years) was one of three Protestants who died when gunmen from the Republican Action Force (believed to be a cover name used by PIRA members) attacked a bar in Templepatrick, County Antrim. A young nurse, Marie Wilson and four other women were among the eleven Protestants killed on Remembrance Day, 1987 when a PIRA bomb exploded during a ceremony in Enniskillen. Marie's father Gordon, a Christian man, comforted her as she lay dying under the rubble and declared later that he 'bore no ill will' towards the perpetrators.

There were cases where women were killed along with male family members who were serving or former members of the security forces. Examples include Emily Bullock (50 years) who was shot dead along with her husband Thomas Bullock at their home – he was a member of the Ulster Defence Regiment (UDR). Violet Mackin was shot dead after she tried to protect her husband, Patrick Mackin who was also killed at their home even though he had retired from the Prison Service. (One thinks also of schoolteacher Mary Travers, shot dead by the PIRA outside a Catholic church during an assassination attempt on her father. He was not a member of the security forces – he was a magistrate.) The PIRA also killed women who joined the security forces. Examples include part-time UDR member Margaret Hearst, a single mother, who was shot while off-duty at her caravan home in the presence of her three-year-old daughter; Gillian Liggett, shot during a sniper attack on a UDR mobile patrol and 19-year-old RUC member Linda Baggley shot while on foot patrol in Derry.

During the Civil War the anti-Treaty IRA at one stage introduced an order prohibiting the execution of youths under the age of 18 years, as mentioned. The PIRA had no such rule, and an early example of a minor being executed as an alleged informer by the organisation occurred in 1973. Fifteen-year-old Bernard Teggart, who was said to have been intellectually challenged, was abducted from a Belfast training centre and found later with hands and feet bound and dying from gunshot wounds to the head. Three Catholic priests issued a statement asking: 'What kind of organisation would feel threatened by a boy with a mental age of eight?'

It is noteworthy that there was one particular way in which the PIRA differed significantly from the Old IRA – the latter disappeared far more persons during the period 1920 to 1922 than did the PIRA during its decades-long campaign, as will be outlined in more detail. PIRA executioners may have found it advantageous to dump the bodies of victims in a public place rather than secretly bury them – it would discourage others from cooperating with the authorities, and remind the public of the consequences of falling foul of the organisation.

Chapter 24: The Disappeared: The Youngest Victim

In later life Martin Corry seemed very happy to talk about the tough interrogation techniques he employed as an IRA officer during the revolutionary period. The feisty, long-serving politician, noted for his combative attitude towards political opponents in Dáil debates, gave interviews describing how he forced a confession from one particular captive who had been abducted as a suspected spy by the IRA. The prisoner was a 15-year-old Protestant boy, William Edward Parsons who had been kidnapped near his Cork city home. He lived at 30 High Street with his parents, English-born Joseph Parsons and wife Florence, who came from Swansea, Wales.

It appears that the youth was taken by his captors to Corry's farm at Glounthaune, east of Cork city, as the underground dungeon in the Knockraha area, 'Sing Sing' was no longer in use. The boy's tender years would not win him mercy and he would not emerge alive from Corry's custody. Like Bridget Noble and Mary Lindsay, the only two women known for certain to have been disappeared by the IRA in the 1920s, Parsons has his own sad place in the history of those turbulent times. He is probably the youngest of the Disappeared of that era, his remains never located. Florence Parsons later denied that her son was involved in anything political. 'He was in no way connected to any Movement, he belonged to the Boys Brigade and the YMCA.'[1]

Corry described in interviews in later life the methods used to get Parsons to admit to being a spy. He gave an account of these methods to Ernie O'Malley, and decades later a more detailed account featured in a Knockraha parish history book for which Corry gave interviews in the 1970s.[2] It appears that Corry told the youth that he would not get out of there alive, and if he did not talk he would get a slow death by hanging, but if he talked he would get a quick death by being shot. To prepare for the hanging, a rope was thrown across a rafter in the roof of a loft at the farm, and a noose was tied at one end. Corry explained to O'Malley: 'He wouldn't talk so I said to the lads, "bring him upstairs". We had the rope ready for him above and we tied a noose around his neck.'[3] According to the Knockraha book, Corry instructed a man to pull the rope and raise Parsons from the ground. The rope had not been raised very far when Parsons indicated he would talk.[4] The reliability of any confession extracted from a minor under such horrendous duress must be open to question.

Senior IRA Cork No 1 Brigade officer Mick Murphy told the BMH how, in November 1920, he had concluded that Parsons was acting as a spy for the enemy as he had often been seen in the vicinity of Murphy's house. On the orders of Brigade O/C Sean O'Hegarty, Murphy had the youth picked up.[5] Murphy went to the location where Parsons was being held, and questioned him. It is alleged that the youth admitted to being a spy in the junior section of the Protestant organisation, the YMCA, and named others in the YMCA who were also spies. Murphy ordered a raid on the Cork home of horticultural instructor James Blemens. James, a widower, and his son Frederick were abducted on 29 November 1920. Murphy stated: 'They were both shot. These two were members of the senior spy section in the YMCA. Their names were given to me by Parsons.' The Blemenses' remains were secretly buried and never found. The following February, James Blemens's son-in-law, James Charles Beal (sometimes spelt as 'Beale') was also shot as an alleged spy by the IRA.

Murphy said they also had information about the Blemenses from letters in the post that were captured, although he did not say if the information was incriminating. Murphy also made the extraordinary claim, in the interview with Ernie O'Malley: 'We got into the back [of the Blemens' house] and we saw them and we heard them.' One wonders what kind of 'spies' would have held discussions while the IRA eavesdropped at the back of their home. Murphy also claimed that Parsons confessed to supplying information to the RIC's District Inspector Swanzy on the whereabouts of Tomás Mac Curtain that led to the Cork Mayor's murder in March 1920. (Parsons would have been aged 13 years at the time.) Murphy, O/C of the 2nd Battalion and a prominent member of the Cork senior hurling team, said that Sean O'Hegarty ordered that Parsons be shot. 'This was done.'

Unfortunately, there is a credibility problem with Murphy's testimony. Thanks to research carried out by historian Gerard Murphy, it is now known that Parsons was not abducted until 23 March 1922, during the Truce, more than a year after the Blemenses were disappeared.[6] The impression given in Mick Murphy's statement was that Parsons had been abducted, questioned and executed in late 1920, during the War of Independence, whereas it is now clear that Parsons was put to death during the Truce when such killings were supposed to have ceased. It was a period when crown forces had withdrawn or were in the course of withdrawing, the RIC was disbanding, and the IRA was about to take over Cork city. It was a time when this 15-year-old youth, even if he had been a spy, could not have been a threat to anyone.

Parsons had been portrayed by Mick Murphy as the IRA's star witness who had first-hand knowledge of the alleged espionage apparatus within the YMCA. The boy was supposed to have given the IRA crucial inside information about members of this Protestant group who were active as spies. He was alleged to have given Mick Murphy the names of the Blemenses who were then executed as spies. But how could Parsons have been a key source of vital information that led to the targeting of the Blemenses? Was the evidence against the Blemenses really as strong as Mick Murphy claimed? Was an alleged confession extracted from a terrified youth in 1922 used retrospectively to help justify the execution of the Blemenses as spies in 1920?

The authors of the authoritative study *The Dead of the Irish Revolution* state that the Blemenses were 'casualties of the spy frenzy that gripped the Cork city IRA' and express scepticism about IRA claims that 'Cork loyalists and Protestants developed a sophisticated information-gathering network and were in league with Crown forces.' The authors go on: 'Dispassionate analysis suggests that informers were neither so ubiquitous nor so organised as the Cork IRA maintained, and that some of those killed were not involved in any way with loyalist spy rings, if such existed, or in anti-republican activities.'[7]

To resolve glaring anomalies in the timescale, a couple of historians have taken the view that Parsons must have been arrested by the IRA in November 1920, admitted to being a spy and named others as spies, and was then released, only to be picked up again more than a year later in March 1922 to be executed. There is no credible evidence for this highly speculative and unlikely scenario. There is no indication from his family or from RIC records that Parsons was taken away by the IRA in late 1920, and Mick Murphy makes no mention anywhere of Parsons being set free from captivity at any stage. It is noteworthy that when Murphy told O'Malley about questioning Parsons concerning the Blemenses and the YMCA 'secret service' groups, he said the 'young lad', who was then shot, was aged 15 years. Parsons turned 15 just weeks before the Truce, so this would also indicate that it was during the Truce that he was taken away and interrogated, before being killed and secretly buried.

Martin Corry, in his interview with O'Malley also says it was 'during the Truce' that the interrogation of Parsons took place – the interrogation under extreme duress that was the prelude to his execution shortly afterwards. While questions have been raised about the credibility of Corry's account of the number of British soldiers executed at Knockraha and other issues, his account of the Parsons saga has the ring of truth about it. He got it right when he described Parsons as a member of the 'junior' section of the YMCA; he was correct about the period when the execution took place, and the account he gave O'Malley is generally consistent with what he related for the Knockraha parish history project many years later. In O'Malley's report of his interview with Corry, Parsons' age is incorrectly given as 26 years, although Corry's description of Parsons as a member of the 'junior' YMCA clearly denotes that he was a teenager.

Mr and Mrs Parsons made strenuous efforts to find out what happened their son, and placed ads in local newspapers. (The *Cork Examiner* carried the ad, titled 'MISSING' in its 25 March 1922 edition.) Possibly due to stress over the disappearance of her son, Mrs Parsons became unwell and the couple moved back to England, residing at Brighton. Britain's Colonial Secretary, the Duke of Devonshire, lobbied the Free State authorities on their behalf.[8] Inquiries were carried out and eventually indications emerged in 1923 that Parsons had been shot as a 'spy' four days after being abducted by the IRA, the sentence having been confirmed by Cork No. 1 Brigade staff. It emerged that Free State investigators had received information from a civilian Stephen Harrington, who had been in 'C' Company, 2nd Battalion and who was said to have had no personal involvement in the Parsons case – his information was presumably second-hand.[9] It was claimed Parsons had two guns when arrested by members of the company, that he was executed by company personnel and buried at an unknown location between Lehanagh and Ballygarvan in the Kinsale Road area.

This latter detail differs from Corry's first-hand account as related in the Knockraha parish history book, which states: 'Corry had Parsons taken outside and executed by firing squad and then buried in Corry's farm'.[10] Information that a 15-year-old boy had been shot and buried on the farm of a well-known anti-Treaty republican would have been highly sensitive. It does not seem like the kind of information that would have been freely shared with Corry's Free State enemies at a time of particular tension and bitterness arising out of the Civil War. Perhaps it was more convenient to convince Free State investigators that Parsons was buried in another location that had no connection to Corry.

It is noteworthy that Jimmy Murphy, who was a member of Martin Corry's Knockraha Company, seemed quite clear in an interview given in the 1970s that a prisoner called Parsons, a member of the YMCA, was shot after he admitted to being a spy, following a hanging incident in an outhouse, and his body buried on Corry's land.[11] As for Martin Corry, he had been arrested by the Free State military at his Glounthaune home in November 1922, and he was an internee during the period in 1923 that Free State investigators were inquiring into Parsons' fate. Corry would not be released until January 1924.

Another Protestant youth, Thomas Roycroft, aged 19 years, a former RIC constable, was also abducted in Cork in March 1922 and, like Parsons, was never seen again.[12] The following June another ex-RIC man, Michael Williams, was abducted, this time in County Laois, and it appears that he was also killed and buried on Corry's farm – he was accused of involvement in the murder of Tomás Mac Curtain,[13] an allegation that his sister Harriette later strenuously denied.

Most Victims Disappeared in County Cork

The historian, Dr Andy Bielenberg of University College Cork (UCC), estimated that the number of people disappeared by the IRA nationwide between 1920 and 1922 to be more than 100. He said that he and fellow academic Jim Donnelly had documented 62 disappearances [including Mrs Noble and Mrs Lindsay] in County Cork during the course of the Irish revolution, adding: 'Undoubtedly, there are a few more out there.' In a lecture at the West Cork History Festival in Skibbereen in August 2018, Dr Bielenberg expressed the view that the scale of disappearances was the 'darkest aspect' of the Old IRA campaign, the 'skeleton in the closet' of the period, with almost four times as many people being disappeared in County Cork alone, as were disappeared during the entire PIRA campaign. [The PIRA admitted to disappearing 13 people; another was disappeared by the INLA; two others were disappeared but no paramilitary organisation claimed responsibility.] It could be argued, of course, that the PIRA did not have the same incentive as the IRA of the 1920s to hide the bodies of those it had put to death. The Auxiliaries and the Black and Tans were no longer around, and reprisal tactics such as destroying houses of those suspected of involvement or complicity in killings or other offences were a thing of the past.

In his talk at the festival, Dr Bielenberg said that the great majority of the disappearances in County Cork, 49 out of the 62, took place during the War of Independence, while the Truce period accounted for the far smaller balance. Of the 62, most were civilians – 28 were from the crown forces. 'The most notable feature of the geography of these disappearances was that over 74 per cent took place in the Cork No. 1 Brigade area.' He said that this brigade resorted to the tactic of disappearing people far more than brigades elsewhere in Ireland or indeed elsewhere in Cork. He referred to Sean O'Hegarty, O/C of the Brigade as a 'very secretive figure, very elusive'. He said that Florence O'Donoghue, the Brigade Intelligence Officer and Adjutant, was 'a highly shrewd intelligence agent and his future wife was one of the moles in the barracks [British military HQ in Cork]. 'They knew everything. Unfortunately for spies and informers that was not good news for a number of them. They [the IRA] did not always get it right, some of these "spies and informers" were innocent, unfortunately.' (In a further study with another researcher, published online in 2020, Bielenberg estimated that the total number of documented IRA disappearances throughout Ireland from 1920 to 1923 was 108.[14])

Another historian, Professor Eunan O'Halpin (Trinity College Dublin), who had relatives in the IRA during the War of Independence, and who is a grand-nephew of Kevin Barry, executed by the British in 1920, worked on a major research project, *The Dead of the Irish Revolution* (ultimately published in 2020). He has also described (in a 2013 newspaper article) how far more people were secretly killed by the IRA in the Cork region than anywhere else. Some were crown forces, some were civilians. 'Most died before the Truce of July 1921, but in Cork secret killings and burials continued as late as June 1922.' He found that on a country-wide basis, crown forces killed more civilians than the IRA, but had no need to hide their victims 'because the law took their side'.[15]

In an essay also published in 2013, O'Halpin estimated that, on a nation-wide basis, 277 civilians were killed by the IRA in the period 1920 to 1921. Of this number, 183 were killed as spies, of whom almost half that number, 47 per cent, were ex-servicemen. He concluded that ex-servicemen were disproportionately targeted by the IRA, especially in Cork. He found that of the 165 civilians killed as spies whose religion was known, 45 were Protestant and 120 Catholic.[16] The sizeable figure for Protestants is noteworthy, as Protestants constituted a minority in the population.

In his introductory remarks to a two-part TV3 series on the Disappeared, broadcast in 2013 and titled 'In the Name of the Republic', O'Halpin stated:

A disturbing aspect of the violence between the years 1919 and 1921 was the fate of civilians deliberately killed by the IRA. Were they spies? Were they informers? Some were, some were not. They were abducted, executed and buried in unmarked graves, or weighed down and dumped in lakes or rivers. They are the forgotten victims of Ireland's struggle for independence. I have spent the last decade researching the dead of the Irish revolution. During that time I have encountered the cases of many people abducted and executed by the IRA, put to death for suspected collusion, often on the flimsiest of evidence. In some cases we don't even know the names of victims, let alone their whereabouts. In the intervening years most of these victims have been conveniently forgotten, their names lost in a maze of records... For me, their deaths at the hands of the IRA cast a very dark shadow over the independence struggle.

In the afore-mentioned 2013 essay, Professor O'Halpin has also referred to indications that 'one or possibly two' women in Carrigtwohill, County Cork were killed and their remains hidden by the Cork No. 1 Brigade, 'although this has not been confirmed'. He comments: 'They belong in the disturbingly large number of probable IRA killings in Cork for which no further information is available at present.'[17] In the Knockraha parish history book, mentioned above, there is a reference to a woman (not identified) being executed by the local Carrigtwohill Company of the IRA. 'Some of the members living today cannot recall the actual reasons for this execution. She was taken down to the lane by Fentons near Slotty and on the riverbank she was executed. It is often said that her ghost haunts the area since. And that on some nights she is seen walking on the strand along by Slotty.'[18]

In 1924 the Free State's Crime Branch investigating the Mary Lindsay case learned from local sources in contact with the IRA in the Knockraha area that her remains were not buried in that district but that 'two women were shot at a place called Reinslaugh [Reenaslough]'.[19] This townland is also in the Knockraha district but the intriguing suggestion that females were among the executed persons secretly buried locally by the Cork No 1 Brigade cannot be verified. Decades later, Sean O'Callaghan, in his book on Mrs Lindsay, remarked that the IRA 'shot several women, mainly prostitutes, for giving information to the authorities', but he provides no sources and once again the claim cannot be verified.[20]

In 1999 the British and Irish governments set up the Independent Commission for the Location of Victims Remains to recover the remains of those disappeared during the recent Troubles. At the time of writing, only three cases remain unresolved – one concerns the British Army officer, Captain Robert Nairac. There was no official body tasked with recovering the remains of the far larger number of persons who were disappeared during the revolutionary era of the 1920s. Relatives had to suffer the agony of not knowing what had happened to their loved ones, and while they might ultimately ascertain the fate of the person who had vanished, recovering the remains could prove far more challenging. According to Professor O'Halpin, during the Truce period, 'GHQ made some efforts to list and investigate IRA killings of civilian spies and of missing military and police, and to locate their remains. But inquiries encountered much local obfuscation, and with the outbreak of the civil war in June 1922 they seem largely to have ceased.'[21]

The afore-mentioned IRA officer Mick Murphy told Ernie O'Malley: 'Every spy who was shot in Cork was buried, so that nothing was known about them. They just disappeared.'[22] While this was a great exaggeration, nevertheless there was a sizeable number of persons disappeared in the area of the Cork No. 1 Brigade, as mentioned. Disappearances were less common in other brigade areas – a notable disappearance in the Cork No. 3 Brigade area being, of course, that of Bridget Noble.

Professor O'Halpin stated that the Cork No. 1 Brigade 'secretly killed and buried an unascertainable number of people whose identities remain unknown' and who do not figure in the data that he was compiling on fatalities during the revolutionary era. Stan Barry, who was a member of the Cork No. 1 Brigade Flying Column, talked of killing and burying 'three or four spies' at Clogheen – he seemed to have lost count. He told Ernie O'Malley how they dealt with one particular Irishman who was condemned to die. The man was 'between tears and acts of contrition when we shot him...' Barry went on: 'Nobody knew where he was buried and nobody but ourselves knew that he had been shot...' Barry, who became a prominent rugby player with Sunday's Well, and Galway manager of the Caltex oil company, considered that the fact that the body was not found 'created uncertainty among the British, and it prevented their reprisals in a particular area'.[23]

During the Truce period, the O/C of the Irish Republican Police in the Cork No. 1 Brigade seemed unwilling to assist in efforts to recover the remains of the disappeared, or to provide information to relatives as to their fate. It appears that he received a letter from the Dáil Éireann Chief of Police in January 1922 pointing out that queries had been received about the disappearance of people 'during the war', and reported to have been 'executed by IRA' and asking if he considered it 'desirable to inform the relatives' of the fate of the parties concerned. The Cork No. 1 Brigade Chief of Police wrote: 'Those shot during the war [are] not to be inquired into as they are all spies in this area.'[24] In fact, basic information would be provided to relatives who inquired about the fate of individuals who had been disappeared in the brigade area, although recovery of remains would be highly problematical.

Anguish of Relatives

The intense anguish of relatives of the disappeared, as they tried to ascertain the fate of their loved ones, is apparent in letters sent to entities such as the Dáil Department of Defence and preserved in the Military Archives. From his home in the Waterville area of County Kerry, Timothy Dennehy pleaded, in September 1921, for information about his son, Constable Michael Dennehy who, as mentioned, was drowned in the Shannon the previous year. It would later emerge that he had been executed 'as a spy' by the IRA. The father refers to himself and his wife as 'sorrow-stricken parents' and says that they have not heard anything further about their son since he was kidnapped, 'so you can imagine how we have felt'. He goes on: 'If we only knew his fate – living or dead, in the latter case we could get him prayed for [i.e. have a Mass said for him]...'[25]

Matilda Blemens and her brother James S. Blemens sent an impassioned plea to the Dáil Minister of Defence in a letter dated 21 December 1921 seeking information about their missing father and brother. As previously mentioned, in November 1920 the father James Blemens senior and their brother Frederick had been abducted by the IRA and never seen again. Then, the following February, their brother-in-law James Charles Beal had been shot dead by the IRA as an alleged spy, as mentioned. Some months later, their sister Sarah, widow of J.C. Beal, died of cardiac trouble aged only 34 years. In the space of just over a year, they lost their father, brother, sister and brother-in-law. In their pre-Christmas letter to the Minister, Matilda and James junior explain that Sarah died the previous day, and in their 'great grief' they 'implored information' about their missing father and brother. 'Our home is desolate and our hearts are breaking. Can you help us?'[26]

Another example of an emotional plea for information about a missing loved one is a letter written by Catherine Ray on 11 December 1921, inquiring about her husband Patrick who had gone missing in Passage West, County Cork the previous January.[27] Patrick Ray (whose name was also spelt 'Rea') was an ex-soldier, reportedly suffering from shell shock and 'not right in the head'.[28] Mrs Ray probably did not have advanced education but her torment seemed to inspire a raw eloquence in her letter pleading for information about her missing husband. Mrs Ray stated:

> Gentlemen, I am taking the liberty of writing to ask you if you could inquire and let me know if the IRA authorities know anything of my

husband, Patrick Ray, who is missing from Passage West, Co Cork on the 21st day of January 1921. I am nearly distracted and thinking from day to day I would hear something. I have 4 children, and my suffering since, I can't describe... Now that peace is on, I am asking you to let me know if you have him as a prisoner, deported, or is he dead or alive. He was an ex-soldier and living in Passage West 7 years. He was up in the city to draw unemployment money and he was back in Passage West at 5.30 and as he came out of the train he met his little boy and told him to go home, and he never turned in home since the 21st day of January. I ask you to see to this, Gentlemen, to see to this and to ease my mind to know if he is dead or alive or if the IRA have him at all. I am heart-broken and only ask you in return to let me know if he is a prisoner or if he is dead or alive. I have 4 young children and am destitute.

Ultimately, about a year after Ray was abducted, the family received a letter dated 15 January 1922 from the Dáil Minister for Defence with the usual form of words, stating that Ray was found guilty on a charge of 'espionage' and 'executed'. The name of Patrick Ray appeared along with Bridget Noble on the same list of missing civilians released in the House of Commons by the Chief Secretary for Ireland in August 1921. Nowadays, the enforced disappearance of a person by individuals acting on behalf of a government, directly or indirectly, is considered by the United Nations to be a 'particularly heinous violation of human rights and an international crime'.[29]

A document produced by the UN High Commissioner for Human Rights makes the following comment that brings to mind the pain expressed by Catherine Ray back in 1921: 'The family and friends of disappeared persons experience slow mental anguish, not knowing whether the victim is still alive and, if so, where he or she is being held, under what conditions, and in what state of health.'[30] The document also states: 'The family's distress is frequently compounded by the material consequences of the disappearance. The disappeared person is often the family's main breadwinner. He or she may be the only member of the family able to cultivate the crops or run the family business. The emotional upheaval is thus exacerbated by material deprivation...' In this regard, one is reminded of the report that emerged of how Bridget Noble's aged father was removed to the workhouse after her abduction. The document also comments on the particular vulnerability of women when they are the direct victims of disappearance. Once again, Mrs Noble comes to mind, and Alexander Noble's embittered comment to de Valera, that it is 'not clean work' to take away 'my lone defenceless wife'.

Chapter 25: Exile from Ireland

Mícheál Óg O'Sullivan, former Vice O/C of the Beara Battalion, travelled initially to Toronto, Canada some time after escaping from prison in Cork in 1923. He then entered the United States, via Buffalo, in June 1926, settling in New York City.[1] Like others linked to the story of Bridget Noble, there would be tragedy in his life. On 10 June 1927, at age 28 years, he married his fiancé Margaret, from County Kerry. A native of Bonane, near Kenmare, Margaret had emigrated to America a couple of years previously, in June 1925. Just over a year after they married, Margaret died from pneumonia in November 1928, aged only 31 years. Mícheál Óg worked as a checker on the docks for a shipping company and at this period resided in the West Harlem district of Upper Manhattan, at 502 West 135th Street. He later lived in The Bronx.

Mícheál Óg kept in touch with his brother, Dr Pronnséas O'Sullivan – they seemed close. While at Freiburgh University in Germany, Pronnséas met a young German woman, Ilse Köhling from Eisenach, Thuringia who, like himself, was awarded a PhD degree. They married and settled in Ireland, where Pronnséas was a teacher and later a schools inspector with the Department of Education. He worked strenuously to promote the Irish language, and continued to be active in Conradh na Gaeilge. During the 1930s, after Hitler came to power, the couple organised Educational Tours to Germany, and many of the Irish who travelled on these tours were teachers. The tours, with the aim of observing the education system in Hitler's new Germany, were organised with the assistance of officials at the German Legation in Dublin – the Minister himself, Wilhelm von Kuhlmann, and the Secretary, Dr Schlemann. The Hitler regime sought to use the schools to inculcate Nazi ideology in the students and from 1933 Jewish teachers were excluded from schools catering for 'Aryan' pupils.

In July 1935 Mícheál Óg was back in Ireland on an extended holiday and spent time with his brother Pronnséas. The *Irish Press* reported on Mícheál Óg's visit, mentioned his education at St Enda's, and stated that it was his first trip back to Ireland in 12 years.[2] The article recalled that he escaped from Cork jail in 1923, succeeded in leaving the country for America, and that he is now engaged 'with a notable firm of shippers in New York'. The article went on: 'The years have not altered Mr O'Sullivan's outlook and he holds fluent conversations with his brother in the Irish language.' While in Dublin, it appears that Mícheál Óg stayed with Pronnséas at the latter's then home at 24 Fortfield Terrace, in an affluent area of Rathmines – this was an address given for Mícheál Óg in Military Service Pension archives.[3] It was a pleasant two-storey, redbrick end-of-terrace house enjoying considerable seclusion at the end of a cul-de-sac, off the Upper Rathmines Road.

At the time of the *Irish Press* story, Pronnséas, obviously on holiday from his job as a schools inspector, was about to depart on one of his trips to Nazi Germany, and there are indications that Mícheál Óg may have travelled with him. The tour was from 28 July to 12 August, costing £15.15s.[4] More than 30 people, mainly teachers, assembled in Galway at the end of July as part of Pronnséas's group. They sailed on the liner *Stuttgart* to the north German port of Bremen where, on arrival, they were given a reception in the town hall. Among the passengers was 'Michael Sullivan' from Bantry, and a ship's passenger list (on the group's return voyage to Galway on the liner *Columbus*) stated that he was aged 37 years and a widower. This may well have been a reference to Mícheál Óg, and while this cannot be confirmed with absolute certainty, the details fit his profile. Mícheál Óg was, of course, a widower, and at the time in question he would have been just days short of his 37th birthday which fell on 16 August, while the postal address for his family home place was usually given as 'Adrigole, Bantry'. One wonders what Mícheál Óg, past pupil of Pádraic Pearse's St Enda's College, would have thought of the educational system under the Hitler regime.

Just over a week after the German trip, Mícheál Óg returned to America on the liner SS *Majestic*, arriving in New York on 27 August.[5] During the 1930s and the Second World War, some Irish nationalists and republicans of various hues were in sympathy with Nazi Germany. Pronnséas reportedly caused uproar when he challenged a speaker at an anti-Hitler public meeting in Rathmines, Dublin in 1935, attended by members of the Jewish community.[6] In 1937 IRA chief of staff Tom Barry travelled to Germany for direct talks with the Nazis. During the war, there was covert cooperation between the IRA and Nazi secret agents who landed in Ireland. While some anti-British republicans may have supported the Germans largely on the basis that 'my enemy's enemy is my friend', it is noteworthy that anti-semitic material featured in the IRA's strongly pro-German publication *War News*.[7]

275

After the downfall of the Nazi regime, Pronnséas O'Sullivan was prominently involved in a charity to help children in war-ravaged Germany. It was known as the Save the German Children Society. The secretary was Hermann Goertz – as a Nazi secret agent he had landed in Ireland during the war to liaise with the IRA. The Fianna Fáil TD, Dan Breen acted as treasurer. Breen, who as mentioned, took part in the killing of two RIC men that started the War of Independence, and who was very active on the republican side in the Civil War, was an ardent admirer of Hitler, and was displaying portraits of the Führer in his Dublin home in the late 1940s, long after details of the Holocaust had emerged.[8]

Meanwhile, Pronnséas's sister Nora O'Sullivan resided with him after he moved to a big three-storey house on Garville Avenue, Rathgar. Nora sought, in vain, an improved Military Service Pension arising out of her Cumann na mBan service. Recalling the destruction of the family home by crown forces in 1921, she declared: 'After the blowing up of my home I had to sleep and live in the open. Is it any wonder that I am now a martyr to rheumatic troubles? Yes, I gave the best of my years working for the cause.'

It is unclear if Mícheál Óg O'Sullivan made a return trip to Ireland after his visit in 1935 - he died at age 65 years in July 1964 in New York City. A death notice in the *Cork Examiner* recorded that he was 'Chief Clerk at Pier 83, N.R.' – a reference to one of the piers on the 'North River', or Hudson, in Manhattan. The notice also recalled his role as Vice Commandant of the 5th Battalion [*recte* 6th Battalion], 3rd Cork Brigade, Old IRA, and as a member of Tom Barry's Flying Column. There was a Requiem High Mass at St Raphael's Church, West 41st Street, followed by interment at Calvary Cemetery. His obituary notice in the *Southern Star* newspaper recalled his education at St Enda's and the connection with Pádraic Pearse.[9] There is no indication that O'Sullivan left behind a memoir of his life and times, and he did not contribute a statement to the Bureau of Military History. He would have had an interesting story to tell, in light of his activities during the revolutionary period and as a pupil of Pearse. Any knowledge he might have had of the Bridget Noble tragedy seems to have gone to the grave with him.

The Passing of Former Comrades

Back in Ireland, the passage of time was also taking its toll among those who had been active in the IRA in West Cork during the Troubles. Both Liam O'Dwyer and Christy O'Connell travelled to Dublin for the funeral of Liam Deasy in August 1974. Deasy's book *Towards Ireland Free*, published the previous year, had been denounced by Tom Barry as a 'travesty of history'.[10] Barry was particularly outraged that Deasy, in describing the Kilmichael ambush, made no mention of a 'false surrender' by Auxiliaries. According to Barry, the 'false surrender' resulted in comrades being killed and was the reason he ordered his men to 'keep firing' and not accept any further surrender. O'Dwyer was troubled by the controversy involving Deasy and Barry, both of whom he greatly admired, and was one of those who defended Deasy. In May 1976 O'Dwyer and Christy O'Connell wrote a letter to the *Southern Star* stating that old age meant they could no longer take responsibility for arranging the flag to cover the coffin at the funeral of an active service member. 'Henceforth it is the responsibility of the families concerned to provide the flags and make their arrangements. We have no further responsibility.'[11]

Just a couple of years later, Christy O'Connell died, in April 1978, at age 81 years. Liam O'Dwyer passed away at age 87 years on 26 April 1983 at his residence in Ardgroom. After funeral Mass in Ardgroom church, he was laid to rest in Gortnabulliga Cemetery. The *Southern Star* paid tribute to him.[12] 'He gave his boyhood, manhood and declining years in the service of his country. By all, even those who differed from him in politics, he was honoured as a fearless, uncorruptible man.' The newspaper recalled the 'dark days' when O'Dwyer and others had to take 'the hillside for a bed and heaven's canopy for a covering'. So far as is known, his only written account of the execution of Bridget Noble was the brief, internal IRA report he sent to GHQ in October 1921.

Connie Healy, who was said to have been the last surviving member of the Beara Battalion, died in February 1999 at age 96 years. As previously indicated, he was connected indirectly by marriage to Bridget Noble, one of his sisters having married a first cousin of Bridget's. Connie had continued to reside at Canfie, Ardgroom, and after funeral Mass in Ardgroom church he was buried at Gortnabulliga cemetery. A local newspaper paid tribute to the late Mr Healy: 'Honest and straightforward, he was a considerate and helpful neighbour who enjoyed the esteem of a wide circle of friends who mourn his passing.'[13] As mentioned, he had been a member of the IRA's Ardgroom Company, and if he had any knowledge of the Bridget Noble tragedy, it seems to have gone to the grave with him.

Exile from Ireland

Some of those in the police and the legal profession who were linked to the saga of Bridget Noble, or who were active in West Cork during the troubled period, did not stay in the new Ireland that emerged after the War of Independence and the Civil War. District Inspector

Thomas J. Oates, the RIC officer who was acquainted with Bridget and who gave evidence at the court hearing for compensation arising out of her death, retired from the force on 10 May 1922 at the time of disbandment. He was aged about 50 years and had 29 years service, qualifying for quite a generous annual pension of £433 6s 8d.[14] He had planned to retire to a farm in his native County Roscommon that he had bought in 1914 for £1,000, but, as he would indicate later, he did not do so due to intimidation, considering it would be 'unsafe' to go there.

Oates moved to England and concern over his personal security may have been a factor in his decision to leave Ireland. As previously mentioned, following the Truce, in various parts of Ireland, there was a series of murders of men who had served in the RIC, while former policemen and their families had also faced intimidation. Threats were made against ex-RIC men, designed to force them out of their homes.[15] (It is likely that there were also many who returned home to 'quiet' areas and were not interfered with.) In Castletownbere, as we have seen, former RIC sergeants Michael Flynn and John Twomey were forced to leave the area. In February 1922 one of Oates's fellow District Inspectors in Cork West Riding, Clonakilty-based Michael Keany, was shot dead. (Subsequently, in 1924, two Clonakilty men who had been active on the anti-Treaty side in the Civil War, John 'Flyer' Nyhan and Thomas Lane were charged by the Free State authorities in connection with a number of murders, including that of D.I. Keany. As previously outlined in an endnote, Lane was also charged in connection with the murder of 16-year-old Robert Nagle, one of the Protestant victims of the Bandon Valley atrocity, but all charges were dropped as witnesses were reluctant to testify.)

After leaving the RIC, and free at last from the tension and danger of police work in troubled Ireland, Oates finally 'tied the knot' in England in early 1923. At Paddington, London, Oates married Bridget Mary Brennan, and they took up residence in Maidenhead, Berkshire. They would live in England for the rest of their lives. Oates seems to have developed a kind of gallows humour to help him cope with the pressures of life in Beara during the troubled times. This is shown by an account given in a diary kept by Malcolm Bickle, an English civil servant based in Castletownbere. Bickle was in charge of the payment of Old Age Pensions, and also acted as Customs & Excise officer. After the burning down of the custom house in May 1920, he described a visit to the town's RIC station. 'It's the first time I've been in. You knock at the door. A gruff voice says who's there and then the door is opened a little on a chain. Seeing we were safe they let us in and we went upstairs to where Oates the District Inspector was. Curley was with him. They greeted us with a great laugh. Oates said every government official would be there before they'd done.'[16] (The man called Curley was probably Mathew J. Curley, an engineer working for the Congested Districts Board for Ireland. Based at Castletownbere, he would later claim compensation from the Irish Free State for 'seizure of bicycle at Ardgroom by IRA members on 14 May 1921'.[17] He subsequently worked for the Land Commission, after the setting up of the Free State.)

The month after receiving the visit from Malcolm Bickle, Oates's lodgings in Castletownbere were raided by a group of men who got away with uniforms and other clothing – a sign, perhaps, of the increasing audacity of local IRA Volunteers. The incident was mentioned in the House of Commons on 20 June 1920, providing Oates with his proverbial 'fifteen minutes of fame'. A Conservative MP, Sir John Pennefeather, asked the Chief Secretary for Ireland about a raid by 'Sinn Feiners' on the house of an RIC District Inspector in County Cork. Mr Henry replied that about noon on 13 June the lodgings of District Inspector Oates, Castletown Bere, 'were entered by about twenty armed and disguised men, who broke the locks of two portmanteaus and three trunks, and took away two suits of uniform and some plain clothes'. Mr Henry added: 'Protection will be given to the houses of the police, as far as practicable.'[18] Protecting the homes of policemen was an earnest aspiration but seemingly unrealistic – the RIC was coming under increasing pressure and was unable even to protect outlying barrack buildings, let alone the private residences of police personnel.

Oates would have had some dark memories of his time in West Cork. Apart from the disappearance of Bridget Noble, he had experience of police colleagues being killed or injured in IRA attacks. As indicated previously, Constable Michael Neenan was fatally injured in the attack on Allihies RIC station in 1920. Later that year Constable Thomas King, off-duty and unarmed, was shot dead while cycling at Snave, near Bantry. A Catholic from Roundstone, County Galway, he was initially wounded and frantically hid in a nearby house, before being dragged out and shot several times. A senior republican later stated that he was executed 'as it was reported that he had taken part in the murder of IRA men at The Ragg, Co. Tipperary'. In fact King had only joined the RIC the previous year after being demobilised from the Royal Navy, and Glengarriff was his first posting.[19] District Inspector Oates was in charge of arrangements for the inquest in Bantry, and he was appalled when only three jurors turned up. He said it showed 'a poor state of society' when they would not attend in a case 'where a poor constable was cruelly murdered'.[20]

A number of jurors also failed to show up for the inquest into the death of Constable James Brett, a father of four who was shot dead by the IRA near Bantry later in June, and once again Oates was appalled. It was yet another reminder that the power of the state that he represented was gradually dwindling away. In apparent revenge for the killing of Constable Brett, who was said to have suffered 'fearful injuries' to his head, a young disabled man called Cornelius Crowley, a member of Sinn Féin, was shot dead in his home, causing much shock and anger in the town.

Oates was one of the former RIC men who applied for compensation to Britain's Irish Grants Committee (IGC) in the mid-1920s in relation to 'hardship or loss' due to his allegiance to the UK government.[21] In his claim, made in November 1926, Oates stated that he was unemployed and living on his pension. He claimed in relation to various items, including losses suffered in relation to his farm in County Roscommon. He had lost a year's rent due to tenants' cattle being driven off. When he tried to sell the farm at auction there was intimidation of potential purchasers and it had to be withdrawn. In November 1921 a 333-yard wire fence was 'totally broken down and destroyed by the Republican Party' and he felt it was 'very unsafe' to go to the place to claim compensation.

Referring to his time as RIC District Inspector in Castletownbere he stated that Cork WR [West Riding] was 'one of the most disturbed counties in Ireland'. During his four years there, he had, in the execution of his duty, 'to arrest and prosecute a number of leading Republicans for various offences against the law, therefore became unpopular'. One of the individuals he named to whom reference could be made was solicitor Jasper Travers Wolfe. Oates was awarded the sum of £125 by the IGC. The former policeman passed away aged about 71 years at his home, Lyndenburg House, Thicket Road, Maidenhead, in June 1942. His widow, Bridget Mary, later went to live in Bournemouth and died there in 1963, aged 79 years.

Thomas J. Oates's friend Malcolm Bickle, referred to above, did not enjoy a long life after leaving Ireland to return to his home city of York. He died in February 1922, aged 34 years, leaving a wife Lillian Alice, and three children who had been born in Castletownbere. District Inspector Forbes le Blount Croke, who was based in Castletownbere for a period in 1921 during Oates's absence, did not live long either after his sojourn in Ireland. Having served as a Captain in the Royal Engineers, he had joined the Auxiliaries in 1920 and was appointed to 'permanent' rank in the RIC in June 1921.[22] Like some other men who had served in the RIC or the Auxiliaries, on the disbandment of these forces he joined the newly-formed Palestine

Gendarmerie, which operated under the British Mandate. (Some of these former RIC men later returned to Ireland to serve with the Royal Ulster Constabulary.) Croke committed suicide by shooting himself in the head at Surafend, Palestine in January 1923, aged 32 years.

County Inspector G.R.W. Patrick

Thomas J. Oates's immediate superior in the RIC in Cork West Riding, County Inspector George R. W. Patrick, did not remain in the Free State on being demobilised from the force in May 1922. Patrick, who as mentioned, made a fleeting reference to the kidnapping of Bridget Noble in his county report for April 1921, moved to Northern Ireland and it appears that he initially stayed with a relative serving as a Church of Ireland clergyman near Belfast. During his time in Bandon, he had experience of appearing at court hearings presided over by local magistrates, including the Earl of Bandon and Charles Sealy-King. These two men were among a number of magistrates kidnapped in West Cork by the IRA and held for a period in 1921 as hostages – if the British executed IRA Volunteers, the magistrates would also be shot. Also kidnapped at this period was Major Henry de Berry, President of the Bantry branch of the Legion of Ex-Service Men – he would later, in 1928, commit suicide.

The abduction of the magistrates must have been a reminder to Patrick that the state authorities that he represented were losing control in West Cork. Having retired from the police with a pension of £600 a year, Patrick later resided at Little Agherton, Portstewart, a seaside town in County Derry. In April 1933 his name figured briefly in a news report when a four-year-old boy ran out in front of his car at Stewartstown, County Tyrone. The boy was injured and Patrick conveyed him to a local doctor for medical treatment. Otherwise, Patrick seemed to live a life of quiet obscurity in his tranquil, seaside retreat. The former County Inspector who had experienced some turbulent times while based in West Cork during the revolutionary period, died at a nursing home in Belfast in December 1936, aged 63 years.

Head Constable Goaley

Michael Goaley, who served in Castletownbere under District Inspector Oates, and who was Head Constable at the time of Mrs Noble's disappearance, moved to England after the RIC was disbanded. As previously indicated, it was probably Goaley to whom Bridget Noble handed the crucial letter naming the men she accused of the 'bobbing' attack on her, the letter that probably sealed her fate. Goaley left the RIC on 9 May 1922 with an annual pension of £233. It was not as generous as Thomas J. Oates's pension but still a very useful addition to his finances. (Goaley's native place, Annaghdown, on the eastern shores of Lough Corrib, is remembered in Irish poetry and song for a great tragedy. In 1828, twenty local people lost their lives when their boat capsized in the lake on their way to Galway. The Irish language poet Raftery wrote the words of the haunting ballad *Anach Cuan* to commemorate those who drowned. One of the victims was named Timothy Goaley – he may have been distantly related to Michael Goaley.) After leaving the RIC, the former Head Constable resided for a brief period in his native County Galway where his wife Annie gave birth to a daughter in 1922. (The couple had married in Galway cathedral in May 1918. At this time he was still a Lieutenant in the British Army, and based in the Machine Gun Corps depot and training centre at Grantham, Lincolnshire.) Goaley and his family emigrated to the English midlands, taking up residence in Nottingham, where another daughter was born in 1930.

It is not known if personal security concerns were a factor in Goaley's decision to emigrate. An assassination carried out by the IRA in March 1920 may have had a particular resonance with Goaley. Members of Michael Collins's special unit, The Squad, took an elderly retired magistrate, Alan Bell, off a tram in Ballsbridge, Dublin and shot him dead. Bell, who was related by marriage to the writer Charlotte Brontë, had apparently been making progress, on behalf of the British, in tracking down the secret funds of the Dáil national loan, sometimes referred to as Collins's 'war chest'. Goaley would have been familiar with the victim as in the years prior to the Great War, Bell had served as a Resident Magistrate in County Mayo, and Goaley had experience of giving evidence as a policeman in court proceedings overseen by Bell.[23] After moving to England, Goaley initially worked as a labourer before going into business, running an off-license in the Nottingham area. His wife Annie died at the young age of 38 years in 1936. Three years later, Goaley married again, this time his bride being Gertrude Mowson. He died in September 1964, aged 76 years, and Gertrude passed away in 1990.

Head Constable Dobbyn

John P. Dobbyn was one of the best-known of the RIC men who served as Head Constable in Castletownbere, having held that post for more than 20 years up to the time of his retirement at the end of 1914. He also left Ireland as British forces withdrew, departing hurriedly for England with his wife in June 1922. A native of County Westmeath and a member of the Church of Ireland, he would later describe how he felt obliged to flee, following a threat. It will be recalled that during the Castletownbere court session in 1915 when Bridget Noble had a neighbour bound to the peace, the magistrate also paid tribute to Head Constable Dobbyn on his retirement. After he left the police, Dobbyn settled in Cork city where he became an accountant with Warren and Mitchell, land agents. He told how, in 1918, four men came to his door, and the leader, with 'a very violent and threatening attitude' told one of his men to 'mark him down'. After this, he felt like a 'marked man'. He felt that the position of loyalists was becoming 'daily more and more perilous'. Then, in early June 1922, a document was pushed through his letterbox stating: 'You have been serving the British all your life and now you are serving the landlords. Fly, you have a fortnight to clear.'[24]

Dobbyn and his wife Margaret quickly left Ireland, and the couple took up residence in England. Margaret died about a year later, on 29 May 1923, at age 69 years. From his home at 14 Bourtonville, Buckingham, Dobbyn applied to the Irish Grants Committee in 1926 for compensation on various grounds, including having to give up his job, the expense incurred in disrupting his home and moving to England, and medical expenses for himself and his wife, arising out of illness 'caused by mental and physical distress'. He was awarded £400. He died in June 1930 aged 76 years, and was laid to rest with his wife in a Buckinghamshire graveyard. The inscription on the headstone includes the words: 'Refugees from Ireland, 1922'.

Sergeant Nugent

Sergeant Thomas Nugent who, like Head Constable Goaley, had served under D.I. Oates, was demobilised from the RIC in April 1922. He was aged 48 years, and with 26 years service was awarded an annual pension of £195.[25] He was one of the RIC men who stayed in Ireland after the force was disbanded. As indicated previously, he was possibly the RIC sergeant who was acquainted with Mrs Noble. Associating with a sergeant on a couple of occasions in Castletownbere was one of the factors that would get her into serious trouble with the IRA. A native of Aughagrania, near Drumshanbo, County Leitrim, Nugent returned to his native county after leaving the RIC. His first posting in 1896 had been to Belfast, where he served in Newtownards Road barracks. He was sent to the Beara peninsula in 1910, having served in Counties Wicklow and Clare. Thomas Nugent died on 10 January 1928 at Aghakilbrack, near Carrick-on-Shannon, County Leitrim, aged 53 years. The cause of death was recorded as Gastritis and Heart Failure. He was unmarried.[26]

The prominent IRA fighter Christy O'Connell was impressed by Nugent's courage when the sergeant and his RIC colleagues were besieged by the IRA in the police barracks at Allihies in February 1920. This was the attack in which one of Nugent's men, Constable Neenan, was fatally injured. In his statement to the BMH, O'Connell reflected that Nugent 'refused to surrender' even though the barracks had been 'completely demolished' [by a bomb explosion] and some of the garrison wounded, including Nugent's pet terrier. Writing in 1956, O'Connell was aware at this stage that Nugent had passed on, and paid tribute to his former opponent as a 'cool, daring man', adding: 'He was a game scrapper – and may he rest in peace.'[27] (One of the Volunteers attacking the barracks, Sean O'Sullivan recalled years later: 'The howls of pain and fright by the RIC men inside was heartrending. Some of us pitied the poor fellows as we had no personal animosity against them, but it was war, which we had to win or lose.'[28])

Judge Hynes

Judge John W. Hynes, who awarded compensation to Alexander Noble arising out of Bridget's death, died in a nursing home in London in July 1930. During his time as a judge, he had resided in Dublin in an elegant Georgian house overlooking the Grand Canal, 17 Herbert Place, and would stay at the County Club, Cork during visits to the south to preside at courts in West Cork. A fervent follower of cricket until he breathed his last, the *Irish Times* reported that when his powers of speech returned a few hours before his death, he used them to discuss the Test match. Another figure from the legal world, John F. Bourke, also known as Jack Bourke, the barrister who represented Alexander Noble in the compensation case, made a new life in England, where he continued with his law career. In 1923, in the county of Worcestershire, he married a young English woman, Eileen W. Beddoes, with whom he had a family. In 1945 he became Recorder of Shrewsbury. In May 1949 his mother, the former Annie Binchy, passed away at Mere Hall, Stroud, Gloucestershire. The obituary notice in the *Cork Examiner* recorded that she was the widow of Matthew J. Bourke K.C., 'the last Recorder of Cork'.

Jasper Travers Wolfe

Jasper Travers Wolfe, the solicitor who had once acted for Bridget Noble in a court case, and who also acted for Alexander Noble when he claimed compensation for Bridget's murder, remained in Ireland and prospered. He became reconciled with former political enemies, such as Neilus Connolly who had once targeted the solicitor for execution during the War of Independence. Wolfe happened to meet Connolly by chance on the steps of the courthouse in Cork city, and inquired after Connolly's daughter who was seriously ill. The two former adversaries shook hands, and afterwards they often had a drink together in Wolfe's favourite pub in Skibbereen.[29] Connolly was elected as a Cumann na nGaedheal TD for Cork West in the 1923 general election, but did not contest the 1927 election, as he preferred farming to politics. In the latter election Wolfe ran as an Independent and took the seat. He would win two further elections, serving in the Dáil from 1927 to 1933, thus playing a very active part in the public life of the new state. His background as a Home Ruler may have helped him adjust to the new Ireland.

One of Wolfe's sparring partners in Dáil debates was the Fianna Fáil TD, Martin Corry. When Wolfe asked if the IRA was prepared to accept responsibility for the various outrages committed in 1921 during the Troubles, Corry interjected that they certainly accepted one responsibility: 'The responsibility of letting Deputy Wolfe go – a very serious responsibility.'[30] The Skibbereen law firm founded by Wolfe survives to this day, and is one of the biggest in West Cork. In 1940 Wolfe had the honour of being elected President of the solicitors' body, the Incorporated Law Society of Ireland, the first Corkman to occupy that prestigious position. When he died in 1952 aged 80 years there was a huge attendance at his funeral – it was said that the cortege was a mile long.

Bridget Noble's Emigrant Sisters

Bridget Noble's sisters passed away in America in the 1930s and 1940s. Mattie Monahan, who continued to live at Myrtle Street in Rockland, Plymouth, Mass., died in 1933 in her 61st year and was buried at Holy Family Cemetery in Rockland. (US records indicate she was now known as Matilda J. Monahan – apparently 'Matilda' being an interpretation of the name 'Mattie' although birth registration records in Ireland show that she was originally named 'Martha'.) Her husband John Monahan died a few years later, in 1938, at age 72 years and was laid to rest in the same plot where family members of succeeding generations would also be buried. In recent years, a small American flag, the 'stars and stripes', stood beside the grey headstone that marks the family grave.

Bridget's other sister Dora Scully, who resided at 439 Hanover Street, Portsmouth, New Hampshire, died in a local hospital in May 1944 aged 74 years. Dora had been a resident of Portsmouth for 44 years, establishing deep roots in the community. She was pre-deceased by her husband, James, who passed away in 1937, aged 73 years, and by her son John, who died in 1941. She was survived by her daughter Mary and three sons, James, Paul and Edward. In stark contrast with the furtive and undignified disposal of Bridget Noble's remains on the

Beara peninsula 23 years previously, Dora was given a funeral with all the liturgical pomp and ceremony that the local Catholic parish could provide.

At the imposing Church of the Immaculate Conception on Summer Street, the Rev. Walter Blankenship celebrated a Requiem High Mass, assisted by Rev. Francis Butler as deacon and the Rev. John O'Leary OMI, as sub-deacon. A choir sang the Latin Mass, the organ was played by Norman Moulton Leavitt, and the obsequies were covered by the local newspaper. Burial was in the family plot at Calvary cemetery, and Father Butler said the graveside prayers. Two of those who helped carry the coffin were Dora's nephews, sons of her late sister Mattie – Harold and Bernard Monahan. This would suggest that the two sisters and their respective families had kept in touch over the years, although residing in different New England states. (Perhaps they also wrote letters to keep in touch with Bridget, back in Reenavaude.) A local newspaper obituary recalled that Dora was a native of 'Castletown Berehaven' and paid tribute to her, stating that she was 'known to her friends as a devoted mother and one much interested in the community'.[31]

Dora's daughter Mary Rutland, after her service in the US Navy in the First World War, resided for many years in Portsmouth, where she was manager of Bernard's Hat Shop on Congress Street. In January 1981 Mary died at a nursing home in Wilmington, North Carolina, where her daughter Marilyn, who had married US Marine John Wojcik, resided with her own family. Mary's war-time service with the navy was not forgotten and Bridget Noble's niece was accorded the honour of being laid to rest with other veterans in Wilmington National Cemetery, which is administered by the US Department of Veterans Affairs. The simple, military-style marble headstone is inscribed: 'Mary Agnes Rutland, Y1 [Yeoman First Class], US Navy, World War 1, Nov 24 1900 - Jan 15 1981.' The headstone inscription gallantly shaved a few years off Mary's age. She was, in fact, born in 1895, not 1900, and was aged 85 years when she passed away.

There is no record of either of Bridget Noble's emigrant sisters returning to Reenavaude. Perhaps there was nothing for Mattie Monahan and Dora Scully to go back to, and maybe there was too much tragedy associated with the home place. It is known that Mattie's son Arthur Monahan did pay a visit to Europe in 1958. Records show that he and his wife Mildred travelled in style, sailing first class on the *Queen Mary* and landing at Southampton. They paid a five-day visit to London, staying at the exclusive Grosvenor House Hotel in Mayfair. Arthur, born in 1900, died in 1979 while Mildred passed away in 1990 – they lived in an attractive house on a pleasant, tree-lined thoroughfare, Queen Street, Falmouth, Mass. As a humble migrant, Mattie would have travelled steerage when she sailed from Queenstown [Cobh] in the 1890s, but she had prospered in America and her family did well too – it was all part of making the American Dream a reality. One can only speculate as to the life Bridget might have had in the US, had she also been given an opportunity to emigrate.

Chapter 26: Alexander Noble's Troubled Life

After his visit to West Cork in 1922, Alexander Noble did not settle permanently back in the area, which must have become a place of horror for him. His father-in-law John Neill probably passed away in the 1920s, although no death registration record has come to light. According to a local source, another person, who was down on his luck, lived in the cottage at Reenavaude for a period before moving to England. (It appears he was called Sullivan – this was almost inevitable in light of this being the dominant name in Beara.) Alexander would eventually become the registered owner of the farm at Reenavaude. The Neill holding was among the properties taken over from the Leigh-White estate by the Congested Districts Board for Ireland (CDBI) in 1911, under the provisions of the Irish Land Act, 1909 – this was part of the process whereby tenants would become the owners of the farms they occupied.

There were long delays in the project being finalised, and the process would drag on into the period after the founding of the Free State. The estate was not vested in the CDBI until March 1923, according to a statement made in the Dáil in February 1929. The Dáil was also told that the holdings of 276 tenants who had signed purchase agreements had been vested in them but the Land Commission was unable to obtain the signatures of the remaining tenants to the agreements, 'which were prepared and ready for execution from the middle of 1928'.[1] Alexander Noble seems to have been one of tenants who delayed signing up – being an 'absentee' tenant may have been a factor in the delay.

A record in the Registry of Deeds in Dublin shows that he was registered for the first time as the owner of the property on 6 November 1929, with a folio number assigned. Intriguingly, the record notes that the property at Ardgroom Inward includes 'five small islands adjacent'. This could be a reference to some uninhabited, grassy islands in the southwest corner of Ardgroom Harbour, close to the coast and in the vicinity of Reenavaude. The registration of the property, now in freehold tenure, would clear the way for Alexander to sell the land, and around this period the few acres were bought by a neighbouring farmer, Florence Sullivan. By now, the thatched roof of the Nobles' cottage had caved in – valuation records show that by 1928 the house was a ruin.[2] While rates would be payable on the land, they would not have to be paid for a house in ruins. The small cottage where Bridget was reared and where she lived with Alexander and which was the only home she ever knew, was gradually claimed back by nature, the ivy-clad walls enveloped by shrubbery and trees.

For a period in the early 1920s, Alexander continued to reside in Grimsby where there were better opportunities to earn a living from his trade as a cooper. He remained a boarder at Mrs Mulligan's redbrick house in the town, 30 Railway Street. It was a convenient location, close to Grimsby docks, while the railway station was just down the street. A few doors away at the street corner, there was a popular public house, the Locomotive Tavern, which no longer survives. Alexander also kept in touch with his family roots in Fraserburgh, where his mother, brother William, and sister Helen still resided. The disappearance and death of Bridget must have weighed heavily on him. He did not have a grave to visit but he may have gained some solace when he placed an *In Memoriam* notice in the local newspaper, the *Fraserburgh Herald*. The notice, in which Alexander paid an emotional tribute to Bridget, appeared on 20 March 1923, close to the second anniversary of her death. The notice stated:

IN EVER LOVING REMEMBRANCE of my dear wife Bridget Teresa Noble, who was kidnapped from her home in Ardgroom, Co. Cork, on the 4th March 1921 by an organisation known as the Irish Republican Army, and shot in Lauragh, Co. Kerry.
Greater love than this hath no man that one should Lay down his Life for another.
Inserted by Alexander Noble, 30 Railway Street, Grimsby.

The following year, around Bridget's third anniversary, Alexander inserted a similar notice in the 18 March 1924 edition of the *Fraserburgh Herald* but this time he included the actual date on which, he stated, his wife was shot at Lauragh – 15 March 1921. The same quote from scripture was included and it was stated that the notice was inserted by 'A. Noble, 1 Finlayson Street'. This was the Fraserburgh address where Alexander's mother was now residing. As previously indicated, it is unclear how Alexander came by the information that Bridget was shot at Lauragh. It will be recalled that a letter from the Department of Defence to his solicitor gave the date of Bridget's death but not the location where she was killed. During his visit to West Cork, Alexander may have picked up some additional information about Bridget's death, either from the RIC or from some other source, possibly a neighbour or a source linked to the IRA.

It is particularly intriguing to note that Alexander included a renowned quote from scripture in his *In Memoriam* notices: 'Greater love than this hath no man that one should Lay down his Life for another.' The line of scripture, John 15:13, is taken from the King James Bible (KJB), with some slight variations. In the original KJB version the line refers to laying down one's life 'for his friends'. In the way the quotation is reproduced by Alexander, the reference is changed to laying down one's life 'for another'. In seeking to interpret Alexander's bible quotation, one is tempted to engage in some speculation. A theory comes to mind, although there is no way of confirming it. Alexander encountered District Inspector Oates during the compensation hearing in Skibbereen, and one wonders if Oates told him that Bridget engaged with members of the crown forces because she was worried about him. In amending the scriptural quote from the plural to the singular, one wonders, as previously indicated, if Alexander meant to convey that Bridget had essentially laid down her life for himself, her husband; that in her love for Alexander she had taken a risk in making contact with the RIC to inquire about him, sparking a chain of events that would lead to her abduction by the IRA, and the 'laying down' of her own life.

Sailing to Australia

Around this period, it seems that Alexander decided to make a fresh start in a very different location at the other end of the world – Australia. By this stage, the question of compensation for the murder of Bridget had been sorted, although the process whereby he would be registered as the owner of the land at Reenavaude had still to be completed. He was no longer in the first flush of youth, and starting a new life 'Down Under' would present certain challenges. Nevertheless, records show that Alexander Noble was one of more than 1,000 passengers who sailed from the port of London on 17 July 1924 aboard the P&O liner *Barrabool* bound for Australia. Alexander's destination was Fremantle, in Western Australia.[3] The passenger list gives his age as 50 years, his occupation as cooper and his address as 1, Finlayson Street, Fraserburgh. It was stated on the list that Alexander's 'country of intended future permanent residence' was Australia.

The voyage aboard the liner, built by Harland & Wolff in Belfast and launched in 1921, would take close on six weeks. Australian records show that Alexander Noble disembarked at Fremantle on 26 August.[4] The records also indicate that he travelled third class, that his marital status was 'widower', his nationality, 'British' and the country of last permanent residence, 'Scotland'. One could speculate that after periods of tragedy and stress, Alexander sought solace in travelling to distant places. After losing his father to a shipwreck and three siblings to TB, and after the difficulties of a paternity suit, he goes to the Beara peninsula, on the edge of Europe, to make his life there, and after the trauma of Bridget's disappearance and death, he goes to an even more faraway location, Australia. (One wonders if he also intended travelling on to Hobart, Tasmania to visit his father's grave.) If he was looking for long-term solace in Australia, it was not to be. Some time after his arrival, it appears he had a change of heart, and decided to return to Europe. Despite his declared intention to settle permanently in Australia, his sojourn 'Down Under' was relatively short. No records have come to light about his return trip to the United Kingdom but he was back in Scotland in 1926.

In that year there was another important milestone in the family history when Alexander's mother, Helen Noble, passed away on 5 August at 1 Finlayson Street, at age 76 years. Among those present at her bedside was Williamina Noble, married to Alexander's brother William – they also lived in Fraserburgh, at 92 Mid Street. It was Williamina who reported Helen's passing to the death registration authorities. The cause of death was stated to be cancer of the liver.[5] Tuberculosis had claimed the lives of four of her children before she herself passed away. Alexander was back in Fraserburgh at this time, having apparently spent some time in Glasgow.[6] There were worrying signs that he was losing control, and that his inner demons were taking over. With the compensation money he received following the death of Bridget, and probably still traumatized by her horrific fate, he was drinking heavily.

Within days of his mother's funeral, he was in trouble with the Fraserburgh police for a public order offence. With an address given as 1 Finlayson Street where his late mother resided, he duly appeared in Fraserburgh Police Court later in August, in front of Bailie [Magistrate] Peterkin. The case was reported in a local newspaper and it was recorded that Alexander Noble, a cooper, 'pleaded guilty to a breach of the peace by cursing, swearing and kicking the door of a dwelling house on Mid Street. A fine of 30s was imposed, the alternative being 15 days.'[7] As indicated above, Alexander's brother William resided at Mid Street but it is unclear if this was the house where Alexander caused a breach of the peace. There would be further difficulties in Alexander's life, arising from his drinking.

Marriage and Prison

In 1927, now aged 53 years, Alexander Noble married again, his bride being a 39-year-old widow, Mabel Vallance, a housekeeper by profession. Although listed as a Catholic in the 1911 Census, on this occasion Alexander did not have a church wedding. He and his new bride were wed at the Register Office in Grimsby on 28 April, the witnesses being Violet Scargall and Frederick Rees. The newly-weds took up residence in a terrace house at 65 Harold Street in the town. While Alexander had previously lived in lodgings in Grimsby, he and his new bride now had a small house to themselves.[8] Alexander and Mabel had factors in common – they were both Scots from Aberdeenshire; they were each married before with no children of either union, and each had lost a spouse under traumatic circumstances.

In 1909 Mabel Chalmers, as she then was, the daughter of whisky traveller John Chalmers, of 119 Union Grove, Aberdeen, married a man from Glasgow, Henry Vallance.[9] They settled at 42 Linwood Drive, Glasgow. According to the 1911 Census, Henry (32) and Mabel (23) had a live-in servant in the house, 21-year-old Catherine McDonald, indicating that the couple enjoyed a certain level of prosperity. Henry served in the British Army during the Great War. (Records show that Henry Vallance, a 'cork merchant', now with an address at 160 Great George Street, Hillhead, Glasgow, joined the Scottish Horse as a Private at age 36 years in 1915. He later transferred to the Machine Gun Corps, was wounded in action on 21 January 1918, and was discharged with a pension. His next-of-kin was stated to be his wife Mabel, with the same address at Great George Street.[10])

Henry was fortunate to survive the war but tragedy was to follow. On 2 April 1922, at 3.35 pm, he was found dead from coal gas poisoning in his bedroom at his residence, 73 Elmbank Street, Glasgow. He was aged 44 years. A local newspaper reported that he was found dead in his bed 'and the gas was turned full on'. The report went on: 'At the time of the discovery, a cat and two kittens were in the room. A curious circumstance is that the cat was dead and the kittens were alive.'[11] The death certificate observed that Vallance, a mercantile clerk and army pensioner, had last been seen alive the day before his death. It was stated that the person who informed the authorities of the death was the deceased man's brother John Vallance, who lived at 56 Queensborough Gardens, Glasgow. The record also noted that the deceased was 'married to Mabel Chalmers'.[12]

Unfortunately, after Alexander Noble wed Mabel, there were soon difficulties in the marriage. Alexander assaulted his wife on the Christmas Day after their wedding. Evidence later given in court seemed to imply that he suspected her of having an affair. It was reported that he was released on bail after being sent for trial for unlawfully wounding his wife, but then went to her home and attacked her again. Charged with aggravated assault, he was sentenced in December 1927 to six weeks hard labour.[13] He appeared in court again the following month. During a hearing at Grimsby Quarter Sessions, on 10 January 1928, Alexander pleaded guilty to maliciously wounding James Ross, on 14 November. In light of this guilty plea, a similar charge in regard to his wife, to which he pleaded not guilty, was not proceeded with. According to police evidence, Noble had been drinking since he received compensation for the murder of his first wife, and on his behalf it was stated that his second wife 'had been behaving immorally'.

While he had some previous 'public order' difficulties, there was no indication that Alexander had ever been in serious trouble with the law, and there were also extenuating circumstances arising out of Bridget's horrendous fate. Nevertheless, the Recorder imposed a sentence of six months hard labour. He told Alexander: 'Your greatest misfortune appears to be that you received £2,000 [sic] when your first wife was murdered by Sinn Feiners.'[14] The case was covered by local newspapers. The headline on the court report in the *Yorkshire Post* read: 'Ruined by £2,000. What Happened To A Man Whose Wife Was Murdered.' The *Leeds Mercury* headline read: 'His Misfortune. Man's Downfall after Receiving Compensation.' The *Hull Daily Mail* had the headline: 'Ruined by £2,000. A Grimsby Wounding Case.' The local prison was Lincoln Gaol, and that's where Alexander probably served his sentence. Ironically, it was also a prison associated with Éamon de Valera, to whom Alexander had appealed for information about Bridget's disappearance. Dev famously escaped from Lincoln Gaol with two other Irish prisoners in February 1919. They had been held in connection with the so-called 'German plot', and got clean away with the help of Michael Collins.

Alexander's marriage may not have survived the difficulties that arose in the relationship, although no record has come to light indicating that he and Mabel divorced. At some stage, Alexander returned to live in his native place, Fraserburgh. He resided with his unmarried sister, Helen Ann Noble, a factory worker, in a stone-built, two-storey terrace house at 51 Hanover Street. In the last five years of her life Helen, known in the family as Nellie, suffered from Parkinson's Disease, and Alexander probably acted as her carer. She died at Thomas Walker

Hospital, Fraserburgh at 7.30 am on 12 May 1939, at age 57 years. The cause of death was given as Paralysis Agitans – a medical term for Parkinson's Disease. It was Alexander who reported her death to the registration authorities.[15] Helen was buried on 15 May at Kirkton Cemetery, Fraserburgh, a Church of Scotland graveyard.

Trouble with the Police

Meanwhile, Alexander was experiencing further troubles in his life. He seemed to find it difficult to cope with personal setbacks, and there were minor brushes with the law for public order matters. On 20 December 1938 at a local court, he was fined 20s or ten days in prison for a breach of the peace. Then, a few months after his sister died, he was up in court again, in December 1939. He seemed to believe that he was being persecuted at his home on Hanover Street by a neighbour, Mrs Annie Hendry, and he verbally abused her. When he appeared before Bailie Trail at a Police Court in Fraserburgh he pleaded not guilty to a breach of the peace. It was alleged that on Thursday, 7 December, within the common passage leading to Mrs Hendry's house at 27 School Street, 'he cursed, swore and used indecent language' to Mrs Hendry, putting her into a state of 'fear and alarm'.

In his own defence Alexander made various allegations against Mrs Hendry. According to the *Fraserburgh Herald* report, he shouted in court, saying: 'I am a poor man. I cannot pay any fines. I will go to jail for it. I have done my best to keep the peace. I am only a poor man and I cannot get peace in my own house for her.'[16] The Bailie asked the accused if he admitted a conviction on 12 December 1938, when he was fined 20s or ten days. 'I was convicted on false evidence,' the accused shouted. The newspaper report noted: 'Accused's manner was so unruly that he was twice cautioned concerning his conduct.' The Bailie imposed a fine of 20s or ten days in prison. Alexander replied: 'I am ready for the ten days.' After some consideration, it was reported that the accused asked for time to pay the fine, and he was given six weeks in which to find the money. According to the *Fraserburgh Herald*, as the accused was leaving the court he shouted: 'I hope the policeman will be warned...' The Bailie once again warned him that he was rendering himself liable for contempt of court.

Alexander Noble moved from the house at 51 Hanover Street where he felt he was being persecuted, and took up residence at another address in Fraserburgh, 73 Frithside Street. He probably lived in rented accommodation here – valuation records for 1930 indicate the property was owned by a landlord who had tenants in the house. The turmoil and the torment in Alexander's troubled life finally came to a close on 26 February 1941. He passed away at 5.25 pm in Woodend Hospital,

Aberdeen, close on 20 years after the disappearance and death of Bridget. The death registration note compiled by the registrar Albert Smith noted that Alexander was aged 67 years, that he was a cooper and that he had been married, first, to 'Bridget O'Neill' and secondly to 'Mabel Chalmers, or Vallance'. The cause of death was given as 'enlargement of the prostate: uraemia'. Alexander's brother William Noble, of 6 Fuller's Circle, Aberdeen, was listed as the person who informed the registry authorities of the death.[17] Alexander was laid to rest on 1 March at Kirkton Cemetery, Fraserburgh, in the same plot at this Presbyterian graveyard where his sister Helen had been buried just a couple of years previously. A few days later, on 6 March, a local newspaper published a brief obituary notice in regard to Alexander, giving only minimal details. The notice stated his address and the place and date of death, and added that he was the 'eldest son of the late Alexander Noble, shipmaster'.[18] There was no mention of Alexander's wife Mabel, nor of the Beara woman to whom he was previously married, Bridget.

One wonders if the son who, according to court records, Alexander fathered back in 1903 was aware of Alexander's passing. Some basic details are known about the boy. He would drop his mother's surname and acquire a different name. He worked as a labourer, married in Aberdeen county in the early 1930s and had a family. His mother Mary Ann never married, but her son was with her as she lay dying in her sixties, and it was he who reported her death to the registration authorities. He himself died suddenly from a heart attack in the late 1960s, and one of his children published a very affectionate *In Memoriam* tribute to him in the local press.

A decade after Alexander Noble's death, his brother William passed away. He was the last survivor of Alexander's siblings, and probably the only one of them who had actually been to the Beara peninsula and met Bridget Noble. Now with an address at 12 Berryden Road, Aberdeen, William died of cardiac failure at age 61 years on 31 January 1951.[19] A death notice was published in the local newspaper, the *Evening Express* and in regard to the funeral, the notice said: 'All friends respectfully invited.' A short funeral service was held at Gordon & Watson's Rest Room, Rosebank Place, and William was buried at Allenvale Cemetery, Aberdeen. William's son, William A.P. Noble of 57 Menzies Road, Aberdeen, reported the death to the registration authorities.

As for Alexander's second wife Mabel, she also returned to her native place, Aberdeen. She had a drink problem, and died alone at age 62 years in 1950, during what should have been a cheerful interlude, the summer bank holiday weekend. The register of deaths recorded that Mabel Noble was found dead at her home, 8 West North Street, at 6.30 am on Monday, 7 August that year – she was last seen alive the previous day at 8.30 am.[20] It was recorded that she was a widow, firstly of '—Vallance' (the first name was unavailable to the registration authorities), and secondly of 'Alexander Noble, cooper'. The person who reported her death was Detective Constable Norman Patterson, of the Aberdeen City Police. Mabel's remains were seen by Dr Robert Richards, and the cause of death was given as 'Cardio Vascular Degeneration' and 'Alcoholism'. One wonders if the terrible fate of Bridget Noble had cast a long shadow, with her bereaved husband turning to drink, followed by difficulties in his second marriage and the lonely death of his second wife, Mabel.

Epilogue

More than 50 years after the death of Bridget Noble, another woman was abducted and killed by republicans. This time, the victim was Jean McConville, a widowed mother of ten who was disappeared and murdered by the Provisional IRA in 1972, as mentioned. There are some parallels. Both women had married across the religious/ethnic divide. Bridget, a Catholic, had married a Scotsman with a Presbyterian background, while Jean, born a Protestant, had married a Catholic who had been in the British Army and was now living in a strongly republican, Catholic area of Belfast, Divis Flats. (Jean became a Catholic on getting married.) Neither woman had the immediate support of a partner or husband. Bridget's husband had moved to England in search of work, and Jean's husband had died, leaving her to look after ten children. Perhaps both female victims were considered 'outsiders' or 'different' by some people in their respective communities. As mentioned, Bridget Noble was one of only two named women known for certain to have been disappeared by the IRA in the Troubles of the 1920s, while Jean McConville was the only female to have been disappeared by the Provisional IRA during the more recent Troubles in Northern Ireland.

Bridget initially attracted adverse attention by making visits to the local RIC station and by her apparent friendship with a police sergeant, and she was the victim of a punishment attack in which her hair was forcibly shorn. As previously outlined, it seems the major reason for her being abducted was that she had given the police the names of the men she accused of attacking her, leading to the arrest of one of them – another would be interned after her death. Jean was also accused of being an informer, but this claim is ridiculed by her family. They wonder how she could have found the time to be an informer, as she was always on her feet looking after ten children.[1] They say one of the reasons she was victimised was that she comforted a wounded British soldier who was crying for help outside her door. The slogan 'Brit Lover' was daubed on her door, and her windows smashed. It is also claimed that she refused to assist in moving paramilitary weapons, and that she became involved in a bitter personal dispute with a republican family. (It was claimed that the family, having sold a second-hand suite of furniture to Mrs McConville, then demanded more than the agreed price.)[2] After carrying out an inquiry, Police Ombudsman Nuala O'Loan found no evidence that Mrs McConville was an informer, stating that she 'is not recorded as being an agent at any time'. The Ombudsman said Mrs McConville 'was an innocent woman who was abducted and murdered'.

In both cases, accounts have emerged as to how the women, while being taken away to their doom, cried out for help but nobody could save them. Bridget made a despairing cry to a neighbour, 'Save me, Jack, save me' as she was being taken down a boreen in a donkey and cart. Jean desperately called out 'Help me' as she was bundled out of her bath at her home, made to dress hurriedly and then hustled away by a gang of masked men and women, while her screaming children tried in vain to protect her.[3] In the case of both women, republicans took them away to a secret location, held them prisoner for a period of time, and then killed them, secretly disposing of their remains. In the immediate aftermath of both killings, the perpetrators seemed reluctant to publicly acknowledge what they had done. Bridget's husband had a struggle to find out what happened his wife, and it took many years for the Provisional IRA to confirm that they had killed Jean McConville. The remains of the 38-year-old widow were finally discovered by a person walking a dog on a beach in County Louth in 2003 after a storm exposed the remains. A forensic examination showed she had been shot in the back of the head.

Republican activist and former hunger striker Dolours Price said before her death in 2013 that, as a member of a special PIRA unit, the Unknowns, she drove Mrs McConville across the border into the Irish Republic, with two other members of the group, and she claimed that they all participated in the actual murder.[4] She identified one of the perpetrators as the head of the Unknowns, Pat McClure. He was an ex-soldier who later emigrated to America where he served the cause of law and order by becoming a prison officer at the Cheshire Correctional Institution in Connecticut – he died in 1986. Ms Price did not identify the third member of the Unknowns who allegedly took part in the killing of Mrs McConville. Dolours' sister Marian, through a statement issued by her solicitor in November 2018, denied any involvement in the murder. Evidence that emerged in court in Belfast in October 2019 suggests that senior republicans, in order to avoid an adverse public reaction, decided to disappear Mrs McConville rather than allow her body to be found – it was said that 'they couldn't take the heat from throwing her on the street'. During the court hearing, former senior IRA member Ivor Bell was found not guilty of soliciting the murder of Mrs McConville.

Following the discovery of the remains of Jean McConville, her children were now able now to give their mother a proper funeral and a Christian burial. There would be no funeral or Christian burial for the two women who were disappeared in 1921, Mrs Noble and Mrs Lindsay as, of course, their remains were never located. According to author Tim Sheehan, men who had served as officers in the local IRA battalion were concerned that the British could exploit, for propaganda purposes, the recovery of Mrs Lindsay's remains. So Jackie O'Leary, Frank Busteed and some trusted helpers exhumed the remains of Mrs Lindsay and her driver James Clarke and buried them in a bog in another location. It appears that one of the helpers was Patrick Sullivan, from Kilmona, Grenagh who worked as a postman and who, as a member of 'C' Company, 6th Battalion, had also been on the anti-Treaty side in the Civil War. In his application for a Military Service Pension, he states that after the ceasefire in the Civil War, he 'helped to remove the decomposed body of a woman spy' and 'interned' [recte interred] her elsewhere. Sullivan, who later resided in New York City before returning to County Cork where he died in 1978, states that the reason for the re-burial was that 'the Free State Army learned where she was buried'.[5] Sullivan makes no mention of Clarke's remains being exhumed and re-interred.

General Richard Mulcahy, who was to succeed Michael Collins as Free State military commander, would have been willing to assist Mrs Lindsay's relatives in the recovery of her remains. In a letter dated 27 March 1922, while serving as Minister of Defence, he told the army's Ard Chongantóir [Adjutant General] that arrangements should be put in place so that they could state they were prepared 'to have her burial place disclosed'. It appears that the letter resulted from representations to the Department of Defence made in February 1922 by a Catholic priest in the Ballinasloe area of County Galway, the Rev. Thomas J. O'Connor.[6] Mrs Lindsay's sisters had apparently enlisted the priest's assistance in their attempts to recover the remains. It may be the case that the covert re-burial operation foiled a move by the Free State army to find the secret grave of Mary Lindsay.

Mrs Lindsay's family were still anxious to give her a proper funeral and in 1924, the year after the Civil War ended, Mrs Lindsay's sister Lady Forde made approaches to people in the Donoughmore area of County Cork, seeking any information as to where the remains might have been buried. Jackie O'Leary who, like Busteed, was on the anti-Treaty side in the Civil War, reportedly became concerned, once again, that the British could benefit from propaganda if Mrs Lindsay's remains were found. (It appears that the IRA in County Tipperary had similar concerns in August 1921 – it was agreed to return the body of executed RIC Inspector Gilbert Potter to his wife Lilias 'on the understanding that no advantage will be taken of this decision for political purposes...'[7]) It was said that O'Leary knew how the remains of the English nurse, Edith Cavell, were exhumed, much to the opprobrium of the German authorities who had executed her. So, according to Tim Sheehan, once again O'Leary, along with some trusted colleagues, secretly dug up the remains of Mrs Lindsay and James Clarke, took them away by lorry and dumped them in a deep pond so that they would never be found.[8] (There have also been reports that the remains were cremated and that it was the ashes that were dumped. A man whose father had been in the local IRA believed these reports were credible – he told me he heard that the remains were incinerated in a tar barrel.) The ultimate disposal of the remains was the final indignity. Mrs Lindsay's grieving sisters would be denied the consolation of giving her remains, and those of James Clarke, a proper burial.

As for Bridget Noble, all those with direct knowledge of her last resting place have passed on, and we are left with rumour and conjecture, and reports that cannot be confirmed. While researching the story of Mrs Noble, I was struck by the accuracy of some of the local anecdotal evidence about her fate. Research in archives showed that oral accounts that had come down over the generations were correct on a number of points. These include the absence of Alexander from the family home at the time Mrs Noble came to the adverse attention of the IRA; the punishment attack in which her hair was forcibly shorn, and the bringing of the priest to her prior to execution. However, as regards the disposal of the remains, the accounts and the theories have varied greatly.

The historian Dr Eve Morrison has remarked on the number of 'ghost stories' that emerged in Ireland, relating to the independence struggle and the Civil War. 'Ghosts of IRA men, civilians, British soldiers and policemen haunted ambush sites or the places where they died, or appeared as "crisis apparitions" to the living at the moment of their deaths.' She described these stories as part of a 'rich fantastical folklore'.[9] (It is noteworthy that Liam O'Dwyer, in his memoir, described a visit from his dead brother Robert, who said 'he would be with me always and that nothing serious would happen to me during the whole struggle'.[10]) Bridget Noble also entered into local folklore. In times past, when people were more inclined to believe in ghostly manifestations, it was said that the 'White Lady', the unquiet spirit of

Bridget Noble, haunted the area of Collorus, the scenic area by the sea where some believe her life was brought to an end.

A local person told me of a female relative travelling with her family by car at night some decades previously. They came to Collorus bridge, over the arch where some believe Mrs Noble met her death. As they were crossing the bridge his relative was startled to see the spectral face of a woman emerging from the darkness and staring in at her, with an expression of great sadness. She had dark hair with streaks of grey and was dressed in black. The woman in the car screamed, 'What was that?' but her husband and children saw nothing. The woman travelling with her family did not know at the time of the Bridget Noble story.

Perhaps the mystical quality of the magnificent seascapes and the haunting sounds of the sea helped to inspire belief in eerie communications 'from the other side'. I was intrigued by how a Canadian-born artist and writer, probably unaware of the Bridget Noble connection, described a memorable visit to the sea caves near Cuas pier, an area also associated with Bridget's time in captivity. Further along the coast is Darrigroe, where Bridget cried out for help as she was being taken away to her death. At the sea caves, Susanne Iles believed she heard the unnerving sound of a woman calling out. She wrote on a blog: 'There were a few times when the hair on our arms stood on end as we listened; we swore we could hear voices talking among themselves; once we were convinced we could hear a woman calling for someone and whispering earnestly...'[11]

During one of my visits to the Beara peninsula, I was told of a 'returned Yank', a man who came from America to visit places associated with his forebears. He was, apparently, a hard-headed individual who did not believe in the paranormal and was not superstitious. He took a taxi to the Doorus area and went walking alone along the path through the shadowy woodlands towards Doorus Point. After a while he began to feel something pressing against him as though to prevent him going further. He became afraid. He had heard about Bridget Noble, and he took his rosary beads from his pocket, hung it on a nearby branch and turned back. The pressure lifted, and all was well. A distant relative believes he may have suffered a slight stroke – nevertheless, the story of his unsettling experience in the woods at Doorus has formed part of the legend of the 'White Lady'.

As earlier indicated, anecdotal evidence suggests that at least one of the republicans involved in the action taken against Mrs Noble was also 'haunted' by the missing woman, but in the sense of suffering a crisis of conscience over what had been done to her. It was said that in old age, he would walk obsessively by the sea, rosary beads in his hands, pleading for Bridget to forgive him. Maybe there were others who also felt regret. Some of those involved in the action against Mrs Noble were very young, in their teens or early twenties, as mentioned, and actions carried out in one's youth can sometimes engender remorse when recalled with the maturity of later years. It is possible that regret over past deeds was a factor in the silence about the fate of the woman from Reenavaude.

Looking back on the story of Bridget Noble, it is apparent that no republican died as a result of anything she did or was alleged to have done – the only person to die was Bridget herself. She lost her life after trying to hit back at the young men who attacked her, forcibly shearing her hair. Summarising points already made in this book, it could be said that in the circumstances of the time, her decision to complain to the police was most unwise but it also showed great courage. She was subjected to a miserable death for 'informing', but it is apparent that she was executed in violation of the IRA's own rules. It can also be said that she took an enormous risk in defending her dignity as a woman. Bearing in mind her husband's tribute to her, his quotation from scripture, and the possible interpretation of the bible quotation as outlined above, maybe it could also be said that she died out of love for Alexander. 'Greater love than this...'

While the exact location of Bridget's remains would remain a mystery, Alexander was at least able to publish some *In Memoriam* notices 'in loving remembrance' of his late wife. Alexander had his faults, he was not a perfect human being, and in the midst of his torment and his drinking, he was violent towards his second wife, but the indications are that he did love Bridget – I believe there is no reason to doubt the sincerity of the *In Memoriam* notices. And, as already outlined, his life went downhill after her death. Bridget is also commemorated in music, through the compassion of the composer Skully, who was moved by her story, who broke the silence and kept her memory alive and who, as mentioned, wrote a piece of music titled *Mrs Noble*. A young American woman called Sandy paid the following tribute on his blog back in 2011: 'Skully, you have brought Bridget's tragedy to the forefront and have given her the justice no one else did. You have exposed this crime for what it is, murder. None of us will forget Bridget Noble now. She is forever emblazoned in my mind and in my heart. Thank you for the tribute you have given her. She may not have a grave, but you have given her a memorial that will live on forever...'

Wherever your remains lie, rest in peace, Mrs Noble.

Acknowledgements

I would like to thank everyone who assisted with this book. In particular I would like to express my great gratitude to some marvellous people on the Beara peninsula who provided enormously valuable guidance and assistance. They know who they are. I am also most grateful to Skully, the musician and composer, for sharing with me his own thoughts and family memories, and for providing me with a copy of the recording made by his grandmother, Mrs Elizabeth Sullivan, in which Eva O'Sullivan tells of the abduction of Mrs Noble. Listening to that recording, with its account of the kidnapping and execution of the woman from Reenavaude, history seemed to come alive, but in a rather chilling way. Details of the first-hand account given by an elderly Beara woman of Mrs Noble's time in captivity were also hugely valuable, and I am most grateful to those who assisted me in this matter. It was important for me to be allowed access to the accounts book that was maintained at the Ardgroom shop/post office where Mrs Noble was a customer, and I am also most grateful to those who gave me assistance with this aspect of my research.

I would like to thank Peter Noble for information on the last resting place in Fraserburgh of Bridget's husband, Alexander Noble, and also for details of the Noble family tree. I am grateful also to Peter Mulready, my fellow-member of the Military History Society of Ireland, for information on District Inspector Thomas J. Oates, gleaned from his own academic studies of the Royal Irish Constabulary. For their valuable help and courtesy, I would like to thank personnel at the Irish Military Archives – research in this facility at Cathal Brugha Barracks, Dublin, unearthed important information. I carried out research at the National Library of Ireland and the Irish National Archives, and am grateful for the courtesy and assistance I was accorded in these establishments. I am also grateful to staff at my alma mater, University College Dublin, for assistance in accessing material held at the archives in Belfield. I would like to thank Cal Hyland for sharing information he gleaned from his own research in the records of the Irish Grants Committee, held at the National Archives in the UK. Jasper Ungoed-

Thomas, grandson of Jasper Travers Wolfe, kindly gave me permission to reproduce a photo of his grandfather – many thanks.

My thanks also to staff at the Cork City and County Archives for their assistance in accessing records of the Castletown Board of Guardians, and to staff at the Valuation Office, Dublin for their advice and assistance in viewing the records for Ardgroom Inward. I am grateful also to staff at the Property Registration Authority, for help in consulting records at the Land Registry and the Registry of Deeds. I would also like to thank staff at the Royal Dublin Society library; the Dublin City Library, Pearse Street; the Jesuit Library, Milltown Park and staff at my own local public library in Terenure, Dublin for their courtesy and help. My thanks also to staff at the National Archives at Kew in Richmond, Surrey for their assistance as I consulted archives during my visit to this facility. I greatly enjoyed attending the West Cork History Festival in Skibbereen in recent years, and talks given at the festival were of great value.

As background to my research, I needed to learn about the history of the Beara peninsula, and in this regard, historian Fachtna O'Donovan very helpfully provided me with books published by the Beara Historical Society, including works by the late Gerdie Harrington. Fachtna is himself an expert on the history of the RIC in Beara and his published work on this topic was of great assistance.

Some of my research was carried out in Irish language publications, and I was reminded of the debt I owe my teachers at O'Connell School, especially the great Bráthair Mícheál Ó Flaitile, for developing my interest in the language.

While many kind people assisted with my work on this book, I would like to emphasise that any conclusions drawn from my research, any comments made in the text, and indeed any errors, are my responsibility alone.

Appendix

Text of internal IRA report on the execution of Mrs Bridget Noble drawn up by the Commandant [Liam O'Dwyer] of the 5th Battalion [Beara Battalion], Cork, No. 5 Brigade, and submitted to Brigade Headquarters in October 1921. The document, a copy of the typed report, is preserved in the Irish Military Archives. (Reference, Bridget Noble, IE/MA/HS/A/649.)

Óglaigh na h-Éireann
HEADQUARTERS,
5TH BATTALION,
CORK No. 5 Brigade
Dept. Adjt.
Octr. 21st 1921
To:
H. Quarters,
Cork No. 5 Brigade

I received your despatch re Mrs Noble asking for further particulars. I have been looking up these particulars for the past three or four days which accounts for delay.
The following details are all that are available:-
No. 1. Officers responsible for execution:-
The Battalion Staff of that time.
No. 2. The then Batt. Comdt. was of course responsible for anything that happened in the Battn. area.
No. 3. Evidence and source from which obtained:-
She was seen by some of the men of C. Company, (CT. Bere) going into the police barracks, on four or five occasions and in conversation with the police sergeant in a private house in C.T. Bere on two occasions.
When she came home from hospital she was bobbed by order of Battn. After a military raid in the district, in the course of which her house was visited by two Officers, a search of her house was made

by order of the O/C H. Coy (Ardgroom) and the following were found:-

Part of a letter from the H. Constable, Castletown, five half torn letters from other members of the R.I.C. and two photos of R.I.C. men.

Information reached us from the R.I.C. that Mrs Noble told them that Liam Dwyer and Pat Crowley were the men who shot William Lehane. This man was shot for land grabbing in Febr. 1920.

After having been 'bobbed' Mrs Noble went into the police barracks in company with another girl Nora Sullivan who, on being questioned afterwards told Pat Crowley, Jerh. Connor, James Malvey, Con Crowley and Tim Rahilly that she saw Mrs Noble handing a letter to the Head Constable containing the names of seven Volunteers and stating that these were the men who bobbed her.

On the 4th March, in a raid on her house a letter was found addressed to Mrs Noble from the Head Constable asking her to meet him in C. Town on that evening. She was arrested on her way to the police barrack.

No. 4.

Date of arrest: 4/3/1921.

Date of trial: 13/3/1921.

Date of execution: 15/3/1921.

No. 5. What resulted from the information which Mrs Noble gave to the police was not too serious as any of the 'murderers' were not caught, but were kept on the run. The district was constantly raided for them until the truce.

One of the men Ml. Sullivan whose name was given by Mrs Noble as having taken part in the bobbing was arrested in the month of May and interned. Another man, John Dwyer, who was arrested on the 4th March, was charged with having bobbed Mrs Noble and got six months imprisonment for same.

No. 6. Mrs Noble admitted guilt on all the charges. She was fortified with the Rites of the Church before being executed.

Commandant

Picture Section

379

Mrs Noble. Keenavauder?

1920 Balance forward	£	s	d
	1	4	2
Nov 15 Paid Cash		10	
	0	14	2
Jan 8 1921 a qur tea and ½ Sugar		2	7
and 2 Candles			6
and a ½ot of Jam		2	
a packet Notepaper and			4
a stamp	0	19	7
Feb 12 Paid Cash		5	
	0	14	7
20 Cash lent		10	
1921 March 2nd a Woollen Shawl	1	4	7
and a Tin Syrup	2	10	
Cash lent		7	3
and a Pillow Case			6
	3	3	
March 4th Paid Cash	4	0	7
	13	10	
Balance £	3	6	9

Bridget Noble's last transaction, 4 March 1921, in the accounts book of the local shop/post office in Ardgroom. (S. Boyne)

The blue-painted house (right) in Ardgroom village that was formerly the shop/post office, which Bridget Noble visited on 4 March 1921 before walking out this road into the countryside where she was abducted. (S. Boyne)

Obscured by ivy and shrubbery, the ruins of Bridget Noble's cottage at Reenavaude with, inset, the fireplace of the dwelling. (S. Boyne)

Liam O'Dwyer, with bandolier and holster, was the Beara Battalion Commandant who wrote an internal IRA report explaining why his organisation 'bobbed' and then executed Bridget Noble. He is pictured here with brother Richard and unidentified young woman holding a rifle. (Private source.)

Ruins of the isolated farmhouse at Feith Bhui, Kilcatherine, where Bridget Noble was held prisoner. (S. Boyne)

The boreen at Darrigroe where Bridget Noble called out to a neighbour to save her as she was being taken to the sea shore en route to the place of execution. (S. Boyne)

Cuas Pier, Beara, an area associated with Bridget Noble's time in captivity – some locals believe she was held in a shed close to the pier for at least one night. (S. Boyne)

Jasper Travers Wolfe, the solicitor who acted for Alexander Noble in his quest to ascertain the fate of his wife Bridget. (Courtesy of Jasper Ungoed-Thomas.)

Daniel T. Sullivan, Quartermaster of Beara Battalion at the time action was taken against Bridget Noble, pictured in the US in 1941. (US National Archives & Records Administration.)

Mícheál Óg O'Sullivan, Vice-Commandant of the Beara Battalion, and former pupil of Pádraig Pearse at St Enda's, pictured with sister Nancy. (Courtesy of Mrs A. O'Grady)

Skully, the musician and composer who kept alive the memory of Bridget Noble, and who wrote a piece of music to commemorate the missing Beara woman. (S. Boyne)

1

Mrs Mary Lindsay, who was disappeared by the IRA in County Cork in 1921.

Bibliography

PRIMARY SOURCES
Irish Military Archives
A/series or Collins Papers
Bureau of Military History
Civil War Operations and Intelligence Reports Collection
Civil War Prisoners Collection
Irish Army Census Records
Liaison and Evacuation Papers
Military Service Pensions Collection

The National Archives (TNA), Kew, Surrey, United Kingdom
Cabinet Papers (CAB)
Dublin Castle records
HM Treasury records re Compensation (Ireland) Commission
Ireland: Colonial Office records re compensation claims
Irish Distress Committee and Irish Grants Committee records
Royal Irish Constabulary records
War Office (WO) records

University College Dublin Archives (UCDA)
Richard Mulcahy Papers
Ernie O'Malley Notebooks

The National Archives of Ireland (NAI)
Census of Ireland, 1901/1911
Other archives consulted include Civil War compensation claims

National Library of Ireland
Catholic parish registers
Ted O'Sullivan Papers

Valuation Office archives, Dublin

Property Registration Authority
Registry of Deeds, Dublin
Land Registry, Dublin

Cork City & County Archives
Castletown Board of Guardians Minutes
Bantry Board of Guardians Minutes

OFFICIAL PUBLICATIONS
Dáil Éireann debates
Hansard House of Commons Debates

REFERENCE WORKS:
Irish Catholic Directories, 1921, 1922.

SECONDARY WORKS
Barry, Tom, *Guerrilla Days in Ireland*, Mercier Press, Cork, 2010.
Borgonovo, John (Editor), *Florence and Josephine O'Donoghue's War of Independence,* Irish Academic Press, Dublin, 2006.
Borgonovo, John, *Spies, Informers and the 'Anti-Sinn Féin Society', The Intelligence War in Cork City, 1920-1921,* Irish Academic Press, Dublin, 2007.
Borgonovo, John, *The Battle for Cork: July-August 1922*, Mercier, Cork, 2011.
Boyne, Sean, *Emmet Dalton: Somme Soldier, Irish General, Film Pioneer*, Merrion/Irish Academic Press, Co. Kildare, 2015.
Clark, Gemma, *Everyday Violence in the Irish Civil War*, Cambridge University Press, 2014.
Connolly, Linda (Editor), *Women and the Irish Revolution*, Irish Academic Press, Co. Kildare, 2020.
Deasy, Liam, *Brother Against Brother*, Mercier Press, Cork and Dublin, 1982.
Deasy, Liam, *Towards Ireland Free*, Royal Carbery Books, Cork, 1973.
Duggan, John P., *A History of the Irish Army*, Gill & Macmillan, Dublin, 1992.
Durell, Penelope & Cornelius Kelly, *The Grand Tour of Beara*, Cailleach Books, County Cork, 2000.
Fanning, Ronan, *Éamon de Valera, A Will to Power*, Faber & Faber, London, 2015.
Ferriter, Diarmaid, *A Nation And Not A Rabble, The Irish Revolution 1913-1923*, Profile Books, London, 2015.

Ferriter, Diarmaid, & Susannah Riordan (Editors), *Years of Turbulence, The Irish Revolution And Its Aftermath*, University College Dublin Press, 2015.

Fischer, Joachim & John Dillon (Editors), *The Correspondence of Myles Dillon 1922-1925,* Four Courts Press, Dublin, 1999.

Fitzpatrick, David, (Editor), *Terror in Ireland, 1916-1923*, The Lilliput Press, Dublin, 2012.

Foster, Gavin M., *The Irish Civil War And Society; Politics, Class and Conflict*, Palgrave & Macmillan, UK, 2015.

Harrington, Gerard, (Compiler), *Beara, History and Stories from the Peninsula*, Beara Historical Society, Castletownbere, Co. Cork, 2005.

Harrington, Gerdie, *Beara, Down Memory Lane*, Beara Historical Society, Castletownbere, Co. Cork, 2008.

Harrington, Gerard, *In The Path Of Heroes*, Beara Historical Society, Castletownbere, Co. Cork.

Hart, Peter, *The IRA & Its Enemies*, Oxford University Press, 1998.

Hatton-Hall, Chiara, *The Galloping Nun*, Paragon Publishing, London, 2013.

Heffernan, Brian, Freedom and the Fifth Commandment: Catholic Priests and Political Violence in Ireland, 1919 – 1921, Manchester University Press, 2014.

Herlihy, Jim, *The Royal Irish Constabulary: A Short History & Genealogical Guide*, Four Courts Press, Dublin, 1997.

Hopkinson, Michael, *Green Against Green, The Irish Civil War*, Gill & Macmillan, Dublin, 2004.

Hopkinson, Michael, *The Irish War of Independence*, Gill & Macmillan, Dublin, 2004.

Jackson, Bob, *A Doctor's Sword, How an Irish Doctor Survived War, Captivity and the Atom Bomb*, Collins Press, Cork, 2017.

Kelly, James & Mary Ann Lyons, (Editors), *Death and Dying in Ireland, Britain and Europe: Historical Perspectives*, Irish Academic Press, 2013.

Kennedy, Liam, *Unhappy the Land: The Most Oppressed People Ever, the Irish?*, Merrion Press, Co. Kildare, 2016.

Kingston, Diarmuid, *Beleagured: A History of the RIC in West Cork during the War of Independence*, Cork, 2016.

Knockraha History & Heritage Society, *Knockraha, Foras Feasa na Paroiste*, County Cork, 2005.

Lyne, Gerard J., *Murtaí Óg*, Geography Publications, Dublin, 2017.

Mac Aodha Bhuí, Iarla, *Diarmaid Ó Súilleabháin, Saothar Próis*, An Clóchomhar, Baile Átha Cliath, 1992.

McCullagh, David, *De Valera, Rise 1882 – 1932*, Gill Books, Dublin 2017.

McKendry, Seamus, *Disappeared: The Search for Jean McConville*, Blackwater Press, Dublin, 2000.

Moloney, Ed, *Voices From The Grave: Two Men's War In Ireland,* Faber and Faber, London, 2010.

Murphy, Gerard, *The Year of Disappearances, Political Killings in Cork, 1921-1922,* Gill & Macmillan, Dublin, 2011.

Ó hAnnracháin, Peadar, *Machtnamh Cime,* Oifig Díolta Foilseacháin Rialtais, 1933.

Ó hAnnracháin, Peadar, *Fé Bhrat an Chonartha,* Oifig an tSoláthair, 1944.

O'Callaghan, Sean, *Execution,* Frederick Muller, London, 1974.

O'Donovan, Donal, *Little Old Man Cut Short,* Kestrel Books, Bray, Co Wicklow, 1998.

O'Dwyer, Liam, *Beara in Irish History,* Vantage Press, New York, 1977.

O'Dwyer, Riobard, *Annals of Beara,* Volumes I, II & III, Gold Stag Publications, Statesboro, Georgia, USA, 2009.

O'Halpin, Eunan & Daithí Ó Corráin, *The Dead of the Irish Revolution,* Yale University Press, New Haven and London, 2020.

O'Hegarty, P.S., *The Victory of Sinn Féin,* The Talbot Press, Dublin, 1924.

O'Malley, Cormac K. H., & Anne Dolan, *'No Surrender Here',* The Civil War Papers of Ernie O'Malley 1922-1924, Lilliput Press, Dublin, 2007.

O'Malley, Ernie, *The Men Will Talk To Me, West Cork Interviews by Ernie O'Malley,* Edited by Andy Bielenberg, John Borgonovo and Padraig Óg Ó Ruairc, Mercier Press, Cork, 2015.

Ó Súilleabháin, Diarmaid, *Dianmhuilte Dé,* Sáirséal agus Dill, Baile Átha Cliath, 1964.

Ó Súilleabháin, Diarmaid, *Ciontach,* Coiscéim, Baile Átha Cliath, 1983.

Ryan, Meda, *The Day Michael Collins Was Shot,* Poolbeg, Dublin, 1995.

Ryan, Meda, *Tom Barry, IRA Freedom Fighter,* Mercier, Cork, 2012.

Sheehan, Tim, *Lady Hostage: Mrs Lindsay,* Dripsey, Co. Cork, 1990.

Sheehan, William, *A Hard Local War: The British Army and the Guerrilla War in Cork 1919 – 1921,* The History Press Ireland, Dublin, 2017.

St Mary's Neighbourhood Reunions Committee, *Butte's Irish Heart, Who Says You Can't Go Home,* Riverbend Publishing, Helena, Montana, USA, 2015.

Ungoed-Thomas, Jasper, *Jasper Wolfe of Skibbereen,* The Collins Press, Cork, 2008.

Verling, Martin, (editor), *Beara Woman Talking: Folklore from the Beara Peninsula,* Mercier Press, Cork, 2003.

Walsh, Maurice, *Bitter Freedom, Ireland in a Revolutionary World 1918 – 1923,* Faber & Faber, London, 2015.

Younger, Calton, *Ireland's Civil War,* Fontana Press, London, 1986.

ARTICLES & STUDIES

Dr Andy Bielenberg (UCC) & Professor Emeritus James S. Donnelly, Jr. (UW-Madison), 'List of Suspected Civilian Spies Killed by the IRA, 1920-21', 2016; also known as 'The Cork Spy Files'. (The Irishrevolution.ie – University College Cork & *Irish Examiner.*)

Dr Andy Bielenberg (UCC) & Professor Emeritus James S. Donnelly, Jr. (UW-Madison), 'Cork's War of Independence Fatality Register'. (The Irishrevolution.ie – University College Cork & *Irish Examiner.*)

Andy Bielenberg, John Borgonovo and James S. Donnelly, 'Something in the Nature of a Massacre' – The Bandon Valley Killings Revisited, *Éire-Ireland*, Fall/Winter 2014.

Julia Eichenberg, 'The Dark Side of Independence: Paramilitary Violence in Ireland and Poland after the First World War', *Contemporary European History*, Cambridge University Press, 2010.

Gabrielle Machnik-Kékesi, 'Gendering Bodies: Violence as Performance in Ireland's War of Independence', Thesis for Degree of Master of Arts, Concordia University, Montreal, Canada, 2017.

Dr Eve Morrison, 'Hauntings of the Irish Revolution', in Chapter Four, M. Corporaal, C. Cusack & R. van den Beuken (eds), *Irish Studies and the Dynamics of Memory*, Peter Lang, Bern, 2017.

Fachtna O'Donovan, 'A History of the Constabulary in Beara', Lecture to the Beara Historical Society, 18 Nov 2002; reproduced in Gerdie Harrington (compiler), *Beara, History and Stories from the Peninsula*, Beara Historical Society, 2005.

Sinn Féin Publicity Department, *The Good Old IRA, Tan War Operations*, Dublin, 1985.

MEDIA

Newspaper and journal archives consulted include: *Aberdeen Journal; Comhar; Cork County Eagle; Cork Examiner; Evening Echo; Fraserburgh Herald & Northern Counties Advertiser; Freeman's Journal; Hartlepool Northern Daily Mail; Irish Independent; Irish Press; Irish Times; Londonderry Sentinel; Portsmouth Herald* (USA); *Southern Star; The Liberator* (Tralee, Co. Kerry); *Yorkshire Post and Leeds Intelligencer.* Also, *An t-Óglach*, Irish Military Archives.

WEBSITES

Ainm.ie (Irish language biographies)
Ancestry.com
Familysearch.org
Findmypast
IrishGenealogy.ie

Irishrevolution.ie (referred to above)
ScotlandsPeople

Notes and References

INTRODUCTION & CHAPTER 1

[1] Sean Boyne, *Emmet Dalton: Somme Soldier, Irish General, Film Pioneer*, Merrion, Sallins, Co. Kildare, 2014.

[2] Maryann G. Valiulis, *Portrait of a Revolutionary: General Richard Mulcahy and the founding of the Irish Free State*, University Press of Kentucky, 1992, p. 258; Eunan O'Halpin, 'Counting Terror: Bloody Sunday and The Dead of the Irish Revolution', in David Fitzpatrick (Editor), *Terror in Ireland, 1916-1923*, The Lilliput Press, Dublin, 2012, p.154; Dr Andy Bielenberg and James S. Donnelly Jr., 'List of Suspected Civilian Spies Killed by the IRA, 1920-21', 2016.

[3] IE/MA/MSPC/CMB/21.

[4] Skully kindly provided me with a copy of the recording, made by his grandmother, of Eva talking about the Noble case.

[5] TNA CO 904/200/106-133.

[6] Bella O'Connell, IE/MA/MSP34REF31400; Leslie Mary Barry, IE/MA/MSP34REF26980.

[7] Letter from Ms Loo Kennedy, Dublin, 21 Oct 1937, in support of Military Service Pension application by Nora O'Sullivan, née O'Neill, IE/MA/MSP34REF20666.

[8] IE/MA/MSP34REF27316.

[9] Liam O'Dwyer, *Beara in Irish History*, Vantage Press, New York, 1977, p. 108.

[10] I am grateful to a confidential source for assistance in this matter.

CHAPTER 2

[1] David McCullagh, *De Valera, Rise 1882 – 1932*, Gill Books, Dublin 2017, pp. 210-11.

[2] 'Inside London', *Irish Times*, 10 July 1973.

[3] 'Bridget Noble, Ardgroom, Cork', IE/MA/HS/A/649.

[4] Tim Sheehan, *Lady Hostage: Mrs Lindsay*, Dripsey, Co. Cork, 1990, pp. 183-84.

[5] Andrew Boyle, *The Riddle of Erskine Childers*, Hutchinson, London, 1977, p. 269; TNA, CO 904/168.

[6] Dr Andy Bielenberg, 'Disappearances in Co Cork 1920-22 and the case of Mrs Lindsay', talk given at the West Cork History Festival, Skibbereen, 19 Aug 2018.

[7] Professor Eunan O'Halpin, 'Problematic Killing During The War of Independence And Its Aftermath: Civilian Spies and Informers', in James Kelly & Mary Ann Lyons, (Editors), *Death and Dying in Ireland, Britain and Europe: Historical Perspectives,* Irish Academic Press, 2013, p. 338-39, quoting Sean O'Mahony Papers, NLI MS 44045/1.

[8] Quote attributed to Michael Collins in Brigadier General F.P. Crozier's book *Ireland For Ever,* Jonathan Cape, London, 1932, as reported in Sean O'Callaghan, *Execution,* Frederick Muller, London, 1974, pp. 188-89.

[9] C.A.J. Coady, *Morality and Political Violence*, Cambridge University Press, 2008, p. 177.

[10] Tom Barry, *Guerilla Days in Ireland,* Mercier Press, Cork, 2010, p. 218.

[11] See Bridie O'Reilly, BMH, WS 454.

[12] *Irish Times*, 2 August 1921; 'Executed At Same Time; Buried In Same Grave', *Cork County Eagle,* 6 August 1921.

[13] Sean O'Callaghan, *Execution,* Frederick Muller, London, 1974.

[14] Tim Sheehan, *Lady Hostage: Mrs Lindsay,* Dripsey, Co. Cork, 1990.

[15] Ernie O'Malley Notebooks, UCDA, P17b/112.

[16] Tim Sheehan, 'Who Erred at Dripsey Ambush?', *Cork Examiner,* 16 Feb 1996.

[17] Sean O'Callaghan, *Execution,* Frederick Muller, London, 1974, p. 14.

[18] O'Callaghan, *Execution*, pp. 99-100.

[19] Dr Andy Bielenberg, quoting entry in General Strickland's diary, in lecture, 'Disappearances in Co Cork 1920-22 and the case of Mrs Lindsay', given at the West Cork History Festival, Skibbereen, 19 Aug 2018.

[20] Eunan O'Halpin, 'Problematic Killing…' in Kelly & Lyons, op. cit. p. 337.

[21] *Nenagh Guardian*, 24 August 1881.

CHAPTER 3

[1] NLI, Catholic parish registers, Eyeries, Diocese of Kerry, Baptisms 1873 to 1881, Microfilm 04286/06.

[2] Riobard O'Dwyer N.T. *Annals of Beara*, Gold Stag Publications, Georgia, USA, 2009, Volume I, pp. 943-94.

[3] Riobard O'Dwyer, op. cit. p. 800.

[4] Riobard O'Dwyer, op. cit., pp. 2197-98.

[5] Tithe Applotment Book for Tuosist Parish, County Kerry, 1824, via genealogy.ie, accessed 13 Jan 2019.

[6] Riobard O'Dwyer, *Annals of Beara*, Volume II, pp. 803-04.

[7] Riobard O'Dwyer, op cit., pp. 578-79.

[8] *Butte Independent*, 14 Dec 1918.

[9] Gerard J. Lyne, *Murtaí Óg*, Geography Publications, Dublin, 2017.

[10] Rudyard Kipling, *A Fleet in Being*, Macmillan, London & New York, 1898, Chapter 4.

[11] *Landowners in Ireland*, Genealogical Publishing Company, Baltimore, 1988. (Originally published 1876.)

[12] Liam O'Dwyer, *Beara in Irish History*, Vantage Press, New York, 1977, p. 93.

[13] *Kerry Weekly Reporter*, 7 Nov 1908.

[14] 'The National Fishing Industry', *Cork Examiner*, 5 April 1895.

[15] 'Irish Fisheries', *Southern Star*, 16 Jan 1902.

[16] 'The Irish Fisheries', *The Daily Nation*, 18 Sept 1897.

[17] *Irish Times*, 28 April 1928.

[18] Old Parish Registers Births, Fraserburgh, p. 179, via ScotlandsPeople website, accessed 31 Jan 2017.

[19] 'UK & Ireland, Masters and Mates Certificates, 1850-1927', via Ancestry.com. See also *Lloyd's List*, 13 April 1881.

[20] *Norfolk News*, 10 September 1870.

[21] Hart's New Annual Army List, 1840 p. 296.

[22] Various family histories on Ancestry.co.uk, e.g. Christine Marshall family tree, consulted 11 June 2020; 'Mercantile Ship News', *The Standard*, 18 Oct 1858.

[23] *Dundee Courier & Argus*, 11 Nov 1879.

[24] See report on the incident by Alexander Sim Noble to *Lloyd's List*, 1 Oct 1888. See also report by William Nicholson, master of the *St Clair* to *Lloyd's List*, 8 Oct 1888.

[25] 'The Gale and Snowstorm', *Dundee Courier & Argus*, 11 Feb 1889.

[26] Attestation of William Noble re joining 5th Battalion, Gordon Highlanders.

[27] TNA, ADM 188/244/164674.

[28] Register of Deaths, Fraserburgh, 1897.

[29] Register of Deaths, Fraserburgh, 1899.

[30] Register of Deaths, Fraserburgh, 1903, via ScotlandsPeople website, accessed 22 March 2017.

[31] Register of deaths, parish of Fraserburgh, 1862.

[32] Peterhead Sheriff Court Decrees, SC4/11/1, p. 184, via Scottish Indexes.

CHAPTER 4

[1] Figures show that in the year 1909-10, fish cured for export at various locations on the Beara peninsula required the use of 7,268 barrels. See 'Report on the Sea & Inland Fisheries of Ireland for 1909', House of Commons Parliamentary Papers, p. 17.

[2] Marriage registered on 16 Feb 1907 in the Registrar's District of Kilcatherine, Union of Castletown, County Cork; see details in Superintendent Registrar's District of Castletown, accessed via IrishGenealogy.ie.

[3] Marriage registers, Parish of Fraserburgh, 1872, Scotland's People website, accessed 15 May 2018, see also John Crenna, *Fraserburgh Past and Present*, Rosemount Press, Aberdeen, 1914, pp. 165-66.

[4] 'Down Memory Lane', *Southern Star*, 4 Dec 2004.

[5] Riobard O'Dwyer, email to rootsweb archive, 1 June 2014.

[6] Riobard O'Dwyer, *The Annals of Beara*, Volume II, Gold Star Publications, Statesboro, Georgia, USA, 2009, pp. 1720, 1803, 1994; see also Volume I, p. 874.

[7] Riobard O'Dwyer, *The Annals of Beara*, Volume II, 2009, p. 844. See also 'Birth Registered in District of Kilcatherine', via IrishGenealogy.ie.

[8] New York, Passenger Lists, 1820 – 1958, via Ancestry.co.uk.

[9] 'Additional Contributors to Irish Victory Fund', *Portsmouth Herald*, 18 June 1919.

[10] 'Dora Agnes Scully', *Portsmouth Herald*, 27 May 1944.

[11] 'New York, Passenger Lists, 1820 – 1957', via Ancestry.co.uk. The 1930 US Census records show that the 'immigration year' for Mattie Monahan [neé Neill] was 1892. Ship passenger records indicate that a female, Mattie O'Neill, entered the US in May that year, having sailed from Queenstown. The records state that her last place of residence in Ireland was 'Kerry' and that her age on arrival in the US was 23 years. [Passenger records, The Statue of Liberty – Ellis Island Foundation.] Bridget Noble's sister Mattie had resided in County Cork, close to the Kerry border, and her age at this stage would have been 20 years. Members of the extended Neill family were sometimes imprecise about ages, and despite apparent discrepancies in the records, it would appear that they refer to Bridget's sister.

[12] Suzanne Lynch, 'Welcome to the most Irish town in America', *Irish Times*, 15 December 2018.

[13] Valuation records for Ardgroom Inward, Kilcatherine, 1933-96, Vol 5., Cork.

[14] Castletownbere Petty Sessions Dog License Registers.

[15] Alan Fernihough, Cormac Ó Gráda & Brendan M. Walsh, 'Mixed Marriages in Ireland A Century Ago', UCD Centre for Economic Research, 2014.

[16] Canon Carmody was filling in a questionnaire issued by the Bishop of Kerry, Bishop Coffey. The canon also stated that there were about 600 houses in the parish, and about 20 Protestant families. Beara Historical Society website, accessed 26 Jan 2017.

[17] P. Ó hAnnracháin, *Fé Bhrat an Chonartha*, Oifig an tSoláthair, 1944, p. 214.

[18] Coimisiún na Gaeltachta Report, 1925, p. 37.

[19] *All-Ireland Review*, 12 Jan 1901.

[20] Peadar Ó hAnnracháin, diary entry for 16 Oct 1921, in *Machtnamh Cime*, Oifig Díolta Foilseacháin Rialtais, 1933, p. 151; see also *Fé Bhrat an Chonartha*, op. cit., p. 202.

[21] Information from local source; see also Riobard O'Dwyer, *Annals of Beara*, Volume II, pp. 865-6.

[22] Riobard O'Dwyer, *Annals of Beara*, Vol. II, pp. 839, 949.

[23] See Thomas Keane, RIC service record, TNA HO184/15/1290.

CHAPTER 5

[1] Castletownbere Petty Sessions Order Book, 12 October 1894.

[2] 'Defendant Acquitted', *Cork Examiner*, 10 June 1907.

[3] 'Castletownbere Sessions', *Cork Examiner*, 15 Jan 1915.

[4] 'Death of Mrs T. O'Sullivan, N.T., Ardgroom', *Cork Examiner*, 13 Jan 1922.

[5] 'Ardgroom Nationalists Rejoice', *Cork Examiner*, 29 May 1914.

[6] TNA, ADM 242/10.

[7] 'Liam Deasy', 'Irish Life and Lore' website, accessed 30 May 2017.

[8] *The Buchan Observer*, 20 Oct 1914.

[9] 'Buchan Territorials in the Trenches: 14 Killed, 31 Wounded', *Fraserburgh Herald*, 15 June 1915.

[10] http://gordonhighlanders.carolynmorrisey.com/HCompany.htm, accessed 6 Sept 2016; TNA WO 372/14/235900.

[11] TNA WO 372/14/235900.

[12] 'Lighting Order Offences', *Aberdeen Journal*, 6 May 1916.

[13] Liam O'Dwyer, *Beara in Irish History*, Vantage Press, New York, 1977, see Dedication.

[14] Liam O'Dwyer, op. cit., p. 68.

[15] O'Dwyer, p. 70.

[16] Liam O'Dwyer, BMH, WS 1527.

[17] Riobard O'Dwyer, op. cit., Volume II, pp. 517-18.

[18] Robert Monteith, *Casement's Last Adventure*, Michael F. Moynihan, Dublin, 1953, pp. 165-66.

CHAPTER 6

[1] 'Some Shocking Facts', *Cork County Eagle*, 15 May 1920.

[2] 'County Cork Farm; Cattle Driving Alleged; Injunction Granted', *Cork County Eagle*, 4 Dec. 1915.

[3] 'Malicious Injuries', *Cork County Eagle*, 20 Oct 1917.

[4] Liam O'Dwyer, Ardgroom to S. Ó Cearnaigh, An Roinn Cosanta, Brainse Airgeadais, Baile Átha Cliath 9, 22 Feb 1967, IE/MA/MD7153.

[5] Charles Townshend, *The British campaign in Ireland, 1919-1921: the development of political and military policies*, Oxford, 1975, pp. 63-4; quoted in Brian Hughes, *Defying the IRA? Intimidation, Coercion and Communities During the Irish Revolution*, Liverpool University Press, 2017, p. 9.

[6] TNA, CO 904/169.

[7] James McCarthy, BMH, WS 1567.

[8] IE/MA/MSP34REF9556.

[9] Dan Breen, BMH, WS 1739.

[10] Ibid.

[11] Oates's RIC record indicates the date of birth as 9 Feb 1872; the 1939 England and Wales Register indicates 9 Feb 1871; the Civil Registration Death Index for England and Wales also indicates 1871 as year of birth.

[12] TNA, HO184/102304589.

[13] 'Policeman's Letters in Breach of Promise Case', *Evening Herald*, 4 June 1918.

[14] Sean O'Sullivan, 'Allihies Attack Recalled', *Southern Star*, 19 Dec 1970.

[15] Fachtna O'Donovan, Chapter Nine, 'A History of the Constabulary in Beara', in *Beara, History and Stories from the Peninsula,* Compiled by Gerard Harrington, Beara Historical Society, 2005.

[16] 'Police Searches in Ardgroom', *Cork Examiner,* 10 March 1920.

[17] The prison records indicate that William Dwyer was committed on 23 January. His offence was recorded as 'Contribute to unlawful association' [sic]. Under the heading 'Marks on Person' the writing is difficult to decipher, but it could refer, in part, to the loss of the tip of a finger 'on left hand'. It was recorded that his address was Eyeries, his occupation, 'farmer' and his next of kin, his father John. He was single, and his religion was 'RC'. On entering the prison, his weight was recorded as 158 lbs and on departure, as 161 lbs. His release date was 22 February 1920.

[18] Liam O'Dwyer, BMH, WS 1527.

[19] Register of Marriages, Fraserburgh, County of Aberdeen, December 1919.

[20] Register of Deaths, Fraserburgh, 1919.

[21] *Southern Star,* 8 January 1972. Patsy Dan Crowley was a prominent member of Ardgroom Company, becoming Captain in 1922. The article in the newspaper describes him as 1st Lieutenant at the time of the raid, although a record in the military archives suggests that he was a Volunteer. See 'Ardgroom Company', in IE/MA/MSPC/RO/55.

[22] Liam O'Dwyer, BMH, WS 1527.

[23] 'Beara and District', *Southern Star,* 19 June 2004.

[24] TNA, CO 904/112.

CHAPTER 7

[1] 'Dr Daniel Lyne and his relatives', *Southern Star,* 4 Dec 2004.

[2] Castletown Board of Guardians minutes, Cork City & County Archives, IE/CCA/BG/59/88, 1919-21.

[3] See list of officers and men, Castletownbere Company, IE/MA/MSPC/RO/55.

[4] Castletown Board of Guardians minutes, Cork City & County Archives, IE/CCA/BG/59/88, 1919-21.

[5] Jasper Ungoed-Thomas, *Jasper Wolfe of Skibbereen,* The Collins Press, Cork, 2008, p. 163.

[6] Castletown Board of Guardians minutes, Cork City & County Archives, IE/CCA/BG/59/88, 1919-21.

[7] *The Men Will Talk To Me, West Cork Interviews by Ernie O'Malley,* Edited by Andy Bielenberg, John Borgonovo and Padraig Óg O Ruairc, Mercier Press, Cork, 2015, Kindle location 1345.

[8] Cork Prison, General Register of Prisoners, 1921.

[9] This is the date given in an article in the *Londonderry Sentinel,* 27 Aug 1921.

[10] Eunan O'Halpin, 'Problematic Killing...' in Kelly & Lyons, op. cit., p.337.

[11] 'Down Memory Lane', *Southern Star,* 17 April 2004.

[12] William O'Neill, BMH, WS 1536; List of officers and men, Castletownbere Company, IE/MA/MSPC/RO/55.

[13] Nora O'Sullivan, IE/MA/MSP34REF20666.

[14] Hannah Hanley, IE/MA/MSP34REF27316.

[15] 'Sinn Fein "Warfare"', *Londonderry Sentinel*, 27 Aug 1921.

[16] IE/MA/MSPC/RO/69. While John Sheehan was Captain of Ardgroom Company on 11 July 1921, confusingly the 1st Lieutenant was also a man called John Sheehan – he later emigrated to the USA.

[17] Riobard O'Dwyer, *Annals of Beara*, Vol II, pp. 439-40.

[18] Eunan O'Halpin, 'Counting Terror: Bloody Sunday and The Dead of the Irish Revolution', in David Fitzpatrick (Editor), *Terror in Ireland 1916-1923*, Lilliput Press, Dublin, 2012, p. 154.

[19] 'Irish Warfare: Rebel Activity in Rural Districts', *Northern Daily Mail*, 4 March 1921; see also 'Rebellious Ireland', *Yorkshire Post and Leeds Intelligencer*, 5 March 1921; 'Items of the Irish Situation', *Irish Independent*, 5 March 1921.

[20] TNA, CO 904/114.

[21] *Northern Whig*, 5 March 1921.

[22] 'Sinn Fein "Warfare"', *Londonderry Sentinel*, 27 Aug 1921.

CHAPTER 8

[1] TNA, CO 904/114.

[2] IE/MA/MSPC/CMB/21.

[3] Riobard O'Dwyer, *Annals of Beara*, Vol. II, p. 467.

[4] The records conflict on various points. Julia Sheehan's MSP application indicates that Katie Sullivan was Captain of Ardgroom Branch of Cumann na mBan and continued in that role during the Civil War, while Julia continued as Secretary. (See Julia Sheehan, IE/MA/MSP34REF56331.) Liam O'Dwyer in his memoir also refers to Julia as Secretary, while Katie Sullivan (as will be shown) in her own application for a Service Medal states that she was Captain of Ardgroom Branch. However, the membership records indicate that Julia was Captain on 11 July 1921 and also on 1 July 1922, while Katie was Adjutant or Secretary on these dates. A list of members of Ardgroom Company has an 'X' marked beside Katie's name, suggesting she was neutral during the Civil War. (IE/MA/MSPC/CMB/21.)

[5] IE/MA/MSPC/RO/69.

[6] 'Berehaven Arrests', *Evening Echo*, 8 March 1921.

[7] *Irish Independent*, 5 March 1921.

[8] James McCarthy, BMH, WS 1567.

[9] Liam O'Dwyer, op. cit., pp. 122-23.

[10] Liam O'Dwyer, pp. 126-27.

[11] Liam O'Dwyer, p. 108.

[12] See death Registration records for Kilcatherine district, via IrishGenealogy.ie; see also entry 'Johnny O'Dwyer & Ellen Lynch (Caolrua)' in Riobard O'Dwyer, *The Annals of Beara*, Volume II, which gives 4 March as date of death.

[13] O'Dwyer, pp. 123-24.

[14] Julia Sheehan, IE/MA/MSP34REF56331.

[15] TNA, WO 35/144.

[16] TNA, WO 35/143.

[17] TNA, WO 35/138.

[18] James McCarthy, Register of Detention Barracks, TNA WO 35/143.

[19] Internees, 6th Division, Cork, 3 August 1921, TNA, WO 35/141.

[20] TNA, WO 35/141. The term '17 I.B' denotes 17 Infantry Brigade, while 476 is the prisoner number assigned to Dwyer.

[21] IE/MA/MSPC/RO/69.

[22] TNA, WO 35/144.

[23] IE/MA/MSPC/RO/69.

[24] See Martin Verling (editor), *Beara Woman Talking: Folklore from the Beara Peninsula*, Mercier Press, Cork, 2003.

[25] Verling, p.123.

[26] IE/MA/MD7153.

[27] TNA HO184/33; HO184/61; HO184/105; WO/372/8.

[28] *Thom's Directory*, 1922; see also TNA HO 184/52;

[29] TNA, HO 184/42.

[30] IE/MA/MSPC/RO-69.

[31] Ted O'Sullivan Papers, NLI, MS 49,668/1-10.

[32] Daniel Crowley, IE/MA/MD7092.

[33] Elizabeth Crowley, IE/MA/MD/19879.

[34] TNA, WO 35/141.

[35] 'Items of the Irish Situation', *Irish Independent*, 5 March 1921.

[36] Spillane would leave the newspaper's reporting staff in 1922, having been recruited by Michael Collins as a Government Information Officer.

CHAPTER 9

[1] Mrs Hannah Hanley, IE/MA/MSP34REF27316.

[2] O'Halpin, 'Problematic Killing...' in Kelly & Lyons, op. cit., pp. 323-24.

[3] *Knockraha, Foras Feasa na Paroiste*, Knockraha History & Heritage Society, 2005, pp. 78-79.

[4] IE/MA/DP2641; TNA WO 35/156/25.

[5] IE/MA/MD7153.

[6] Martin Fallon, BMH, WS 1,121; John Walsh, BMH, WS 966; Seumas O'Meara, BMH, WS 1504.

[7] Regarding John Coughlan, see Bielenberg & Donnelly, 'List of Suspected Spies Killed by the IRA, 1920-21'.

[8] Liam O'Dwyer, BMH, WS 1527.

[9] The allegation that Patsy Dan Crowley shot Bridget Noble first entered the public domain on 29 August 2017 when the recording of Eva O'Sullivan's account was played for the audience at the West Cork History Festival in Skibbereen, County Cork, during a talk by academic Dr Eve Morrison on 'Cork Ghosts of the Irish Revolution'.

[10] *Londonderry Sentinel*, 27 Aug 1921.

[11] John P. Haran, BMH, WS 1458; Marie Coleman, 'Women Escaped the Worst Brutalities in the War of Independence', *Irish Examiner*, 27 Nov 2015; 'Report of the Labour Commission to Ireland', 1921, p. 81.

[12] Ernie O'Malley, *On Another Man's Wound*, Anvil Books, Cork, 2002, p. 177.

[13] Liam O'Dwyer, op. cit., pp. 110-11; Riobard O'Dwyer, *Annals of Beara*, Vol. III, p. 1099; see also marriage registration record, showing that John Mulligan, a policeman, residing at Castletownbere, married Hanna Dwyer, also of Castletownbere, daughter of John Dwyer, shopkeeper, at St Joseph's Church, Cork city, on 6 October 1903.

[14] TNA, HO184/15/1290; HO184/119.

[15] Nora O'Sullivan, IE/MA/MSP34REF20666.

[16] Louise (Louie) O'Connell, IE/MA/MSP34REF55471.

[17] TNA, WO 372/6/124332.

[18] RIC Service Records, TNA, HO184/61.

[19] TNA, HO184/15/1290.

[20] *Freeman's Journal*, 26 July 1920; see also *The Kerryman*, 31 July 1920.

CHAPTER 10

[1] Liam O'Dwyer, in a 1943 letter supporting the MSP application of Frances Smyth, describing how her area of Lauragh was a regular 'hang-out' for men on the run, IE/MA/MSP34REF60031.

[2] TNA WO 35/139.

[3] See note re William Dwyer, in 'Easter Rising & Ireland Under Martial Law', Findmypast website, accessed 11 May 2017.

[4] See, for instance, Patrick A. Murray, BMH, WS 1584.

[5] TNA, WO 35/139.

[6] TNA HO 144/1734/376829. One of the other internees on the list is John Allen, of Newcestown, County Cork, a brother of Brother William Allen, who taught at O'Connell School, Dublin and who became a noted collector of books and rare historical items to do with the revolutionary period. See also receipt for prisoners 'committed from Cork' from officer acting on behalf of prison governor to Lt. R.C. Woodbridge, 16 March 1920, TNA WO 35/139/00633; see also TNA WO 35/139/00666.

[7] TNA, HO 144/1734. A note on the document stated: 'Forwarded to the Home Office for the information of the Secretary of State. 3.5.20.'

[8] *Knockraha, Foras Feasa na Paroiste Cnoc Ratha*, Knockraha History & Heritage Society, 2005, p. 150.

[9] Michael Hopkinson, *The Irish War of Independence*, Gill & Macmillan, Dublin, 2004, p. 111.

[10] O'Halpin, 'Problematic Killing...' in Kelly & Lyons, op. cit. p. 327.

[11] Dr Andy Bielenberg (UCC) & Professor Emeritus James S. Donnelly, Jr. (UW-Madison), 'List of Suspected Civilian Spies Killed by the IRA, 1920-21', 2016.

[12] Martin Corry TD, letter in support of application for a Military Service Pension by Edward Moloney, IE/MA/MSP34REF27648.

[13] Ernie O'Malley Notebooks, UCDA, P17b/112.

[14] Ibid.

[15] Sean Healy, BMH, WS 1643.

334

[16] Ernie O'Malley, *On Another Man's Wound*, Anvil Books, Cork, 2002, p. 343.

[17] James Holohan, BMH, WS 1586.

[18] Ernie O'Malley, *Raids and Rallies*, Mercier Press, Cork, 2011, p. 212.

[19] P.S. O'Hegarty, *The Victory of Sinn Féin*, The Talbot Press, Dublin, 1924, pp. 54-56; Tom Garvin, 'Patrick Sarsfield O'Hegarty', *Dictionary of Irish Biography*, Royal Irish Academy/Cambridge University Press.

CHAPTER 11

[1] *Kerry Weekly Reporter*, 26 Feb 1887; 'A Troublesome Eyeries P.P.', *Southern Star*, 23 April 2005; 'P.P. Went All the Way in Law', *Southern Star*, 30 April 2005; 'Father O'Callaghan and the Pikemen', *Freeman's Journal*, 16 Sept 1926.

[2] Bella O'Connell, IE/MA/MSP34REF31400; Louise O'Connell, IE/MA/MSP34REF55471.

[3] Hannah Hanley, IE/MA/MSP34REF27316.

[4] For details of clergy in Eyeries parish, see *Irish Catholic Directory*, 1922, p. 255.

[5] "Sergeant Shot Dead', *Cork Examiner*, 5 May 1920.

[6] Brian Heffernan, *Freedom and the Fifth Commandment: Catholic Priests and Political Violence in Ireland, 1919-21*, Manchester University Press, 2014, pp. 138-40.

[7] James Quigley, BMH, WS 692; Thomas Crawley, BMH, WS 817.

[8] Sean Boylan, BMH, WS 1715; J. Anthony Gaughan, *Austin Stack, Portrait of a Separatist*, Kingdom Books, 1977, p. 112.

[9] See 'Denis "Dinny" Lehane', in Andy Bielenberg & James Donnelly, 'Cork Spy Files', The Irish Revolution website. See also Ernie O'Malley Papers, UCDA P17b/108, referenced in Cork Spy Files.

[10] O'Halpin, 'Problematic Killing...' in Kelly & Lyons, op. cit. p. 331.

[11] 'News from Ireland', *The Tablet*, 4 Dec 1920.

[12] See *Irish Independent*, 26 November 1920; also, Brian Heffernan, *Freedom and the Fifth Commandment*, Manchester University Press, 2014, pp. 138-39.

[13] Tom Barry, *Guerrilla Days in Ireland*, Mercier Press, Cork, 2010, p. 57.

[14] Heffernan, p. 140. See also, Michael Sheerin, BMH, WS 803.

[15] 'How Attack Was Made', *Irish Independent,* 23 March 1921.

[16] T. Ryle Dwyer, *The Kerryman*, 14 June 2001; Manus Moynihan, BMH, WS 1066.

[17] TNA CO 904/115.

[18] 'Letter from Father Daly PP', *Cork Examiner*, 12 Nov 1923.

[19] IE/MA/MSP34REF27316.

CHAPTER 12

[1] House of Commons, Hansard, 19 Aug 1921.

[2] IE/MA/CP/5/2/6/ (CCLXVI).

[3] 'The Missing List', *Irish Times*; 'In IRA Custody', *Freeman's Journal*, 22 August 1921.

[4] IE/MA/HS/A/649.

[5] Thomas Reidy, BMH, WS 1422.

[6] IE/MA/MSPC/RO/64.

[7] Liam O'Dwyer, BMH, WS 1527.

[8] Liam O'Dwyer, BMH, WS 1527 – the relevant information is in a table outlining the Beara Battalion staff officers in place at particular times; O'Dwyer, op. cit., p. 130.

[9] Liam O'Dwyer, IE/MA/MSP34REF9556; Ted O'Sullivan Papers, NLI, MS 49,668/1-10; see also, IE/MA/MSPC/RO/69.

[10] O'Dwyer, *Beara in Irish History*, p. 120.

[11] Artist Mike O'Donnell found the document while searching through family papers at his home in Tralee. He told how his granduncle Father Leonard Boyle came across the school report by chance when it fell out of a second-hand book he had bought in Oxford in 1953. In 1982 Father Boyle, then based in Toronto, sent the document as a gift to Mike's father.

[12] Joe Duffy,Prologue, *Children of the Rising: The Untold Story of Young Lives Lost in Easter 1916*, Hachette Books Ireland, 2015.

[13] 'Letters of 1916' website, Maynooth University, consulted 7 Oct 2018; letter from UCD Archives.

[14] 'Remarkable Case', *Freeman's Journal*, 29 May 1918.

[15] 'Berlin in 1933', *Irish Times*, 30 Jan 1938.

[16] Christopher O'Connell, BMH, WS 1530.

[17] 'IRA Veteran Dies', *Southern Star*, 15 Aug 1964.

[18] Minutes of Castletown Board of Guardians meeting, 9 March 1921, IE/CCA/BG/59/88, 1919-21.

[19] Death details registered in Castletown District; 'Beara News', *Southern Star*, 11 Dec 1948.

[20] Christopher O'Connell, BMH, WS 1530.

[21] Ms Margaret O'Neill, IE/MA/MSP34REF40784.

[22] Liam Deasy, op. cit., p. 354; Julia Sheehan, IE/MA/MSP34REF56331.

[23] 'West Cork Round-Up', *Southern Star*, 7 May 1921.

[24] Sean T. O'Sullivan, 'Planning for an ambush on the Beara peninsula', *Southern Star*, 20 April 1974.

[25] Tom Barry, *Guerrilla Days in Ireland*, Mercier Press, p. 167.

[26] See article by Jerry O'Neill in *Beara, History and Stories from the Peninsula*, compiled by Gerard Harrington, Beara Historical Society, 2005, p. 281.

[27] 'Unarmed Soldiers Murdered', *Irish Times*, 13 June 1921.

[28] Jerry O'Neill, op. cit.

[29] IE/MA/MSPC/A/3/1.

[30] Tom Barry, *Guerrilla Days in Ireland*, pp. 116-17.

[31] 'Echoes from Beara', *Southern Star*, 19 Oct 1963.

[32] Liam O'Dwyer, BMH, WS 1527.

[33] TNA, WO 35/89.

[34] *The Men Will Talk To Me, West Cork Interviews by Ernie O'Malley*, Editors, Bielenberg, Borgonovo & Ó Ruairc, op. cit., Kindle Location 1629.

[35] Statement by Nora Mary Healy, Ted O'Sullivan Papers, NLI, MS 49,668/11-22.

36 'Sister of Butte Man Tells About Warfare in Erin', *The Anaconda Standard*, 27 June 1921.

37 Gerard Lyne, Tuosist Parish Newsletter, 2016.

38 IE/MA/CP/4/11/XXIX.

39 TNA, WO35/74.

CHAPTER 13

1 Travers Wolfe to Captain Thomas Healy, Liaison Officer, Bandon, 28 Nov 1921, IE/MA, LE/11/1.

2 'Liaison Officers', *Irish Independent*, 15 July 1921.

3 'Thomas Bernard Barry', TNA, WO 35 206/005.

4 See 'Thomas Barry', IE/MA/MSP34REF57456.

5 'Offences Against Police', TNA CO 904/148.

6 Grand Lodge of Freemasons of Ireland, Membership Registers, 1733 – 1933; Jasper Ungoed-Thomas, *Jasper Wolfe of Skibbereen*, The Collins Press, Cork, 2008, p 211.

7 'Lists of Freemasons in the Brigade Area; list of Provincial Grand Officers for year 1920', Florence O'Donoghue Papers, NLI MS 31,200.

8 'Masonic Hall Raid', *Irish Times*, 26 Jan 1935; Meda Ryan, *Tom Barry, IRA Freedom Fighter*, Mercier Press, Cork, 2012, p. 293.

9 Jasper Ungoed-Thomas, op. cit., pp. 124-25.

10 'Berehaven', *Cork Examiner*, 13 May 1920.

11 Wolfe to Healy, 28 Nov 1921, IE/MA, LE/11/1.

12 Healy to Chief Liaison Officer, 10 Nov 1921, IE/MA, LE/11/1.

13 IE/MA/MSPC/RO/51; see also Thomas Healy, IE/MA/MD5258.

14 Travers Wolfe to Captain Thomas Healy, Liaison Officer, Bandon, 26 Nov 1921, IE/MA, LE/11/1.

15 Comdt. Dalton, Acting Chief Liaison Officer to Healy, 9 Dec 1921, IE/MA, LE/11/1.

16 Healy to Dalton, 6 Dec 1921, IE/MA, LE/11/1.

17 Dalton to Healy, op. cit.

18 Gavin M. Foster, *The Irish Civil War And Society; Politics, Class and Conflict*, Palgrave & Macmillan, 2015, pp. 136-37.

19 Wolfe to Captain Thomas Healy, 26 Nov 1921, IE/MA, LE/11/1.

20 'Cork Farmers Murdered', *Irish Times*, 21 Feb 1921.

21 Sir Hamar Greenwood, House of Commons, Hansard, 28 April 1921.

22 Summary of proceedings of military court of inquiry in lieu of inquest into the death of William Connell, April 1921, TNA CO 904/189.

23 Jasper Ungoed-Thomas, op. cit., pp. 115-16.

24 IE/MA/CP/4/40.

25 Patrick O'Sullivan, BMH, WS 1481.

26 Sources include: Tim Herlihy & seven others, BMH, WS 810; John Sullivan Lynch, IE/MA/MS/A/649; Ex-Soldier Kidnapped: "Executed for Spying"', *Irish Times*, 14 Jan 1922.

27 Sources include: Comdt. E. Quinlan, 27 Jan 1922, IE/MA, LE/11/1; RIC Inspector General's Confidential Report for May 1921, TNA, CO

904/115; Con Spain, BMH, WS 1464; 'Reburial of RIC', *Nenagh Guardian*, 14 Feb 1925.

CHAPTER 14

[1] See 'Dublin Castle Statements, May 1921', TNA CO 904/168.

[2] The Local Government Board for Ireland, in its report for the year ended 31 March 1920, states that under the Poor Relief (Ireland) Act, 1914, they have authorized the 'boarding out' of certain classes of the 'destitute poor' from certain, specified Unions, to the Workhouses of adjoining Unions. Under this arrangement Castletown Union was permitted to have 'healthy' inmates 'boarded out' in Kenmare Workhouse. See pp. xxvii to xxviii.

[3] *Cork County Eagle*, 28 Jan 1922.

[4] 'The Murdered Cadets; Claims by Dependents and Relatives; Shocking Story Told in Court; Bodies Mutilated After Death', *Irish Times*, 12 Jan 1921.

[5] TNA, CO 905/15.

[6] Under-Secretary of State for the Colonies (Lord Arnold), House of Lords debate, 5 March 1924, Vol 56, cc535-65.

[7] Bridget Noble, IE/MA/HS/A/649.

[8] Ibid.

[9] Ibid.

[10] D. Nagle, IE/MA/HS/A/649.

[11] Jasper Ungoed-Thomas, op. cit., pp. 141-44.

[12] Ibid.

[13] Barry Keane, *Massacre in West Cork, The Dunmanway and Ballygroman Killings*, Mercier Press, Cork, 2014, Chapter Six.

[14] *Irish Independent*, 5 May 1928.

[15] Hugh Brady, BMH, WS 1266; Bernard Sweeney, BMH, WS 1194; see also 'Sinn Fein Rule in Ireland', *The Spectator*, 3 June 1922.

[16] Only one of the murders, that of Robert Nagle, resulted in an individual facing charges. In 1924, two republicans who had been on the anti-Treaty side in the Civil War and who had acted as an escort to Tom Barry, the Flying Column leader while fighting Free State forces in County Tipperary, (see Dan Breen, BMH, WS 1763) were arrested by Free State authorities in connection with a number of murders. The accused men were John 'Flyer' Nyhan, who had been a member of Barry's Flying Column and his comrade Thomas Lane, both from Clonakilty. Lane was the younger brother of Jim Lane, Clonakilty Battalion engineering officer. One of the charges against Thomas Lane was for the murder of Robert Nagle. (See, for instance, 'Accused in Court', *Cork Examiner*, 7 March 1924.) The State did not proceed with the prosecutions, a judge stating that some witnesses refused to come forward and give evidence. (See 'Informations Refused', *Freeman's Journal*, 2 May 1924.)

[17] Professor David Fitzpatrick, *Descendancy: Irish Protestant Histories since 1795*, Cambridge University Press, 2014, p. 169.

[18] IRP Superintendent Daniel O'Neill was a brother of Michael O'Neill, whose shooting is believed to have sparked the attacks on Protestants. According to a Free State military intelligence report, Daniel O'Neill was an 'unscrupulous individual' who took part 'in the murder of several Protestants in West Cork'. (Letter from Col. M. Costello to Dept. of Defence, 30 Sept 1925, IE/MA/DOD/2/21085.) Another brother, Denis 'Sonny' O'Neill took part in the IRA ambush at Bealnablath on 22 August 1922, in which the National Army Commander-in-Chief, Michael Collins, was killed. (See IE/MA/MSP34REF4067.) Some believe that Sonny O'Neill fired the shot that killed Collins. (See, for instance, Meda Ryan, *The Day Michael Collins Was Shot*, Poolbeg, Swords, Co. Dublin, 1989, Chapter 13.) Relatives of Sonny O'Neill denied he shot Collins. It has been claimed that another brother, Jackie O'Neill, was also at Bealnablath, 'minding the landmine after it had been laid'. (See interview with Tom Foley, 2 Sept 1989, in Sean O'Mahony Papers, NLI MS 44,104/4.)

[19] *An t-Óglach*, 18 May 1922. The RTE TV documentary, *An Tost Fada*, 2012, was produced by Gerry Gregg for Praxis Pictures.

[20] *Irish Times*, 1 May 1922.

[21] *Cork Examiner*, 1 May 1922.

CHAPTER 15

[1] Brian Hanley, *The IRA, A Documentary History 1916 – 2005*, Gill & Macmillan, Dublin, 2010, p. 18.

[2] Ernie O'Malley, sworn testimony re Tom Barry's pension appeal, 19 April 1940, IE/MA/MSP34REF57456.

[3] In his statement to the Bureau of Military History, Ted O'Sullivan recalls that during the first week in March 1921 he travelled to Castletownbere 'to select 12 replacements for men who were to be demobbed from the [flying] column'. At Eyeries, he met Sean O'Driscoll, Christy O'Connell, Michael O'Sullivan 'and nine others whose names I cannot recall'. See Ted O'Sullivan, BMH, WS 1478.

[4] John O'Driscoll, BMH, WS 1250.

[5] O'Halpin, 'Problematic Killing…' in Kelly & Lyons, op. cit., p.335.

[6] IE/MA/CP/4/40.

[7] Liam Deasy, *Towards Ireland Free*, Royal Carbery Books, Cork, 1973, p. 210.

[8] Patrick Beagan, BMH, WS 612.

[9] Jennie Scannell, IE/MA/MSP34REF59791.

[10] RIC County Inspector Report, Cork, for December 1920, TNA CO 904/113.

[11] Sean Healy, BMH, WS 1643.

[12] O'Halpin, ' Problematic Killing…' in Kelly & Lyons, op. cit., p. 324.

[13] Catriona Crowe, RTE radio programme, 'What If?', 17 Feb 2008; Ernie O'Malley, *The Singing Flame*, Mercier Press, Cork, 2012, p. 136.

[14] O'Malley to Chief of Staff, 4 July 1921, UCDA, P7/A/21, cited in Brian Hughes, *Defying the IRA?*, Liverpool University Press, 2016, p. 137.

[15] 'Cork Courtmartial', *Cork Examiner*, 31 May 1921.

[16] IE/MA/CP/4/40.

[17] Constabulary List, Issue 159, 1921, TNA, HO184/104.

[18] RIC Inspector General's Report to Dublin Castle for April 1921, TNA, CO 904/115.

[19] 'Berehaven Arrests', *The Liberator*, 12 March 1921.

[20] 'Berehaven Releases', *Cork Examiner*, 16 March 1921.

[21] IE/MA/MSPC/RO/55.

[22] 'Berehaven Arrests and Releases', *Cork Examiner*, 31 March 1921.

[23] See 'Thomas Barry', IE/MA/MSP34REF57456.

[24] Cork War of Independence Fatality Register, UCC/*Irish Examiner*, accessed 28 June 2017.

[25] TNA, CO 904/149.

[26] TNA, HO184/102276536.

[27] TNA, CO 904/114.

[28] TNA, CO 904/115.

[29] Ibid.

[30] See Bielenberg & Donnelly, Cork Spy Files, The Irish Revolution

[31] This quotation and details of Thomas's time at Dunboy are from his own account, which features in a book, Penelope Durell and Cornelius Kelly (compilers), *The Grand Tour of Beara*, Cailleach Books, Allihies, County Cork, 2000, pp. 162-69.

[32] *Plight of Southern Irish Loyalists*, Publicity Office, Duke of Northumberland's Fund, Boswell Printing and Publishing Co., London, 1921; TNA CO 904/27.

[33] Ted O'Sullivan Papers, NLI, MS 49,668/1-10.

[34] IE/MA/HS/A/649.

[35] Correspondence re this case can be found in 'John McNamee, Longford', IE/MA/HS/A/649.

CHAPTER 16

[1] TNA, WO 35/112/17; see also, for instance, *Meath Chronicle*, 4 Sept 1920, and *Anglo-Celt*, 4 Sept 1920.

[2] Volunteers with the names Patrick Kane and James Dalton were listed as members of the 4th Battalion, 2nd Meath Brigade, IRA at the time of the Truce, 11 July 1921. According to lists supplied to the Military Service Pension authorities in the 1930s, Kane, listed as 'dead', was a member of Martry Company; Dalton, from Knockumber, Navan, was a member of Ardbraccan Company. See IE/MA/MSPC/RO/488.

[3] See local newspaper reports, e.g. 'Girl's Hair Cropped', *Connacht Tribune*, 15 May 1920, and 'The Evidence of Identification', *Connacht Tribune*, 12 June 1920. Men called Peter Joyce and Michael Leonard were recorded as being members of the 1st (Tuam) Battalion, IRA on 11 July 1921 – see IE/MA/MSPC/RO/239.

[4] 'Summary of Outrages Against Police', 2 May 1920, TNA, CO 904/158.

[5] 'Alleged "Bobbing" of Girl's Hair', *Cork County Eagle*, 30 Oct 1920; see also TNA WO 35/208.

6 Marie Coleman, 'Violence Against Women During The Irish War of Independence', in Diarmaid Ferriter & Susannah Riordan (Editors), *Years of Turbulence, The Irish Revolution And Its Aftermath*, University College Dublin Press, 2015, p.141.

7 BMH, WS 1682.

8 *Limerick Leader*, 11 April 1921.

9 Linda Connolly, 'The war against women', *Irish Times Magazine*, 3 June 2020.

10 *Leitrim Observer*, 29 May 1920.

11 TNA/HO184/15/1290.

12 'Summary of Outrages against Police, April-July 1920', TNA, CO 904/148.

13 Ibid.

14 Ibid.

15 IE/MA/CP/4/40/F.

16 *Leitrim Observer*, 4 Sept 1920.

17 Leo Buckley, BMH, WS 1714.

18 Professor Linda Connolly, 'Sexual Violence a dark secret of War of Independence and Civil War', *Irish Times*, 10 January 2019.

19 James Maloney, BMH, WS 1525.

20 William Sheehan, *A Hard Local War: The British Army and the Guerrilla War in Cork 1919 – 1921*, The History Press Ireland, Dublin, 2017, p. 31.

21 'Catalogue of Crime in Ireland', *Weekly Irish Times*, 25 Sept 1920.

22 General Macready, Report on Situation in Ireland for Week Ending 16 April 1921, TNA, CAB/24/122.

23 TNA, CO 904/115.

24 Diarmaid Ferriter, *A Nation And Not A Rabble*, Profile Books, London, 2015, pp. 241-43; TNA CO 906/19.

25 *Connacht Tribune*, 14 Jan 1922.

26 Julia Eichenberg, 'The Dark Side of Independence: Paramilitary Violence in Ireland and Poland after the First World War', *Contemporary European History*, Cambridge University Press, 2010.

27 Gabrielle Machnik-Kékesi, 'Gendering Bodies: Violence as Performance in Ireland's War of Independence', Thesis for Degree of Master of Arts, Concordia University, Montreal, Canada, 2017.

28 *Cork Examiner*, 11 June 1921; 'Young Girl's Death', *Irish Independent*, 22 March 1921; *Freeman's Journal*, 22 March 1921.

29 'The Death of Miss Elizabeth Scales', *Irish Times*, 29 Jan 1921.

CHAPTER 17

1 'Mrs Lindsay's Fate', *Irish Times*, 30 July 1921; 'Maria Georgina Lindsay', National Probate Calendar, England & Wales.

2 Busteed is reported to have said to Mrs Lindsay: "Listen you old bitch, you think you are dealing with a bunch of farm labourers, the men who will touch their caps to you and say "Yes Madam" and "No Madam". Well, we're no bunch of down-trodden tame Catholics. My grandfather was Protestant and my bloody cousins are Protestants all over West Cork.

This is not a religious war we're fighting. I don't give a damn for any religion.' See Sean O'Callaghan, *Execution*, Frederick Muller, London, 1974, p. 133.

3 Tim Sheehan, *Lady Hostage*, p. 176.

4 Sean O'Callaghan, *Execution*, pp. 177-79.

5 Tim Sheehan, *Lady Hostage*, p. 176.

6 Tim Sheehan states in *Lady Hostage* (p. 24) that the National Volunteers [who were aligned with the Irish Parliamentary Party] 'supported conscription'. In fact the Irish Parliamentary Party and its supporters strongly opposed moves by the British to extend conscription to Ireland in 1918. Sean O'Callaghan states that Mrs Lindsay was 'reared in the bigoted Unionism of the north of Ireland' and that she was the 'daughter of a Linen Lord'. (*Execution*, pp. 109-10.) In fact as previously indicated, she was the daughter of a County Wicklow solicitor – it is reported that she also lived in County Mayo. She married wealthy Ulster linen merchant John Lindsay and lived in Banbridge, County Down before moving to County Cork.

7 As a hard-working Parliamentary Secretary in the Department of Health during the 1930s, Dr Ward concentrated resources on overhauling and extending the hospital system. A man of his time, he consulted on health matters with members of the Catholic hierarchy and in 1944, at Episcopal behest, he banned the sale of newly marketed sanitary tampons because of concerns over the sexual arousal of girls at an impressionable age. (See Lawrence William White, 'Francis Constantine Ward', *Dictionary of Irish Biography*, Cambridge University Press/Royal Irish Academy.) In 1946 a tribunal of inquiry cleared Dr Ward of all charges related to alleged misconduct in the management of his family bacon-curing firm, and alleged local government corruption. However, the tribunal found that he and other directors had made incomplete tax returns relating to income from the firm, and he resigned his office.

8 O'Duffy would go on to serve in a number of posts – Chief of Staff of the National Army, Commissioner of the Civic Guard (An Garda Síochána), and head of the Blueshirts, who adopted the paramilitary-style uniforms and salutes of fascist groups on the continent. He led an Irish brigade to fight for Franco in the Spanish Civil War. He died in November 1944, aged 54 years. (See Patrick Long, 'Eoin O'Duffy'', *Dictionary of Irish Biography*, Cambridge/Royal Irish Academy.)

9 Report from RIC County Inspector's Office, Enniskillen, to Inspector General, 19 July 1920, in RIC file re 'Owen [sic] O'Duffy', TNA CO 904/211/325-328.

10 'Woman's Struggle With Raiders', *Irish Independent*, 20 April 1921.

11 O'Halpin, 'Problematic Killing…', Kelly & Lyons, op. cit., p. 336.

12 Thomas Brennan Papers, notebook marked 'IRA', Monaghan County Museum, cited in O'Halpin & Ó Corráin, *The Dead of the Irish Revolution*.

13 'Monaghan Woman Shot: Court of Inquiry's Finding', *Anglo-Celt*, 7 May 1921.

[14] Hansard, House of Commons Debates, 19 April 1921.

[15] Supt. James McKenna, BMH, WS 1028.

[16] O'Halpin, 'Problematic Killing…', Kelly & Lyons, op. cit., p. 336, quoting notes by Nuala O'Neill (daughter) in NLI, O'Mahony Papers, MS 44064.

[17] See 'Dublin Castle Statements, May 1921', TNA CO 904/168.

[18] 'Sir Basil Clarke', *The Times*, 13 Dec 1947.

[19] According to academic D.M. Leeson, police patrols had begun to 'reconnoitre by fire', shooting ahead blindly when they came to a likely location for an ambush. Leeson records that the day after the incident, RIC Headquarters issued an instruction banning indiscriminate firing by 'parties travelling by motor'. (David Leeson, 'The Black and Tans', Thesis, McMaster University, 2003, pp. 65-6.) See also 'A Priest's Story', *Freemans Journal*, 19 Nov 1920.

[20] The 1911 Census indicates that there were 1,137 people in Ireland called Noble, with only 212, or 18.6 per cent, described as Roman Catholic.

CHAPTER 18

[1] *Cork County Eagle*, 17 Sept 1921.

[2] 'Coomhola Aeridheacht', *Southern Star*, 27 Aug 1921.

[3] 'Rollicking Reunion', *Southern Star*, 2 Sept 1921.

[4] 'Castletown Bere Sports', *Cork County Eagle*, 24 Sept 1921.

[5] 'Interesting Cases', *Cork County Eagle*, 25 March 1922; 'Ardgroom Company', IE/MA/MSPC/RO/55. '

[6] TNA CO 904/178.

[7] TNA CO 904/150.

[8] See, for instance, letter dated 14 June 1922 from Dublin Castle official Norman Loughnane to Officer in charge, Evacuation, listing RIC pensioners 'who have been ordered to leave their homes', IE/MA/LE/11/3.

[9] 'Summary of Outrages Against the Police, during the Week ended 6 Nov 1921', TNA, CO 904/150.

[10] Cal Hyland, 'Considering the Situation of Protestants in West Cork, 1920-1925', West Cork History Festival, 19 Aug 2018; see also, Cal Hyland, letter, *Irish Times*, 12 Aug 2017.

[11] Riobard O'Dwyer, *Annals of Beara*, Vol. II, p, 552.

[12] 'Pádraig Ó Súilleabháin', Ainm.ie.

[13] Michael J. Crowley, BMH, WS 1603.

[14] TNA CO 762/107/14.

[15] TNA/CO 762/68/23.

[16] 'Berehaven', *Cork Examiner*, 19 Dec 1921.

[17] In 1952 James McCarthy was residing at Yonkers, New York when he successfully applied for a 1917-21 Medal (IE/MA/MD20071); when he gave a statement to the BMH in 1957, he had an address in the Glasheen Road area of Cork. (BMH, WS 1567.)

[18] Eugene Dunne, BMH, WS 1537.

[19] Ibid.

[20] 'Berehaven', *Cork Examiner*, 2 Jan 1922.

[21] 'Berehaven Meeting', *Cork Examiner*, 20 March 1922.

[22] 'Munster Cleared', *Irish Independent*, 15 April 1922.

[23] Margaret O'Neill, IE/MA/MSP34REF40784.

[24] Michael Laffan, *Judging W.T. Cosgrave*, Royal Irish Academy, Dublin, 2014, p. 105; Liam Lynch to Tom Lynch, 12 Dec 1921, in Cormac K. H. O'Malley & Anne Dolan, *'No Surrender Here', The Civil War Papers of Ernie O'Malley 1922-1924*, Lilliput Press, Dublin, 2007, p. 12.

[25] Ronan Fanning, *Éamon de Valera, A Will to Power*, Faber & Faber, London, 2015, p. 136.

[26] IE/MA/CP/4/40.

[27] King's College London: Liddell Centre for Military Archives, Fuller/1/1/63.

[28] 'Gradation List of Officers of the British Army', Jan 1939, p. 430.

[29] 'Captain to pay £300 damages', *The Pall Mall Mail and Globe*, 4 May 1921.

CHAPTER 19

[1] Liam O'Dwyer, *Beara in Irish History*, Vantage Press, New York, 1977, p. 105.

[2] Liam O'Dwyer, op. cit., p. 129.

[3] Liam Deasy, *Brother Against Brother*, Mercier Press, Cork, 1982, p. 43.

[4] Richard English, *Armed Struggle, The History of the IRA*, Pan Books, London, 2004, p. 34.

[5] Liam O'Dwyer, op. cit., pp. 130-31.

[6] Ibid.

[7] Liam O'Dwyer, op. cit., p. 129.

[8] See details re Ardgroom Company, IE/MA/MSPC/RO/55.

[9] In his application for a Military Service Pension, Patrick Joseph Murphy states that Sean O'Driscoll, who was his IRA O/C prior to the Truce, 'served in the National Forces until May 1923'. IE/MA/24SP667.

[10] Irish Army Census Collection 1922, Irish Military Archives; Eyeries Company, IE/MA/MSPC/RO/55.

[11] Patrick Joseph Murphy, IE/MA/24SP667.

[12] 'Eyeries Man Active During Civil War', *Southern Star*, 31 Jan 1981.

[13] 'Big List of Awards', *Freeman's Journal*, 11 Feb 1924.

[14] Margaret O'Neill, IE/MA/MSP34REF40784.

[15] See '2nd Bureau, Occupation of Barracks by Irregulars etc., 1922', IE/MA/LE/15/1.

[16] 'Beggar's Bush Reports', *Irish Examiner*, 17 May 1922.

[17] 'Berehaven Incident', *Cork Examiner*, 8 July 1922.

[18] 'Camp Buildings Burned', *Cork Examiner*, 8 August 1922.

[19] Details of Flynn's experience are given in letters to the RIC Tribunal, seeking compensation, TNA HO 144/22575.

[20] John Twomey, TNA, CO 762/30/6.

[21] 'West Cork Happenings: Reports of Irregular Tyranny from Castletownbere', *Freeman's Journal*, 25 July 1922.

[22] For details of individual compensation claims, see NAI FIN/COMP/2/4.

[23] Eoin Neeson, *The Civil War, 1922-23*, Poolbeg, Dublin, 1989, p. 224.

[24] Frank Busteed, IE/MA/MSP34REF4903.

[25] Meda Ryan, *The Day Michael Collins Was Shot*, Poolbeg, Dublin, 1995, p. 114.

[26] This is the estimate of John P. Duggan in his book *A History of the Irish Army*, Gill & Macmillan, Dublin, 1992, p. 113.

[27] Ernie O'Malley, The Singing Flame, Mercier Press, Cork, 2012, p. 226.

[28] UCDA, P17a/57, cited in Richard English, *Ernie O'Malley, IRA Intellectual*, Oxford University Press, 1998, p. 81; IE/MA/CW/OPS/01/03/03.

[29] IE/MA/2D245; see also IE/MA/MSPC/RO/69.

CHAPTER 20

[1] Liam O'Dwyer, op. cit., p. 132.

[2] TNA, T 160/146.

[3] Nora Sullivan, IE/MA/MSP34REF21522.

[4] Hannah Hanley, IE/MA/MSP34REF27316.

[5] Dr Patrick Valentine Thomas Murphy, IE/MA/MD8306.

[6] TNA/CAB/24/138.

[7] "Parliament Meets', *Anglo-Celt*, 16 Sept 1922.

[8] John Linge, 'The Royal Navy and the Irish Civil War', *Irish Historical Studies*, May 1998, p. 68, quoting, 'Report of Proceedings, *Vanity* to Admiralty, 31 Aug 1922, (PRO, ADM 1/8632/173.'

[9] 'Artillery Man's Suicide', Western Morning News, 8 March 1923.

[10] TNA, T 160/146.

[11] Dr P.V.T. Murphy, IE/MA/MD8306.

[12] 'Irregular Tactics', *An t-Óglach*, 7 Oct 1922.

[13] 'Irregular Tactics, Treatment of a Cork Medical Officer', *An t-Óglach*, 7 October 1922.

[14] Cork City & County Archives, Minutes of Castletown Board of Guardians, Sept 1921, IE/CCCA/BG59.

[15] O'Malley & Dolan, op cit., *'No Surrender Here'*, p. 505.

[16] O'Malley & Dolan, p. 506.

[17] O'Malley & Dolan, p. 511.

[18] 'Youth Shot Dead', *Cork Examiner*, 20 March 1923.

[19] Ted O'Sullivan told Ernie O'Malley that McCarthy was executed 'more or less unofficially'. 'He used to show the Free State the houses so they could raid them so our lads shot him on St Patrick's Day 1923 without sanction.' (*The Men Will Talk To Me, West Cork Interviews by Ernie O'Malley*, op. cit., Kindle edition location 1710.)

[20] *Irish Times*, 17 March 1923.

[21] William Levingston Cooke, Freemason and Justice of the Peace, who ran a bicycle shop, was shot dead at his home on the Old Blackrock Road on 21 August 1922. Walter Hailes, a post office official and Freemason, was shot the following month near his Cork home and severely wounded.

In Kinsale, Eric Wolfe was shot dead on 19 December 1922. After the Civil War, Theo Creber was shot dead on 21 August 1923 at Kerry Pike, near Cork City. Cooke was a Methodist; the others were Church of Ireland.

CHAPTER 21 & CHAPTER 22

[1] 'Towns Taken', *Freeman's Journal*, 20 Dec 1922.

[2] 'Castletownbere: Occupied by National Troops', *Cork Examiner*, 18 Dec 1922.

[3] 'Items of the Fighting', *Irish Independent*, 6 Jan 1923.

[4] IE/MA/MSPC/RO/69; see also Matthew Sullivan, IE/MA/MSPC/34REF1835.

[5] IE/MA/MSPC/RO/69.

[6] Hannah Hanley, IE/MA/MSP34REF27316.

[7] Margaret O'Neill, IE/MA/MSP34REF40784.

[8] Bella O'Connell, IE/MA/MSP34REF31400.

[9] IE/MA/CW/OPS/04/01. O'Dwyer stated (IE/MA/MSP34REF9556) that the ambush occurred in April but this seems erroneous.

[10] IE/MA/CW/OPS/04/01.

[11] IE/MA/ CW/P/13/07.

[12] John Murphy, IE/MA/MSP34REF1834.

[13] *Irish Independent*, 11 April 1923.

[14] 'Adrigole Lady's Death: Inquest Adjourned', *Cork Examiner*, 21 April 1923.

[15] Pádraig Óg Ó Ruairc, 'The Women Who Died For Ireland', *History Ireland*, Sept-Oct 2018.

[16] 'Funeral of Miss M. Dunne', *Cork Examiner*, 23 March 1923.

[17] 'Trigger Mine Found In A Cork Dump', *Freeman's Journal*, 21 May 1923.

[18] IE/MA/MSPC/RO/64.

[19] IE/MA/CW/P/13/07.

[20] 'Numerous Arrests', *Irish Times*, 24 May 1923.

[21] Statement by Nora Mary Healy, Ted O'Sullivan Papers, NLI, MS 49,668/11-22.

[22] Liam O'Dwyer, op. cit., pp. 132-3.

[23] Nora Mary Healy, IE/MA/MSP34REF60764.

[24] See 'News of Beara Exiles', *Southern Star*, 19 Feb 1972.

[25] IE/MA/MSPC/RO/69.

[26] Calton Younger, *Ireland's Civil War*, Fontana Press, London, 1986, p. 415f.

[27] Francis J. Friel, IE/MA/24SP6861.

[28] IE/MA/CW/P/13/07.

[29] *Cork Examiner*, 4 June 1923.

[30] Liam O'Dwyer, p. 134; see also Riobard O'Dwyer, *Annals of Beara, Volume II*, p. 788.

[31] Dáil Éireann Debates, 22 June 1923.

[32] Ted O'Sullivan, IE/MA/MSP34REF2092.

[33] *The Men Will Talk To Me, West Cork Interviews by Ernie O'Malley*, Edited by Andy Bielenberg, John Borgonovo and Padraig Óg O Ruairc, Mercier Press, Cork, 2015, Kindle locations, 1472-1516; see also locations 1661-1682.

[34] IE/MA/CW/P/13/07.

[35] Louise O'Connell, IE/MA/MSP34REF55471.

[36] IE/MA/MSPC/RO/64.

[37] 'Prominent Irregular Arrested', *The Liberator* (Tralee), 29 Sept 1923.

[38] IE/MA/CW/P/02/02/06.

[39] Ted O'Sullivan, IE/MA/MSP34REF2092.

[40] Nora O'Sullivan, IE/MA/MSP34REF21522.

[41] Hannah Hanley, IE/MA/MSP34REF27316.

[42] NAI, FIN/COMP/2/4/938; 'Bantry Compensation Awards', *Cork Examiner*, 11 July 1924.

[43] Michael Flynn to Paymaster General, 1 August 1930, TNA, HO144/22575.

[44] IE/MA/CW/P/02/02/06.

[45] Julie Ann Crowley, 'The Crowley Family', in *Butte's Irish Heart, Who Says You Can't Go Home*, authored by St Mary's Neighbourhood Reunions Committee, Riverbend Publications, Helena, Montana, USA, 2015. See also Ancestry Family Trees, Ancestry.com.

[46] Ernie O'Malley, op. cit., Kindle locations 1661-1682.

[47] *Kerry Reporter*, 28 June 1924.

[48] 'Late Mr P. Crowley', *Southern Star*, 28 June 1924.

[49] 'Criminal Injury Claims', *Cork Examiner*, 14 Jan 1924; *Irish Independent*, 10 Jan 1924.

[50] 'Irish Free State: Compensation for injury to persons and property'. Memorandum, House of Commons, Cmd. 1844, April 1923.

[51] Lord Danesfort, House of Lords debate, 17 June 1925.

[52] Fachtna O'Donovan, 'A History of the Constabulary in Beara', lecture given to the Beara Historical Society, 18 Nov 2002.

[53] 'Ardgroom Incident', *Cork Examiner*, 25 March 1924.

[54] Foster, op. cit., p. 279.

[55] From Detroit, Michigan, Liam O'Dwyer wrote to the Chairman of the IRA Army Council making various criticisms of the US-based republican organisation, Clan na Gael. The Chairman wrote back to him on 13 January 1927 defending Clan na Gael. Moss Twomey Papers, UCDA, P69/183.

[56] US Immigration Officer, list of arrivals, Boston, 3 Sept 1926.

[57] Liam O'Dwyer, op. cit. p. 135.

[58] Records of the Immigration & Naturalization Service, via FamilySearch, accessed 5 Oct 2017.

[59] Iarla Mac Aodha Bhui, op. cit., p. 185.

[60] US Dept of Labor records, declaration of intention to become a citizen, 6 Feb 1928, via Findmypast, accessed 16 March 2018.

[61] *Southern Star*, 19 Feb 1938.

[62] Daniel Harrington, IE/MA/MD7452.

[63] Canada Ocean Arrivals, 1919-1924, Ancestry.com, accessed 22 June 2017.

[64] IE/MA/MSPC/RO-69.

[65] Patrick Malvey, US Dept. of Labour Immigration Service, 14 Sept 1926.

[66] Patrick Joseph Malvey, Malvey Family Tree, Ancestry.com, accessed 16 June 2017.

[67] New York Naturalization Records, 1882 – 1944, via Ancestry.com, accessed 23 June 2017.

[68] Riobard O'Dwyer, *Annals of Beara*, Vol. II, pp. 963-63; see also 'Beara Echoes', *Southern Star*, 1 Aug 1964.

[69] 'Beara Echoes', *Southern Star*, 1 Aug 1964.

[70] Riobard O'Dwyer, *Annals of Beara*, Vol. II, pp. 439-40.

[71] 'New York New York, Extracted Death Index, 1862-1948', accessed via Ancestry.com, 30 June 2018.

[72] IE/MA/MD49240.

[73] IE/MA/DP42026.

[74] Liam O'Dwyer, p. 136.

[75] Liam O'Dwyer, p. 136.

[76] Liam O'Dwyer, p. 137.

[77] Meda Ryan, *Tom Barry*, p. 295.

[78] IE/MA/MSPC/RO/69.

[79] Riobard O'Dwyer, *Annals of Beara*, Volume II, Gold Stag Publications, Statesboro, Georgia, USA, 2009; see section headed 'Johnny O'Dwyer & Ellen Lynch (Caolrua)'.

[80] See Michael Dwyer, petition for naturalization to US District Court, Boston, Mass., 14 Oct 1938.

[81] Riobard O'Dwyer, *Annals of Beara*, Volume II; see section headed 'Johnny O'Dwyer & Ellen Lynch (Caolrua)'.

[82] Julia Sheehan, IE/MA/MSP34REF56331.

[83] Liam O'Dwyer, *Beara in Irish History*, p. 137.

CHAPTER 23

Dr Eve Morrison, 'Bridget Noble' in 'Hauntings of the Irish Revolution', in Chapter Four, M. Corporaal, C. Cusack & R. van den Beuken (eds), *Irish Studies and the Dynamics of Memory*, Peter Lang, Bern, 2017.

[2] Articles by Sean T. O'Sullivan were published in the *Southern Star*.

[3] Bella O'Connell, IE/MA/MSP34REF31400.

[4] IE/MA/MSP34REF9924.

[5] Seán Mac Stiofáin, 'An Súilleabhánach mar Óglach', *Comhar*, Dec 1986.

[6] Iarla Mac Aodha Bhuí, *Diarmaid Ó Súilleabháin, Saothar Próis*, An Clóchomhar, Baile Átha Cliath, 1992, pp. 184-85.

[7] Timothy O'Donoghue, IE/MA/MSP34REF4270; Patrick Michael Ahern, IE/MA/MSP34REF652; James Gannon, IE/MA/24SP5435; Maurice Quinn, IE/MA/MSP34REF12835.

[8] Tim Sheehan, *Lady Hostage: Mrs Lindsay*, Dripsey, 1990, p.147.

[9] Tim Sheehan, 'Who Erred at Dripsey Ambush?', *Cork Examiner*, 16 February 1996.

[10] See 'Civilian James Clarke' in Bielenberg & Donnelly, 'List of Suspected Spies Killed by the IRA in 1920-21'.

[11] Sean O'Callaghan, *Execution*, p. 127.

[12] Tim Sheehan, *Lady Hostage*, pp. 117-18.

[13] IE/MA/MSP34REF4903.

[14] Sean O'Callaghan, *Execution*, p. 31.

[15] Denis Dwyer, BMH, WS 713; Daniel McCarthy, WS 1257; Dan McCarthy, WS 1957. See also quotation from 'Record of Services in Ireland' of the 1st Battalion, Manchester Regiment, in 'The Case of Mrs Lindsay', Military Service Pensions Collection, Irish Military Archives, 11 March 2018.

[16] Sean O'Callaghan, *Execution*, pp. 189-92.

[17] Sean O'Callaghan, p. 182.

[18] Daniel Corkery, BMH WS 1719; James Murphy, BMH, WS 1633.

[19] Andy Bielenberg, John Borgonovo & James S. Donnelly Jr., 'Something in the Nature of a Massacre, The Bandon Valley Killings Revisited', *Éire-Ireland*, Fall/Winter 2014.

[20] *Irish Press*, 26 February 1977.

[21] I should declare an interest here. I was the young reporter sent to interview Mr and Mrs Goldin. So far as I can recall, the initiative for the interview came from Mr Goldin, who valued publicity. I found Mrs Goldin to be a very charming, likeable lady. I did not see anything shocking about the photo, but then I was of a younger generation than Liam O'Dwyer.

[22] *The Green Book*, p. 33. The quotation is from an original version of the handbook – shorter versions have appeared in more recent years on various websites.

[23] Liam O'Dwyer, op. cit., pp. 105-06.

[24] *The Good Old IRA, Tan War Operations*, issued by the Sinn Féin Publicity Department, Dublin, November 1985.

CHAPTER 24

[1] NAI, TSCH/3/S3033.

[2] *Knockraha, Foras Feasa na Paroiste*, Knockraha History & Heritage Society, 2005, pp. 150-52

[3] Ernie O'Malley Notebooks, UCDA, P17b/112.

[4] *Knockraha*, op. cit., p. 151.

[5] Michael Murphy, BMH, WS 1547.

[6] Gerard Murphy, *The Year of Disappearances, Political Killings in Cork, 1921 – 1922*, Gill & Macmillan, Dublin, 2011, Chapter 32.

[7] Eunan O'Halpin & Dáithí Ó Corráin, *The Dead of the Irish Revolution*, Yale University Press, New Haven & London, 2020, see entry re 'James Blemens'.

[8] NAI, TSCH/3/S3033.

[9] Gerard Murphy, *The Year of Disappearances*, pp. 193-94; IE/MA/A/7431.

[10] *Knockraha*, op. cit., p. 152.

[11] Gerard Murphy blog, 'The Year of Disappearances', 30 April 2020, quoting from the 1977 edition of Jim Fitzgerald's *Knockraha, Foras Feasa na Paroiste*, p. 77.

[12] It is unclear why Thomas Roycroft was abducted and killed – he had joined the RIC in August 1920 but was discharged as 'unsuitable' in June 1921. (TNA HO184/15/1290.) The disappearance of Roycroft is among the issues dealt with in considerable detail in Gerard Murphy's book, *The Year of Disappearances*.

[13] *Knockraha*, (2005) op. cit., pp. 155-56.

[14] Andy Bielenberg & Pádraig Óg Ó Ruairc, 'Shallow graves; documenting & assessing IRA disappearances during the Irish revolution 1919-1923', *Small Wars & Insurgencies*, 2020.

[15] Eunan O'Halpin (TCD), *Irish Independent*, 25 March 2013.

[16] O'Halpin, 'Problematic Killing…', Kelly & Lyons, op. cit., pp. 329-32.

[17] O'Halpin, ' Problematic Killing…' in Kelly & Lyons, op. cit., p. 337, citing as source 'Martin Corry recordings, 1976, courtesy of Jim Fitzgerald of the Knockraha Historical Society'. See also Gerard Murphy, *The Year of Disappearances*, Chapter 8.

[18] *Knockraha* (2005) op. cit., p. 137.

[19] Andy Bielenberg, 'Female Fatalities in County Cork during the Irish War of Independence and the Case of Mrs Lindsay', in Linda Connolly (Editor), *Women and the Irish Revolution*, Irish Academic Press, 2020, quoting Crime Branch to Private Secretary, Minister of Home Affairs, 9 May 1924, Sean O'Mahony Papers, NLI MS 44,045.

[20] Sean O'Callaghan, *Execution*, p. 151.

[21] O'Halpin, 'Problematic Killing…', Kelly & Lyons, op. cit., p. 338.

[22] Mick Murphy, Ernie O'Malley Notebooks, UCDA, P17b/112.

[23] Stan Barry, O'Malley Notebooks, UCDA, P17b/111, quoted in Professor Eunan O'Halpin, '*Probematic Killings…*', op. cit., p. 339.

[24] IE/MA/A/0649.

[25] IE/MA/HS/A/535. The Military Archives file includes details of a report from the O/C, 3rd Brigade, IRA (North Roscommon) indicating that Constable Dennehy was taken prisoner on 23 November 1920 and executed 'as a spy' the following day.

[26] James Blemens and Frederick Blemens, IE/MA/HS/A/535.

[27] Patrick Ray, Cork, IE/MA/HS/A/649.

[28] Gerard Murphy, *The Year of Disappearances*, p. 44.

[29] 'Declaration on the Protection of All Persons from Enforced Disappearance', proclaimed by the United Nations General Assembly in its resolution 47/133 of 18 December 1992.

[30] Office of the United Nations High Commissioner for Human Rights, 'Enforced or Involuntary Disappearances'.

CHAPTER 25

[1] New York Naturalisation Records, 1882 – 1944, via Ancestry.com accessed 15 May 2017.

[2] 'Michael Og O'Sullivan', *Irish Press*, 27 July 1935.

[3] See letter from Ted O'Sullivan to Office of the Referee, Griffith Barracks, Dublin, 12 Dec 1935, IE/MA/MSPC/RO-64.

[4] See advertisement, *Irish Press*, 6 July 1935.

[5] Mícheál Óg is listed as 'Michael Sullivan', a 37-years-old widower, of 502 West 135 Street, New York City, and a naturalised US citizen.

[6] 'Where is Her Toller? Anti-Hitler Mystery; Contradictory Reports; Stormy Meeting in Rathmines', *Irish Times*, 4 Jan 1935.

[7] Brian Hanley, 'Oh here's to Adolph Hitler' – the IRA and the Nazis', *History Ireland*, May-June 2005.

[8] For account of Dan Breen reportedly weeping at Hitler's death, see Eunan O'Halpin, *Defending Ireland*, Oxford University Press, 1999, p. 152; for account of portraits of Hitler on show in Breen's home, see 'An Irishman's Diary', *Irish Times*, 24 Feb 1997.

[9] *Cork Examiner*, 6 Aug 1924. See also 'Beara Echoes', *Southern Star*, 15 August 1964.

[10] Tom Barry, *Reality of the Anglo-Irish War 1920-21*, Anvil Books, Tralee and Dublin, 1974.

[11] 'Flags At Veterans' Funerals', *Southern Star*, 22 May 1976.

[12] 'Late Liam O'Dwyer, outstanding Beara freedom fighter', *Southern Star*, 7 May 1983.

[13] 'Late Connie Healy', *Southern Star*, 13 March 1999.

[14] TNA PMG48/66; PMG48/75.

[15] See, for instance, letter from Dublin Castle official Norman Loughnane to Evacuation Office, re RIC pensioners 'ordered to leave their homes', 14 June 1922, IE/MA, LE/11/3.

[16] Peter Hart, *The IRA & Its Enemies*, Oxford University Press, 1998, p. 75.

[17] NAI, FIN/COMP/2/4/2812.

[18] 'Theft of Police Clothing, Castletown Bere', House of Commons Hansard, 17 June 1920.

[19] See Ted O'Sullivan, BMH, WS 1478; 'Bantry Policeman Murdered', *Cork County Eagle*, 19 June 1920.

[20] 'A Shocking Crime: Wounded Man Dragged Out and Shot Dead', *Weekly Irish Times*, 19 June 1920.

[21] Thomas J. Oates, TNA CO 762/19/22.

[22] TNA, HO 184/42; HO 184/102240609.

[23] See prosecution in County Mayo court by Constable Michael Goaley, Partry, of John Middleton, Cappaghduff, on 11 September 1911, for not having light on vehicle after dark, with Alan Bell RM on the bench; Petty Sessions Order Books CSPS 1/868, accessed via Findmypast, 24 Aug 2017.

[24] John P. Dobbyn, TNA, CO 762/35/1.

[25] TNA, HO 184/76; PMG48/74.

[26] Death registration records for Drumshanbo district, 1928.

[27] Christopher O'Connell, BMH, WS 1530.

[28] Fachtna O'Donovan, Chapter Nine, 'A History of the Constabulary in Beara', in *Beara, History and Stories from the Peninsula*, Compiled by Gerard Harrington, Beara Historical Society, 2005.

[29] Jasper Ungoed-Thomas, *Jasper Wolfe of Skibbereen*, op. cit., p. 153.

[30] Dáil debates, 20 March 1928; quoted also in Jasper Ungoed-Thomas, op. cit., p. 217.

[31] 'Mrs Dora Agnes Scully', *Portsmouth Herald*, 27 May 1944.

CHAPTER 26

[1] Dáil Éireann Debates, Vol. 28, No. 4, 27 Feb 1929.

[2] Valuation records for Ardgroom Inward, Kilcatherine, 1933-96, Vol 5., Cork.

[3] 'Passenger Lists Leaving UK 1890 – 1960', Findmypast, accessed 21 Oct 2017.

[4] National Archives of Australia, K269, 26 Aug 1924, BARRABOOL.

[5] Register of Deaths in Fraserburgh Parish, 1926.

[6] Aberdeen Electoral Registers – there is an entry in the Fraserburgh register for 1925 indicating that Alexander Noble is registered at 1 Finlayson Street, but located in Glasgow.

[7] *Aberdeen Press & Journal*, 28 August 1926.

[8] The 1927 Electoral Register shows Alexander and Mabel Noble as the only electors located at 65 Harold Street. The register codes indicate that the two were entitled to vote in both Parliamentary and local elections.

[9] *Aberdeen Daily Journal*, 19 April 1909; see also Register of Marriages for the Blythswood district of Glasgow, April 1909.

[10] 'British Army Service Records, 1914-1920', findmypast; 'WW1 Service Records', fold3 website.

[11] 'Glasgow Gas Poisoning Victims', *The Courier*, 4 April 1922.

[12] Register of Deaths in the District of Anderston, Glasgow, 1922.

[13] *Northern Daily Mail*, 31 December 1927.

[14] 'Ruined by £2,000. A Grimsby Wounding Case', *Hull Daily Mail*, 11 January 1928; see also court reports on same date in *Yorkshire Post* and *Leeds Mercury*.

[15] Register of Deaths in District of Fraserburgh, 1939.

[16] 'Guilty of Breach of the Peace: Cooper Wanted to Go to Jail', *Fraserburgh Herald*, 26 Dec 1939.

[17] Register of Deaths in the Northern District of Aberdeen, 1941.

[18] *Aberdeen Weekly Journal*, 6 March 1941.

[19] Register of Deaths in the Northern District of Aberdeen, 1951.

[20] Register of Deaths in the Eastern District of Aberdeen, 1950.

EPILOGUE

[1] 'Where the Bodies are Buried', *The New Yorker*, 16 May 2015.

[2] Seamus McKendry, *Disappeared: The Search for Jean McConville*, Blackwater Press, Dublin, 2000, pp. 14-15.

[3] *New Yorker*, op. cit.

[4] Interview for film *I, Dolours*, produced by Ed Moloney and directed by Maurice Sweeney, screened in 2018; Gerry Moriarty, 'Dolours Price told

film-makers of her direct involvement in murder of Jean McConville', *Irish Times*, 25 July 2018; Patrick Radden Keefe, *Say Nothing: A True Story Of Murder And Memory in Northern Ireland*, William Collins, London, 2018, Chapter 27.

[5] Patrick Sullivan, IE/MA/MSP34REF17863.

[6] Mrs Lindsay, IE/MA/HS/A/649.

[7] Diarmaid Ó hÉigeartaigh, Secretariat Department, Dáil Éireann, to Mrs Lilias Potter, Apsley House, Cahir, Co. Tipperary, 23 Aug 1921, IE/MA/HS/A/649.

[8] Tim Sheehan, *Lady Hostage: Mrs Lindsay*, Dripsey, 1990, pp. 186-189.

[9] Eve Morrison, 'Hauntings of the Irish Revolution', op. cit.

[10] Liam O'Dwyer, op. cit., p. 127.

[11] Susanne Iles, 'Cuas Pier Caves', posted on 'The Ring of Beara Blog', 11 Dec 2010, accessed 24 July 2017.

Index

Bandon Valley atrocity, 158-161.
Banishment by IRA, 164, 166-67, 213-14, 221, 223.
Barry, Tom, 21, 22, 65-66, 83, 101, 121, 135, 137, 141-42, 144, 148, 159, 171-72, 249, 252, 275.
Breen, Dan, 60-61, 165, 167, 276.
Benson, Ethel, 19, 21-22, 25, 190.
Bielenberg, Dr Andy, 20, 23-24, 112, 115, 268-69.
'Bobbing', see 'Hair shearing attacks on women'
Brugha, Cathal, 21.
Busteed, Frank, 20, 22-23, 115, 190-91, 216, 255-58.

Carroll, Kate, 2, 5, 19, 76, 156, 165, 178, 191-94.
Casement, Roger, 56, 120.
Childers, Erskine, 19, 195.
Clarke, Basil, 194.
Clarke, James, 18-24, 190-91, 255-58, 300.
Coleman, Dr Marie, 184-85..
Collins, Michael 19-21, 50, 141, 145, 156, 204, 210, 216-17, 236, 261, 282.
Congested Districts Board for Ireland (CDBI), 30, 58, 279, 288.
Connolly, Professor Linda, 185.
Corry, Martin, 93, 109, 112-15, 264-68.
Cotter, Edward 'Ned', 235-36.
Croke, District Inspector Forbes le Blount (RIC), 88, 280.
Crossbarry ambush, 65, 101, 135, 163, 171, 211-12.
Crowley, Michael, Adjutant, Beara Battalion, 68, 108, 127-28, 133-34, 254..
Crowley, Patsy Dan, 14, 64-65, 75, 83, 89, 101-03, 107-08, 110-11, 138, 234-37, 240-41.
Crowley, Sean [Seán Ó Crualaoich], Jack or Jackessy, 46-47.

Dalton, Emmet, 2, 141, 146-48, 203, 215-16.

Daly, Rev. Michael, 83, 117-19, 121-23.
De Valera, Éamon, 16-21, 71, 125-26, 204, 248-49.
Dobbyn, Head Constable John P. (RIC), 49, 282-83.
Du Maurier, Daphne, 28.
Dunne, Margaret, 203, 230-31.
Dwyer, John, Cailroe, 81-82, 84, 86-89, 129, 202, 231-32, 250, 306.

Eichenberg, Dr Julia, 188.

Fish curing industry, 30, 33, 37.
Forde, Lady Annie Catherine, 24, 299.
Furious Pier, British military camp, 82-83, 86, 136, 139, 170-71, 206, 213, 222.

Goaley, Head Constable Michael (RIC), 88, 281-82.
Goodman, Rev. James, 55.

Hair shearing attacks on women, 9, 70-71, 75-76, 81, 129, 184-89, 255.
Hanley, Hannah (née O'Neill), Cumann na mBan (CnB), 12-13, 74, 92, 105, 119, 124, 170, 219-21, 229, 238, 254.
Harrington, Gerdie, 304.
Harris, Eoghan, 160.
Hatton-Hall, Lieutenant Hubert Christopher, 206-08, 222.
Healy, Connie, Ardgroom Company, 83-84, 89, 259, 277.
Hyde, Douglas, [Dubhghlas de hÍde], 46.
Hynes, John W., Judge, 143, 152-54, 284.
Holland, Dan, 9-10.
Hurley, Charlie, Commandant Cork No 3 Brigade, IRA, 62, 73, 129, 142, 163.

Irish Grants Committee, 200, 214, 280, 283.

Kelly, Captain C.J. O'Connor, 108, 125.
Kipling, Rudyard, 29.
King's Own Scottish Borderers (KOSB), 138-39, 206, 222.
King's Own Yorkshire Light Infantry (KOYLI), 105.

Lehane, William, 14, 57-59, 74-75, 78, 94, 102, 104-107, 110-11, 118-19, 164, 177, 207, 306.
Leigh-White Estate, 42, 58, 288.
Lindsay, Mary, 1-2, 5-6, 18-24, 76, 112, 114-15, 125, 152, 178, 190-91, 195, 255-58, 270, 299-300.

Lloyd George, David, 17-18, 21.
Lynch, Liam, Anti-Treaty IRA Chief of Staff, 126, 204, 217, 225-26, 232.
Lyne, Gerard J. 28, 138.

McCarthy, Brigid, 7, 46, 232.
McConville, Jean, 2, 5, 262, 297-99.
Monahan, Martha (Mattie or Matilda), née Neill, 41, 285-87.
Monteith, Robert, 56, 174, 248.
Mulcahy, Richard, Chief of Staff, Irish Volunteers/IRA; Defence Minister, 60, 126-27, 156, 165, 169, 299.
Murphy, Dr. Patrick V. 57, 85-86, 135, 219-20; banishment of, 221-25; 240.

Neill, John, 7, 15, 26-27, 42, 47, 69, 77, 151, 288.
Neill, Mary, 26-27 , 50, 55.
Noble, Alexander, 2, 6, 15, 16, 17-20, 24, 30-36, 37-45, 47, 51-52, 64, 67, 71-72, 77, 97, 125-26, 140, 145-46, 151-58, 273, 288-96.
Noble, Alexander Sim, 32-35.
Noble, Bridget, née Neill or O'Neill, 1-6, abduction 7-16; family background 26-28; marriage, 37-39; life on the farm, 41-43; personality, 44-45; 47; court case, 48-49; 50; punishment attack, 67-72; allegations against her, 74-76; complaint to RIC, 79-81; cry for help, and fate, 91-94; disposal of remains, 95-100; Lehane shooting, 107-11; church rites, 117-19; husband's quest for information, 125-27; responsibility for death sentence, 128-30; compensation for death, 151-56; information about fate, 156-58; death sentence against IRA rules, 162-64; 172-73; 175-180; Dublin Castle statement,194-96; excluded from accounts of conflict, 253-55; *In Memoriam*, 289-90; ghost reports, 300-31.
Noble, Charles, 31, 33.
Noble, Isabella, 31, 33-34.
Noble, Jessie, 31, 64.
Noble, John 31, 33.
Noble, William, 31, 33-34, 38, 50, 53-54, 64, 289, 291, 295.
Nugent, Sergeant Thomas, (RIC), 59, 63, 74, 283-84.

Ó hAnnracháin, Peadar, 45-47.
Oates, District Inspector Thomas J., (RIC), 11-12, 58-62, 88, 151-55, 173, 198-99, 277-80.
O'Connell, Bella, CnB, 12, 13, 119, 138, 219, 229, 237-38, 234.
O'Connell, Christopher, 12, 53, 64, 83, 135, 138, 175, 197, 210, 237-38, 239, 243, 253, 276-77, 283-84.

O'Donoghue, Florence, Intelligence Officer, Cork No 1 Brigade, IRA, 20, 142, 269.

O'Driscoll, Sean, 12, 54, 62-63, 135, 197, 211, 255.

O'Dwyer, Liam, Commandant, Beara Battalion, IRA, 11, 13, 28-29, 54-55, 56, 59, 60, 63-64, 66, 70, 72, 75-76, 81, 82, 83-87, 90. 93-94, 95, 101, 103-04, 107-11, 127-30, 136, 140, 143, 157, 162, 175, 177, 209-11, 218, 210-21, 223-24, 229, 231-33, 239, 242, 247, 248-54, 259-60, 276-77, 300, 305-06.

O'Friel, Commandant Frank, 216-17, 234-36.

O'Halpin, Professor Eunan, 72, 92-93, 269-71.

O'Hegarty, Sean, Commandant, Cork No 1 Brigade, IRA, 20, 114-15, 265, 269.

O'Malley, Ernie, 22, 103, 113-14, 120, 163, 169, 237, 263-67, 271.

Ó Súilleabháin, Diarmaid, writer, 243, 254-55.

O'Sullivan Beare, Donal, 27-28.

O'Sullivan, Eva, 8-11, 56, 97-99, 101-03, 145, 174.

O'Sullivan, Jack, 56.

O'Sullivan, Mícheál Óg, Vice-Comdt., Beara Battalion, 68, 121, 128, 130-33, 135-37, 139, 144, 197-98, 219-22, 223, 228, 231, 238-39, 274-76.

O'Sullivan, Murty Óg, 28.

O'Sullivan, Pronnséas, 130-32, 139, 274-76.

O'Sullivan, Ted (IRA officer, later Fianna Fáil TD), 47, 69, 129, 137, 163, 176-77, 235-37, 238, 241, 252.

Parsons, William Edward, 6, 264-68.

Patrick, County Inspector George R.W., RIC, 144, 171-72, 281.

Pearse, Pádraic, 3, 130, 134.

Price, Leslie, 11, 21.

Puxley, John, 28.

Redmond, John, 30-31.

Royal Navy, 30, 33, 46, 51-52, 65, 203, 219-20.

Scully, Dora, née Neill, 39-41, 196, 285-86.

Scully, Mary Agnes, (US Navy), 52, 286.

Shea, Rev. James Bartley, 46.

Sheehan, John, Ardgroom Company, IRA, 11, 64-65, 75, 82, 85, 88, 89, 101, 135, 202, 212, 246, 251.

Sheehan, Julia, née O'Sullivan, Ardgroom CnB, 81, 84, 85, 88, 136, 202, 26, 251-52.

Skully (composer & musician), 3, 9, 44, 56, 302, 304.

Sullivan, Daniel T., Quartermaster, Beara Battalion, 70, 128, 134-35, 207, 215, 222, 223, 243, 246.
Sullivan, George P., 174-75, 200.
Sullivan, Katie, Ardgroom CnB, 81, 85, 88, 247-48.
Sullivan, Mark, 68, 73, 74, 108, 197, 220, 222, 223, 243-44.
Sullivan, Michael, Gurteen, 87, 144, 211.

Treacy, Sean, 60, 61.

Waters, Samuel, (RIC), 28-29.
Wolfe, Jasper Travers, solicitor, 48-49, 68, 141-48, 151, 154, 156-58, 260, 280, 284-85.

About the Author

Sean Boyne was born in Dublin and educated at O'Connell School and University College Dublin, graduating with a degree in History and Politics. He worked as a journalist and has a particular interest in Irish history, and military history. He has written a number of books, including *Emmet Dalton: Somme Soldier, Irish General, Film Pioneer*, published by Merrion in 2014.

Printed in Great Britain
by Amazon

79511755R00210